COMPARING PUBLIC POLICIES
*United States, Soviet Union,
and Europe*

The Dorsey Series in Political Science
Consulting Editor   SAMUEL C. PATTERSON   *University of Iowa*

COMPARING PUBLIC POLICIES

United States, Soviet Union, and Europe

RICHARD L. SIEGEL

and

LEONARD B. WEINBERG

both of the
Department of Political Science
University of Nevada—Reno

1977 **THE DORSEY PRESS** *Homewood, Illinois   60430*
Irwin-Dorsey Limited, Georgetown, Ontario   L7G 4B3

© THE DORSEY PRESS, 1977

First Printing, February 1977

ISBN 0-256-01935-5
Library of Congress Catalog Card No. 76–49318
Printed in the United States of America

To
Clara and Samuel Siegel
Rose and Max Weinberg
Faye and Herman Rappaport

Preface

This book has been conceived and written in the hope that it will serve three fundamental purposes. First, we have sought to help mesh the burgeoning study of public policy, especially comparative public policy, with the long-established field of comparative politics. These two subjects tend to be strengthened when integrated with each other. Contributors to comparative politics, especially those focusing on advanced industrial countries, have tended to neglect the products, or results, of politics while emphasizing structures and processes. The study of public policy, at least in the United States and Great Britain, has tended to be parochial in its analysis of national and local policy outcomes. We hope that both fields can be furthered by a book that provides relatively detailed comparisons of major public policy patterns in eight of the world's leading industrialized nations.

Our second major purpose is to synthesize and fill in gaps in the evolving subfield of comparative public policy. Despite the limits noted above, comparative public policy is now one of the significant fields of growth in political science and social science generally. Outstanding recent work with cross-national emphasis has been produced by an array of scholars from numerous disciplines. These include economists Frederic Pryor, Gaston Rimlinger, and

Richard Musgrave; sociologists Harold Wilensky, Phillips Cutright, and Odin Anderson; and political scientists Hugh Heclo, Arnold Heidenheimer, Bruce Russett, Alexander Groth, Larry Wade, and Cynthia Enloe. Yet we found it necessary to go beyond synthesis of such work to primary research in many areas.

Third and last, since you our readers are affected daily by government policies, we hope this book will make you more conscious of the various options that confront political decision makers. Potentially at least, the comparison of different countries' approaches to similar problems can contribute to concrete steps toward improving living conditions around the world.

Acknowledgments

We wish to express our gratitude to numerous persons who assisted this project. Most personally and directly, our wives, Joan Siegel and Ellen Weinberg, provided active encouragement, tolerance, and support. A heroic typing effort was completed, with uncommon grace, by Kenna Boyer.

The University of Nevada, Reno, provided financial support to both authors in the forms of grants from its Research Advisory Board and sabbatical leaves. The Center for International Studies of the London School of Economics hosted Richard Siegel as a visiting fellow and Leonard Weinberg enjoyed the facilities of Florence, Italy. The staff of the Getchell Library at the University of Nevada, Reno, the British Library of Political and Economic Science, and the Bancroft Library at the University of California, Berkeley, were eager to promote our efforts. As the resourcefulness of the University of Nevada, Reno, librarians was indispensable we wish to single out the following among them for special thanks: Anne Amaral, Joyce Ball, Joan Chambers, Barbara Fleming, Naoma Hainey, Yoshi Hendricks, Lenore Kosso, Dorothy McAlinden, Mary Nichols, Sharon Prengaman, and Jack Rittenhouse.

Finally, we gratefully acknowledge Samuel Patterson, Dorsey's advisory editor. David Abernethy of Stanford University, Michael Baer of the University of Kentucky, Brian Silver of Michigan State University, and Michael King of Pennsylvania State University joined Samuel Patterson in reading the entire manuscript and pointing us toward numerous improvements. Useful criticisms and suggestions were also offered by Michael Banks and Paul Taylor of the London School of Economics and by the University of Nevada, Reno's, Francis Hartigan, Neal Ferguson, Allen Wilcox, Joseph Crowley, M. Richard Ganzel, Glen Atkinson, and Eleanore Bushnell.

January 1977   RICHARD L. SIEGEL
                                  LEONARD B. WEINBERG

Contents

munity and Culture: The Context of Policy-Making. Interest Groups. Political Parties. The Political Executive. Parliaments. Executive Bureaucracies. The Judiciary. Conclusion.

1 *Introduction*

Most of the time we experience political life vicariously, as if we were viewing a continuing theatrical performance. The presentation may be alternately boring or exciting, tragic or comic, superficial or profound, yet a performance nevertheless. Every now and then we become aware, as in a modern play, that the separation of actors and audience is not complete. Certain scenes seem to require our participation even if the roles we are assigned are marginal and small.

The drama of political life also has its professional critics, people who earn their livelihoods by evaluating the performance. Among these analysts are individuals known as political scientists. Until quite recently, American political scientists tended to focus their assessments of the performance on three of its components. First, they devoted great attention to what we might call stage management—the various props, costumes, lighting arrangements, and other paraphernalia which provide the setting or background for the theatrics.

The leading actors have also come under scrutiny. Political scientists have tried to discern the meaning, style, and quality of their renditions. To do this, political scientists have often sought, rather like gossip columnists, to uncover biographical information about the

1

players' social backgrounds and even their personality character-istics. Some political scientists have concluded, though, that this approach is a less meaningful path to understanding than one which is focused on the script and on the characters these actors are asked to play. The assumption here is that the performance will be pretty much the same, given the script, no matter which particular actors are in the cast.

We in the audience, those of us who are occasionally brought on-stage, have not been ignored. Our opinions have been surveyed; our knowledge about and interest in the central characters have been tested. Political scientists have found our apparently curious customs, habits, and tastes relevant in understanding the overall performance and our reaction to it. Why do we vote? Why do we riot? Why do we so often fall asleep during scenes that political scientists find so stimu-lating? All are questions which political scientists have asked, investi-gated, and argued over for decades. Some have even speculated about whether we count at all. Obviously there would be little reason to put on the play if there were no audience. But does our presence really make much difference in determining the flow of action onstage? Some say yes, some say no; still others say that it depends on the play and the setting.

If we attend a Broadway production, what may we expect from our exposure to this experience? The rewards, if any, are likely to be in-tangible. That is, if the play is well written and the performance effec-tive, the production may evoke an emotional response within us. Whether the feeling aroused is faint or strong, positive or negative, ephemeral or long-lasting, the effect on the members of the audience is primarily psychological.

This is not true, however, for the drama of political life. There are, to be sure, certain similarities. A large part of our reaction to politics be-longs in the emotive realm. If you do not think this is so, ponder for a moment your responses to the assassination of a prominent national leader or to the election of a presidential candidate with whom you are particularly enthralled. But political life clearly has an effect on us beyond its ability to arouse sensations. The central characters pos-sess a capacity to reward and punish us in ways denied to Broadway actors.

The officials of a modern state can affect our lives in a myriad of ways. To name a few, they can tax our incomes, compel us to spend years in military service, and limit our ability to express our political views. Indeed, their decisions concerning abortion and contraception, health care, educational and employment opportunities, and old-age pensions have an influence in shaping the entire cycle of our lives.

DEFINING PUBLIC POLICY

Public policies are shaped when governments or comparable authorities (including some ruling political parties) decide whether or not to alter aspects of community life. Policies are public to the extent that they involve governmental or quasi-governmental decision-making and determine the interests of the community. The line between private and public policy is not now and never has been a sharp one.

Public policy has both foreign and domestic components. Foreign policy involves decisions and actions by national governments in support of essentially domestic interests.[1] For example, U.S. energy policies, designed to maximize domestic supplies, are directed at both Middle Eastern governments and American citizens. The present volume clearly emphasizes domestic policy. Yet, as in discussions of military capabilities and conscription, foreign policy is also considered.

The bulk of the research conducted by political scientists has tended to focus on *input* and decision-making activities rather than *output* or policy. Public opinions, interest groups, political parties, and policy-making institutions have been extensively investigated both for the United States and for most other industrialized societies. Our primary interest in this book is with *output* and *outcomes*. We will examine environmental patterns and policy-making practices in different countries essentially in their role as influences on output. We are less concerned with *how* various political systems produce what they do than with *what* they produce. In particular, we are going to be concerned with three areas of public policy: (1) the extraction and mobilization of resources; (2) the distribution of public resources; and (3) the regulative policies that political systems impose on their respective environments.[2]

Extraction

We mean by the term extraction the policies which establish the tangible costs citizens are asked to pay for the various public goods and services provided for them by the political system. How much of what individuals or business firms earn is taxed? How fairly is the tax bur-

---

[1] James N. Rosenau, "Adaptive Strategies for Research and Practice in Foreign Policy," in Fred W. Riggs, ed., *International Studies: Present Status and Future Prospects* (Philadelphia: American Academy of Political and Social Science, 1971), pp. 218–45.

[2] We have adapted these categories from Gabriel A. Almond and G. Bingham Powell, *Comparative Politics: A Developmental Approach* (Boston: Little, Brown & Co., 1966), pp. 190–212; and Joyce M. Mitchell and William C. Mitchell, *Political Analysis and Public Policy: An Introduction to Political Science* (Chicago: Rand McNally & Co., 1969), pp. 11–132.

den distributed in the population? What are the primary objects of tax assessments (for example, personal income, consumption, property)?

In addition to taxation we also intend to treat involuntary service to the state as a tangible cost. Does the system, for example, require you to spend a given period of time in its armed forces? If this is so, how long must you serve? How much are you paid for such service? What are your chances of getting killed or disabled in the course of your time of service? These questions must be part of a rational assessment of benefits and liabilities.

Distribution

Under the rubric distribution we intend to scrutinize the policies of political systems with respect to what they give you by way of tangible benefits. To what extent does the system reinforce the social and economic advantages of the elites? To what degree does it redistribute resources so as to assist the poor and incapacitated segments of the population? Is the effort at redistribution accomplished by the direct provision of goods and services or by reliance on income assistance, or both?

We also intend to look at a range of fundamental distributional choices that systems make and that affect their capacity to distribute tangible benefits. For instance, we want to know the relative emphasis assigned by various governments to private sector as opposed to governmental provision of services. How do governments differ in regard to their relative budgetary allocations for military versus civilian purposes?

We shall stress long-term patterns of governmental distribution that have direct effects on individuals. Included here are levels of support for education, social security, and health services. If you are old, sick, out of work, or seek governmental assistance in pursuing educational goals, which systems have the most to offer, which the least?

Regulation

To varying degrees all political systems seek to regulate the conduct of individuals, groups, and institutions in their environments. Indeed, the breadth and intensity of such regulation are frequently taken to be among the most important criteria in classifying political systems. In the Western liberal tradition a minimum of regulation is typically equated with freedom and a democratic order, whereas systems which regulate widely and intensively tend to be viewed as tyrannical. In our view, the individual should evelute regulations in a more flexible manner.

It occurs to us that in complex, industrialized societies the state or the political system need not be the sole source of extensive and intensive control. In the United States, for example, decisions made by private institutions, such as large business corporations and trade unions, will frequently have as constraining an effect on individual conduct as many authoritative allocations made in the political system. Potentially at least, state regulation of private or nonpolitical institutions (that is, industrial, commercial, agricultural, educational, philanthropic, and mass media institutions) may actually maximize individual choice.

We have chosen to illustrate the vast field of regulation with discussions of the extent and limits of government control over individual and group political activity, efforts by enterprises to restrain trade, worker involvement in business management, and pollution control. An effort has been made to provide a broad view of the objects and tools of regulation.

Welfare, Warfare, and Post-Industrial Policies

This book also discusses policy in terms of its relationship to objectives and priorities. *Welfare* policies relate to the provision of basic goods and services in the interest of sustaining health and providing opportunities for decent lives. Housing, income maintenance, the foundations of education, and social services are among the ingredients of the welfare state. *Warfare* or *military-industrial* policies relate to a mobilization and allocation of resources for national security. Such policies include military conscription and the share of taxes directed to the military establishment; the share of spending and the distribution of resources for military-related manpower, research, and equipment; and the regulations imposed in the name of national security. *Post-industrialism* is a complex concept which is elaborated further in Chapter 7. We note here only that it refers to an emerging agenda of current and future political issues dominated by such concerns as environmental quality, privacy, control over bureaucracy and technology, equality for women, and more meaningful participation in political and business decision-making.

DETERMINANTS OF POLICY

In the first few chapters of this book we discuss the factors that determine the content of public policies. In order to manage the large number of contributing influences we have categorized them under the headings domestic, international, and historical. Domestic factors, basically current influences that develop within national boundaries, are further subdivided under the headings political and environmental, the latter with an emphasis on the socioeconomic. We seek to evaluate each set of domestic factors and to compare the impacts of these sets. International determinants are given a greater place in this book than in most studies of public policy. Included are discussions of the results of wars, international economic advances and dislocations, actions of particular national governments, and the emergence of intergovernmental organizational authority. Finally, we seek to suggest how historical experience intrudes on contemporary policy and to trace some of the main directions of evolving governmental roles in Europe and North America during past centuries.

THE EIGHT SURVEY STATES

Our search for similarities and differences in policies will focus on the records of eight nation-states, including seven European countries, primarily because this number seemed optimal for providing adequate analysis of a substantial range of cases without generating an unwelcome catalog of national patterns.

But why the particular eight nation-states, namely the United States, the Soviet Union, the United Kingdom, France, Italy, Sweden, the German Federal Republic (West Germany), and the German Democratic Republic (East Germany)? We sought to compare countries with important similarities in such aspects as socioeconomic development, cultural traditions, and geographic situation. This is not to suggest that our group of eight represent a common pool of states in any narrow sense. Major similarities and differences are set out in Chapter 5. However, we have chosen North American and European states which are among the world's most industrialized and affluent. Except for the Soviet Union they share major elements of a common Western historical and cultural tradition, and even Russia has maintained significant ties with that heritage.

Two of the states are the military and political superpowers of international politics. Four are the major member states of the European Communities (the interlinked European Economic, Coal and Steel, and Atomic Energy organizations), a structure that features prominently in this study. East Germany is included because direct comparison of the two Germanies promised to be interesting and fruitful and because it has emerged as an industrial and technological leader in East-Central Europe. Finally, Sweden is included largely because its economic and public policy innovations and progress outweigh its relatively small population. By such criteria as level of scientific and technological innovation, energy consumption, and military prowess, these nations have an enormous impact on the rest of the world.

We do not insist that only these choices could have been made. Such relatively populous European countries as Spain and Poland have been omitted. The exclusion of such smaller countries as the Netherlands and Yugoslavia limits the presentation of policy experiments. Among others Japan, South Africa, Norway, Denmark, Switzerland, Israel, Canada, Australia, and New Zealand would each have been an interesting addition to an analysis of public policy in advanced industrial states.

OUTPUT AND OUTCOME

Having identified the chosen policies and nation-states, we will proceed to suggest some major distinctions emphasized in this project. The first is *outputs* and *outcomes*.

The term *output* is a basic element of systems analysis as related to political science by David Easton and others.[3] According to Easton, the structural elements of the political system, including the personnel and their methods of operation, process and convert inputs into outputs described as allocational decisions and implementing actions. In other words, outputs are policies as conceived and carried out. *Outcomes* are the effects or impacts that a policy has on the conditions that it is designed to affect. These impacts may be positive, negative, conflicting, or nonexistent. For example, a given law or a change in administrative approach may alleviate or aggravate the situation that was its source.

Weighing the outcome of public policies is, of course, easier said than done. As several commentators on the subject have pointed out, it is exceedingly difficult to demonstrate cause and effect relationships between particular policies and significant changes in a political system's environment.[4] One can rarely be certain that changes in the system's environment were brought about by particular policy efforts. For instance, was a higher rate of employment in a country stimulated by a certain governmental policy, such as the forcing of lower bank interest rates, or was it a result of other, nonpolitical, environmental changes or if some combination of both factors? Moreover, policies intended by their authors to produce one set of outcomes may evoke other unintended consequences. The U.S. Civil Rights Act of 1964 may have stimulated urban ghetto rioting by raising black expectations about substantive improvements which were not immediately forthcoming.

---

[3] For Easton's framework see David Easton, *A Framework for Political Analysis* (Englewood Cliffs, N.J.: Prentice-Hall, 1965); and *A Systems Analysis of Political Life* (New York: John Wiley & Sons, 1965).

[4] Thomas R. Dye, *Understanding Public Policy* (Englewood Cliffs, N.J.: Prentice-Hall, 1972), pp. 291–99; Yehezkel Dror, *Public Policymaking Reexamined* (Scranton, Pa.: Chandler Publishing Co., 1968), pp. 25–57; and Easton, *Systems Analysis*, pp. 351–52.

The effort to assess the outcome of policy on the environment, although fraught with hazards, is essential to the task which we have defined for ourselves. Given the complexity of the problem, however, the best we can do is report measured associations or correlations between outputs and outcomes rather than demonstrate cause and effect relationships.

PUBLIC AND PRIVATE

By dwelling on public policies, we focus on governmental actions and the consequences that flow from them. To do this is inevitably to render judgments about the performance of political systems. Nevertheless, it may be that public needs are being met as well or better through private sector means than through political or public means.

In the light of these considerations it becomes evident that in evaluating the outputs and outcomes of public policies we are not, at the same time, judging how well all public needs are being met in particular countries. This is true, in the first place, because we cannot be certain about the precise nature of public needs. They can vary from one country to another, and they can also vary over time in the same country. Second, governmental response to public needs is not the same thing as or equivalent to societal response. The latter encompasses both public and private response. The focus of this book is on the political component and not the overall societal reaction.

PROBLEMS AND PITFALLS IN POLICY COMPARISONS

Major problems emerge when we seek to acquire and interpret information about the content of public policies and the nature of outcomes. Social scientists have had enough experience with cross-national research to know that the problems and pitfalls of such efforts are frequently overwhelming. One walks through quicksand just to obtain the necessary data. Among the specific problems are the unavailability of data and the distortion of data.

The Unavailability of Data

One of the most intensive efforts to collect data for cross-national research was the Dimensions of Nations project associated with Harold Guetzkow, Jack Sawyer, and R. J. Rummel.[5] Their original effort to acquire usable data on 236 variables reflecting the characteristics of 82

---

[5] R. J. Rummel, *The Dimensions of Nations* (Beverly Hills, Calif.: Sage Publications, 1972), p. 14.

nations led to a claimed 83 percent success rate. However, this project was able to obtain well over 90 percent of the desired information for most Western European states and as high as 90 percent for several Eastern European countries.

The reasons given for absent data include: (1) the lack of statistical resources, human and mechanical; (2) the lack of need for certain information in the view of some governments; (3) the desire of a government not to compile or disclose information that could be expected to reflect negatively on its actions; and (4) the resistance of nongovernmental institutions, groups, and individuals to disclosing information that they considered confidential or were afraid to disclose. Even such an advanced program as that of the U.S. Bureau of the Census reflects each of these problems.

These barriers did not, however, prove insuperable. We obtained a wide range of statistics, the largest part from intergovernmental organizations. This was supplemented by national government data and interpretations by independent sources.

The Distortion of Data

Distorted data probably pose greater problems for an undertaking such as this than do unavailable data. As noted by Rummel, distortion may result from clerical error, methodological inadequacy, definitional inconsistency, and political intent. Methodological inadequacy may derive from the assumption that nationwide opinion samples can be accurately drawn from just the urban or economically favored sectors of a population. Definitional inconsistency may arise when two states use different interpretations of such subjective terms as substandard or such seemingly objective terms as *minority race.* Political intent to distort can lead to the falsification of data at either the collecting or dispensing stages. This will happen so long as the release of information can weaken or strengthen a government's popularity and hold on the levers of power. As Rummel notes, "With such difficulties, few have been brave, or foolhardy, enough to 'dirty their hands' in the data." Nonetheless, we think that the effort, no matter what the problems involved, was worth making. In difficult cases we have provided several versions of statistical truth or have avoided presenting data on one or more countries because of our suspicions concerning their accuracy.

VALUES

Few of us develop an ideology—a "system of values and beliefs"—concerning public policy priorities. Not even Roman Catholicism or Marxism-Leninism points all adherents to totally common value preferences. Yet most of us have at least a rough ordering of priorities that guide our judgment of governmental actions.

Like public officials, the authors and readers of this volume must make value choices. No political system has yet been able to provide all things to all people. Liberty to keep one's wealth can easily conflict with equality and social justice for many others. Many personal freedoms are often incompatible with the security and stability of an ordered society. Economic growth may be advanced, at least in the short term, by ignoring damage to the physical environment.

Our own value preferences are a product of our socialization as and identification with what Leonard Freedman terms the "liberal critics" of American politics.[6] As such, we fall between the radical left and the "moderate" center. In terms of particular values this means that we tend to emphasize civil liberties more than domestic security, environmental quality more than economic growth, and equal opportunity together with high minimal living standards when these conflict with privilege. We approach the welfare state positively and the military-industrial state skeptically. At the same time we wish to see social justice coupled with pragmatism. All government programs benefit from a high level of efficiency. Further, each sound program requires substantial support from those who implement it and from the broad public that is affected. We are elitist enough to want the majority to be educated to accept the viewpoint of liberal critics. Yet we are democratic enough not to want programs imposed in the face of mass opposition.

The domestic and international determinants of public policy will be discussed in the next two chapters. This will be followed by a chapter in which the eight selected countries are compared in relation to these determinants. We then offer some historical background concerning the development of the primary kinds of policy discussed in this book. After that, we undertake the survey of current policy in the selected nations, in chapters entitled "Distributions: The Welfare State"; "Distributions: Military-Industrial and Post-Industrial"; "Extraction: Military Draft and Taxation"; "Regulating and Protecting Civil Liberties and Rights"; "Antitrust Policy and Worker Participation: Aspects of Industrial Regulation"; and finally, "Protecting the Environment: Pollution Control Policy."

---

[6] Leonard Freedman, *Power and Politics in America*, 2d ed. (North Scituate, Mass.: Duxbury Press, 1974), p. 3.

2 Domestic Influences on Public Policy

In this chapter and the next we intend to explore the various factors which shape public policies. Although, as we indicated in Chapter 1, our major focus is on output and outcome, on what political systems do and how their actions affect citizens, we nevertheless consider it crucial for us, the consumers of policy, to understand the circumstances out of which variations in public policies arise. Why?

Suppose for the moment that you are the citizen of a country whose government, in your estimation, consistently allocates too little of its resources for the provision of adequate housing facilities. Assuming that you have the desire to do something about this failure, it seems likely to us that you would want to exert your energies so that they would have the maximum payoff. In order to act rationally under these circumstances you should have some understanding of just what factors in your society produced the particular pattern of policy-making with which you are so dissatisfied. To do otherwise is in our view the equivalent of tilting at windmills. Such a course of action may be personally therapeutic, but it is unlikely to lead to the slaying of any real dragons.

11

How much difference does it make, in terms of policy output, that the political leaders of a country are devout Communists rather than Roman Catholics? Does it really matter whether a nation has one, two, or many political parties? Do countries whose economies exhibit rapid rates of growth have governments that spend more of the countries' disposable resources on public health facilities than is spent by the governments of countries with slow-growth economies? The ability to answer these questions, and many more like them, is obviously fundamental for an individual who wants to see certain public policies initiated, changed, or continued unaltered.

Such questions have often been asked by social scientists, but the answers have tended to be partial, tentative, and contradictory. Up to this point much work has been directed at refining the sets of variables to be examined as possible influences. It has not been easy to select potentially important factors, to measure them, or to isolate their independent impacts.

Perspectives or influences on public policy can be organized sensibly and reported to you within the context of an environmental-political framework. Specifically, we intend to arrange our review of that framework in approximate accordance with David Easton's systems framework. Easton views the political system as operating in an environment that is divided into two broad categories: intrasocietal and extrasocietal.[1] In other words, Easton conceives the political system as operating in both a domestic and an international context. Both the intra- and extrasocietal environments are subdivided into several constituent categories. In this chapter we are going to examine arguments and evidence concerning the effects of intrasocietal economic, sociodemographic, physical environmental, and overtly political factors on nation-to-nation variations in policy output. The next chapter will be devoted to discussion of extrasocietal influences.

We seek to convey the reasons why it has been believed that each of these kinds of factors influences major areas of public policy. In many cases leading scholars have argued about the relative impacts of particular factors. These disputes are reported and evaluated here to allow readers to judge for themselves. Emphasis is placed on contentions about the independent influence of particular variables. Although questions of relative importance are touched upon here, we do this only in an introductory way and leave more specific determinations to the chapters dealing with particular public policy issues.

---

[1] David Easton, *A Framework for Political Analysis* (Englewood Cliffs, N.J.: Prentice-Hall, 1965), pp. 69–75.

ENVIRONMENTAL SOURCES OF VARIATIONS
IN PUBLIC POLICIES

Economic Factors

The view that the structure of a nation's economic enterprise, the level of its technology, and its relative wealth are the crucial determinants of the policies its political system produces has long been widely held. From Aristotle and Marx to such contemporaries as Marcuse and Galbraith, numerous scholars have maintained that the ways by which a country produces goods and services determine both how its political system is likely to be organized and, in turn, how that system is likely to allocate its available resources. This fundamental perception has been shared both by philosophers, whose major tools of analysis were the principles of logic and the historical record, and by modern social scientists whose principal instruments of investigation are multivariate statistical procedures and the computer.

Because the extant writing on this theme is so voluminous, we think it essential to impose a somewhat arbitrary order on our discussion of it. Initially, in evaluating economic influence, we suggest that three separate factors must be considered: (1) the structure of a country's economic enterprise, that is, the issue of who owns the major means of production in society and what policy consequences flow from this; (2) the reputedly independent influence on policy of technology, the physical implements by which goods and services are produced in the economics system; and finally, (3) the relationship between a country's wealth (for example, per capita income) and the shape and direction of its public policies.

Next, in saying that economic factors influence or even exclusively determine policy, we must stipulate what kinds of policies we are talking about. In this regard, we think it useful to distinguish the *agenda* for policy-making from the specific content of policy. Let us illustrate the nature of this distinction. It seems likely that two countries in which large numbers of people own automobiles will have political systems that will develop rules to regulate the conduct of drivers. The content of these driving regulations may be substantially different in the two countries, but both will seek in some fashion to regulate automobile driving. Contrast this situation, if you will, with that of a country in which the major means of conveyance is the horse or the camel. Here it seems unlikely that there will be any public policy dealing with the driving of automobiles. In this situation such regulations are not on the *agenda* for policy-making.

Public policies themselves, that is, their content, may be clustered (see Chapter 1) under three broad headings: extraction, regulation, and distribution. *Extraction,* it will be recalled, refers to the tangible costs citizens are asked to pay for public goods and services. By the term *regulation* we mean the breadth and intensity of political control of individual, institutional, and group conduct. And we use the term *distribution* to designate public policies which allocate political system resources, in the form of goods and services, to a country's population.

The Structure of Economic Enterprise. Much of the writing dealing with the impact of the structure of economic enterprise on public policy—private versus public ownership or capitalism versus socialism—is highly polemical in character. Advocates of socialism have demonstrated, at least to their own satisfaction, that capitalism inevitably causes political systems to pursue policies of imperialism and aggression in foreign affairs, and racial, sexual, and class discrimination on the home front.[2] Conversely, defenders of free enterprise have asserted that an inevitable linkage exists between socialism, at least in its Soviet "communist" version, and police state tactics.[3]

Each side in the argument has developed rejoinders to cope with the attacks of the other. Many defenders of socialism maintain that the deficiencies in the Soviet system are an outgrowth of historical peculiarities unique to Russian society rather than the inevitable result of the application of socialist economic doctrines. Similarly, writers sympathetic to capitalism have denied the existence of an inextricable link between private ownership and imperialism, citing Switzerland, or between private ownership and racial, sexual, and class oppression, pointing to Scandinavia in this instance.[4]

As public policy analysts we think it best to drain at least some of the emotional fervor from the issue in order to evaluate our choices dispassionately. The crux of the argument seems to revolve around the relative emphasis to be assigned regulatory and distributive policies. Supporters of what can be termed the classical or traditional "liberal" capitalist model have long believed that general prosperity and individual liberty are best secured if the state directly regulates individual, group, and institutional conduct as little as possible.[5] Against this position, proponents of socialism, public ownership, and comprehensive state planning invert the order of policy priorities. They suggest

[2] Richard C. Edwards, Michael Reich, and Thomas E. Weisskopf, eds., *The Capitalist System* (Englewood Cliffs, N.J.: Prentice-Hall, 1972).

[3] Milton Friedman, *Capitalism and Freedom* (Chicago: University of Chicago Press, 1962).

[4] Robert C. Heilbroner, "The Human Prospect," *New York Review of Books* 26 (January 24, 1974): 21–34.

[5] Adam Smith, *The Wealth of Nations* (Harmondsworth, England: Penguin Books, 1970).

that first priority be assigned to achieving a high level of economic productivity and that the fruits of this productivity be distributed on a relatively equal basis to the working population. To achieve these objectives the political system must play an intensive regulatory and distributive role in society. From the socialist viewpoint, real liberty, that is, maximum personal discretion, follows from rather than precedes equally apportioned economic abundance.[6]

Devotees of private ownership respond to these assertions by claiming that no matter how well intentioned state policy-makers are, individual liberty is inevitably diminished under socialism because of the concentration in comparatively few hands, under state auspices, of so much economic and political power. On the other side, the socialists maintain that such libertarian policies as exist under capitalism are uneven and illusory. For instance, they argue that although the state may directly regulate conduct relatively less under capitalism, ordinary individuals have their personal and working lives regulated for them by the owners and managers of private firms, in whose selection they have taken no part.

Despite this authentic dispute there are, surprisingly, a number of matters on which both capitalist and socialist scholars agree. First, there is agreement on the desirability of industrialism and economic growth. Capitalism and socialism may be seen as competing strategies for bringing about these commonly endorsed, and largely unquestioned, objectives.

Next, both sides to the argument would agree that the agenda for policy-making is more extensive under socialism, that under socialism the political system is called upon to do more. Concomitantly, both socialist and capitalist enthusiasts accept the fact that private ownership economies restrict the breadth of public policy-making in the political system.

Moreover, both sides agree in large measure about the extractive consequences of the two types of economic arrangements. Specifically, socialism, given its egalitarian thrust, implies a steeply graduated "soak the rich" approach to taxation, whereas capitalism encourages minimal taxation levels. Instead of soaking the rich, the defenders of private ownership stress the importance, for purposes of stimulating economic growth and general prosperity, of encouraging the rich to invest their funds in various business and commercial endeavors. This savings and investment function is performed by the state under socialism.

In recent years the entire relevance of the conventional debate be-

---

[6] Michael Harrington, *Socialism* (New York: Saturday Review Press, 1972); and Oskar Lange and Fred M. Taylor, *On the Economic Theory of Socialism* (New York: McGraw-Hill Book Co., 1964).

tween the proponents of capitalism and the proponents of socialism has been called into question by such observers as Galbraith, Burnham, Djilas, Lindblom, and Dahl.[7] These writers see the structure of enterprise question, at least as it applies to the matter of private versus public ownership, as dated. According to their conception, in countries with advanced industrialized economies the question of who "owns" large productive units, the government or private shareholders, Air France or American Airlines, is less significant that the question of who runs them. These writers argue that in cases of both private and public ownership, control over the operation of large-scale enterprise rests in the hands of managers, a separate class of individuals who are distinguished by their possession of indispensable technical and managerial skills. For those holding this viewpoint it makes little difference whether the enterprise be public or private because in both instances control rests with the managers.

Given this understanding, the central public policy problem becomes one of regulation. Here the discussion has to do with the accountability of the managers to some other force (for example, the public) or institution (for example, the regime) in society. Left alone, the managers, whether in the United States, Great Britain, or the Soviet Union, will seek to regulate the rest of society, including its political system, in the name of technological rationality and on behalf of their respective enterprises. Assuming that this is a bad idea, it then becomes essential to find some lever of control by means of which the managers can be made accountable, their decisions regulated by other elements.

Here leaders of the consumer movement in the United States stress the need for having public interest representation on the boards of directors of major corporate enterprises and the desirability of reforming election campaign practices so as to restrict the influence of corporate wealth in the candidate selection process. Some of those fearful of managerial domination rally around the idea of worker participation. Partially inspired by Yugoslavian experiments along these lines, they advocate the introduction of a worker presence at all levels, including the highest, of enterprise decision-making. Contemporary efforts to give workers a voice in the selection of management will be discussed further in Chapter 10.

Technology. The second economic source of influence on public policy which we wish to examine is that of technology, particularly ad-

---

[7] John Kenneth Galbraith, *The New Industrial State* (Boston: Houghton Mifflin Co., 1967); James Burnham, *The Managerial Revolution* (Bloomington: Indiana University Press, 1960); Milovan Djilas, *The New Class* (New York: Praeger Publishers, 1957); Robert A. Dahl, *After the Revolution* (New Haven: Yale University Press, 1970); and Dahl and Charles E. Lindblom, *Political, Economics, and Welfare* (New York: Harper & Row, 1953).

vanced technology. By technology we mean the application of science to the production of goods and services in the economic system. It is obvious that the level of a society's technological development is related to our other two factors: the structure of enterprise and wealth. Nevertheless, in recent years there has been a considerable body of commentary, directed especially at the problems of advanced industrialized societies, which encourages readers to believe that beyond a certain level of sophistication technology takes on a life of its own. From this perspective technology itself shapes politics and policy instead of being shaped by them.

Contemporary views on the relationship between technology and politics may be sensibly organized under three headings: technological determinism, technology as a conditioning variable, and a technology-politics interaction system. According to the first, determinist interpretation, "not only is technology an uncaused, unwilled cause which causes other things, but technological change is the sole and irresistible cause of all changes in all other fields of human activity."[8] The second view—which sees technology as a conditioning variable—awards it a more modest role. It sees technology as an independent factor which, along with other forces, serves to shape, constrain, or condition public policies. Finally, technological advances may be seen as playing an interactive, reciprocally influencing role vis-à-vis politics and policy. Advocates of this approach believe that, though the requirements of technological advance shape political decisions, so too do political needs, and hence policy, influence the course of technological development.[9]

Just as there are disagreements over the degree to which contemporary technology molds political life, there are also conflicting views over the moral and ethical consequences of technology. Some observers see the phenomenon as a primarily liberating force in society. Modern technological developments, among other things, have the potential to free individuals from deadening, repetitive work and of liberating humanity from the effects of diseases which previously caused enormous suffering. For other observers technology's impact on the human condition has been essentially evil in character. Their arguments often stress two themes: first, that modern technology acts to produce an artificial environment which causes human relationships to lose their warmth and spontaneity, becoming cold, machinelike, and impersonal.

[8] Victor C. Ferkiss, "Man's Tools and Man's Choices: The Confrontation of Technology and Political Science," *American Political Science Review* 67 (September 1973): 974. See, for example, Alvin Toffler, *Future Shock* (New York: Random House, 1970); and Zbigniew Brzezinski, *Between Two Ages* (New York: Viking Press, 1970).

[9] Kenneth Boulding, *The Meaning of the Twentieth Century* (New York: Harper & Row, 1965).

Second, thanks to technological "advances," the weapons of modern warfare have become infinitely more destructive. Political systems that possess nuclear weapons now have the capacity to destroy all life on this planet.

Still another position concerning the moral consequences of sophisticated technology holds that they are ethically neutral. According to this view, the tools which men use to produce things are physical objects which do not have the ability to think, reason, or express intent. If this is true, then it follows that tools should be neither praised nor blamed for the purposes to which they are put. Instead, judgments of approval or disapproval should be directed at the tool-users or tool-makers. The atom bomb that exploded over Hiroshima in August 1945 cannot be accused of inhumanity or for that matter praised for astute strategic planning; the bomb was, after all, the instrument of a political purpose, not its cause.

Our discussion to this point has been general: we have not as yet explicitly linked technology to public policy questions. Using the above commentary as a background or context-setting effort, we should now like to turn to the problem of the relationship between technological development and public policies.

First, with respect to the impact of modern technology on the agenda for policy-making, it seems clear that the number of technological items requiring some form of political response has increased enormously. For instance, the Swedish economist Gunnar Myrdal argues that the entire array of governmental services which we associate with the term *welfare state* derives from the unsettling social consequences of the industrial revolution. The mere existence of devices like automobiles, airplanes, and television sets evokes the need for some form of policy output. Moreover, pollution, a largely unanticipated consequence of technological development, is becoming an increasingly significant area of policy concern. Indeed, technological development itself has become a policy-relevant issue in a number of countries. Figures such as the French journalist-politician Servan-Schreiber and the Russian physicist Andrei Sakharov have argued that Western European and Soviet political leaders are not, for a variety of reasons, pursuing policies of technological innovation and growth vigorously enough.[10] It has become a widely articulated view in advanced industrialized societies that rapid technological innovation is symptomatic of societal vitality—that was the symbolic meaning of the American space effort—whereas slow rates of technological innovation

---

[10] J. J. Servan-Schreiber, *The American Challenge* (New York: Atheneum, 1968); and Andrei Sakharov, *Progress, Co-Existence, and Intellectual Freedom* (New York: W. W. Norton & Co., 1968).

and deployment are often taken to be signs of societal decay. In this connection, the emigration of substantial numbers of British scientists to the United States, the brain drain, stimulated a public debate in Great Britain some years ago. It was then argued that unless the government pursued policies designed to make professional life more pleasant for the country's scientists, Britain would fall into a condition of irreversible decline. Similar views were expressed in the United States in the aftermath of Russia's initial space successes in 1957 and 1958.

The impact of modern technology on the capacity of political regimes to regulate individual conduct has been widely discussed. Many writers on this theme express the fear that the application of sophisticated technology increases immeasurably the state's capacity to damage human liberty. Here the major disagreement has generally not been between those who view the impact as beneficial versus those who see it as harmful, but instead the discussion has centered on the question of the degree of extent of harm. It seems to us that there is a group of observers who emphasize the technology-enhanced ability of political regimes to scrutinize and control the external behavior of individuals through such techniques as computer-based record keeping and electronically assisted surveillance. Still worse, there are those—Herbert Marcuse is a notable example—who believe that the most devastating impact of modern technology on state regulatory capacities is primarily intrapersonal in character. This line of reasoning has it that technology's influence on people's lives is so pervasive that it shapes and dominates their consciousness so as to rob them of the will and the ability to act in ways regarded as dangerous by governmental authorities.[11]

It would be unfair to move on without at least mentioning a more optimistic interpretation. Some students of the Soviet political regime have contended that the requirements of rapid technological development are such that scientists, engineers, and other practitioners in technology-related fields must pursue their work free from the constraints of regime-inspired ideological imperatives. Whether or not the long-run effect of allowing spheres of freedom to arise in scientific research will be a spillover of freedom into political and social areas remains to be seen.[12] Certainly current trends are far from encouraging.

Although the views concerning the impact of technology on regulatory capacities have generally been pessimistic, those which treat the association between technological advance and distributive policies have not. Indeed, some commentators see the increasing application of modern technology in the economic realm as stimulating a new era of

---

[11] Herbert Marcuse, *One-Dimensional Man* (Boston: Beacon Press, 1964).

[12] Zbigniew Brzezinski and Samuel P. Huntington, *Political Power: USA/USSR* (New York: Viking Press, 1963).

abundance in society.[13] If the history of all previously existing political systems has been built around the problem of scarcity and how to allocate scarce resources, political regimes in nations where technology has advanced the farthest are likely to be simultaneously confronted by conditions of both abundance and scarcity. As Galbraith points out in *The Affluent Society,* the public sector may still be starved in situations of private affluence for reasons having to do with a country's historical political values. In addition, the existence of technology-inspired wealth does not necessarily mean that the poor or least privileged strata in the population will be major beneficiaries. But what it does mean, if the forecasts are accurate, is that the potential exists for improving the quality of public services and for providing a less materially impoverished life for the poor.

On the other hand, and unfortunately there is another hand to this argument, two major socioeconomic problems attend the effort to stimulate abundance through the application of sophisticated technological means. First, automation and advanced technology have disturbing consequences for the occupational structure of a nation's economy. Some have contended that as the proportion of unskilled or semiskilled jobs declines, industries rely more on technology. Thus, in the long run the political systems of advanced industrialized societies are going to be confronted by a large mass of technologically superfluous individuals.[14] Unless meaningful work and/or recreational alternatives can be devised for these individuals, or the tie between income and employment is broken, there will be an increased likelihood of massive social unrest with associated forms of individual and collective violence, such as has been experienced recently in the United States.

Although this picture of the future remains open to challenge, what does seem relatively certain is that the proportion of the work force in primary occupations (for example, farming, mining) and secondary occupations (for example, manufacturing), that is, occupations involving the production of goods, is going to decline. Long-term trends suggest that employment in service-related fields (for example, education, health services, government) is likely to grow. Nonprofit institutions — schools, hospitals, governmental agencies, private foundations — are likely to absorb a growing proportion of job-seekers. This shift in the occupational structure, from the production of goods to the provision of services, carries with it a host of related changes, ranging from the

---

[13] Herman Kahn and Anthony J. Wiener, "The Next Thirty-Three Years: A Framework for Speculation," in Daniel Bell, ed., *Toward the Year 2000* (Boston: Beacon Press, 1969), pp. 73–99; and A. F. K. Organski, *The States of Political Development* (New York: Alfred A. Knopf, 1965), pp. 186–211.

[14] David Apter, ed., *Ideology and Discontent* (New York: Free Press, 1964), pp. 17–43.

increasing difficulty of tying wage increases to increases in productivity, with inflationary consequences, to a possible decline in the influence of organized labor, whose major bastions of strength in the economy have been in the industrialized sector.[15]

The second problem deriving from the abundance through technology equation has to do with the consumption of nonrenewable natural resources. To the extent that abundance is pegged to the continuously expanding technology-based production of goods for mass consumption, the rate at which advanced industrialized societies use up the earth's nonrenewable resources increases. Thus, without the implementation by governments of long-range social and resource plans or the development of resource-saving technological innovations, the ultimate result of short-term technology-induced abundance will be long-run technology-stimulated scarcity.

Wealth. Many observers have emphasized the linkages between the relative wealth of nations, as measured by such indicators as per capita income, and the patterns of their public policies. Let us, first of all, consider the relationship between national wealth and regulatory policy, especially the regulation of individual conduct.

Under this rubric, the work of such researchers as Lipset, Dahl, Cutright, and Russett points to the following generalization: the more economically developed or the wealthier the nation, the greater are the chances that its political regime will be supportive of strong civil libertarian policies.[16] Or, put the other way, the poorer a country, the less likely are its citizens to enjoy freedom of speech, press, and assembly. To be sure, there are deviant cases. India is a very poor nation whose political regime long supported civil liberties; East Germany, in contrast, is relatively wealthy and, at the same time, highly restrictive when it comes to the regulation of its citizens' conduct. Despite the existence of such deviant cases, by and large the generalization holds.

The next question is, Why do we find a strong association between wealth and civil libertarian guarantees? One line of explanation has it that the wealthier countries are more inclined and better able than the poorer ones to support systems of mass primary and secondary education and that, for a variety of reasons, a highly literate population is more likely to develop the political skills necessary to assert and defend

[15] Daniel Bell, *The Coming of Post-Industrial Society* (New York: Basic Books, 1973), pp. 123–164.

[16] Seymour Lipset, *Political Man* (Garden City, N.Y.: Doubleday & Co., 1960), pp. 45–76; Robert A. Dahl, *Polyarchy* (New Haven: Yale University Press, 1971), pp. 62–80; Phillips Cutright, "National Political Development: Its Measurement and Social Correlates," in Nelson Polsby, Robert Dentler, and Paul Smith, eds., *Politics and Social Life* (Boston: Houghton Mifflin Co., 1963), pp. 569–81; and Bruce M. Russett et al., *World Handbook of Political and Social Indicators* (New Haven: Yale University Press, 1964), pp. 293–303.

liberal democratic freedoms. A complementary argument is that wealth lowers the level of political antagonism in a society. Nations torn by bitter social and political cleavages are typically nations in which the various contending forces, including the governmental authorities, are likely, by definition, to be deeply mistrustful of their opponents. Therefore, the authorities tend to wish to silence their antagonists. In such situations the legally prescribed rights of citizens rest on shaky ground. To the degree, then, that economic scarcity is a source of political antagonism, and politics a conflict between haves and have-nots, it follows that a wealthier nation, all other factors aside, will exhibit lower levels of political hostility and hence be more likely to sustain civil liberties than will a poorer one.

However, when we introduce the time dimension into the discussion and raise questions about causality, the picture becomes both more complex and less rosy. First, some theorists argue that countries undergoing the process of economic development, which typically means becoming industrialized, are likely to be subjected to a whole series of strains and tensions that raise the level of political antagonism and, in turn, reduce the chances of introducing, extending, or maintaining civil libertarian policies. In that case the association between wealth and individual liberty may be seen as applicable to nations which are already relatively wealthy. Second, for some writers it is by no means clear whether wealth per se causes libertarian policies or is itself a result of such policies. These observers contend that economic growth is as much stimulated by as it is a cause of liberal democratic freedoms. On the face of it, then, these arguments appear to be self-contradictory. It would seem that economic growth and industrialization can either weaken the chances for civil libertarian guarantees or be stimulated by such guarantees. Certainly they cannot do both simultaneously.

As we see it, there are basically two ways out of this dilemma. First, it may be argued that a large percentage of the countries which are at the same time wealthy and staunchly civil libertarian got that way as a result of uniquely Western cultural-historical patterns, that is, are countries whose underlying values were most strongly affected by the Protestant Reformation. Thus the association between wealth and liberty is the spurious result of a third, cultural variable. The non-Western countries around the world where one can find a wealth-liberty combination may be seen as products of yet another historical accident, the accident in this case being conquest and/or colonization by strongly libertarian but self-aggrandizing Western powers whose imposition of certain institutional structures and value patterns facilitated economic growth and libertarian political rules. This is, to put it mildly, a culturally biased, Kiplingesque point of view.

An alternative explanation, which we regard as more plausible, is built around the importance of timing. From this perspective it is the rapidity of change rather than economic development per se that is inimical to civil libertarian guarantees.[17] Rapid industrialization rather than industrialization itself is seen as producing the stresses and strains damaging to the cause of freedom. A correlative account of the relationship, based on review of the history of Western nations, suggests that certain civil liberties, particularly the franchise and the rights of trade union organization and collective bargaining, were denied to the bulk of the population (that is, the working class) until the process of industrialization was well along. Thus it was only after Western countries were already relatively wealthy that full civil libertarian guarantees were extended to most citizens.

With respect to the question of the association between economic development and the distributive policies of political systems, a good deal of evidence has been accumulated which suggests that the wealthier the nation, the greater the proportion of its gross national product that will be spent for public consumption purposes.[18] Against a background of research on the public expenditure policies of American state governments suggesting the same kind of relationship, these findings are rather impressive.

However, a significant qualification should be brought to the reader's attention. The relationship between wealth and the expenditure of resources for public purposes appears to be strongest for nations undergoing the process of industrialization; beyond a certain level of economic development (where annual per capita income exceeds $600) the strength of the association diminishes somewhat. Why should this be the case? According to the American economist Frederick Pryor, the answer appears to lie in the fact that countries undergoing a changeover from agricultural to industrial dominance must confront a series of structural problems which can only be met through greater public exertions.[19] The agenda for public policy-making expands dramatically as a country undergoes economic development. Infrastructural needs arise for highways, railroads, port facilities, and so on, which typically require an increase in public outlays so as to encourage industrialization. At the same time, industrialization creates numerous social dislocations which call forth increased governmental expenditures. Problems that in a traditional agricultural setting were met by family,

---

[17] John H. Kautsky, *Communism and the Politics of Development* (New York: John Wiley & Sons, 1968), pp. 184–201; and Robert P. Clark, Jr., *Development and Instability* (New York: Dryden Press, 1974).

[18] Frederick C. Pryor, *Public Expenditures in Capitalist and Communist Nations* (Homewood, Ill.: Richard D. Irwin, 1968).

[19] Ibid., pp. 280–312.

church, or local community become objects of public concern and hence public expenditure during this stage of a country's development. In addition, a host of new social problems (for example, crime, delinquency, sanitation) emerge as a result of the industrialization-stimulated concentration of large numbers of people in relatively small areas. And these problems also call forth greater public expenditures.

After countries are relatively wealthy and industrialized, however, the ability of subsequent increases in per capita income to produce variations in the level of public expenditures decreases in importance relative to other factors. Pryor, using data derived from the United States and 13 European countries, concludes that expenditures for internal security, foreign aid, and research and development remain strongly linked to wealth. But "for military, welfare, education, and health expenditures, on the other hand, this per capita income variable has little explanatory power."[20] In other words, as compared to the effect of per capita income on public outlays in the American states, in relatively wealthy nations per capita income is not an especially important determinant of public spending for most of the leading spheres of distributive policy.

Another explanation of why per capita income declines in importance, as against other factors, when nations reach comparatively advanced stages of economic development involves the shifting status of the citizen. It is generally true that the wealthier the country, the higher its per capita income, the more evenly that income is distributed among the population. Thus in wealthy nations an increasingly large proportion of citizens begin to see themselves as "haves," not "have-nots." As a result growing numbers of people begin to perceive themselves as taxpayers, individuals from whom resources are being extracted, and not exclusively as the beneficiaries of their political system's distributive policies. Thus we would expect to find progressively stronger resistance to proportionately greater public expenditures in nations where large numbers of citizens come to see themselves as paying the bill, through taxation, for these public allocations. Correlatively, it may also be true that the development of preferences for private consumer goods and services lowers the level of popular tolerance for proportionately greater public spending in wealthy nations. Indeed, taxpayer resistance has become a live issue in the wealthiest of industrial countries.

We may conclude that national wealth is an important determinant of variations in regulative, distributive, and extractive policies. But for reasons which we have just expressed, it appears to be far from being the exclusive or predominant constraining factor.

---

[20] Ibid., p. 287.

The Physical Environment and Public Policies

Until recently, most commentary on the relationship between people's physical surroundings and their political behavior dealt with two things: first, the impact these surroundings were alleged to have in determining what kind of political regime would rule; and second, the significance of these surroundings on the regime's military and foreign policy orientations. Only relatively recently, as an outgrowth of growing concern in the Western world with pollution and problems involving nonrenewable natural resources, have we witnessed intense discussion of the direct link between the physical environment and domestic public policy matters.

Illustrative of the first type of argumentation noted above are the works of the 16th century French philosopher Jean Bodin, his 18th century countryman Montesquieu, and the 20th century American political scientist Karl Wittfogel.[21] For these observers, certain aspects of a society's physical circumstances, climate for Bodin and Montesquieu and water resources for Wittfogel, determine to a large extent the kind of political regime that is likely to develop in different areas of the world. Assertions about the second relationship of physical surroundings to foreign policy and military considerations have been advanced by some observers of international relations. Those who claim that physical conditions are decisive influences on the international behavior of political systems advocate "geopolitics." These individuals have claimed that the geographic location of a nation imposes certain enduring constraints on its foreign policy. De Gaulle, for example, once remarked to Churchill that, in the final analysis, France was at the edge of a continent, Britain an island, and America another world. And these geographic truisms, as he saw them, were to be decisive in determining French foreign policy under his leadership.[22]

More pertinent to our present concern, however, is the effect of what has come to be called the ecological crisis on patterns of domestic public policies. In this connection it should hardly come as a surprise that the political systems of the various industrialized countries have for some time produced policies directed at and constrained by the availability of material resources. These policies were largely based on two assumptions. First, it was believed that an inexhaustible supply of material resources was available for exploitation — either domestic

---

[21] Jean Bodin, *Six Books of the Commonwealth* (Oxford: Basil Blackwell, n.d.); Baron de Montesquieu, *The Spirit of the Laws* (New York: Hafner Publishing Co., 1949); and Karl Wittfogel, *Oriental Despotism* (New Haven: Yale University Press, 1957).

[22] Quoted in Ronald Steel, *The End of Alliance* (New York: Viking Press, 1962), p. 71.

resources or resources that could be obtained via international trade and/or conquest. Second, the unlimited exploitation and conversion of these resources for industrial and commercial purposes were defined as being necessary ingredients in promoting economic growth and general prosperity.

It is no wonder then that public policies in this realm were primarily facilitative in character. Generally, policies were designed so as to promote the rapid exploitation of natural resources for economic development purposes. In addition, given the assumption of inexhaustibility, these resources were defined more as the objects of policy than as the crucial constraining elements in policy-making. The problem was viewed essentially as having to do with devising the forms of human organization and technologies that could most effectively exploit the resources.

Now it is becoming apparent that the resources themselves are far from inexhaustible. Indeed, there are projections which show that at current consumption rates a fair share of the world's nonrenewable natural resources will be used up in from 50 to 100 years.[23] If this is true, the flow of causality may reverse itself. That is, if we assume long-run resource depletion instead of inexhaustibility, then policies must be constrained by this fact. The problem becomes one of shaping and adjusting policies so as to take account of the immutable fact of diminishing supply. If policy-makers in industrialized societies do what environmental experts generally say they should do, present policies will be altered considerably. The need, as environmentalists see it, for comprehensive economic and resource planning will inevitably incline governments to play an increasingly intensive role in all forms of social behavior. Taxation levels will be raised in an effort to reduce the consumption of goods which require scarce resources for their production. Individual and group behavior will be regulated more intensively and in new ways (for example, no Sunday driving). And the distributive patterns of public spending will be redirected so as to promote such things as energy-saving mass transportation and the development of recycling techniques to conserve scarce metals and fibers.[24]

If policy-makers do not do what the environmentalists want them to, what will they do? They will probably bet that resource consumption rates can be maintained at their present or even increased levels until such time as scientific and technological breakthroughs solve the problem. If the policy-makers lose this bet, and vital resources are used up

---

[23] Donella H. Meadows et al., *The Limits to Growth* (New York: Universe Books, 1972).

[24] Richard A. Falk, *This Endangered Planet: Prospects and Proposals for Human Survival* (New York: Random House, 1971).

and technological solutions prove impossible or of only limited value, the industrialized nations will face collapse.

We may well ask why policy-makers would be inclined to gamble in this fashion. They may reason that the doomsday forecasts of the environmentalists are wildly exaggerated. Or they may believe that the rapid consumption of nonrenewable resources has an intimate association with continued economic growth, which, in turn, is linked to full employment and higher per capita income. Many political leaders fear that policies designed to restrict resource depletion would evoke massive popular resistance. Moreover, politically influential business and labor forces are unlikely to sit still while expansion-restricting policies threaten the profitability of their enterprises or the availability of jobs.

To this point we have commented on only one segment of the problem posed by the ecological crisis. If we assume for the moment that the environmentalists' advice will be rejected and that the decision-makers will persist in policies designed to maximize economic growth and minimize resource saving, then it seems likely that the decision-makers will be increasingly constrained to take the problem of pollution into account. The authors of *Limits to Growth* suggest that as economic growth increases, the amounts of carbon dioxide, thermal energy, radioactive waste, and toxic metals released into the environment also increase at an exponential rate. The consequences in terms of the planet's ability to sustain plant and animal life, including human life, are likely to be, if they are not already, disastrous. And it is clear that, relative to population size, the industrialized societies contribute disproportionately to the pollution problem.

Public policy remedies which require more stringent regulatory and distributive policies encounter the same set of difficulties we have described previously. To the extent that pollution-control policies threaten economic growth and prosperity, they are likely to meet both popular and business community resistance. Thus, unless technological innovations intervene, policy-makers, as well as the populations on whose behalf they act, may soon be confronted by almost insurmountable problems. Current efforts by the eight nations to regulate their physical environments are discussed in Chapter 11.

Social and Demographic Influences on Public Policy

The major problem we confront in discussing the linkage between the social characteristics of societies and the policy outputs of their political systems has to do with the flow of influence. In this chapter we are principally concerned with describing how certain environmental and political system attributes explain variations in public policies among nations. Therefore, we have chosen to see policy patterns as being caused by various antecedent economic, ecological, social, and political factors. But it is also perfectly obvious that the flow of cause and effect can operate the other way. Specifically, the policies themselves can produce variations in the environmental and political milieus of society.

Given this logic, we have been willing to view public policies as more amenable to substantive change, relatively less fixed, than the environment in which they are generated. We have therefore treated the policies as more effects than causes. Now with respect to the relationship between the social characteristics of society and public policy, it seems to us that certain social features are more easily changed than others. That is, variation in the literacy rate of a country's population may be seen as caused by or as explicable in terms of public spending levels for education. Here the policy is more cause than result of environmental change. On the other hand, take the case of a nation whose population is divided into various tribal or linguistic groupings. In this situation, the social characteristics are likely to be far more enduring and difficult to alter than is the literacy rate, and hence more likely to cause public policies to be pursued than to be modified by public policies.

In this light, we think that the particular social characteristics of industrialized societies which are likely to evoke variations in policy include the following: (1) population density, (2) population size, and (3) social cleavage patterns.

As everyone knows, the size of the world's population is increasing at a substantial rate. However, the rate of increase in the industrialized nations is lower than that found in the preindustrial or industrializing countries. In addition, the world's population is becoming progressively more urban. A larger and larger proportion of the total population is composed of people who reside in cities of over 100,000 residents. What public policy consequences follow from these observations?

Population Density. High population density has been linked by social scientists to an elaborate array of social disorders. Among these are high rates of delinquency, suicide, mental disorders, alcoholism, and tuberculosis. Moreover, the concentration of more and more people in cities creates certain structural or ecological problems having to do with public health, sanitation, transportation, pollution, and violence.

To say all this is to suggest that the agenda for policy-making appears to expand enormously as a result of urbanization. As Philip Hauser puts it:

> The increasing size and density of population, the increasing interdependence of the social order, the breakdown of traditional social controls, and the inability of inherited social institutions to cope with the new problems of urban life have led inexorably to the manifold expansion of government functions and powers.[25]

To deal with these problems governments have created whole new sets of institutions to make and implement regulatory and distributive policies in such areas as transportation, recreation, education, public housing, urban renewal, sewerage, water, solid waste disposal, and fire and police protection. Thus, to indicate that urbanization is increasing rapidly in the industrialized world is also to suggest the need for an expanding role for governmental activity and policy-making in social life. Although not all urbanologists share this view—Edward Banfield is a notable dissenter[26]—most believe that more funds must be extracted to pay for expanded services, that more types of personal and group conduct must be subject to public regulation, and that more public goods and services must be provided.

Indeed, the enormity of the problems involved strain the capacities of existing governmental structures. As a result of these strains efforts have been made by policy-makers in several of the most industrialized and urbanized societies (for example, Great Britain, France, Italy, and the United States) to reorganize local governmental institutions along more economically and demographically rational lines. Because of recent growth patterns, the boundaries and jurisdictions of local political units, often defined in past centuries, have been found to compound the already difficult dilemmas confronting urban policy-makers. Yet despite the efforts to create new regional or metropolitan political units in Western Europe and the United States, the reformers have generally not met with much success. In the United States, for instance, for reasons stemming from the federalist requirements of the Constitution and the "home rule" provisions of many state constitutions, efforts to create comprehensive metropolitan area–wide governments have typically failed.

One public policy question worth speculating about here is that of the association between urbanization and regulatory policies. A number of scholars have argued that urbanization, especially rapid urbanization, encourages the formation of mass political movements, frequently with revolutionary aspirations, which, in turn, give rise to repressive "law and order" policies from authorities who see their rule

---

[25] Philip M. Hauser, "Urbanization: An Overview," in Hauser and Leo F. Schnore, eds., *The Study of Urbanization* (New York: John Wiley & Sons, 1965), p. 28.

[26] Edward C. Banfield, *The Unheavenly City* (Boston: Little, Brown & Co., 1970).

as threatened by revolutionary upheaval or other forms of collective violence.[27] In short, rapid urbanization and derivative phenomena pose great dangers for the maintenance of individual freedom.

However, if we rank the nations of the world in terms of the percentages of their populations living in cities of 100,000 or more, we can come to somewhat more sanguine conclusions about the regulatory consequences of urbanization. Almost all the nations whose political systems have produced regulatory policies which we would judge as freedom-supportive are among the most thoroughly urbanized, whereas none of the 50-odd least urban countries meet conventional libertarian standards.[28]

Our explanation for these seemingly disparate findings has to do with the speed of urbanization and with the varying capacities of economic and political institutions to cope with the phenomenon. That is, in situations where for economic and technological reasons, large numbers of people are suddenly expelled from agricultural pursuits, and where insufficient jobs are available for them as they seek to become city dwellers, and in addition, where housing and urban services are inadequate, then we have all the crucial ingredients for turmoil, disorder, and governmental repression. Such a combination of forces characterizes present-day urbanization patterns in several Latin American countries.

> The formation of a marginal and sub-marginal population, often living on the very edge of subsistence levels, was the most obvious price that the major Latin American towns had to pay for reconciling their high rates of population growth with the low levels of productivity of their economic structure. The *barriadas,* slums, shanty towns, *favelas* and so forth, . . . spread and multiplied within the bounds of the urban horizon, must be regarded as indicators of a more general phenomenon: a huge sector of the urban population was living in economically, socially, and politically marginal conditions.[29]

Where the city's population grows at a slow pace, or where a high proportion of urban residents are old-timers — second- or third-generation urbanites — as against unintegrated newcomers, there is no necessary link between urbanization, social unrest, and governmental repression. In fact there is some evidence that over the long run city

---

[27] William Kornhauser, *The Politics of Mass Society* (Glencoe, Ill.: Free Press, 1959).

[28] Charles Taylor and Michael C. Hudson, *World Handbook of Political and Social Indicators,* 2d ed. (New Haven: Yale University Press, 1972), pp. 219–21.

[29] UN Economic Commission for Latin America, "Some Consequences of Urbanization for the Total Social Structure," in Gino Germani, ed., *Modernization, Urbanization, and the Urban Crisis* (Boston: Little, Brown & Co., 1973), p. 159.

life promotes a variety of societal changes—high social mobility, enhanced educational opportunities, a participatory change-oriented outlook on life, and the breakdown of traditional rural-based forms of domination—which stimulate popular demands for strongly civil libertarian public policies. Therefore, we may conclude that in and of itself high population density need not mean heightened levels of governmental control over individual and group political behavior; in fact the trend may be in the opposite direction. Unfortunately, however, this generalization may not apply to other modes of personal conduct. Large numbers of people living in close proximity to one another impel diverse kinds of regulatory policies which inhibit devil-may-care land usage, transportation, and recreational practices.

Population Size. The overall size of a nation's population also serves as a source of constraint on public policy. As things now stand, the evidence points to a continued exponential rate of growth on a worldwide basis.[30] The time it takes for the earth's population to double in size is becoming shorter and shorter. Yet it is the poorer, preindustrialized countries which contribute disproportionately to the continued growth rate. The population size of the industrialized societies is expanding much more slowly.

In terms of public policy concerns, the major issue confronting decision-makers in the preindustrial nations has to do with the elemental matter of producing sufficient food to sustain life for vastly expanded populations. In India, for example, recent innovations in farming techniques have resulted in substantial increases in crop yields. But these advances have been partially nullified because the increased food supply has been largely absorbed by intervening population growth. As a result there has been relatively little net improvement in the average Indian's diet.

Although population growth in industrialized societies is substantially slower, the problems it presents for policy-makers are no less troublesome. For as Richard Falk points out, "In terms of garbage production, pollution, land use, and resource depletion each additional person to the United States is equivalent in ecological terms to the addition of at least 25 people to India."[31] In other words, despite the fact of slower growth, the per person impact of population increase is considerably greater among the industrialized nations than in the rest of the world. The problem then is really part of, and serves to exacerbate, the ecological crisis whose dimensions and policy influences we have discussed previously.

What sort of regulatory role should political authorities in indus-

---

[30] Paul R. Ehrlich, *The Population Bomb* (New York: Ballantine Books, 1968).
[31] Falk, *Endangered Planet,* p. 139.

trialized societies assume in confronting the problem of population growth? Up to now the major issue in this area has been whether or not and the extent to which governments should legalize and/or make available contraceptive information and devices and abortion services. Various representatives of racial and religious groups have raised moral objections to governmental toleration and support of birth control. The general working assumption of both the advocates and opponents of these policies is that the increased availability of birth control services will result, in the long run, in a reversal of present population trends. If there is a choice in the matter, a large enough number of people will choose to limit family size so as to restrict population growth. There is indeed some evidence that this is already occurring in the industrialized countries. Alternatively, if policies based on free choice and voluntary cooperation do not have the desired impact, then the prospect of involuntary regulation of family size is raised, and with it a whole array of profound moral and ethical dilemmas will be placed on the agenda for public policy consideration.[32]

Social Divisions.   The degree to which a country's population is divided along racial, religious, ethnic, and linguistic lines is typically an important influence on the shaping of its public policies. If certain peoples emphasize subnational identities and/or are treated distinctively by other groups, the political system's agenda is likely to be crowded by a host of issues not present in more socially homogeneous nations. For one thing, as observers of recent events in the United States, Northern Ireland, Lebanon, and Nigeria can attest, the existence of major subnational cleavages frequently provides sources of intensive domestic violence and civil strife.

We think that the central policy influences relatable to social cleavages are broadly regulatory in character. And here we have in mind the regulation of group as opposed to individual conduct. The crucial problem facing policy-makers has to do with finding strategies and pursuing policies which promote social stability in society. This goal may be achieved in several different ways.

First, in some nations the social divisions in the population tend to be overlapping or cross-cutting. In Switzerland, for example, one can find German- and French-speaking Protestants as well as German- and French-speaking Catholics. Thus the two major social divisions in the country, religious and cultural-linguistic, cut across each other. When this occurs naturally, the chances of the population being divided into

---

[32] Daniel Callahan, "Ethics and Population Limitation," in Robert Roelofs, Joseph Crowley, and Donald Hardesty, eds., *Environment and Society* (Englewood Cliffs, N.J.: Prentice-Hall, 1974), pp. 338–57.

warring camps is minimized, and so are the regulatory problems confronting policy-makers. But even in Switzerland policy formulas have been devised, built around subnational cantonal governments and decentralization, to limit the potential for the development of social cleavage–based political antagonisms.

Where the natural social divisions of a nation do not exhibit this Swiss-type overlap, but instead tend to be isolative and recurrent, the regulatory problems facing policy-makers are substantially increased. We have in mind here such situations as the racial division in the United States, the problem of French- versus English-speaking Canadians, and the separation of Belgium into Flemish and Wallonian ethnic communities. In these and similar instances, four basic policy options are available to decision-makers: integration, consociation, segregation, and elimination.[33]

With integration, regulation is achieved by seeking to remove the source of social division itself through the pursuit of policies (for example, in education and housing) designed to reduce the affected group's distinctiveness and, in some instances, to meet its demands for greater social justice. We think that the racial integration movement in the United States during the 1950s and early 1960s had these goals in mind.

Although ostensibly benign in intent and execution, on many occasions the integrationist goal has been pursued by governmental tactics of violence and coercion. In Fascist Italy the German-speaking minority in the northern part of the country (Alto Adige) was subjected to considerable pressure to abandon its non-Italian cultural and linguistic character. Similarly, and with greater vengefulness, the forcible integration of Estonian, Latvian, and Lithuanian populations occurred in the Soviet Union after World War II at Stalin's direction. In the United States coercion has been occasionally directed since 1954 at groups that opposed peaceful integration of blacks.

The principal liberal alternative to integration is consociation. By this we mean efforts to achieve group regulation that are based on the recognition by policy-makers of the legitimacy of the affected group's right to retain its socially distinctive attributes. Policies of consociation, such as have been employed in the Netherlands, Belgium, Lebanon, Austria, and now Northern Ireland, involve the development of certain economic and political rules—federalism, proportional representation in elections, local autonomy, quota-based hiring practices, and elite-devised coalition governments—whose purpose is to award the affected

---

[33] Arend Lijphart, *The Politics of Accommodation* (Berkeley: University of California Press, 1968), pp. 1–15.

group or groups political and economic strength roughly equal to what their relative size in the population would warrant. In addition, the consociation strategy typically involves the encouragement, or at least the tolerance, of group-based cultural and educational facilities. Public support for instruction in an affected group's language or dialect in the school system would be an example.

Violence, both by governmental authorities and by elements in the population, may also occur when consociational policies are utilized. Here the major stimulants to civil strife are questions of how fair and equitable the consociational arrangements are perceived to be by the particular group and other elements in the population. For instance, the recent consociational settlement in Northern Ireland has spurred claims from Catholic extremists that the arrangements do not go far enough, whereas militant Protestants have maintained that the British government has capitulated to unreasonable Catholic demands.

Segregation, like consociation, involves the retention by racial, religious, ethnic, or linguistic minority groups of their socially distinctive characteristics. However, in this case the underlying premise of public policy-makers is the inherent inferiority of the affected group. Regulation is achieved by designing rules and procedures or by legitimating customary practices which are intended to deny members of the group access to and influence in the political system. Evidently the preconditions for the "success" of segregationist policies are: (1) the acceptance by the segregated group's members of their own inferiority; and/or (2) the fear that stepping out of line (that is, violating segregationist practice) will being instantaneous retaliation. When these perceptions break down, as has occurred with blacks in the United States in recent years, so too does the regulatory capacity of the segregationist policies. The long-run consequences of segregation are likely to be quite violent, involving coercive efforts by the authorities to maintain the old arrangements and violence by group members to alter the underlying policies defining their inferiority.

Finally, there is the alternative of elimination. This may be achieved either by expelling the affected group from the nation's territory or by physically exterminating the group. The latter policy was employed by the Nazi regime in Germany against the Jewish minority. Although patently inhuman and criminal, elimination may be a successful regulatory strategy if the bulk of the country's population is either indifferent or supportive. The major barriers to the implementation of this ghastly approach, aside from the consciences of the political authorities, are: (1) the affected group's size — the bigger the group, the greater the difficulty; and (2) pressure from the international community. However, the invocation of international legal principles has rarely been effective.

POLITICAL SYSTEM SOURCES OF VARIATIONS
IN PUBLIC POLICIES

One of the ironies of contemporary political research and speculation about developments in industrialized nations is the inclination to
view variations in public policies, and indeed political systems themselves, as essentially the passive consequences of environmental forces.
This perspective has been adopted by scholars of diverse philosophic
persuasions and methodological inclinations. Thus futurists stress the
impact of technology, Marxists the ownership of productive forces and
the class struggle, and students of American state politics the level of
industrialization, as the crucial environmental determinants of policy.
Yet it is difficult to deny that in industrialized nations a growing percentage of the work force is employed by government and that public
policies are playing an increasingly pervasive role in the lives of ordinary citizens. Now it may very well be that these occurrences derive
from environmental changes. Yet we find it difficult to believe that progressively larger and more intrusive political systems exercise no independent influence in shaping public policy, but are instead simply like
billiard balls shot into pockets by different environmental cues. As
Samuel Beer has argued:

> The modern state has served and has been served by various types of
> economy. Its main traits of structure and development have not been a
> mere reflection of an autonomously developing economy, but, on the con-
> trary, have displayed their own dynamic, often dictating the course of
> economic development itself.[34]

The political system, as conceived by Easton, includes three components: the political community, the regime, and the authorities.[35] By
political community he has in mind the sense of shared identity and
commitments that members of a society have toward one another and
toward their nation taken as a whole. The identification of Americans
with one another, as distinct from other nationalities, and with the
United States as a country, as distinct from other countries, is an illustration of the kinds of relationships that Easton has in mind. For our
purposes, though, we intend to emphasize the idea of shared commitments by regarding the influence of political ideology and public opinion on policy output, and by treating these as the crucial aspects of political community.

---

[34] Samuel Beer, "Modern Political Development," in Beer and Adam Ulam, eds.,
Patterns of Government, 3d ed. (New York: Random House, 1973), pp. 70 and 82.

[35] David Easton, *A Systems Analysis of Political Life* (New York: John Wiley & Sons,
1965), pp. 171–219.

Second, the regime component of the political system refers to the fundamental organization or basic constitutional arrangements, formal and informal, through which political decision-making occurs. The organization of the American national government into three relatively separate branches can serve as an example of regime characteristics.

The third component is the group of people who wield decision-making power: the authorities, or incumbents. On the American political scene, incumbent congressmen, senators, the president, federal judges, and bureaucrats are among the authorities. These individuals are, in short, the occupants of important authority roles in the political regime.

Using this categorization, we should now like to examine some arguments concerning the influence of political system characteristics in structuring public policy.

The Political Community

Under this heading we consider two separate but interrelated elements: ideology and public opinion. *Ideology* may be defined in a variety of ways.[36] We mean by this term widely shared and basic beliefs which stipulate how a society, including its political system, is and should be organized, what its goals are, and how they should be achieved.[37] Elements of ideologies are often set forth without meeting this broad test. What place do ideology and value systems have in molding public policy?

In a recent series of articles in the *British Journal of Political Science*, Anthony King scrutinizes a variety of distinctive policies adopted by five western democracies — West Germany, France, Great Britain, Canada, and the United States — in an effort to explain the timing of their original implementation and the level of current financing.[38] Among the social services he considers are old-age pensions, unemployment insurance, sickness pay, medical services, housing, and education. He finds that, with the notable exception of education, the United States tended to introduce all of these services later and to spend less on them, relative to GNP, than did its counterparts. In his view the underlying reason for the rather distinctive American policy response has to do with the enduring antistatist bias in the American liberal

---

[36] George Lichtheim, *The Concept of Ideology and Other Essays* (New York: Random House, 1967).

[37] Adapted from Zbigniew Brzezinski, *Ideology and Power in Soviet Politics*, rev. ed. (New York: Praeger Publishers, 1967), p. 5.

[38] Anthony King, "Ideas, Institutions, and the Policies of Governments: A Comparative Analysis," *British Journal of Political Science* 3 (July and October 1973): 291–313, 409–23.

ideology—as described, for example, in Louis Hartz's *The Liberal Tradition in America*. King contends that in none of the other countries examined did public debate concerning these services involve the role of the state itself. Moreover, he goes on to explain the relatively stronger performance of the American system in education, both secondary and postsecondary, largely in terms of the country's traditional liberal commitment to individual self-advancement and equality of opportunity.

In a related, though noncomparative, analysis of fundamental American political values, Donald Devine contends that one of consensual liberalism's functions for the American political system is to screen and frame issues in such a way as to restrict the agenda for public policy-making.[39] He argues that the antistatist component of the liberal ideology encourages the resolution of societal problems in the private sector and, concomitantly, prevents the overloading of public sector decision-making.

Such ideological determinism has played an even stronger role in explanations of public policy in the Soviet Union and other Communist-ruled states. Unlike most of the regimes of North America and Western Europe, those of Eastern Europe constantly proclaim their fidelity to an ideology. Led by theorists of totalitarianism, most post-1945 Anglo-American writing on the Soviet Union long emphasized the strength of the ideological factor—especially in central areas of domestic policy. The professed Communists and their critics differed in their interpretations of which elements of the ideology were decisive and the reasons for this. Yet those critics, including Merle Fainsod and Zbigniew Brzezinski, stressed the role of ideology in consolidating dictatorship in areas ranging from the organization of authority to the politics of agriculture and literature.[40]

However, skepticism about the impact of ideology on Western and Eastern societies has grown in recent decades. Harold Wilensky recently sought to refute widely held contentions about the influence of ideology on welfarism. He disputed the existence of major differences in values held by elites in industrialized nations and devised an empirical test which showed that approaches to equality and opportunity "consistently add nothing" to understanding variations in social security systems.[41]

Wilensky's skepticism was preceded by the rise of a school of thought

---

[39] Donald J. Devine, *The Political Cultures of the United States* (Boston: Little, Brown & Co., 1972).

[40] Brzezinski, *Ideology and Power;* and Merle Fainsod, *How Russia Is Ruled,* rev. ed. (Cambridge, Mass.: Harvard University Press, 1963).

[41] Harold I. Wilensky, *The Welfare State and Equality* (Berkeley: University of California Press, 1975), pp. 42–49.

which stressed that ideology was declining or dead as an influential force.[42] Among Sovietologists, such earlier skeptics of Marxism-Leninism's impact as Barrington Moore, Jr., were joined by Alfred Meyer, a partially converted Brzezinski, and many others.[43] Marxism-Leninism is now often portrayed as a source of rationalization of pragmatically based policy or as a refuge of neo-Stalinist reactionaries. Yet few argue that it is totally irrelevant to Soviet policy-making.

To the extent that they are held by individuals — ordinary citizens and especially key decision-makers — ideological precepts contribute to perceptions of the world and help people decide what is good and bad, what is desirable and undesirable, and what priorities should be assigned to different tasks. With variations of time and place ideological considerations help answer the question of what is to be done.

The linkages between public opinion and public policy are both complex and important. So far as the importance of public opinion is concerned, we believe along with the late V. O. Key that

> all governments, we may set out axiomatically, must concern themselves with public opinion. They do not maintain their authority by brute force alone; they must seek willing acceptance from most of their citizens. Popular governments may be considered as a special case of governments in general. Popular government has its peculiarities, one of which is the basis for the exercise of its authority: that governors shall seek out popular opinion, that they shall give it weight if not the determinative voice in decision, and that persons outside the government have a right to be heard. This legitimization of the view that the preferences of the governed shall be accorded weight by governors constitutes the moral basis of popular government, an ethical imperative that in mature democracies is converted into consistent habits and patterns of action among those in places of authority and leadership.[44]

Public opinion, that is popular opinions about issues, events, and personalities, is a product of three elements. First, it is partly, and only partly, molded by forces present in the political system's environment, such as those we have described earlier in the chapter: for example, the prevailing economic conditions of the country. Second, it is also partly a reaction to proposed or existing governmental policies and actions. But public opinion is also, and this gives it its independent status, the mixing of these environmental and governmental elements with the underlying beliefs, values, and predispositions of individuals.

---

[42] Daniel Bell, *The End of Ideology: On the Exhaustion of Political Ideas in the Fifties* (New York: Free Press, 1960).

[43] Barrington Moore, Jr., *Soviet Politics — The Dilemma of Power* (New York: Harper & Row 1950); Brzezinski, *Between Two Ages;* and Alfred G. Meyer, *The Soviet Political System* (New York: Random House, 1965).

[44] V. O. Key, Jr., *Public Opinion and American Democracy* (New York: Alfred A. Knopf, 1961), p. 412.

Typically the impact of public opinion on policy is indirect. In democratic regimes there exist institutional arrangements — political parties, competitive elections for public office, and interest groups — whose function is to translate popular sentiment into governmental policy. The role of these units and procedures will be described in greater detail shortly. In modern or modernizing autocratic regimes rulers tend to rely more on their intuition, frequently based on ideological presuppositions, in gauging public sentiment as well as on monopolistic political education campaigns in molding it. Yet few, if any, regimes dare to completely ignore the priorities of their citizens.

With the advent of national opinion polling in the United States in the 1930s, and later in all the other industrialized Western democracies, the distribution of public opinion has come to have a more direct influence on public policy. Elected officials may now be apprised of public sentiment on most major issues of the day. The extent to which they choose to act in conformity with that sentiment can vary substantially, but certainly any democratic politician who values reelection will ignore it at his or her peril.

To argue that mass opinion is an influential determinant of policy requires us to look into the nature of the phenomenon. First, not all public policy matters are of sufficient significance to the public to evoke opinions. Most routine governmental actions fall into this category. But it has also been found that relatively important policy decisions, those having to do with American foreign trade, for example, may evade popular concern.[45] Even issues which are vigorously debated in the mass media may elicit modest interest from the broad public. This has led some scholars to differentiate between attentive and inattentive publics, the former being composed of individuals whose fortunes are most immediately affected by the outcome of governmental deliberations. And naturally, the sentiments of the attentive public are far more likely to carry weight in determining the policy result.

It has also been observed that public opinion may be inconsistent, contradictory, and uninformed. Inconsistency is suggested by the lack of strong statistical associations between the distribution of sentiment on various policy issues. For example, in *Political Change in Britain,* Butler and Stokes make an effort to relate the British public's reaction to a variety of problems which faced that country in the late 1960s (for example, nationalization of industry, retention of nuclear weapons, entry into the Common Market, abolition of the death penalty, and treatment to be accorded immigrants from the Commonwealth countries).[46]

---

[45] James J. Best, *Public Opinion* (Homewood, Ill.: Dorsey Press, 1973), pp. 216–64.

[46] David Butler and Donald Stokes, *Political Change in Britain* (New York: St. Martin's Press, 1969), p. 199.

They discovered that knowing an individual's position on one issue, say nationalism, was of little help in predicting how he or she would stand on any other. The most people do not confront the world of public decision-making with a set of broad, underlying principles whose effect would be to govern their views on a set of particular issues so as to make them consistent with one another. The resulting inconsistency in the mass public's political beliefs — and the phenomenon is by no means restricted to Britain — lessens the impact of public opinion on those in authority.

This difficulty is compounded when public sentiment is not merely inconsistent or even ephemeral but is actually contradictory. For instance, Angus Campbell and his associates discovered, in sampling American public opinion during the 1950s, that many people who endorsed higher levels of public spending for social services were equally enthusiastic about the idea of lowering taxes.[47] As we all know, doing the former makes it exceedingly difficult to simultaneously accomplish the latter.

Yet other findings indicate some positive attributes of public opinion. According to Key:

> In American presidential campaigns of recent decades the portrait of the American electorate that develops . . . is not one of an electorate strait-jacketed by social determinants or moved by subconscious urges triggered by devilishly skillful propagandists. It is rather one of an electorate moved by concern about central and relevant questions of public policy, of governmental performance, and of executive personality.[48]

Key and other students of public opinion consider U.S. and Western European voters sufficiently sophisticated to identify those political parties and candidates for office whose stands on salient policy issues correspond to their own and then to act accordingly in the voting booth. Let us take an illustration drawn from the Butler and Stokes analysis of British public opinion. In 1963 a random sample of British voters were asked whether they favored the expansion or curtailment of social service programs and then, which party — Labour or Conservative — was more likely to accomplish the preferred goal. The results suggest that the British public was by and large successful in identifying the Labour party as more likely to expand services and the Conservative party as more likely to retrench in this policy domain. What is more, those voters

---

[47] Angus Campbell et al., *The American Voter* (New York: John Wiley & Sons, 1960), pp. 168–87.

[48] V. O. Key, Jr., *The Responsible Electorate* (Cambridge, Mass.: Harvard University Press, 1966), pp. 7–8.

who had voted Conservative in the 1959 general elections and who, by 1963, favored an expansion of government services, were much more likely to report having switched to Labour in the 1964 contest.[49]

Similar findings have been adduced from recent studies of American public opinion and electoral behavior. Gerald Pomper, in the course of his analysis of popular sentiment in the last several presidential elections, provides evidence that increasingly large segments of the electorate have been successful in identifying the alternative stands of the Republican and Democratic candidates on such policy issues as aid to education, school integration, medical care, fair employment practices, and foreign aid. And like their British counterparts, American voters were prone to cast their ballots for the candidates whose views on these matters, which they successfully perceived, most closely paralleled their own.[50]

Finally, a study of the relationship between constituency attitudes and the roll-call voting record of members of the U.S. House of Representatives in 1958 found relatively strong positive associations between the constituents' policy preferences and their representatives' voting record on such issues as civil rights and social welfare.[51] However, the link was far more tenuous in the area of foreign policy, and it was not clear from this study whether constituents' opinions exerted a direct influence on the representatives' behavior.

We would maintain, in sum, that despite problems having to do with the complexity and visibility of policy-related issues, as well as the problems stemming from the mass public's cognitive capacities, democratic public opinion does constitute a constraining influence on policy outcomes. The influence may most often be indirect, mediated by political parties and their candidates; and it may also vary in intensity and power, depending on the importance and clarity of the issues involved; but that it exists seems indisputable.

As for such nondemocratic countries as the Soviet Union and East Germany, we can offer little empirical evidence to support the contention that public opinion acts as an important constraint on policymakers. "Revisionist" analyses of Soviet politics have made a strong case for group pressures, but not yet for diffuse mass input.[52] Yet the

---

[49] Butler and Stokes, *Political Change,* pp. 345–46.

[50] Gerald Pomper, "From Confusion to Clarity: Issues and American Voters, 1956–1968," *American Political Science Review* 66 (June 1972): 415–28.

[51] Warren Miller and Donald Stokes, "Consistency Influence in Congress," in Angus Campbell et al., eds., *Elections and the Political Order* (New York: John Wiley & Sons, 1966), pp. 351–72.

[52] H. Gordon Skilling and Franklyn Griffiths, eds., *Interest Groups in Soviet Politics* (Princeton: Princeton University Press, 1971).

Nazi and Italian Fascist regimes were often surprisingly responsive to mass attitudes; the popular will has been responded to directly and dramatically in Poland; and we anticipate that future Western scholarship will confirm Soviet claims of strong patterns of responsiveness in numerous areas of domestic policy.

Political Regimes

Do the kinds of political regimes which rule in different nations make much difference in determining what types of extractive, distributive, and regulative policies are produced? If we assume that the regime type is itself simply a reflection of underlying environmental social and economic forces, as many have, then the answer must obviously be negative. But if we adopt the view that political regimes are able to alter in diverse ways the social and economic milieus in which they operate, the response to our question has to be more open and tentative, at the very least. Let us explore the matter from the perspective of an author who does work on the assumption that political regimes make a difference.

In *Comparative Politics: A Distributive Approach,* Alexander Groth classifies regimes into three types: established democracies, innovative-mobilizational autocracies, and traditional autocracies. He identifies as democratic those regimes in which there is generally both popular and open participation in the political process, and he considers such regimes as "established" if they have exhibited these attributes since before the end of World War II (for example, Australia, Canada, Great Britain, Ireland, Sweden, Switzerland, and the United States). Groth takes autocracy to mean rule by one or a few persons, and distinguishes between innovative-mobilizational versions, such as the Soviet and Nazi regimes, and traditional autocracies, such as those which have recently been deposed in Greece and Portugal and the one which is presumably in the process of disestablishment in Spain.

> Innovative-mobilizational regimes seek to change the inherited social order, popular values, traditional institutions and the distribution of resources and gratifications in society. . . . Within this category the Right regimes, such as the Nazi and Fascist, carry out most of these objectives without simultaneously destroying the socioeconomic elites of *status quo ante* — that is, without massively redistributing economic resources from the old elite to the nonelites. In contrast, the Left regimes are outwardly committed to destroy the perquisites of all *status quo ante* socioeconomic elites and to redistribute economic resources to the heretofore nonelites. . . . Traditional autocracies are regimes that continue a long-established inherited social order; they de-emphasize popular participation and involvement in political affairs. . . . They are oriented to the maintenance

of a traditional structure of power and generally do not tamper with age-old customs, beliefs and attitudes.[53]

Having identified these three regime types, Groth goes on to argue that their extractive, distributive, and regulatory policies are substantially different from one another. First, with respect to extraction, he contends that the established democracies are more inclined to rely on direct and progressive forms of taxation and to exhibit budget-making procedures that are at once more open and less arbitrary than the procedures of their autocratic counterparts. Although this observation may come as a shock to readers familiar with the "tax loopholes" in the United States, it is nevertheless Groth's view that progressive taxation, based on personal income and the ability to pay, is more prevalent among the established democracies than it is in either type of autocracy.

By contrast, Groth found that traditional autocracies are more inclined to rely on regressive indirect taxing methods which place a disproportionate share of the burden on those least able to bear it. Correlatively, these regimes tend to undertax the property and income of the economically and socially privileged elites in the population to whose interests they are especially sensitive.

While the emphasis of the traditional autocracies is on the maintenance of the existing social order, this is decidedly not the case, at least when they come to power, with innovative-mobilizational regimes. So far as their extractive policies are concerned, Groth contends that the principal thing which sets them apart from the established democracies is their propensity to rely on arbitrary, confiscatory means. "Authoritarian regimes of the twentieth century have significantly supplemented the resources available to them through taxation by large-scale confiscation and expropriation of private resources. Both in extent and method such appropriations have far exceeded anything realized by any of the effective democracies."[54] By confiscating without compensation the property of proscribed segments in the population, kulaks or Jews, these regimes buttress their tax revenues.

Aside from this common characteristic, Groth finds significant policy differences between right-wing (that is, Fascist, Nazi) and left-wing (that is, Communist) versions. He argues that the Fascist and Nazi regimes approximated traditional autocracies in the preferential treatment they accorded to the wealthy and wellborn, at least so long as these groups were politically congenial. This is supported by the following account by Richard Grunberger in *The 12-Year Reich:* "From 1933

---

[53] Alexander J. Groth, *Comparative Politics: A Distributive Approach* (New York: Macmillan Co., 1971), p. 15.

[54] Ibid., p. 80

onwards government statutes enormously strengthened the organizational power of cartels. Armed with unlimited arbitrary powers of cartelization, the Ministry of Economics bestowed official sanctions on what had previously been private organizations, for restricting capacity and subordinating whole industries to the wishes of monopolists."[55]

Alternatively, the ideological thrust of Communist regimes is radically egalitarian, and their principal beneficiaries are supposed to be working classes instead of private sector monopolists. As against the right-wing pattern these regimes do, in fact, eliminate tax and other advantages enjoyed by the traditional upper strata. Yet under Communist rule income differences based on skill, performance, and political orthodoxy are by no means eliminated. This fact has certain consequences for tax policy. As Groth points out, the Soviet regime has tended to rely not on income taxes but on consumption or turnover taxes on food, clothing, and other perishable and durable commodities as the major source of its revenue. This approach to taxation, evidently intended to restrict mass consumption of private goods, does not work to the advantage of the ordinary Russian worker; it does reward technological, administrative, and scientific elites. "It is a matter of fact that high taxes on bread, milk, vegetables, tobacco and clothes impose far heavier burdens on the man who earns 400 rubles a month than one who earns 4,000."[56]

Based on Groth's analysis, if we rank the three regime types in terms of their distribution of public goods and services in relation to national income or wealth, the order would be as follows: left-wing innovative-mobilizational autocracy, established democracy, right-wing innovative-mobilizational autocracy, and traditional autocracy. The performance of traditionalist regimes in terms of the amount of money allocated, relative to GNP, for education, medical services, social welfare, and public housing is far and away the worst. On the other hand, the output of most European Communist regimes, but not of Fascist or Nazi regimes, in most of these areas of distributive policy has been impressive. What is more, the Communist regimes have made substantial efforts to ensure that previously deprived elements in the population, always with the qualification of political congeniality, obtain access to such customarily upper-class services as professional health care and higher education.

The major difference, in Groth's view, between the distributive policies of Communist and democratic regimes lies in the greater propensity of the former to impose long-term investment policies which promote the expansion of heavy industry at the expense of consumer

---

[55] Richard Grunberger, *The 12-Year Reich* (New York: Ballantine Books, 1971), p. 194.
[56] Groth, *Comparative Politics*, p. 81.

goods. The relatively greater impact of public opinion on policy choice in the established democracies makes such a course of action exceedingly difficult to sustain, except under emergency conditions.

The matter of regulatory policy should be sufficiently familiar to the reader as to require little elaboration. Briefly, despite a certain unevenness in performance in the judicial systems of established democracies, groups and individuals in these democracies are generally freer of governmental restraint in most spheres of conduct than are groups and individuals under either type of autocracy. In addition, there appear to be vast discrepancies among the regime types in regard to the severity of the punishments that are imposed on criminal offenders. For instance, while the range of crimes punishable by death has been substantially reduced in the established democracies in recent years—where capital punishment has not been completely abolished—individuals may still be executed in the Soviet Union for such activities as forgery, the violation of currency regulations, looting public property, and giving or taking bribes.

Our willingness to accept Groth's findings, particularly those concerning extractive and distributive policy differences, is qualified by the fact that his evidence is often dated and fragmentary. As he himself admits, "Our inquiry is handicapped by a dearth of data."[57] Nonetheless, his work offers an interesting counterweight to arguments which stress the role of economic and other environmental indicators in determing public policy variations among nations.

To this stage in our discussion we have reported policy differences which appear to be attributable to variations between democratic and authoritarian regimes. We now want to consider some arguments which ascribe differences in policy output to internal variations among democratic regimes. Specifically, we want to explore the question of why the United States has lagged behind other Western democracies (for example, Great Britain, Sweden, West Germany) in the provision of many public goods and services.

As we indicated earlier, with the exception of education the United States has tended to introduce these social goods and services at a later date and to spend proportionately less on them than has been the case with comparable Western European democracies. Why should this be so? Several regime-related arguments have been advanced. Heidenheimer suggests a number of explanatory factors.[58] First, the professionalization of the public administration occurred later in America

---

[57] Ibid., p. 11.

[58] Arnold J. Heidenheimer, "The Politics of Public Education, Health, and Welfare in the USA and Western Europe: How Growth and Reform Potentials Have Differed," *British Journal of Political Science* 3 (July 1973): 315–40.

than in similar European political systems, and as a consequence the public administration has enjoyed less esteem. A reputation for incompetence at the national level and/or corruption at the local level made the American public leery about investing the despised bureaucrat with substantial power. Second, "it is evident that the defensive strength of competing private suppliers of services was immensely greater in the American setting."[59] Interest groups anchored in the business community and the professions and opposed to public spending for and especially public control over these social goods and services, were organized earlier and came to enjoy greater prestige in the United States than in Western Europe.

On the other side of the ledger, the forces pushing for the welfare state were comparatively weaker in the American system. As Heidenheimer and Andrew Martin contend, the American labor movement has been organizationally more fragmented and ideologically more sympathetic to capitalism than have typical European labor unions.[60] In addition, there failed to develop in the United States a separate working-class or union-based political party, such as the Labour party in Britain or the Social Democratic parties in Scandinavia and Germany, capable of attaining power and implementing welfare state programs or, at a minimum, of being a sufficient political threat to conservative parties as to induce them to initiate such programs.

More broadly, certain institutional features of the American political regime seem to be linked to the retardation of the welfare state. In this connection both Heidenheimer and Martin refer to the fragmentation of policy-making institutions and the decentralization of political parties. The importance of federalist and separation of powers doctrines is stressed. The dispersion of formal authority for policy-making makes it relatively easy for groups seeking to block welfare state policies to do so, while making it difficult for the proponents of such policies to have their wishes enacted into law. Moreover, the fact that American parties are composed of diverse groups with frequently conflicting goals has made it hard for these parties to compensate for the institutional fragmentation through disciplined and coordinated efforts at policy-making.

The Authorities

In the final analysis, public policies are made by individuals. No matter what forces are at work in the political system's environment,

---

[59] Ibid., p. 323.

[60] Andrew Martin, *The Politics of Economic Policy in the United States* (Beverly Hills, Calif.: Sage Publications, 1973).

and no matter how much ideology, public opinion, and regime characteristics constrain their decisions, it is literally true that policies are made and implemented by individuals with the authority to act. It is impossible to discuss patterns of French, German, and Russian policymaking in this century without mentioning de Gaulle, Hitler, and Stalin. In addition to being molded by significant individuals, policies are also molded by groups of men in authority whom we will designate collectively as political elites.

Those who address the question of the linkage between an individual political leader and his or her policy enactments are typically engaged in a dialogue over the relative importance of the psychological versus the environmental and political constraints on the person's behavior. For example, a series of biographies of Hitler emphasizes the extent to which his actions were guided by internal psychological or personality imperatives having little to do with immediate external societal or political forces. On the other side, there are interpretations of Hitler's conduct, particularly in foreign policy, which down play the psychological and stress instead the historical circumstances of post–World War I Germany. This view may be summarized as follows: no German defeat no Hitler or no Depression no Hitler. That is, if the circumstances had not been propitious, Hitler might have ended his career as a minor Bavarian politician or architect, in which case the personality-molding relationship he developed with his parents and his subsequent sexual exploits, or lack thereof, would be of little general interest. Similar observations have been made about the careers and actions of Churchill, Roosevelt, de Gaulle, and indeed all "great men."

It strikes us that this issue cannot be resolved in either-or terms. Obviously, psychological and environmental-political elements interact with one another to produce particular policy decisions. We think, however, that under certain kinds of conditions the psychological attributes of political leaders are especially important. First of all, personality is likely to count for a great deal in crisis situations. Where past precedent and routine provide no clear-cut guidelines for action, then the role of personality or character is likely to be significant. Take the case of France during the 1958 Algerian crisis. Here we have a figure, de Gaulle, who was brought to power by the forces in French society which wished to preserve a French Algeria. Yet the same de Gaulle was maintained in power in 1962, after he had decided on Algerian independence, by the forces in France which were sympathetic to that position. Could any other French politician have performed this feat? Probably not.

Second, we agree with Fred Greenstein that "personality variations will be more evident to the degree that the individual occupies a position free 'from elaborate expectations of fixed content.' "[61] In other words, personality will not usually be an important determinant of policy decisions where the job or role is relatively fixed by rule or law and where, therefore, the individual exercises little discretionary authority. Conversely, with major leadership positions—president, prime minister, party secretary—where there is room to interpret the role in a variety of different ways, as did Chamberlain and Churchill, Hoover and Roosevelt, the potential significance of personality variations is maximized.

We come now to the status of political elites in the policy-making process. The focus of discussion in the extensive literature devoted to this matter is somewhat similar to that treating individual political leaders. It is only somewhat similar because psychological issues, except in such work as the Italian elite theorist Vilfredo Pareto and the American political scientists Harold Lasswell and Lucien Pye, rarely become the center of attention. Instead, the debate is built around the question of the degree to which national political elites are responsible to other segments of society.[62]

As we conceive it, there are basically three positions concerning the relationship between elite policy-making and environmental-political factors. The first view, in either its Marxist or non-Marxist form, holds that political elites are composed and reflect the preferences of dominant social classes and/or economic institutions in society. In societies where the military, landed aristocrats, religious hierarchs, or business notables enjoy wide power and esteem, the political elite will be drawn from these groups and will pursue policies compatible with their interests. Significant changes in policy are seen as deriving from changes in the composition of the political elite, which, in turn, is caused by shifts in the pattern of social stratification in society—the rise of certain groups and the decline of others—as well as alterations in the organization of economic activities.

The crucial features of this position are (1) that it ties the elite and its policies to minority segments in the population while (2) simultaneously ascribing to the elite an essentially passive role. A second conception of the political elite's role in policy-making retains the idea of passivity, by and large, but changes the understanding of accountability. This view has also been employed to characterize the distribution of power in Western, industrialized, and ostensibly democratic nations. Here the social composition and policy orientations of the

---

[61] Fred I. Greenstein, *Personality and Politics* (Chicago: Markham Publishing Co., 1969), p. 56.

[62] Geraint Parry, *Political Elites* (New York: Praeger Publishers, 1970); and Peter Bachrach, *The Theory of Democratic Elitism* (Boston: Little, Brown & Co., 1967).

political elite are subject to popular, majoritarian control through the mechanisms of periodic elections and competing political parties. Although not exercising close scrutiny over the day-to-day operations of government, the public is able to control the broad direction of public policy by its ability to replace the incumbent elite, from time to time, with politicians whose programs are more to its liking.

The final perspective on elite policy-making that we wish to note might appropriately be called elite autonomy. This argument, deriving for the most part from the work of writers on post-industrialism and bureaucracy, holds that for reasons stemming from the complexity of modern policy issues, a shift from parliamentary to bureaucratic arenas of decision-making, and the growing importance of science and technology, a new kind of political elite has arisen.[63] This post-industrial political elite is or will be socially heterogeneous — its recruitment based on meritocratic principles — but ideologically homogeneous. It does or will formulate public policies based on the values of efficiency and rationality. Instead of being responsible to the owners of the means of production or the mass electorate, it will control and manipulate its environmental-political milieu in the name of its underlying science-derived values. To the extent that this elite is accountable at all, it will be receptive or open to advice from the nation's scientific-engineering community, from which it will also draw its members. However, it is our impression that as yet this type of autonomous elite exists only in the minds of its devisers. Although scientists and engineers are becoming functionally indispensable in modern industrialized societies they will not necessarily come to play a predominant, uncontrollable elite role in policy-making.

CONCLUSIONS

The research findings and speculations which we have discussed in this chapter vary considerably in terms of specificity and consistency. Given this unevenness, are we still able to say anything worthwhile about the causes of variations in public policies? We think so, but the conclusions will be affected necessarily by the state of the art.

What we have done, generally, is present findings and arguments which assess the independent influence that an array of environmental and political factors have on policy outcomes. We have followed this procedure for reasons of clarity and simplicity. Yet in the real world things are not that simple. The various environmental and political

---

[63] Bell, *Post-Industrial Society*, pp. 341–67; and Merle Fainsod, "Bureaucracy and Modernization: The Russian and Soviet Case," in Joseph LaPalombara, ed., *Bureaucracy and Political Development* (Princeton: Princeton University Press, 1963), pp. 233–67.

factors which influence the shape and direction of policy interact with one another, rather than act independently or in isolation, so as to produce varying results.

For instance, in discussing findings concerning the source of U.S. distributive policies, we cited research which pointed to the importance of ideology, trade unionism, interest groups, political parties, and regime organization as independent constraints. It seems sensible to believe, however, that these elements do not operate in isolation from one another, but rather that they mix or interact with one another to evoke the retarded welfare state pattern.

Next, a similar line of reasoning may be adopted with respect to the environment versus politics argument we reported at the beginning of the chapter. The advocates of environmental determinism have been concerned largely with extraction and distribution. It seems possible to us that even if the predominance of environmental factors were confirmed in relation to the greater part of these policy categories, political considerations may still be more important in regulatory matters. We cite in support of this pluralist possibility the work of Theodore Lowi and C. Alexander Smith, which emphasizes that "arenas of power" and political processes vary in response to the type of policy under consideration.[64] Further, Cynthia Enloe has demonstrated that the politics of the physical environment is distinguishable from that of other issue areas in terms of structures, processes, and influential factors.[65] In subsequent chapters we will point out unique patterns of influential factors in several different policy areas.

Another path to resolving the politics and environment issues is Heclo's conclusion that while socioeconomic factors provide "the underlying conditions calling forth a policy response," only the political process provides "the energizing agents by which specific responses have been made."[66] This position is, for us, congenially politics-centered while giving environmental factors at least some of their due. Yet we are aware that Heclo has not systematically disproved the independent contribution of socioeconomic factors in the development of political responses.

To compound the problem of causality further, there is the question of cross-national uniformity. Many writers on public policy have tended to assume that the same combination of environmental and/or

---

[64] Theodore J. Lowi, "American Business, Public Policy, Case Studies, and Political Theory," *World Politics* 16 (July 1964): 677–715; and T. Alexander Smith, *The Comparative Policy Process* (Santa Barbara, Calif.: ABC-CLIO, 1975).

[65] Cynthia H. Enloe, *The Politics of Pollution in a Comparative Perspective* (New York: David McKay Co., 1975).

[66] Hugh Heclo, *Modern Social Politics in Britain and Sweden* (New Haven: Yale University Press, 1974), p. 288.

political conditions will produce the same kind of policy output in different countries. Yet B. Guy Peters, Samuel Huntington, and Brzezinski suggest that this need not be the case.[67] For reasons relating to unique historical experiences and traditions, a single constellation of environmental and political factors may yield one set of policy outputs in one nation while producing a quite different result in another.

Therefore, regarding the question of what causes variations in public policies with which we began this chapter, we propose some subsidiary questions to serve as investigatory devices. Which policies — extractive, distributive, regulatory — are you talking about? At what point in time? And with which nation or nations are you concerned? It may only be possible to answer the big question after the little ones have been answered.

---

[67] B. Guy Peters, "The Development of Social Policy in France, Sweden, and the United Kingdom: 1850–1965," in Martin Q. Heisler, ed., *Politics in Europe* (New York: David McKay Co., 1974), pp. 257–92.

3 External Influences on Public Policy

In January 1974, millions of Americans lined up for hours at gasoline stations and had time to consider the cause of their inconvenience. Blame often fell on the major multinational oil companies and the Arab governments, though other candidates were also suggested in the press. This was a time when the masses of people in Western industrialized states became much more aware than ever before that decision-makers beyond their borders had enormous power to shape their lives.

The study of comparative politics, and particularly an approach that stresses policy, cannot be content with the analysis of factors that are situated within the individual nation-states. Governments increasingly respond to suggestions, demands, and other influences which derive from events and actors based outside the domestic society. This responsiveness is made necessary by the development of a community of nation-states that has become "interdependent" in a vast range of economic, cultural, social, political, military, and physical environmental relationships. Most national governments usually retain the greater part of the autonomy and control that is accorded to them by their own constitutions and in some traditional studies of national politics. Yet the study of public policy and its context cannot be restricted by the boundaries of the nation-states.

Externally based developments, forces, and structures with a strong capacity to influence national domestic policies include wars, global depressions, multinational oil companies, near-universal international organizations like the United Nations, regional structures like the European Communities, the Roman Catholic church, the American Central Intelligence Agency, and the remnants of the Soviet- and Chinese-based groupings of Communist parties and their auxiliary organizations. The aims of this chapter will be to classify such forces, to consider their weight in particular countries and in individual sectors of public policy, and to throw some light on the ways in which their influence is exerted. We are interested in the factors outside national societies that have direct or indirect impact on the setting of national political agendas and policies and on the ability of national authorities to implement chosen policies. One of the main results of the increasing interdependence of peoples and governments has been a blurring of the lines between domestic and foreign policy. Some policies that are traditionally considered domestic, responding to and seeking to influence national society, are in fact wholly or partly responses or adaptations to external influences. Traditional domestic policy structures in national governments, including ministries of finance, agriculture, and labor, are increasingly involved in activities that combine foreign and domestic aspects.

Classifying External Influences

We welcome a growing recognition that external structures and forces other than national governments and intergovernmental organizations influence interstate and national politics. Robert O. Keohane and Joseph S. Nye, Jr., suggest *transnational relations* as a term that incorporates "contacts, coalitions and interactions across state boundaries that are not controlled by the central foreign policy organs of governments."[1] They exclude those "interstate interactions" that "are initiated and sustained entirely, or almost entirely, by governments of nation-states," and insist that transnational interactions, must include nongovernmental actors.[2] Their conception comprises a wide range of movements of things across state boundaries, including the movements that characterize communications, transportation, and finance. Their conception emphasizes the activities of organizations that

---

[1] Robert O. Keohane and Joseph S. Nye, Jr., *Transnational Relations and World Politics* (Cambridge, Mass.: Harvard University Press, 1971), p. xi.

[2] Ibid., p. xii.

participate in such interactions, but also includes movements of goods, funds, persons, information, and ideas that may not depend on organizations.

Although the concept of *multinational policies* advanced by the German political scientist Karl Kaiser excludes phenomena that are not directly political, it is in several ways broader than Keohane and Nye's transnational relations.[3] Kaiser specifically includes such possibly unorganized interaction as movements of persons across frontiers if it substantially affects governments, as well as the interaction between governments and such nongovernmental organizations as multinational corporations. He adds some formal and informal patterns of intersocietal collaboration that are excluded by Nye and Keohane's concept of transnational relations, including "direct horizontal transactions between societal actors of different nation-states, transactions which bypass the institutions of government but strongly alter their margin of maneuver; the various forms of mutual penetration of formally separate entities; and the growing activities of a number of nonstate actors."[4] Kaiser conceives of transnational relations, defined largely in Nye and Keohane's terms, as constituting a part of his larger conceptions. His is a very broad conception of such interaction, and we will henceforth utilize his term, *multinational,* to refer to the less official forces and interactions that impinge on domestic policymaking.

Enough structures, forces, and patterns have been mentioned to suggest a very complex pattern of multinational policies. We will seek now to focus our analysis in such a way as to isolate certain leading aspects of these phenomena and make the subject more tangible. In order to do this we will organize our discussion on the basis of the character, essentially structural in nature, of the sources of multinational influence. Our classification of these sources distinguishes, first, major multinational developments that shape the domestic policies of all or some of the industrialized states. Second, we analyze patterns of involvement in the domestic affairs of other countries by particular foreign governments as well as institutions linked to such governments, including multinational corporations and political parties and movements. Finally, we illustrate some of the patterns of multinational cooperation and organization that have developed as products of and re-

---

[3] Karl Kaiser, "Toward a Theory of Multinational Politics," *International Organization* 25 (Autumn 1971): 790–817; and Karl Kaiser, "Interdependence and Autonomy: Britain and the Federal Republic in Their Multinational Environment," in Kaiser and Robert Morgan, eds., *Britain and West Germany: Changing Societies and the Future of Foreign Policy* (New York: Oxford University Press, 1971). A similarly broad concept, that of "world society," is developed in John W. Burton, *World Society* (London: Cambridge University Press, 1972).

[4] Kaiser, "Multinational Politics," p. 790.

sponses to these and other kinds of multinational interdependence. In this regard we must note a wide range of structures, from participation by a few European states in joint technical projects to sophisticated agencies of multilateral coordination of numerous policy areas and the emergence of a degree of "supranatural" authority in such institutions as those of the European Communities, which now links nine states of Western Europe. We do not presume to incorporate every aspect of multinational politics into this framework, and we recognize some danger of overlapping in our categories. However, it is a framework that assists us in the exploration of a wide range of external influences in each of the functional spheres of public policy.

INTERNATIONAL DEVELOPMENTS AND FORCES

The multinational environment is periodically dominated by certain developments that change the basic context of much of domestic as well as foreign policy. In our century such phenomena have included two general international wars, the Great Depression that began in 1929, the Cold War that emerged after 1945, and such technological breakthroughs as atomic energy. A case has also been made for the epochal character of developments in computers and telecommunications.[5]

Other events and developments may affect particular countries on a more selective basis. These include certain dramatic disasters in the physical environment, such as oil spills, and international financial crises that threaten to force a devaluation of currencies as well as accompanying adjustments in various aspects of the national economic policies of the states under pressure.

Such events are far from being fully independent of the national and multinational organizations discussed in later sections of this chapter as separate sources of multinational policies. Wars, depressions, and other crises can all be viewed as the creations of such organizations, especially national governments. However, they can also be seen as having a force of their own as they move beyond the effective control of these organizations. It is for this reason that we view them separately from the organizations that create and sustain them.

Major International Military and Political Developments

World War II. Probably no phenomenon has as great an effect on domestic policies as a general international war. World Wars I and II were enough like "total war" to force basic changes in national patterns of extraction, distribution, and regulation. The unparalleled ef-

---

[5] Zbigniew Brzezinski, *Between Two Ages* (New York: Viking Press, 1970).

fects of these wars included extraordinary levels of destruction, whole-
sale changes in regimes and constitutions, and major shifts in the
international division of wealth. Traditional patterns of public policy
are often among the first casualties of war, since war dramatically
alters national policy agendas and makes possible a vastly broader
range of policy responses.

Responses to the pressures of World War II were particularly consistent across national lines in such areas as government borrowing and
taxation, the conscription of military manpower, restrictions on the
civilian use of material resources, the development of industrial planning, marked increases in overall national governmental spending, and
sectoral increases in defense and related spheres. These common patterns tend to be more apparent than do the dissimilar policies that can
be ascribed to that war.

However, during its course World War II contributed to such disparate policies as increased German and decreased Soviet pressures
against organized religion. The war years resulted in increased employment opportunities for women everywhere, and for such minorities as the American blacks, but it also resulted in the physical extermi-
nation of Jews and other minorities in the German-occupied countries.
Each of these steps was justified by the national authorities as necessary to the war effort, though the validity of some of the claims is
obviously doubtful. Although World War II intensified the mobilization of resources in such nations as the United States and the United
Kingdom, respite from some of the more onerous state burdens and
patterns of control was granted in Nazi Germany and the Stalinist
Soviet Union in order to solidify mass support for the war effort. Nazi
Germany was surprisingly slow to demand the total mobilization of
human resources, including female labor, and the Stalinist regime
recognized the need to liberalize its policy on private agricultural
production.

The variations in wartime policy can be explained in part by the
specific character of the war's impact on particular countries and also
by the interaction of the war's effects with domestic influences. It is
obviously important to consider whether the war years brought a new
regime or new leaders to power as well as the number of lives and the
amount of property lost at home and abroad. For some neutrals, such
as Sweden and Switzerland, but also for such combatant countries as
the United States, the economic benefits of World War II were substantial. In the United Kingdom, the loss of lives and property led to
great increases in both national solidarity and the national debt.

The patterns of public policy were also influenced by the subsequent effects of the war experience. The major common factor was a
continued mobilization of tax and other material resources to sustain

levels of overall government spending that were, at the least, significantly higher than the prewar levels and in some cases, such as that of the United States, dramatically greater than the prewar levels.[6]

However, the sectoral distribution of this new level of spending varied considerably. For most of Western Europe, as noted by Walter Laqueur, "this was a new age of social reforms, and although some of them had been initiated well before the first World War, their full impact was felt only after 1945 when the social security services expanded in new directions and became far more comprehensive."[7] As Maurice Bruce has noted, "The decisive event in the evolution of the [British] Welfare State was the Second World War."[8] The war ended with a Labour government, elected with a parliamentary majority for the first time, in the process of developing a program that included large-scale expansion of both nationalized industry and social insurance and services. The National Health Service came into existence, and British social service spending rose from 37.6 percent to 46.1 percent of total government expenditures between 1938 and 1950. National defense fell from almost 30 percent to less than 20 percent of total spending in the same period.

British writers have given much attention to the war's impact. Alan J. Peacock and Jack Wiseman view World War II as a primary example of the kind of exceptional national experience that helps raise the level of taxation generally deemed tolerable by the voters and helps create a new threshold for peacetime spending.[9] In terms of both extraction and distribution they assign to World War II a role "in actually stimulating changes both in ideas and in actual policies."[10] These changes are viewed primarily in regard to the stimulation of the welfare state, as Peacock and Wiseman point to such impacts of the war as the exposure of the inadequate physical and social conditions of soldiers and civilians and the unavoidability of blending social services with postwar reconstruction. Richard M. Titmuss points to an even more direct relationship when he views the development of such programs as family allowances and National Health Insurance as "in part an expression of the need of war-time strategy to fuse and unify the conditions of life of civilians and non-civilians alike."[11] The ma-

---

[6] Solomon Fabricant and Robert Lipsey, *The Trend of Government Activity in the United States since 1900* (New York: National Bureau of Economic Research, 1952), pp. 62–63.

[7] Walter Laqueur, *Europe since Hitler* (Harmondsworth, England: Pelican, 1972), p. 243.

[8] Maurice Bruce, *The Coming of the Welfare State* (London: B. T. Batsford, 1968), p. 326.

[9] Alan J. Peacock and Jack Wiseman, *The Growth of Public Expenditures in the United Kingdom* (Princeton: Princeton University Press, 1961), p. xxiv.

[10] Ibid., p. 94.

[11] Richard M. Titmuss, *Essays on the Welfare State*, 2d ed. (Boston: Beacon Press, 1963), p. 84.

jority of European states were also moved toward further welfare state development by their involvement in World War II and the recovery from its consequences.

It is noteworthy that a quite different pattern of change in public spending occurred in the United States. Between 1939 and 1949 the federal government's combined spending on national defense, veterans' pensions, diplomacy, foreign aid, and debt interest, all reflecting the new role of the United States as military and diplomatic leader of the Western alliance, rose as a proportion of total federal expenditures from under 20 percent to over 80 percent of the sharply increased total.[12] Social welfare, broadly defined, fell from a level of almost half of federal spending shortly before the war began in Europe to a level in the range of 10 percent. The American case stands as an example of war failing to make a major contribution to the emergence of a welfare state.

The effects of the war-created conditions on national regulatory policies were also strong but variable. The most consistent pattern was one of postwar continuation of controls over movements of people and numerous aspects of economic life. This was prompted by the existence in war-shattered Europe of material shortages, nonfunctioning enterprises, internationally nonconvertible and inflation-prone currencies, immense numbers of refugees, and other elements that defied the prewar patterns of economic and social management. As Walter Laqueur states, "In the given economic situation there was little scope for the traditional advocates of laissez-faire liberalism; planning and the demand for nationalization had many powerful supporters."[13] Western European nationalization of critical or bankrupt economic sectors tended to proceed before the renewal of comprehensive postwar planning. Substantial governmental planning in Western Europe awaited the utilization of American Marshall Plan aid, beginning in 1948. However, stronger central government involvement with private business enterprises increased, and moves were made to reduce business monopoly power.

In numerous European countries postwar social and political freedom for individuals and groups varied primarily in response to the policies of occupying powers which were in a position to define the terms of economic and political rights. With the vital assistance of native Communists the regulative patterns of the Soviet Union were extended throughout Eastern and East-Central Europe. Almost immediately after the military victory the Soviet Union itself reverted to

---

[12] Fabricant and Lipsey, *Trend of Government*, pp. 62–63.

[13] Laqueur, *Europe since Hitler*, p. 40. For comments on this effect among the West German political parties see Peter Merkl, *The Origin of the West German Republic* (New York: Oxford University Press, 1963), p. 104.

many of the harsh patterns of police state control that had been developed in the 1930s under Joseph Stalin. Some spheres of life, including many fields of science, were put under even more intensive control than had prevailed during that period.

On the other hand, the pattern for most of Western Europe was the enjoyment of greater political and social freedom and rights. New forms of political representation and welfare state benefits combined with the effects of purges of Nazi and Fascist collaborators to set a tone of liberation and increased opportunity. Earlier restrictions on Communist and other far-left political activity were eliminated as a consequence of the strong Communist role in the Resistance in several states and in deference to the Soviet role in the victory.

The enormous effects of World War II were uniformly dramatic in consequence but tended to vary greatly according to particular national situations and experiences. It can be argued that if such a phenomenon can be said to produce a more developed welfare state in some countries and to foster the flowering of a warfare state in others, to give rise to Stalinist patterns of subjugation in some and new democratic procedures in others, then its causative role is dubious. Yet a general international war is both the product of the actions of national political systems and a cataclysmic development that moves beyond the control of any and all such national systems. It makes certain outcomes possible and others impossible, and many of its results are undreamed of when the first shot is fired.

The Cold War and Recent Limited Wars. The post-1945 East-West Cold War was a very potent cause of renewed state interventions in the economic life of Western countries. It was, perhaps, equally influential in maintaining Communist patterns of state intervention. Gunnar Myrdal emphasizes as offshoots of the Cold War increased armaments expenditure and the provision of "reasons for redirecting investment, production, and, indeed, the whole life and work of each national community into line with the governments' pursuance of the Cold War and the safeguarding of state security interests."[14]

As is true of all such global developments, the impact of the Cold War varied considerably from state to state. Some nations, including Japan and several in Western Europe, could hide inexpensively behind the American nuclear umbrella. Although even the United States could not absorb a defense burden of tens of billions of dollars without weakening its ability to raise the level of public services nearer to the level of its private affluence, it was the living standards of the Soviet Union and other Communist-ruled states that suffered most from the dis-

---

[14] Gunnar Myrdal, *Beyond the Welfare State* (New Haven: Yale University Press, 1960), p. 27.

tortions of investment priorities linked to the Cold War.[15] Such distortion in favor of heavy industry and arms was definitely not new to the Soviet system, but the departure from Stalinist priorities was certainly delayed by the Cold War developments. The Cold War brought the need to adjust to cutoffs in the flow of people, capital, and trade across East-West lines, changes that were quite painful for some continental states.[16] Among its other apparent consequences were a broadening of the sectors of science in the service of the state, greater concern for secrecy and loyalty, and a heightened role for state propaganda.

The limited shooting wars that have played a major role in East-West relations since World War II are not easily separable from the Cold War which they helped to fuel and which, reciprocally, played a major role in their development. The Korean War can be most closely associated with the Cold War insofar as it greatly intensified the arms race and mutual distrust. During 1950–53 the cost in lives and funding of the Western effort in the Korean War fell overwhelmingly on the United States. Yet Western European countries faced the great burden of responding to the international economic consequences of that war, including the scarcity and resultant increased cost of vital commodities, at an early stage of their economic recovery. During this period the Soviet Union and its allies in Eastern Europe substantially intensified their investments in munitions and metals production, thus allowing the war to further reduce welfare and consumer expenditure.

By the time events in Indochina reached the level of a major war in 1965, America's allies were in a position to withstand much of its negative economic effects, whereas the United States itself faced a major social and political disruption. The countries of Western Europe were able to continue a pattern of economic growth that brought them closer to American living and production levels. America's role in the Indochina war sharply increased its defense allocations, restricted previously contemplated levels of financing for the "War on Poverty," and helped create a climate conducive to new regulations on individual and group political activity.

Western Europe has tended to suffer more than North America from Middle Eastern crises because of its greater dependence on the oil and trade routes centered in the Middle East. The 1956 Suez War directly involved the armed forces of France and Britain in an abortive action. The 1967 Six Day War led to the closing of the Suez Canal, a development which contributed to the substantial disruption of British

---

[15] Harold L. Wilensky, *The Welfare State and Equality* (Berkeley: University of California Press, 1975), pp. 74–80.

[16] Gunnar Myrdal, *An International Economy: Problems and Prospects* (London: Routledge & Kegan Paul, 1956), pp. 137–38.

finances, among other outcomes. The effects of the 1973 Arab-Israeli War on European and worldwide economic life were even greater, since the war was linked to the subsequent oil embargo, nationalization of Western investments, and price increases. The impact of these developments will be discussed further under the heading "Economic Crises and Trends."

Economic Crises and Trends

A high degree of economic interdependence has resulted from marked growth in international commodity trade, travel, and capital movements, and the resultant influence on national "domestic" economic policy of changes and pressures imposed from abroad.[17] The international economic system allows the export and import not only of goods and services, but also, directly or indirectly, of interest rates, money available for credit, inflationary increases and deflationary decreases in prices, shortages and excesses of commodities, and international payments deficits and surpluses. These flows can often outweigh domestic factors as considerations in the formulation of economic policies and can help determine the outcome of these policies. Our emphasis here is on the situations in which such interdependence creates the conditions of crisis or major strain for national economies, and thereby becomes a dominant factor in shaping economic policies even in the stronger states.

The Great Depression. The Great Depression of 1929–39, the greatest peacetime economic crisis of the 20th century, saw the spread across national boundaries of enormous decreases in wages and prices, increased unemployment, a collapse of investments, a decline of trade, and other disastrous economic consequences.[18] As such, it brought on a great challenge to national governments to seek new policy measures that would make possible the survival of political regimes and of the national societies themselves.

Rather common national economic policies in the face of the Great Depression included efforts to minimize unwelcome economic impacts from other countries through such system-closing devices as higher tariffs and greater restrictions on the entry of foreign labor. Other policies that were attempted in states with differing political systems

---

[17] Richard N. Cooper, "Economic Interdependence and Foreign Policy in the Seventies," *World Politics* 24 (January 1972): 161. See also Richard N. Cooper, *The Economics of Interdependence: Economic Policy in the Atlantic Community* (New York: McGraw-Hill Book Co., 1968).

[18] The perspectives on the Great Depression offered here are largely adapted from Charles P. Kindleberger, *The World in Depression, 1929–1939* (London: Allen Lane/Penguin Press, 1973).

included increases in the money supply, governmental encouragement of monopolistic business organization and practices, new controls on other business prerogatives, subsidies and production limits
in agriculture, labor-intensive public works, the discouragement of
female employment (this most strongly in Germany), and toward the
end of the Depression period, major spending on rearmament. However, these policies were applied in different states in differing mixtures and at varying levels of intensity. They were applied most boldly
in Nazi Germany, though there many of the policies would probably
have been tried in the absence of acute unemployment and other economic difficulties. New policies toward labor unions had to be developed in most countries due to violence or threats to production
schedules, though the actual policies varied from the breakthrough in
labor rights achieved in the United States to repression in Italy, Germany, and the Soviet Union.

As the calculated use of government budgets and other financial
instruments for the purpose of increasing and decreasing levels of demands for goods and money — economic policies identified with John
Maynard Keynes — had not come into general acceptance during this
period, government fiscal policies varied from traditional budget balancing through increased taxation and decreased expenditures to unplanned deficit financing. Sweden was one of the few countries to consciously apply Keynesian techniques, though others, including the
United States, adopted aspects of these approaches before 1940.

Recent Financial Pressures.   At present few nations are invulver-
able to such pressures on their domestic economic system as result from
the cycles of international trade and finance. The states in this study
are less threatened than are most less developed countries. However,
even these states have recently been affected greatly by changes in the
cost and availability of commodities ranging from food to petroleum,
in the flow of labor and capital across national boundaries, and in the
distribution of monetary reserves among the nations.

Among the leading influences on national policies, affecting most
severely countries which are struggling with other economic problems
and are greatly dependent on other countries for trade and other
economic relations, are the pressures of foreign debts and of challenges
to the exchange value of national currencies. These pressures can develop over long periods of time in response to basic trends in national
economic growth, trade, and interest rates, or can suddenly attack a
particular currency through speculative financial activity.

Even before the end of World War II the victorious governments
recognized the need to recreate an international monetary system
capable of sustaining expanded world trade and postwar reconstruction. With some strains and subsequent adjustments this system did

assist the economic reconstruction of Western Europe, while allowing an enormous increase in trade among the industrial countries of the West. This international monetary system was based on holdings of the British pound and American dollar as reserve currencies, and on the adjusting influence of such international institutions as the International Monetary Fund. For many years after World War II the system allowed other industrial states to benefit from deficits in the balance-of-payments accounts of the United States, while Washington maintained levels of reserve gold far above its actual needs. However, in the late 1950s long-term pressures on the American dollar began to develop, and these led to significant changes in the domestic and foreign economic policies of the United States and the other states that were large-scale holders of dollars.

In the late 1950s the patterns of international exchange forced the need for reconsideration of numerous aspects of American economic policy.[19] The period of the Eisenhower Administration saw the net liquidity position of the United States, that is, the surplus of its gold reserves to dollars held officially abroad, fall from more than $11 billion to a little more than $3 billion. Progress toward stabilization was made by the Kennedy Administration, but the full blossoming of the Vietnam War accentuated America's problems. Ultimately, the situation prompted basic changes in America's policy toward the convertibility of its reserves, the exchange value of the dollar, and the institution of controls over wages and prices. Such changes were viewed during the Kennedy and Johnson years as steps to be avoided through the successful application of such lesser steps as encouragement of investment in advanced industrial processes, governmental assistance to export-oriented businesses, noncompulsory governmental influence on wages and prices, encouragement of foreign investment and travel in the United States, restrictions on custom-free purchases by American travelers, and modifications in foreign exchange outlays by the military. The lesser steps did not work because of forces within the U.S. economy and because foreign countries maintained conflicting policies.

During the past 30 years the international monetary system has benefited and harmed all of the Western states in our survey. West Germany and Sweden, which have long been strong currency countries, have often been required to maintain exceptionally high domestic interest rates in order to avoid distortions in the prices of their exports. Britain and Italy have been periodically, and most acutely at this writing, subjected to severe strains on their credit, monetary reserves, and currency values. Their present problems reflect their exceptional vulnerability to such multinational economic forces as sharp rises in

---

[19] Robert V. Roosa, *The Dollar and World Liquidity* (New York: Random House, 1967).

petroleum prices and the need to compete for exports during a major international recession. The causes and consequences of such economic pressures are discussed further under the headings "International Monetary Fund" and "Organization of Petroleum Exporting Countries."

Physical Environment: New Perceptions

Numerous disastrous developments affecting the physical environment in various parts of the world, magnified in their impact by modern telecommunications, have dramatically increased public and governmental sensitivity to what has typically been a slow but steady process of environmental deterioration in industrial countries. Air pollution inversions from Pennsylvania to London, the deaths of both bodies of water and people due to chemical water pollution in Japan and the United States, and oil spill damage to coasts throughout the world have been among the more dramatic and well-publicized environmental events of the past quarter century. Perhaps in combination with the American and Soviet achievements in space exploration these events have helped create an increased consciousness of a common global environmental dependency on our "Spaceship Earth," and have had an immediate and direct effect on national environmental policy by raising the priority given to such values as purity, natural beauty, conservation, and quiet in relation to economic growth. Many of the great number of recent international conventions and national policy changes, statutes, and regulations concerning the physical environment can be traced directly to the impact of such events.

Group awareness and international communications worked to move the various states toward some common institutional and policy developments, and later furthered the institutionalization of an international movement for the protection of the global environment as well as national environments. This is not to say that the primacy of environmental values has been established. By the early 1970s, governments of industrialized states conceded a substantial legitimate place for environmental values even when these appeared to be in direct conflict with immediate economic goals.[20] Nonetheless, Richard Falk is probably correct when he states that "the governors of most states are so absorbed by the tasks of maintaining their own control that they have little excess capacity to absorb the significance of those fundamental, but also more remote and very recently perceived, threats

---

[20] Since 1973 energy shortages have reduced the emphasis on environmental values in some respects, but even as pollution controls are relaxed the overall conservation ethic seems to be gaining some new impetus in the face of the shortages.

arising from the cumulative effects of technology upon the environment."[21]

Cultural and Social Trends

Multinational cultural and social trends do not tend to sweep in on national political systems with the suddenness of the developments previously noted. Yet they can have a widespread impact in a remarkably short time. Among the most obvious of these trends have been the increased consciousness of inequalities affecting the opportunities of racial minorities and women, new attitudes toward old standards of educational opportunity and old standards of living, and the rise of alternative life-styles and new variations on religious values.

The most dramatic impacts on public policy have been in those areas in which new levels of consciousness are mobilized by national and international political movements, as in the cases of racial minorities, women, and students. As with physical environmental issues, groups in one developed country after another have generated new criticism of their respective societies. The media have often readily given considerable attention to the new ideas and to their foreign as well as their domestic exponents. Contemporary communications have also made possible frequent and intense international contact among the advocates of these ideas.

As a result of these developments new political issues can sweep across the developed states, though rarely without substantial resistance. Although the impact of new policies often takes decades to become evident, and much of the "new politics" may be empty or symbolic action, results have already been substantial in regard to the granting and reinforcement of rights and opportunities for such groups as women, racial minorities, youth, pornographers, and sexual deviants. All of these groups have benefited from multinational flows of communications.

PATTERNS OF INFLUENCE FROM FOREIGN NATION-STATES

Having noted the impacts of major multinational forces and developments, we now proceed to the impacts that can be traced directly to particular nation-states. Such interactions are so extensive and varied that we can illustrate only a small proportion. Major influences have emanated from each of the eight survey countries, and none has been

---

[21] Richard A. Falk, *This Endangered Planet: Prospects and Proposals for Human Survival* (New York: Random House, 1972), p. 225.

immune from such effects. Perhaps the most widely discussed impacts have been those of the United States on Western Europe and of the Soviet Union on Eastern Europe.

The "Americanization" of Western Europe and the emergence of the Soviet sphere in Eastern Europe are primary examples of political processes that involve the multinational roles of governments, political parties and movements, business enterprises, and trade union organizations, among other agents. The effects of this interaction tend to be most direct in states that are dependent on the leadership and resources of the superpowers, but the domestic processes and policies of the United States and the Soviet Union themselves are also affected. Both Soviet and American patterns of influence reach deeply into many functional areas of European society. As within its own borders, Moscow has sought to extend its influence into all spheres of East European life, including broad areas of cultural and social experience. "Americanization" also tends to suggest to people in Western Europe effects across the spectrum of all spheres of life, including the effects produced by American films, television programs, management and merchandising techniques, technological exports, and overseas military personnel. Direct American influence in Western European policy-making processes is perhaps less obvious than its Soviet counterpart in Eastern Europe, and it operates through substantially different styles and structures.

Yet the superpowers are not the only sources of pressure and suggestion in Europe and North America. The United States has built its basic political and social institutions on European models and is today actively studying Western European approaches to complex issues ranging from taxation to social security. Eastern Europe turns its face increasingly to the West and has begun to serve as a tutor to an increasingly interested audience of Soviet officials in such spheres as industrial management.[22] The diffusion of policy innovations among Western European countries is aided by intense communications and exceptionally well-developed multinational institutions. Eastern European regimes show signs of increased willingness to learn from one another despite Soviet pressures against many kinds of innovations. Although the largest number of examples presented below represent flows from the United States to Western Europe, it is not suggested that this has been or is at present the dominant relationship or that the other associations are not producing flows of policy innovations.

---

[22] Zvi Y. Gitelman, "The Diffusion of Political Innovation: From Eastern Europe to the Soviet Union," *Sage Professional Papers in Comparative Politics,* vol. 3, no. 27 (Beverly Hills, Calif.: Sage Publications, 1972).

Multinational processes of interaction and influence are viewed here in relation to James N. Rosenau's categorization of multinational "linkages" as *penetrative, reactive,* or *emulative.*[23] We choose to interpret quite broadly Rosenau's definition of *penetration* as processes in which "members of one polity serve as participants in the political processes of another," sharing the authority to allocate its values. The stress here is on participation by externally based actors in the selection of goals, the allocation of costs, and the mobilization of resources and capabilities. This penetration may be set in a cooperative or a coercive framework, or in a mixture of the two. We would include participation that takes certain indirect forms, among them the precluding of certain options to national decision-makers. Nationally and internationally based governmental and nongovernmental individuals and organizations, but not external events or developments, are viewed as instruments of penetration. Thus we are considering only some penetrative processes in this section and will discuss other processes under the heading "International Organizational Cooperation."

Rosenau's other categories of linkages go far to round out the patterns of multinational processes in which one state's policies or actions respond to the prior behavior of a multinational actor. *Emulative* processes occur when policy-makers copy or adapt an element of policy demonstrated in another country. *Reactive* processes occur when developments in one nation prompt a policy response in another, the reaction usually differing from the stimulus.

These three kinds of processes are not always easy to distinguish. When a superpower like the United States or the Soviet Union elicits a reaction it does so substantially because its economic, military, and political instruments of penetration are in place. Further, the distortion factor is often high, particularly in regard to penetration. Both the penetrating structure and the penetrated political system may benefit from misrepresenting the scale and nature of the external participation. For example, many of the details of Soviet control within the Czechoslovak party-state policy-making and policy-implementing agencies remained secret until the 1968 events in Czechoslovakia. Multiple international influences tend to interact with one another and with numerous domestic factors. Social scientists and national decision-makers will usually differ in their estimates of impacts. Finally, the published documentary evidence on this subject is not extensive. The "evidence" of responsive or emulative processes may include the close timing of the apparent influence and the response or, in regard to emulation, the fact

---

[23] James N. Rosenau, ed., *Linkage Politics: Essays on the Convergence of National and International Systems* (New York: Free Press, 1969), pp. 44–49.

that one policy appears to be modeled on another. In some cases, co-incidence or a lack of alternative policy choices may be at work, and the emulation may be nonexistent or less significant than it seems to be.

Penetrative Processes

With the exception of the occupying regimes in West Germany, Italy, and Austria, American penetration of Western Europe has proceeded without most of the kinds of trappings employed by Moscow for the pervasive penetration of its bloc. Western Europeans have not had Americans or American-installed agents placed within their ministries, American ambassadors with the right to be consulted on all substantial acts of domestic and foreign policy, or tightly interlocked political party structures.[24] Although such instruments of penetration are still used in all Eastern European-bloc states, structural penetration varies considerably from country to country.[25] In contrast to the American position in Western Europe, the pattern of Soviet control of Eastern Europe has been characterized by threats and the use of severe economic, military, and political sanctions, most notably in East Germany in 1953, in Hungary in 1956, and in Czechoslovakia in 1968. Through such methods Moscow has succeeded in maintaining a high degree of control over most of the countries brought within its sphere in the wake of World War II, affirming distinct limits regarding the monopoly of Communist party power, the existence of domestic dissent and autonomous organizations, and the speed and scope of economic decentralization and rationalization. Substantial liberalization has been tolerated in certain countries for varying periods of time, but eventually draws pressures from Moscow and from such relatively "hard-line" East European regimes as that of East Germany.

However, this contest between Soviet and American methods of penetration does not mean that the role of the United States in Western Europe is minor. The major instruments of the American presence are U.S. governmental agencies, civilian and military, and multinational business enterprises based in the United States. Such penetration, though often benevolent in intent and outcomes, has been increasingly regarded by Western European governments and the Western European public as a mixed blessing. We discuss below some of the major

----

[24] See Zbigniew Brzezinski, *The Soviet Bloc,* rev. ed. (Cambridge, Mass.: Harvard University Press, 1968); and Barbara Wolfe Jancar, *Czechoslovakia and the Absolute Monopoly of Power* (New York: Praeger Publishers, 1971), especially pp. 241–74.

[25] Albania and Yugoslavia should be regarded as largely independent of these structural patterns of penetration, these states now being essentially outside the Soviet sphere of domination.

examples of American penetration of Western Europe since World War II.

The Occupation of Western Germany. Beginning with the closing months of World War II, much of continental Europe was occupied by the victorious Allied armies. Soviet forces moved deeply into Eastern and Central Europe together with other elements of Soviet power, while parallel American, British, and French occupations were carried out in Germany, Austria, and Italy. The effects of Soviet penetration have proved to be more lasting and deep in regard to regime character and public policy. Yet the imprint of the Western Allies on the areas occupied by them was far from negligible. We illustrate this from the case of the occupation of Germany.[26]

Most of the administrative structures established by the United States and its Allies in West Germany had economic functions. The amalgamation of the Western zones was undertaken principally to coordinate economic policy, and such central issues of the occupation as the dismantling of industry for reparations, the decartelization of industry, and production quotas were largely economic in character. The Western Allies pulled in separate directions in regard to several major aspects of economic policy. The British Labour government emphasized the nationalization of industry, and the French were strongly disposed to demand reparations. Britain and the United States, but not France, were interested in German economic recovery at a quite early stage because of the perceived Soviet threat and the burden of financial subsidy made necessary by conditions in their zones. Dramatic Allied contributions to German recovery included Marshall Plan support and a currency reform in June 1948 that resulted in a major degree of financial stabilization. The ending of industrial dismantling and the raising of industrial production goals embodied the overall policy of economic recovery.

On some constitutional issues, such as the clever concept of a constructive no-confidence vote protecting the tenure of the chancellor by requiring the simultaneous election of a successor before his ouster, the American contribution to German political practices proved decisive and durable. In other constitutional matters, such as the nature of German federalism, the outcome probably differed little from what would have been produced by intra-German bargaining. The overall legacy of the American presence in Germany on the character of the West German political system is visible but not broad or intense.

---

[26] The major sources for this discussion include: John Gimbel, *The American Occupation of Germany: Politics and the Military, 1945–1949* (Stanford, Calif.: Stanford University Press, 1968); John Ford Goley, *The Founding of the Federal Republic of Germany* (Chicago: University of Chicago Press, 1958); and Merkl, *Origin*.

For such reasons as their lesser place in Allied priorities and the more entrenched German attitudes in these spheres, occupation policies had even less permanent impact on German cultural life or the German social system. Such great changes as the post-Nazi Christian revival cannot be credited to any Allied thrust. Other changes, such as the influx of millions of refugees from East Germany, Poland, Czechoslovakia, and elsewhere, were affected primarily negatively by the Allied decisions to concentrate relocation in areas that were underpopulated but could not readily absorb large numbers of people. Although American and French officials sought to prompt major changes in German education, the effects of their efforts in such areas as structure, standards, availability, and curriculum were spotty and often short-lived. The strong reaction of many Germans to American interference in school affairs may have set back such reforms for decades.

It is noteworthy that the occupation is not merely a subject for historical study, but has left a degree of penetration that survives to this day under the terms of the 1954 Paris Agreements. As argued by Kaiser in 1971, "Even today (and despite the Federal State of Emergency legislation of 1968), the restriction of West Germany's sovereignty takes the form of a penetrated system."[27] In addition to the broad responsibility of the three Western Allies in West Berlin, they maintain rights concerning the stationing of troops in the Federal Republic as well as powers relating to reunification and peace settlements. The Federal Republic has emerged as a fully recognized member of the international community, but it is still affected by legacies of the occupation.

The Marshall Plan, Mutual Security, and Movement toward Equality. The American government which shared its role as occupying power in Germany with the governments of France, Britain, and the Soviet Union had a unique position as the only postwar source of substantial economic and military assistance in Western and Southern Europe. Between 1946 and 1966 American aid to Allied states in Europe totaled more than $45 billion, and more than half of that amount was provided between 1945 and 1952, the period of Europe's greatest need (see Table 3–1).

Such levels of aid intensified American penetration of the recipient countries. American aid represented, especially during the first six or seven years of its existence, a significant proportion of the recipients' overall resources and their only means for acquiring crucial commodities that were unavailable without dollars. The Marshall Plan also involved a structure for sustained intervention, albeit within a highly

---

[27] Karl Kaiser, "Interdependence and Autonomy," p. 29.

TABLE 3–1

U.S. Military and Economic Assistance to NATO Allies, 1946–1966 (in millions of dollars)

Country	Postwar Relief 1946–48	Marshall Plan 1949–52	Mutual Security Act 1953–57	Mutual Security Act 1958–61	Foreign Assistance Act 1962–65	Foreign Assistance Act 1966	Total 1946–66
France	$1,909.1	$ 3,561.8	$ 3,467.1	$ 352.0	$ 96.4	$ 11.8	$ 9,398.2
United Kingdom	3,836.9	3,252.8	1,290.3	289.0	289.8	86.0	9,044.8
Italy	1,271.2	1,690.0	1,852.5	642.1	564.4	68.0	6,088.2
Turkey	113.3	461.0	1,374.3	1,287.6	1,280.2	257.5	4,773.9
Federal Republic of Germany	1,344.4	2,491.8	759.9	395.5	3.3	2.4	4,997.3
Greece	723.6	1,056.9	707.3	594.8	461.6	85.5	3,629.7
Netherlands	238.2	1,121.6	835.2	178.3	94.0	0.1	2,467.4
Belgium-Luxembourg	163.4	740.9	891.4	112.5	73.8	19.2	2,001.2
Norway	75.0	354.7	428.8	151.3	124.2	42.8	1,176.8
Denmark	21.0	346.7	315.5	120.7	89.4	20.1	913.4
Portugal	–	61.8	241.2	64.1	133.0	5.4	505.5
Berlin	–	–	101.9	30.0	–	–	131.9
Iceland	–	29.4	16.7	23.1	7.0	7.7	83.9
Canada	–	14.4	12.7	9.1	–	–	36.2
Total	$9,696.1	$15,183.8	$12,294.8	$4,250.1	$3,217.1	$606.5	$45,248.4

Source: Reproduced from *Integration and Disintegration in NATO: Processes of Alliance Cohesion and Prospects for Atlantic Community*, by Francis A. Beer, a publication of the Mershon Center of the Ohio State University (Columbus, Ohio: Ohio State University Press, 1969), p. 146.

cooperative framework, in the policy-making and policy-execution processes of all recipient states.[28]

The primary vehicle of American penetration from 1948 to 1952 was the Economic Cooperation Administration (ECA), the uniquely independent Marshall Plan agency. The ECA, with offices in each recipient's capital, was responsible for coordinating the utilization of the $13.6 billion of Marshall Plan aid in Europe. This was to be achieved in cooperation with the recipient countries and the Organization for European Economic Cooperation (OEEC), which was created as a vehicle for European multinational participation in the utilization of the aid. The ECA's role involved stimulating and pressuring substantial changes in the structure of the European economy and in the economic policies of recipient governments. An ECA-initiated study described as one of ECA's two main "businesses" "attempting to bring about changes in the plans, policies and actions of the participating countries and OEEC."[29] Changes were brought about at all stages of aid utilization and affected broad areas of national economic policy. The ECA could also reach into social policy, as in promoting the interests of "democratic" labor through its Office of Labor Advisors, its programs for increased manpower utilization, and its insistence on giving priority to industrial, agricultural, transport, and infrastructure investment in lieu of possibly equally necessary welfare facilities. Without much success American policy-makers also sought to pressure their clients into making substantial shifts toward investment in defense, beginning soon after the outbreak of the Korean War in 1950.

Although such issues of distribution were the main objects of American attention, ECA officials were also concerned with extraction and economic regulation. One notable case was the ECA's insistence in 1948 that French officials agree to adopt such measures aimed at fiscal stability as additional taxes, limits on the national debt, and controls over private credit.[30] Further, Marshall Plan implementation combined strong influence on national economic policy with potent pressure on the recipients to move toward international cooperation in such areas as trade and payments.[31]

The European Recovery Program represents a high point of sustained institutional penetration of European policy and processes by

---

[28] Harry Bayard Price, *The Marshall Plan and Its Meaning* (New York: Cornell University Press, 1955).

[29] Harry H. Fite, L. W. Hoelscher, Arthur R. Mosler, and W. J. Sheppard, *Survey of Relations of the Parts of ECA* (Washington, D.C., 1949), p. 9, as cited in ibid., p. 314.

[30] Ibid., p. 105.

[31] See Max Beloff, *The United States and the Unity of Europe* (Washington, D.C.: Brookings Institution, 1963).

American governmental officials. Later American assistance gravitated away from general economic support toward military aid that was not felt by the recipient states to be equally vital. This change combined with the end of the "dollar gap" in international payments and the related strengthening of the European economies to reduce American leverage on the economic policies of the recipient states. Despite a continuing expensive American military presence in Western Europe and American provision of NATO's main nuclear shield, or perhaps because of this support, Washington has generally been frustrated in such continuing efforts as persuading its allies to divert more resources to the military sector to meet agreed NATO force levels.[32] Although Western European publics and governments have been made quite nervous by U.S. threats to reduce the American presence in Europe, the tangible response to these threats has not been considerable outside West Germany.

By the late 1960s it could be said that "in the course of recent years the [European Economic] Community has rendered monetary aid to the United States on a very large scale."[33] This was not the kind of direct assistance noted above, but it took such very real forms as the advance repayment of debts, special purchases of U.S. government securities, and "offset agreements" for West German purchases of American goods and services to help balance American foreign exchange deficits incurred as a result of the military presence in the Federal Republic. This partial reversal of financial roles has resulted in a significant degree of Western European influence in U.S. economic policy-making, beginning in the 1960s.[34]

Multinational Business Enterprises. The attention of American and European observers shifted in the 1960s from discussion of the direct influence of the U.S. government in Europe to the impact of multinational businesses based in the United States and to some extent controlled and supported by the U.S. government.[35] Such enterprises, especially those with direct investment in European manufacturing subsidiaries and those providing financial services, have become the most important nongovernmental instruments of the American presence,

---

[32] Francis A. Beer, *Integration and Disintegration in NATO* (Columbus: Ohio State University Press, 1969), pp. 62–63.

[33] M. Albert, "Repercussions of the Economic Policy of the United States on the Policies of the European Economic Community," in Charles P. Kindleberger and Andrew Shonfield, eds., *North American and Western European Economic Policies* (London: Macmillan, 1971), p. 71.

[34] Stephen D. Cohen, *International Monetary Reform, 1964–69: The Political Dimension* (New York: Praeger Publishers, 1970), p. 169; and Brian Tew, *International Monetary Cooperation, 1945–70*, 10th rev. ed. (London: Hutchinson, 1970), p. 135.

[35] Jean-Jacques Servan-Schreiber, *The American Challenge* (New York: Atheneum, 1968).

providing a penetrative capability through their own actions and as vehicles for the transmission of U.S. governmental authority.

Multinational businesses are marked by the existence of a base of operations in a "home country" and a set of subsidiaries, established under the laws of other countries, which tend to share a common pool of financial, technological, and managerial resources.[36] Some authorities insist on such additional criteria as a substantial number of subsidiaries and a huge level of assets or sales. Although the contemporary multinational corporation is predominantly an American-based phenomenon, Western European and Japanese multinational firms are also important. As recently as 1956, European companies had greater direct holdings in the United States than vice versa. By the early 1970s, however, total American direct investments in Europe exceeded $30 billion, and the amount of such investments in the nine states of the European Communities was four times as great as the direct investments of those countries in the United States.[37] American firms controlled 40 to 50 percent of all foreign investment in the Community countries, and thus represented almost half of a foreign firm presence in the Community states that was collectively responsible for between 9 and 33 percent of sales in particular Community countries, between 4 and 18 percent of manufacturing jobs, and even higher proportions in the sensitive spheres of exports and high-technology industry. Although the larger Community states tend to have a smaller part of their industry under the control of such multinationals, even in Britain, France, and West Germany American-based multinationals control major or controlling shares of the national markets in such individual sectors as chemicals, electronics, and automobiles. American companies have definitely taken greater advantage than their European counterparts of the opportunities provided by free movement of capital in the expanding European Communities.

Rebated profits provide both revenue and help for international payments accounts (though investment outflows to other countries can be costly in initial payments impact and employment). Since most receiving countries profit from jobs, exports, and the introduction of advanced technology, multinational investment is actively sought by most Western European states.

---

[36] Raymond Vernon, "Multinational Business and National Economic Goals," in Keohane and Nye, *Transnational Relations,* p. 344.

[37] Christopher Tugendhat, *The Multinationals* (London: Eyre and Spottiswoode, 1971), p. 24; and *European Communities* (Brussels: European Communities), January–February 1974, p. 16. Western European investment in the United States has tended to be greater in such "portfolio investments" as purchases of corporate stocks and bonds and government securities.

In the view of all West European governments these advantages out-weigh some definite disadvantages that relate to penetration. First, the multinational enterprises are widely considered to be capable of frus-trating governmental action in such areas as exchange rates, techno-logical development, competition, bank lending, taxation, labor, price and incomes controls, and planning in general.[38] They achieve this mainly because of their ability to operate on a larger geographic scale than can be policed by any one government. They can act in the cor-porate interest against a national interest by manipulating currencies and profits among subsidiaries, shifting production and research from one state to another, offering bribes to secure contracts, and financing new investment in other states or through "Eurodollar" and "Euro-bond" money markets that are outside the direct control of the regulat-ing state. Their capacity to frustrate varies in accordance with the size of their operations, their company organization, and the existence of alternative opportunities.

The second major dimension of the problem which multinational enterprises present to their host governments is the role played by these enterprises as agents of their "home governments." American multi-national corporations can treat the agencies of the U.S. government as their own instruments, as the International Telephone and Telegraph Company (ITT) apparently sought to do in Allende's Chile. Students of American corporate penetration of Western Europe have put more emphasis on the reverse role, in which the U.S. government seeks to use its power over American-based companies to force acts of omission and commission by subsidiary companies incorporated under Euro-pean national law, creating an as yet unresolved question of juris-diction.

Washington has insisted, usually successfully in the short run, that European subsidiaries of American-based corporations, and fully autonomous European companies in some instances, accept U.S. gov-ernmental authority in such areas as antitrust laws, information dis-closures, the transmission of nuclear and other sophisticated tech-nology, trading with Communist-ruled states, the financing of invest-ments, and rebating profits to the United States. This has meant that France has been denied computer technology and nuclear raw materials on the ground that these would contribute to French nuclear capability, that the growth of Western European trade with Communist states has been somewhat slowed, and that European companies have been dis-couraged from certain types of mergers and trade agreements that

---

[38] See Jack N. Behrman, *National Interests and the Multinational Enterprise: Tensions among the North Atlantic Countries* (Englewood Cliffs, N.J.: Prentice-Hall, 1970), pp. 71–82.

could affect the American market. European governments have had to accept some additional limits to their autonomy in domestic and foreign economic policy in exchange for the advantages brought by the multinationals.

No one aspect of American extraterritorial authority presents an alarming problem to any Western European state, and the situation as a whole is still more one of occasional political embarrassment to host governments than one of loss of great spheres of authority. However, the multinationals contribute to the unequal interdependence between the United States and Western Europe. Kenneth Waltz has concluded that "if means for bringing other countries into compliance with professed American policies are desired, the American government does not have to look far to find them."[39] It can be expected that such instruments, particularly multinational corporations, will become increasingly available to Western European governments and Japan. As a result, American sensitivity may lead to international agreements that limit the use of multinationals for direct and indirect penetration.

Intelligence Organizations. The time spent in writing the present volume coincided with the Watergate and intelligence agency investigations carried out in the United States. These investigations, especially the ones conducted by the special committees on intelligence activities in the two houses of the U.S. Congress, confirmed some important dimensions of American penetration in Western Europe as well as the rest of the world.

The most notorious disclosures, those concerning assassinations, did not relate to Europe. However, official information was disclosed concerning widespread interference in Western European economic and political systems, this centering on efforts to use U.S. financial support and bribes to alter the normal process of competition among trade unions, political parties, and individual candidates.[40] In the pursuit of anti-Communist goals, payments have been extended to nonprofit organizations and multinational corporations. Although such operations have affected each of the Western European countries in our sample they have apparently been concentrated in Italy in recent decades. Faced with a serious threat of Communist party control in that country, the United States has spent millions of dollars to sustain non-Communist political and economic forces.

---

[39] Kenneth N. Waltz, "The Myth of National Interdependence," in Charles P. Kindleberger, ed., *The International Corporation* (Cambridge, Mass.: MIT Press, 1970), p. 222.

[40] Jerry J. Berman and Morton H. Halperin, *The Abuses of the Intelligence Agencies* (Washington, D.C.: Center for National Security Studies, 1975). See also the series of reports released in 1975 and 1976 by the U.S. Senate Select Committee to Study Governmental Operations with Respect to Intelligence Activities.

While the American effort has involved many organizations other than the Central Intelligence Agency, it is also true that the intelligence organs of the United States are not at all alone in their presence or methods. Throughout the contemporary world, intelligence agencies of numerous countries interact with domestic groups and institutions. Although the major participants include the Soviet, British, French, Iranian, and Israeli agencies, the field is crowded.

It is necessary to recognize that much of the American activity in Western Europe is a reaction to a large Soviet effort to promote Communist and pro-Communist elements there and to weaken certain competing institutions. However, it is also important to differentiate the clearly parallel operations of such Soviet intelligence agencies as the Committee for State Security (KGB) from the far more complex nature of organized "international Communism" and the roles of particular Communist parties.

The Soviet Communist party maintains liaison with other Communist parties through intelligence agents, formal meetings, and operations of a section of its Secretariat. However, a former Soviet-controlled Communist movement has long since been replaced by one in which Communist parties, often several in a given non-Communist state, adopt variations of pro-Soviet, pro-Chinese, and neutralist-independent postures. Some of the most biting criticism of Soviet actions has come from Western European Communists, including assaults on Moscow's invasion of Czechoslovakia and the suppression of Soviet dissidents. At times Western Communist influence on Soviet developments seems to equal or exceed that flowing in the opposite direction. Moscow can rebuke and censure Western Communist parties, but it can no longer order the French or Italian parties to adopt a particular electoral campaign posture or to change leaders. It has no power directly analogous to the U.S. government's extraterritorial jurisdiction over the multinational corporations, except perhaps in regard to some minor parties that have little influence in their own countries. Although the future of some Western European Communist parties appears bright in the mid-1970s, that future is tied closely to the image of those parties as autonomous national parties.

The Roman Catholic Church. The question of the Roman Catholic church as a vehicle for multinational penetration is less clouded by matters of organizational control. The authority of the Vatican, or Holy See, functions within an organization that is much more disciplined, cohesive, and centralized than the international Communist movement, though it has also had its severe schisms. The Vatican's efforts have different consequences at the national level, depending on the issue, the importance of Catholics in the society, the history of the national church's posture toward Rome, the relative degree of Catholic unity, and the strength of the Catholic infrastructure in such sectors as trade unions and political parties.[41] The Vatican acts most directly on the Italian and Spanish regimes, with particular weight in areas of cultural and social policy, and has had an impact on most countries with substantial proportions of Catholics on such moral issues as abortion.

Reactive Processes

Although penetration is generally regarded as in conflict with aspects of national sovereignty, it is considered normal for countries to react to many pressures which have their source in other nations. Current trends point to a decreasing emphasis on penetration together with an increased interreaction among such countries as those in our survey.

Most of Western Europe has continually responded to U.S. policies. An official of the European Communities noted at the beginning of the present decade, "The choice of measures to be used in their [the Communities' member states] policy mix is today strongly subject to the influence of the decisions taken on the other side of the Atlantic in response to a situation peculiar to the United States."[42] The major new development is that, in relation to such areas of economic policy as interest rates and agriculture, Western European governmental decisions now have a stronger reciprocal impact on American public policy.[43] Further, Western European nations sometimes seem too preoccupied with other pressures, such as those generated by the Organization of Petroleum Exporting Countries (OPEC), to react to American initiatives.

Reactive policies are often highly predictable. In the nuclear weapons field, each possible "breakthrough" by the Soviet Union or the United States was used to justify the next round of atmospheric tests until 1963, and continues to be used as a justification for underground testing by these states and for the "catch-up" tests of China and France. A more benevolent pattern of response may have been the slowing of the worldwide race for the development of the supersonic transport (SST) after the U.S. Congress decided that the economic and environmental risks were too great and the oil-exporting states further decreased the economic viability of the project by raising fuel costs.

One of the more interesting patterns of governmental reactions has been prompted by the direct and indirect impacts of multinational

---

[41] Ivan Vallier, "The Roman Catholic Church: A Transnational Actor," in Keohane and Nye, *Transnational Relations*, p. 140.

[42] Albert, "Repercussions," p. 140.

[43] Cooper, *Economics of Interdependence*, p. 142.

business enterprises. Such enterprises remain quite welcome throughout Western Europe and are becoming more significant as direct in-
vestors in the United States and project developers in the Soviet Union.
Although not as restrictive as Canada or the United States, Western
European host governments have taken some steps to limit the multinationals' scope for independence and disruption. These steps have
included restrictions on entry and operating conditions, such as special
permits for investment, bans from some particularly sensitive sectors
of industry, special treatment of the multinationals' taxes to discount
some of their capital-shifting advantages, and national laws designed
to counter the effects of foreign legislation in such areas as antitrust.[44]
Moves like these have been designed to ensure independence from their
neighbors and Japan as well as from America. Christopher Tugendhat
writes of the "running battle of wits between multinational companies
and governments," a struggle that the companies may choose to break
off in favor of a more favorable situation elsewhere if pressures from a
host government become too strong.[45] Although national governments
may make some progress in the expansion of effective controls on the
multinationals in such areas as taxation, they are not likely to make
the multinationals equal to domestic companies in this regard. Acting
as individual governments, they can do even less to prevent the
sporadic use of foreign extraterritorial authority. Such threats will be
vastly augmented in the near future as a result of huge new investments
by oil-producing states.

Emulative Processes

From the beginning of their existence nations have sought to borrow
and adapt structures and policies from other societies. Western European emulation of American practices since 1945 extends into virtually
every aspect of societal life. Imitation is most evident in such nonpolicy
areas as language, business organization and techniques, and mate-
rialist dimensions of "the good life."

However, some Europeans consider policy emulation to be as extensive as other aspects of Americanization. The European Communities
economist M. Albert has argued, "The American example is . . . at the
root of the frame of reference adopted in Europe, especially in such
matters as education policy, the relations between industries and the
universities, and a better awareness on the part of the government of its
responsibilities towards workers and firms."[46] On the other hand,

---

[44] Behrman, *National Interests*, pp. 130–45.

[45] Tugendhat, *Multinationals*, p. 131.

[46] Albert, "Repercussions," p. 66.

numerous studies of European government have ignored such emulation. Our feeling is that imitation and stimulation should be taken into account, though we view the patterns of emulation to be limited to particular issue areas and to vary in intensity from one state to another.

It is probably not surprising that in recent decades Britain has adopted more from American policy than has any other European nation. Between the United Kingdom and the United States there exist both unique traditional ties and intense links in communication between national elites and through the mass media. The United States is not as prone to act on what it learns about British experience, though some British influence has been brought to bear on recent American consideration of capital punishment, the treatment of homosexuals and drug users, health care, urban air pollution, the minimum age for voting and majority status, and incomes policy, to suggest a few areas. The British are more likely than Americans to formally cite the other's experience with problems and attempted solutions, as the record shows in such varied issues as race relations, women's rights, and capital market regulation.

British emulation of American policy can be found in the development of the British Race Relations acts of 1965 and 1968 closely following the 1957–65 period of major U.S. legislation in this field. In a thorough study of the development of these two British statutes, which were designed to ameliorate the social pressures resulting from majority discrimination against black and South Asian immigrants into Britain, Anthony Lester and Geoffrey Bindman cite strong evidence that the American example was of critical importance for the British decision to apply legislative and judicial remedies and for the defining of those remedies. As summarized by Lester and Bindman, "It was the sudden awareness of the danger that the second generation [of immigrants] might become a coloured underclass, given heightened consciousness by the racial crisis of the northern cities of the United States, which strengthened the case for the new legislation, modelled not surprisingly, upon American statutes."[47] British proponents of what Americans call civil rights legislation cited evidence from U.S. congressional hearings and adapted American state law as well as federal legislative and judicial approaches. In such areas as employment, commercial services, public accommodations, and housing, the United Kingdom adapted the U.S. and Canadian emphasis on the use by special administrative agencies of education, persuasion, and conciliation and only in the last resort, of legally enforceable orders. The sum of the two main British antidiscrimination laws does not go quite as far or

---

[47] Anthony Lester and Geoffrey Bindman, *Race and Law* (Harmondsworth, England: Penguin Books, 1972), p. 17.

promise to be quite as effective as the American legislation as rein-forced by American court rulings. But neither the intensity and scope of British racial problems nor the political pressures on behalf of minor-ities were nearly as great as in the United States.

In some areas, such as wage-price control, the United Kingdom–U.S. relationship is reciprocal. The former chairman of the British National Board for Prices and Incomes referred to the United States as "the coun-try which most clearly studied the British experiment of 1965–70 and came to follow it, just as she has also preceded it."[48] Britain adopted in 1965 the wage-price "criteria" developed in 1962 by the U.S. Council of Economic Advisers, and subsequently developed three stages of wage and price policy that borrowed heavily from similar multistage American policies. Washington was encouraged by British legislation to move toward compulsory restraints in 1971, and the seeming failure of such British policies was later offered by the Nixon Administration as one excuse for moving back toward a decontrolled economy in 1974.

Emulation of the United States is, of course, not limited to Britain. Outstanding examples of continental Western Europe's borrowings from American economic policy include stricter control of monopolistic business practices and the development of a system of subsidized agri-culture. In the important sector of industrial policy, Jacques R. Hous-siaux of the University of Paris claims that "what is new is that Euro-pean governments are now trying to imitate the methods used in the United States to develop new technologies and spread them through-out their industries."[49] He refers here to the sponsorship of such ser-vices as the provision of professional management education, subsidies for research and development, and the increased use of government contracts to prime industry. Western European states have adopted such policies partly to support domestically based industries in compe-tition with American multinationals. These governments have also found much to emulate in the restrictive approach of the United States toward conditions of entry and operation by multinationals, including access to U.S. security markets, as well as in the development of in-ducements for multinational investments in depressed regions.

Both American awareness of physical environmental deterioration and American approaches to solutions have influenced continental Western Europeans.[50] Apparent emulation of American environmental policies can be traced back to the 19th century, though most of our ex-

---

[48] Aubrey Jones, *The New Inflation: The Politics of Prices and Incomes* (London: André Deutsch, 1973), p. 147.

[49] Jacques R. Houssiaux, "American Influence on Industrial Policy in Western Europe since the Second World War," in Kindleberger and Shonfield, *Economic Policies*, p. 353.

[50] Michel Phipponeau, "The Environment," in Richard Mayne, ed., *Europe Tomorrow: 16 Europeans Look Ahead* (London: Fontana, 1972), pp. 131–63.

amples are more recent. Nicholson cites the American National Park Service, Soil Conservation Service, Tennessee Valley Authority, and Fish and Wildlife Service as among "main administrative innovations which have had most marked influence internationally."[51] The American conception of national parks, adapted to New Zealand, Australia, and colonial Africa before the turn of the 20th century, has now reached France and other European states. More recently, the technical standards of American pollution control laws have been copied or adapted in Western Europe. American legislation has forced higher worldwide standards in automobiles, in terms both of safety and of emission control.

In some cases the lesson from America is to avoid certain developments, such as high-rise public housing or what is viewed as excessive racial heterogeneity. No contemporary Western European public acknowledges a desire to build a society which duplicates all of America's political, aesthetic, social, and cultural dimensions. Europeans have been disturbed and shocked by such American phenomena as race riots and the repressive response to them, political assassinations, toleration of high unemployment levels, and acceptance of poverty and slums.

Of course, Europeans borrowed from one another long before they came to see the United States as a possible source of innovations. This record is highlighted by developments relating to prisons, social security, military conscription, and taxation. What is probably the most pervasive pattern of international emulation in the world today, ranging systematically into virtually every major field of domestic policy, operates among Norway, Denmark, and Sweden. In Scandinavia, and to a lesser degree in the larger Nordic region which includes Finland and Denmark, routine contacts among government officials at all levels are supplemented by intense ties among political party, trade union, corporate, and other elites.[52] The result is an exceptional degree of "harmonization" and joint development of policies in the Scandinavian and Nordic regions.

Present trends suggest that Western European countries will increasingly emulate other European states more than the United States. Numerous innovations exist, including Dutch prison reform, West German labor-management relations, Swedish employment policies, and Italian regional development.[53] In some instances a search for European alternatives to rejected American models can be observed, as

---

[51] Max Nicholson, *The Environmental Revolution: A Guide for the New Masters of the World* (Harmondsworth, England: Penguin Books, 1972), pp. 205–6.

[52] C. Robert Dickerman, "Transgovernmental Challenge and Response in Scandinavia and North America," *International Organization* 30 (Spring 1976): 213–40.

[53] John Pinder, "Economic Growth, Social Justice, and Political Reform," in Mayne, *Europe Tomorrow*, p. 283.

in the French adaptation of the British "New Towns," partly out of fear of the "Manhattanization" of Paris.[54]

A critical question relates to the basis for such emulation as exists. Richard N. Cooper suggests that one source is the coming together of national economic objectives. He notes that virtually all North Atlantic countries, despite varying standards and priorities, are committed to comparable objectives of economic growth, low unemployment, and price stability.[55] Many other common policy objectives have emerged in such spheres as education, political processes, and environmental policy, in the face of common problems that threaten societal stability in many states.

A tendency exists for emulation to arise out of necessity or convenience where movements of trade and capital, but especially people, create a demand for common regulations and benefits. P. R. Kaim-Caudle has found evidence of tendencies toward common social insurance policies in such country sets as West Germany and Austria, Britain and the Republic of Ireland, and to a lesser degree, the United States and Canada.[56]

The choice of policy areas for emulation is also influenced by the experience gap among governments in particular policy areas. The British government had dealt with racial discrimination in its colonies and at home for many years, but felt inclined to learn from American experience with a broadly conceived antidiscrimination program when such a policy was to be applied within Britain itself. This factor seems particularly strong in the development of regulations regarding the use of the physical environment, an area linked with difficult new questions of technological and economic impact.

Finally, governments and political movements are prone to look beyond their borders for answers when domestic remedies have failed. Numerous problems often seem to be intractable, among them inflation and crime. It is only natural that political systems should look toward those governments which have had the most success in particularly difficult areas, though this is not done as often as one might think.

INTERNATIONAL ORGANIZATIONAL COOPERATION: ASSISTANCE AND PRESSURES

Pressures and stimuli like those that have been described thus far have contributed to the creation and development of structures of intergovernmental and nongovernmental international organization and

---

[54] John Ardagh, *The New France: A Society in Transition, 1945–73* (Harmondsworth, England: Penguin Books, 1973), p. 275.

[55] Cooper, *Economics of Interdependence*, p. 8.

[56] P. R. Kaim-Caudle, *Comparative Social Policy and Social Security: A Ten Country Study* (London: Martin Robertson, 1973), especially pp. 306–12.

cooperation on a scale of membership or participation ranging from bilateral to virtually universal. Such association is both an additional source of external influence on national domestic and foreign policy and a means to moderate the impact of other pressures. Several intergovernmental organizations appear to have been created substantially to channel American and Soviet influence. Others, including several based in Western Europe, have been developed in part to minimize the effects of superpower dominance.

No international organization has superseded the national regimes of Europe and North America as masters of their own domestic policy. Yet some organizations, using a variety of approaches, involve themselves effectively in particular spheres of public policy. The beginnings of supranationalism, a term defined below, have emerged together with many structures for international collaboration, coordination, and conciliation. The institutions affecting the European and North American states have an Eastern or Western European, a North Atlantic, or a global scope, the last further divisible into those which the Communist-ruled states have either joined or avoided. These institutions range in functional area from narrow and technical spheres, such as the post and railroads, to organizations with sweeping jurisdictions, such as the United Nations and the Council of Europe, with some in between dealing with varied aspects of a single functional sphere, such as economics or military affairs. Nongovernmental international organizations tend to be more limited in their fields of interest, though they are important in such areas as transportation, athletics, religion, labor, and science.[57]

We are principally interested in how national public policy is affected by the institutional capacity and functional scope of the international organizations. The role of these organizations as instruments of political or economic integration is clearly related to their ability to influence national governments.

Joseph S. Nye has proclaimed as his "law of reverse salience" for international organizations that "the less the task politically, either because of its technical nature or limited impact, the greater the prospects for the growth of the organization's authority vis-à-vis the member states."[58] Others have noted a weakness of international organizations in *high politics*, a term that usually centers on national security issues. Yet substantial organizational capabilities are evident even in some important domestic policy areas.

Political scientists have learned that the powers of international

[57] See Kjell Skjelsbaek, "The Growth of International Nongovernmental Organization in the Twentieth Century," in Keohane and Nye, *Transnational Relations*, pp. 70–92.

[58] Joseph S. Nye, *Peace in Parts: Integration and Conflict in Regional Organization* (Boston: Little, Brown & Co., 1971), p. 24.

organizations do not have to be formally "supranational" in order to be significant. Supranationalism refers to power over national governments. Charles de Gaulle argued that the essence of supranationalism was the power of officials of an international organization or of a majority of national government representatives acting through the organization to override or ignore the objections of individual member governments. Supranationalism also exists when an international organization is given some authority to tax, distribute to, and regulate individuals and corporate structures that are normally within the jurisdiction of national governments, whether the organization's authoritative allocations of values are conducted through processes of policymaking, policy-implementation, or rule-adjudication.

Both of these approaches to the term *supranational* suffer from a degree of distance from the real problems of analyzing the powers of international organizations. Such organizations have differing formal and actual patterns of interaction with member governments. Some organizational staffs and coalitions of member governments have accrued some very real power in relation to member governments and their subjects despite the absence of formal authority.

The analysis of the power of international organizations must be specific in order to be meaningful. Nye suggests the following as possible forms of authority possessed by officials of international organizations:[59]

1. Gathering, analyzing and distributing of information.
2. Recommending national laws and actions.
3. Evaluating activities of states in terms of the goals of the international organization.
4. Creating and administering regulations.
5. Performing specific actions involving expenditure of funds that have an important impact on the resources of some members.
6. Helping to determine their own budget and staff.
7. Initiating new policies that expand the scope of organizational tasks.

The ability to participate in policy-making processes and to promulgate administrative rules can be as important as formal approval of the basic policies of such organizations.

Additional measures of the institutional capacity of an international organization include the levels of its voluntary and compulsory jurisdiction over governments, domestic groups, and individuals; the size of the organization's budget relative to its assigned tasks and the separate resources of its members; and whether the member governments can veto the initiatives of the organization's staff or coalitions of other member governments. The sources of the power and weakness of

---

[59] Ibid., pp. 39–40. Nye credits William Coplin with the first five of these criteria.

international organizations are diffuse, and it is easy to be misled by an incomplete picture. Predecisional involvement may represent considerable power in both national and international political structures.

This broad approach to the issue of the institutional capacity of international organizations will now be applied to an analysis of international organizational impact on domestic policies of governments. We deal with economic policy first and then discuss human rights and the physical environment.

Economic Policy

If Nye is right in saying that among international organizations an inverse relation exists between political significance and institutional capacity, organizations with responsibilities for important areas of economic policy, including areas which inevitably have social and environmental aspects, should be among the less significant international agencies in terms of institutional capacity and impact on national governments. The record in this regard is mixed. The leading economic organizations which deal extensively with developments in North America and Europe include the International Monetary Fund, the Organization for Economic Cooperation and Development (the successor to the Marshall Plan–stimulated Organization for European Economic Cooperation), the All-European (with North American participation) United Nations Economic Commission for Europe, East Europe's Council for Mutual Economic Assistance, and the European Communities, which links nine Western European states.

International Monetary Fund. Some impacts of international financial pressures have been discussed above. Stronger international cooperation in the financial field has proved unavoidable in the wake of the Great Depression, World War II, and the efforts of more than 150 national governments to cope with volatile postwar economic and political conditions. The International Monetary Fund (IMF), created in 1944 largely on American and British initiative, is the principal agency for adapting the system of international payments to sustain expanding world trade and maintain economic development and stability among the non-Communist states. The IMF is part of a larger system of international financial institutions that also includes the Bank for International Settlements (BIS) and the International Bank for Reconstruction and Development (World Bank), and it is also closely involved with national central banks, private banks, and other financial organizations and governments.

In the IMF's routine operations, its relatively strong international staff is a substantial presence as guardian against exchange rate manipulations by member states, and is particularly strong in the leverage that it can exert on less developed states possessing minimal exchange reserves and financial expertise. As noted earlier, even major countries have shown a capacity to fall into deep financial trouble, as reflected by pressure on their currencies on exchange markets and the accompanying buildup of serious deficits in their international payments balances. In these circumstances the IMF, through both its intergovernmental Board of Directors and its international staff, wields substantial power based on its access to some of the reserve currency needed to stabilize the finances of a country in difficulty. Even if the country can avoid drawing on discretionary IMF funds at a given moment, perhaps relying instead on IMF credits to which it has guaranteed access, or on BIS and foreign central bank arrangements, it must face the possibility of future dependence on short-term credits that are provided at the discretion of the IMF. Consequently, a national government can become almost as dependent on this source of credit as a near-bankrupt private debtor.

When a government requests IMF support above its level of automatic entitlement it becomes subject to a process of review, negotiation, and supervision of its financial affairs by that organization. Until the mid-1950s this control was effectively directed by the U.S. government, which supplied the desired dollars through the Fund. However, since that time, as other currencies came into demand, the IMF staff has been delegated increasing authority by the Fund's Executive Board for negotiating drawings and standbys, establishing "performance criteria" in various areas of national economic policy as set out in "letters of intent," and allowing subsequent drawings only on the condition that action be taken in conformity with such pledges.[60] The IMF's power involves all economic policies affecting national payments solvency and government measures concerning expenditures, tax programs, and economic regulation. According to the former British Prime Minister Harold Wilson, his request for IMF assistance in 1967 led to proposed conditions that included "strict credit control, a tightening of prices and incomes policy—presumably statutory—a limitation on growth, and an agreement that, while we might during the currency of the loan decide to devalue, we must pledge ourselves never to float."[61] Although the British were able to avoid such an arrangement in 1967 at the cost of immediate devaluation, they have at other times utilized various kinds of IMF support, including loans from the "General Agreement to Borrow," created by the leading IMF financial powers, in conjunction with support from foreign central banks and the Bank for International

---

[60] Tew, *Monetary Cooperation*, pp. 123–24.

[61] Harold Wilson, *The Labour Government, 1964–1970: A Personal Record* (London: Weidenfeld and Nicholson and Michael Joseph, 1971), p. 453.

Settlements. A very strong IMF "letter of intent" was negotiated with Italy in early 1974, and publicity concerning this contributed to the fall of an already wobbly Italian Cabinet.

The present system of floating currencies, long resisted by the IMF but now managed in part by it, may help avoid immediate currency crises, but the exceptional financial strains felt since 1973 in several major industrial states has made them increasingly dependent on the support of foreign banks and governments as well as international financial institutions for the means to forestall financial collapse. This has brought greater efforts to reform the international financial system that makes such wrenching crises necessary or possible, efforts dominated by the leading financial states which constitute the "Group of Twenty" (formerly the "Group of Ten") at the core of the IMF. The IMF's success now depends heavily on the actions of new oil-producing financial powers as well as on agreement among the industrialized states. Pressure by multinational institutions for policy coordination and their demands in times of crisis have not been matched by multinational solutions to the financial problems that threaten the stability of individual states and the world economy in the 1970s.

OEEC–OECD. The Organization for European Economic Cooperation (OEEC) was pointedly limited to intergovernmental cooperation, but developed this to a high level of effectiveness in its work focusing on productivity, trade, and international payments. Although the Organization for Economic Cooperation and Development (OECD), created in 1961, has not been credited with effectiveness equal to that of its smaller predecessor, it has continued with some success the use of the OEEC-developed processes of intergovernmental "confrontation" to secure a degree of coordination of economic policies among the industrialized states. Confrontation requires national policy-makers to report to and meet periodically with their opposite numbers in other governments and to take cognizance of their suggestions and criticisms. Sometimes this assumes the form of "mutual prodding or even nagging," which in the view of one authority "have proved their worth in the OECD, as in the OEEC."[62]

Such procedures are used by various working committees of the OECD, as well as its executive organs, and have been credited with influencing numerous concrete changes in national fiscal, monetary, and manpower policies, as well as changes in such related fields as science and education. However, member states are not required to consult the OECD committees before implementing policies, and the authority of the organization is based more on psychological pressure and the expectation of future reciprocity than on enforcement procedures. The

---

[62] Henry G. Aubrey, *Atlantic Economic Cooperation: The Case of OECD* (New York: Praeger Publishers, 1967), p. 105.

role of the organization's staff is low-key in regard to initiatives for task expansion, and the nature of the organization leaves little room for staff development of organizational policy, rules, or international agreements. The OECD does provide a broad range of research and advice to governments, and makes recommendations for multinational action through other organizations.

Council for Mutual Economic Assistance. Between 1956 and 1964 Nikita Khrushchev sought to transform the two major Soviet-bloc intergovernmental organizations, the Council for Mutual Economic Assistance (CMEA) and the Warsaw Treaty Organization, into strongly integrative and somewhat supranational organizations that would have necessarily become significant influences on the domestic and foreign policies of all members. But neither the Khrushchev- nor the Brezhnev-era Soviet leaderships have attained such objectives as supranational planning or major production specialization in the bloc through CMEA.[63] Joseph Stalin could have created such integrative structures when he authorized the creation of CMEA in 1949, but he did not require them at that time. When Moscow began in 1956 to actively seek stronger bloc institutions, its plans fell victim to the economic disparities and separate political aspirations of East European states, particularly Rumania, which surprised the world with their success in forestalling major bloc economic and military integration. Moscow does not yet effectively combine its extensive economic planning processes with those of its allies, and the CMEA staff has been slow to develop an international character or the capacity to affect organizational or national decisions. The Soviet bloc in Eastern Europe remains underdeveloped in regard to the movement of capital, labor, and trade across frontiers, thereby maintaining the autarky and isolation that also characterize Soviet economic affairs. The Soviet Union is given little assistance through CMEA in such very real areas of need as technological advancement and the rationalization of production and prices. Except for recent steps toward generous petroleum prices Moscow has offered few economic or political concessions to its associates because of or through CMEA.

United Nations Economic Commission for Europe. The United Nations Economic Commission for Europe, the only organization with broad economic concerns that links the North Atlantic states with Communist-ruled Eastern Europe, has been a force for moderating the isolation of the Soviet economy. It has worked with some success to break down barriers to East-West economic intercourse imposed by both sides. Its excellent research and anticipation of future problems are evidenced by its comparatively early response to environmental

---

[63] On CMEA see Andrzej Korbonski, "Comecon," International Conciliation, no. 549 (September 1964); Michael Kaser, COMECON: Integration Problems of the Planned Economies (New York: Oxford University Press, 1965); and Sandor Ausch, Theory and Practice of CMEA Cooperation (Budapest: Akademii Kiado, 1972).

degradation. Yet it can do little more than propose joint planning and coordination, barred by the suspicions engendered by Cold War antagonisms from direct involvement with substantial areas of national domestic policy outside a few fields, including inland transport.

European Communities. The European Communities, based on separate treaties that led to the creation of the European Coal and Steel Community (ECSC) in 1952 and the European Economic (EEC) and Atomic Energy (Euratom) Communities in 1958, represents the farthest thrust of multinational cooperative action and institutional capacity in the economic and related spheres. The establishment of the Communities reflected a determination on the part of the six founding states that it should develop into a vehicle for economic if not political union, and it has been provided with some strong tools with which to achieve its goals.

The European Coal and Steel Community, the first of the Communities to be established, was provided by its founding treaty with more specific supranational authority than was allowed to the others. Its executive High Authority was entitled to tax production, subsidize production and structural improvements, and regulate competition. It could act directly on enterprises and, with the concurrence of the intergovernmental Council, impose its will on member governments. Governments could become subject to compulsory adjudication on the initiative of the Community structures. The ECSC set many of the main directions for action later taken up by the European Economic Community (EEC), an organization with a much wider functional scope. Yet its center of supranationalism, the High Authority, did not develop much beyond its original range of powers and actually minimized its supranational actions in practice, as by frequent consultation with the government representatives of the Council.[64] Although the limited scope of its jurisdiction made the task virtually impossible in any case, the ECSC has been criticized for failing to move its membership close to a common energy policy. By 1957 the ECSC structures had substantially settled into the routine management of specific rules.

The political and legal character of the European Economic Community, created in 1958, and of the European Communities system, created in 1967 with the fusion of the main structures of the three Communities, defies brief summary. Leon Lindberg and Stuart Scheingold conclude, "It is neither federal nor confederal, intergovernmental or supranational, sovereign or dependent, but it shares some of the characteristics of all."[65] They cite Walter Yondorf's term for this political system, *sector integrated supranational system*, a label which em-

---

[64] Leon N. Lindberg, *The Political Dynamics of European Economic Integration* (Stanford, Calif.: Stanford University Press, 1963), pp. 52–53.

[65] Leon N. Lindberg and Stuart A. Scheingold, *Europe's Would-Be Polity: Patterns of Change in the European Community* (Englewood Cliffs, N.J.: Prentice-Hall, 1970), p. 307.

phasizes the sharing of authority between national and supranational actors on differing bases, depending on the functional sector involved.

The power of the present European Communities is not based on a high degree of formal supranational authority in the hands of the Communities institutions. Even such maximizers of the role of the presumably supranational Commission of the EEC (and now the three Communities) as Lindberg, Scheingold, and Pickles tend to emphasize its informal, indirect, and implied powers.[66] The three Community treaties empower the Commission to serve as watchdog over the application of the treaties, detecting breaches by individuals, enterprises, and governments, and taking remedial action. The Commission can bring violators before the Communities' Court of Justice, though it has usually been sufficient for it to issue a formal opinion concerning transgressions. Under the authority of the treaties, it can issue and enforce regulations, directions, and decisions, and put forward recommendations and opinions, these differentiated according to the degree to which the action is enforceable, the policy area involved, and the party being regulated. Although technically corresponding to the administrative decree, these powers tend to overlap into the policy-making sphere, most notably in the area of competition (antitrust) policy. Such authority is significantly augmented by the Commission's power to implement Council rules and policies. The scope of the accumulated "administrative power" is extended with every enlargement of the Communities' tasks.

The Commission performs its most important role by working to enlarge these tasks. This involves both completing the timetable for Community development set out in the treaties and proposing new areas for Community activity that were not foreseen when the treaties were written. The Commission can effectively initiate new policy and reject Council amendment of its proposals (overridden only by a unanimous Council). It dominates the predecisional and policy-implementation activity of the Communities and intrudes deeply into the main decision-making processes as well. The Communities depends to a critical extent on the Commission's ability to propose acceptable policies and to mediate and maneuver with the government representatives until compromises and areas of agreement emerge.

Although the formal and informal powers noted here are still essentially intact, they have been restrained since 1965 by a French-led effort to keep the Commission from using self-developed supranational authority. France has also sought to limit nonunanimous policy-making by the Council, though this has been used in a very limited sphere. The

---

[66] William Pickles, "Political Power in the European Economic Community," in Carol Ann Cosgrove and Kenneth J. Twitchett, eds., *The New International Actors: The United Nations and the European Economic Community* (London: Macmillan, 1970), pp. 201–21.

January 1966 "Luxembourg Compromise" agreed to by the Council resulted in the beginning of a shift away from supranationalism in the Communities' policy-making processes, with increased power to the permanent representatives and ministers of the member states and the Commission more careful not to appear to be acting like a government. A shift has taken place "away from Community-level centralized administration and policy-making, and toward programs conceived in Community-wide terms with implementation largely decentralized and the responsibility of member states."[67] Although some believe that the Commission has lost its effective policy-making capacities and has become just another bureaucracy,[68] it appears to be working as hard as ever in the mid-1970s to expand the programs of the Communities. The "Eurocrats" now have a more realistic approach to the problems involved in gaining national government support for those programs. The Commission has not been able to form the remarkable compromises and coalitions that made its major successes possible, as in agriculture and tariff reduction, during its first decade. Yet this may well result as much from the limits of its original powers as from its bureaucratization or the Luxembourg Compromise.

In contrast to the Commission, the other substantially supranational Communities organ, the Court of Justice, has continued to increase its authority. As the Commission has increased its use of administrative powers which require Court of Justice review, the Court has repeatedly, though not invariably, interpreted the Community treaties to stretch the supranational authority of the Communities organs and has maximized the applicability and supremacy of Community law.[69] It has authority over the other Communities organs, member governments, and private parties, and its influence is extended through the acceptance of Community law by national courts. It has sanctioned substantial control over enterprises and has ruled in a number of cases that the existence of Community acts in given fields bars parallel or conflicting national action. According to Pickles, the Court of Justice may ultimately secure a role in the Communities system greater than that of the U.S. Supreme Court in the American political system.[70] Few observers would go this far, but it is already the most powerful and the busiest international court in the world.

Authoritative assessments of the Communities accomplishments are marked by considerable disagreement. A minimalist position was

---

[67] Lindberg and Scheingold, *Europe's Would-Be Polity,* p. 290.

[68] David Coombes, *Politics and Bureaucracy in the European Community* (London: George Allen, 1970), p. 299.

[69] See Anthony Perry and Stephen Hardy, *EEC Law* (New York: Matthew Bender, 1973), pp. 69–155.

[70] Pickles, "Political Power," p. 218.

stated by former French President Georges Pompidou when he referred to the Communities as not much more than a customs union plus a farm policy.[71] The political scientist Helen Wallace supports Pompidou, observing that "Community policies have been restricted so far either to sectors like agriculture and tariff policy, which are relatively well insulated from other sectors, or to fairly limited aspects of other sectors."[72] In her view spillover from sector to sector has not occurred, and such policies as the free movement of labor and capital have had less impact than many anticipated.

A considerably broader impact is suggested by Lindberg and Scheingold. They examine 12 "economic functions" of government, and suggest through the use of a scale the relative importance for each function of Community decision-making processes as compared with national processes. They designate influences in each sector as (1) all national; (2) only very beginning Community; (3) both, national predominates; (4) both, Community predominates; or (5) all Community. Their evaluation seems rather subjective, with only enough evidence to suggest the existence but not the extent or the intensity of Community roles. Table 3–2 presents their assignments of rank values for the 12 "economic functions" as of 1968. Although Community "dominance" is suggested

TABLE 3–2
Rating of Locus of Decision-Making in Designated Areas of Economic Policy

	Rank Value – 1968
Countercyclical policy	2
Regulation of economic competition and other government controls on prices and investments.	3
Agricultural protection	4
Economic development and planning	2
Exploitation and protection of natural resources.	2
Regulation and support of transportation.	2
Regulation and support of mass media of communication	1
Labor-management relations	1
Fiscal policy	3
Balance-of-payments stability	3
Domestic monetary policy	2
Movement of goods, services, and other factors of production within the customs union	4

Source: Leon N. Lindberg and Stuart A. Scheingold, *Europe's Would-Be Polity: Patterns of Change in the European Community*, © 1970, p. 71. Reprinted by permission of Prentice-Hall, Inc., Englewood Cliffs, New Jersey.

---

[71] *Economist,* March 30, 1974, p. 52.

[72] Helen Wallace, "The Impact of the European Communities on National Policy," *Government and Opposition* (Autumn 1971): 535.

for only the same two sectors noted by Wallace, agriculture and tariffs, a beginning of Community involvement is seen in five other areas, and a substantial Community role is put forward for three other spheres. On the other hand, Lindberg and Scheingold foresaw a stalling of the Community's progress in the 1970s.

It seems to us that Lindberg and Scheingold are correct in regard to the broad *scope* of the European Communities' economic activity, but that they overestimate the *intensity* of that impact. The treaties constitute an agenda and guidelines for subsequent action by the Communities organs. However, the treaties are not self-executing, and it has been the task of the Communities institutions and the member governments to give them concrete expression. These include the economic sectors noted by Lindberg and Scheingold and such other fields as social security, manpower, energy, company administration, aid to depressed regions, education, research, and protection of the physical environment.

The December 1969 and October 1972 summit meetings of the Communities heads of state and government approved what can be termed a second program. This carried the tasks of the Communities significantly beyond the treaties in some respects and promised the early fulfillment of most of the remaining explicit treaty commitments. A loosely defined economic, monetary, and political union was set forth as the target for 1980. The financing of the Communities administration and programs from its own revenues and a share of its members' value-added tax was scheduled. Promised expansion of the social, regional, and industrial investment funds suggested sharply increased distributions within the region.

Finally, the critical test has been the ability of the Communities institutions and member governments to agree to specific acts and policies that implement this impressive dream of unity. It is this task that has been, in the majority of areas, beyond the capacities of these parties. Some of the major summit-endorsed programs have been or are clearly on their way to implementation in the 1970s, including a stronger base for funding Communities administration, a major degree of national tax harmonization, and the Monetary Cooperation Fund. These sectors join the Common Agricultural Policy and the incomplete common transport (primarily road and rail) policy as major areas of Communities accomplishment. However, most of the hopes of 1969 and 1972, many of these originating even before the 1957 signing of the Treaty of Rome, have largely fallen victim to global political and economic pressures, inadequate will on the part of the member governments, a resurgence of nationalism, and a decline in emotional and idealistic commitment to a united Europe. Intensive efforts by the Commission helped make possible the breakthroughs in tariff reductions and agriculture in the 1960s.

In the 1970s coordination of energy and counterinflation policies seems doubtful and the regional, social, and investment funds continue to be victimized by intense politics and resulting inadequate resources.

How can we sum up the impact of the European Communities on its members' economic autonomy and problems? The Communities' greatest contribution to helping its member states has probably been in free trade. Although no conclusive proof has been presented concerning the Communities' contribution to the member states' economic advancement since 1952, this progress has been enormous and has outstripped that of most other industrial states. The Communities has developed conditions and rules that encourage penetration by multinational enterprises, but has done little to help the member states control these enterprises more effectively. Assistance has been provided to member states facing balance-of-payments difficulties, but efforts toward monetary integration have been halting. While agriculture has been stabilized, subsidies have been costly and inadequate attention has been given to the structural reform of European farming. The Communities' transfer payments, running to $3.5 billion yearly, are very high by the standards of international organizations; yet these payments are concentrated overwhelmingly in agriculture. Greater balance can be expected in the course of the 1970s, but not distributions that rival those of the national governments even in sectors, such as regional and social fund aid, in which governments negotiate reciprocal and often counterbalancing advantages and disadvantages.

The impacts of the Communities' work have been indirect as well as direct. John Pinder argues that "the harmonization of taxes, the fixing of common agricultural prices, and the free movement of goods and people cannot but influence member countries' policies of redistributing incomes and helping deprived groups by means of taxation and benefits."[73] The European Communities has been a strong conscious agent of multinational emulation of policy in such areas as worker participation in management, value-added and corporate taxation, antitrust law, "indicative planning," regional development, manpower training, industrial safety, and social security.

Organization of Petroleum Exporting Countries (OPEC). The greatest sudden redistribution of wealth was engineered in 1973 and 1974 by the Asian, African, and South American member states of the Organization of Petroleum Exporting Countries (OPEC). This organization originated in 1960 and was slow to develop adequate capability to set world oil prices. Yet by 1974 it had demonstrated a virtually unchallenged power over prices and the separate Organization of Arab

---

[73] Pinder, "Economic Growth," p. 275.

Petroleum Exporting Countries (OAPEC) had proved its ability to restrict the flow of oil as a political instrument.

The result of the embargo and the oil price increase of nearly 400 percent was the most severe dislocation of the economies of non-Communist industrialized states since the 1930s. By 1975 the OECD states faced unprecedented outflows of gold and currencies and few Western states were able to avoid severe recession combined with exceptional inflation in prices. The countries most dependent on imported oil, such as Japan and Italy, tended to fare worst, but even the more self-sufficient United States saw its economy move in parallel directions.

The priorities of domestic and international politics in the developed states shifted to such questions as financing oil imports, protecting the international financial system from the huge holdings accumulated by oil-exporting countries, regulating the foreign investments of OPEC states, and providing protection against future restrictions on supplies. These pressures and the initial national efforts to stabilize the situation helped increase the levels of unemployment and inflation that accompanied negative national economic growth in much of the industrial West.

The response of the principal oil-consuming nations included the creation in late 1974 of the International Energy Agency (IEA) under the aegis of the OECD. This agency has coordinated significant steps in areas ranging from financing to precautions against new emergencies.[74] Its achievements have been more limited in energy conservation and price adjustment.

It is notable that new intergovernmental institutions have been at the center of the current politics of energy and finance. Although neither the IEA nor OPEC emphasizes supranational authority, they demonstrate that national governments cannot achieve their goals on a bilateral basis and reflect the growing merger of international and domestic policy.

Human Rights Policy

Multinational cooperation and enforcement in protecting human rights reflect both strong national government resistance to external interference and countervailing multinational pressures to establish a meaningful role for international organizations in this sphere that bridges political and social policies. The world has not been able to act as if genocide, forced labor, and governmental use of torture and extralegal detainment never existed. Yet neither national governments nor

---

[74] See Ulf Lantzke, "The OECD and Its International Energy Agency," *Daedalus* 104, no. 4 (Fall 1975): 217–27.

international organizations have been able to exert consistently effective influence against such practices.

The United Nations has sponsored a Universal Declaration and several covenants on human rights. Its Human Rights Commission yearly receives thousands of complaints concerning the denial of such rights. In recent years the UN has refined its processes for dealing with these complaints. Yet charges against only a few "outcast" countries are taken seriously and little of consequence results from those that are judged valid. Although reports and protests have been issued against South Africa, Chile, and Israel, most other nations have been able to rest easy.

The UN Declaration provided the impetus for action in Western Europe under the auspices of the Council of Europe, one of the earliest organizations created (1949) to work toward European union. The Council has failed to fulfill the aspirations of many of its founders, who hoped it would provide a keystone for institutional and policy development for a united Europe. However, it has created such useful international structures as the European Human Rights Commission and the European Court of Justice (separate from that of the European Communities), which function together with the Council's Committee of Ministers and Parliament as a single system for processing complaints from individuals, organizations, and governments concerning alleged violations of the European Convention for the Protection of Human Rights and Fundamental Freedom. This system is based on the fact-finding and mediating role of the Commission, but it also provides for binding decisions by the Court of Justice and political pressure from the Committee of Ministers and Parliament. Although tangible pressures are limited to expulsion from the Council of Europe, governments have been reluctant to defy the findings of the Council's structures. Recent cases have dealt with British detention policies in Northern Ireland and the definition of British citizenship. A significant number of specific changes in constitutions, statutes, and administrative procedures have been made in response to the Council of Europe's Human Rights Convention and the interpretation of the Council's structures. These have centered on issues of due process of law and freedom of expression.

The work of the Council of Europe in the sphere of human rights was preceded by that of the International Labor Organization (ILO), an agency created in 1919 with representatives of labor, management, and government. The ILO has pioneered methods of reviewing government reports by expert committees as the basis for the supervision of compliance with its conventions and has authorized international labor noncooperation with offending states and their commerce.[75] Both the

---

[75] E. A. Landy, *The Effectiveness of International Supervision: Thirty Years of I.L.O. Experience* (London: Stevens and Sons, 1966).

Council of Europe and the ILO have functioned with considerable difficulty in many other spheres of activity, but have had some measurable impact in the area of human rights.

Foreign governments and intergovernmental organizations have usually been restrained by a sense of futility and a reluctance to upset the Communist regimes when confronted with evidence of persecutions in Eastern Europe. Some nongovernmental organizations have sought to take up the slack. The demands and protests of these organizations have brought some relief and forestalled worse treatment in some situations. Yet even the successes reveal weaknesses in the global system for protecting the rights of individuals and groups.

Physical Environmental Policy

The role of international organizations has been uniquely important in the area of the physical environment. Though the responses of most organizations to environmental problems have been deplorably slow to take shape, they developed earlier than did the responses of most national governments. As a result, such worldwide organizations as the United Nations, World Health Organization, UNESCO (United Nations Educational, Scientific, and Cultural Organization), Food and Agriculture Organization, World Meteorological Organization, Intergovernmental Maritime Consultative Organization, World Bank, and International Atomic Energy Agency have been able to make a large contribution to worldwide, regional, and national activity. The United Nations Environmental Secretariat, the administrator of the UN's Environmental Program and Environmental Fund, developed out of the 1972 Stockholm Conference on the Human Environment. That conference has been the single most dramatic attempt to mobilize national and international effort to maintain and improve environmental quality and the conservation of resources.

Virtually all of the European and North Atlantic organizations discussed in relation to economic and social issues have become committed to environmental protection, but only in the past decade. These include the OECD, the Council of Europe, the UN Economic Commission for Europe (which has given environmental issues the highest priority for the longest period), and the North Atlantic Treaty Organization (for which such work can be viewed as image-building). Their work has emphasized the sponsorship of research and experimental projects, the compilation of scientific information, the collection and comparison of national government environmental policies, and the drafting of model legislation and international agreements. Often lacking in expertise and information, and aware of particularly strong multinational linkages to their own environmental problems, most governments of industrial nations have been eager to develop environmental policy within a multinational framework. Pressures from international organizations have given national government agencies little choice but to coordinate and cooperate on a multinational basis. Between the date that national environmental reports were requested by the UN's ECE in late 1970 and the date of submission of the reports, "a surprising number of changes occurred in the legal and institutional approaches to environmental problems in many ECE countries, some quite sweeping."[76] A similar speeding of momentum was associated with the 1972 Stockholm Conference. The impetus of international organizations combined with newly powerful domestic pressures to foster rapid processes of multinationally influenced institutional and policy development throughout the industrialized states.

The European Communities was late in developing an environmental program, its Commission initiating work in this field in July 1971. The Communities' Environmental Program, approved by the Council of Ministers in July 1973, suffers from this late start, as the Commission had to tread around the multiplicity of efforts by other organizations. The program also suffers more directly than do other programs of international organizations from apparent conflicts between its environmental ideals and such economic objectives as industrial and energy development. The Communities organs have the troublesome responsibility of ensuring that national environmental regulations and subsidies for environmental purification do not give enacting states trade advantages in the Common Market. As a result, it is possible that the Communities' program may have some retarding impact on its members' environmental policies.[77] Yet no organization can match the Communities' capacities to require coordination of policy and impose regulations directly on both member governments and enterprises. Such regulations have already begun to flow from the Communities' decision-making machinery.

CONCLUSIONS

Domestic policy is affected by a wide range of external forces and organizations, including great international crises, transnational trends, foreign governments and movements, multinational enterprises, and international organizations. The impacts of these forces and organizations have grown as national governments and peoples have become

---

[76] Amasa S. Bishop and Robert D. Munro, "The UN Regional Commissions and Environmental Problems," in David A. Kay and Eugene B. Skolnikoff, eds., *World Eco-Crisis: International Organizations in Response* (Madison: University of Wisconsin Press, 1972), p. 363.

[77] Phipponeau, "The Environment," pp. 131–63.

more interdependent. National efforts to control domestic affairs without sufficient attention to multinational forces and organizations have frequently been frustrated.

Such states as the Soviet Union and the United States are less subject than most others to the impacts of international pressures. The Soviet Union has limited and regulated many kinds of multinational flows, and both superpowers are self-sufficient in many kinds of resources and reluctant to borrow ideas from other states. Yet even these superpowers have felt the effects of the processes of penetration, reaction, and emulation described in this chapter. However, those processes have weighed much more heavily on the policy-making of the Western European states.

Our evidence has led us to stress external impacts on domestic economic, social, and environmental policies. Political processes have been somewhat protected from multinational influence by the tendency of most countries to view interference in this area as illegitimate. States also create stronger barriers to foreign advice or models in cultural areas that are close to their roots and souls, such as religion and education. On the other hand, we have been able to establish that nations are increasingly looking outward for solutions to problems for reasons that include national inexperience and failure as well as the common nature of the objectives and tasks facing industrial states. Even such spheres as human rights and education are increasingly subject to multinational influence.

The processes and instruments of external influence have been shown to vary widely, depending on the source and the recipient of the effects and the particular moment in history. In general, formal penetration by governments through occupation and aid programs, and also through the Communist movement, has declined in comparison with processes of reaction, emulation, and multinational cooperation.

International organizations show strength outside purely technical spheres. They demonstrate substantial capability in regard to economic and environmental issues, though less capability in relation to human rights. These international structures can be expected to have increasing impact on major areas of national domestic policy. Multinational emulation and collaboration have become increasingly important, and this trend can be expected to accelerate. It may well be that unnecessary crises and catastrophes will occur before multinationalism is markedly improved. However, cooperation will almost surely grow, given the trends and problems that we have outlined in this chapter.

4 Environmental and Political Influences on Public Policy in Eight Nations

To this point we have dealt in a general way with what many observers believe to be the major determinants of public policy. Now we shall investigate the crucial characteristics of those nations whose current policies will be compared in the remainder of this book. Those countries are the United States, Great Britain, France, Italy, Sweden, the German Federal Republic (West Germany), the German Democratic Republic (East Germany), and the Soviet Union. Specifically, we intend to examine the similarities and differences in the physical social, and economic environments and the political systems of these eight nations which are likely to have a bearing on their patterns of public policy.

PHYSICAL RESOURCES

Numerous students of foreign policy, especially those of the geopolitical school, have emphasized the role of such physical factors as area and natural resources.[1] Although such elements of national power are not always ob-

---

[1] Klaus Knorr, *The Power of Nations* (New York: Basic Books, 1975).

101

viously relevant to domestic policy, associations of this kind are very significant. The size of a nation helps determine accessibility of resources and ability to regulate the society. The availability of energy sources and other commodities helps decide whether a country will look inward or outward in its economic development. Inadequate resources can be overcome, as has been done by Japan. Yet the pace of industrialization and the drive toward affluence will usually be affected by resource availability.

In terms of area (see Table 4–1) we find that the eight countries include two of the largest countries in the world. Both the Soviet Union and the United States are continental in scope, the former being uniquely huge. The five Western European states are medium-sized in comparative terms, and East Germany alone is small.

TABLE 4–1
Area

Country	World Rank (N = 133)	Area (sq. km.)
Soviet Union.........	1	22,403,000
United States.........	4	9,363,387
France..............	44	551,208
Sweden.............	48	449,682
Italy................	58	301,226
West Germany	66	247,960
Great Britain........	68	244,016
East Germany........	96	197,431

Source: Bruce Russett et al., *World Handbook of Political and Social Indicators* (New Haven: Yale University Press, 1964), pp. 139–41.

The present awareness of an energy crisis has highlighted the distribution of fuels and related technology. At this writing and for many years to come the industrialized world will depend primarily on such fossil fuels as coal, petroleum, and natural gas. When we analyze the distribution (see Tables 4–2, 4–3, and 4–4) of these three resources among the eight nations, it is clear that they are far from being evenly dispersed. The vast wealth of the Soviet Union is striking. The United States invariably ranks second behind the USSR, but given its substantially greater energy use America is much farther from self-sufficiency. Following the two giants, Great Britain, with recent and continuing discoveries of impressive quantities of oil and natural gas in the North Sea, ranks third and will evidently join the Soviet Union as a net exporter of fuel. West Germany and France appear to be moderately endowed, and East Germany, Italy, and Sweden lag behind. Several of these states have improved their situations by developing hydroelectric and nuclear power. Yet the line between energy haves and have-nots is basically determined by fossil fuels.

TABLE 4–2
Coal Reserves

Country	Rank among the Eight	Total Reserves (million metric tons)
Soviet Union 1		4,121,603
United States 2		1,100,000
West Germany 3		70,000
Great Britain 4		15,000
France 5		2,800
Sweden 6		90
East Germany........... 7		50
Italy 8		–

World total, 1972 = 6,641,200

Source: *United Nations Statistical Yearbook, 1973* (New York: UN Publishing Service, 1974), pp. 166–67.

TABLE 4–3
Crude Petroleum Reserves

Country	Rank among the Eight	Total Reserves (million metric tons)
Soviet Union........... 1		5,716
United States.......... 2		4,899
Great Britain.......... 3		716
West Germany 4		71
Italy.................. 5		35
France................ 6		13
East Germany 7.5		–
Sweden 7.5		–

World total, 1972 = 76,800

Source: *United Nations Statistical Yearbook, 1973* (New York: UN Publishing Service, 1974), pp. 170–71.

TABLE 4–4
Natural Gas Reserves

Country	Rank among the Eight	Total Reserves (million metric tons)
Soviet Union........... 1		18,633
United States.......... 2		7,535
Great Britain.......... 3		1,303
West Germany 4		351
France................ 5		187
Italy.................. 6		170
East Germany 7.5		–
Sweden 7.5		–

World total, 1972 = 54,100

Source: *United Nations Statistical Yearbook, 1973* (New York: UN Publishing Service, 1974), pp. 172–73.

Area and energy supplies certainly do not reveal all of the critical differences among the eight states in regard to physical resources. Other notable findings include the enormous food-growing capacity of the United States and the chronic shortages in the Soviet Union; the unique Soviet access to virtually every important mineral; and the high degree of dependence of all the smaller states on an often volatile and politically controllable world market in many commodities.

DEMOGRAPHIC AND SOCIAL PATTERNS

Let us turn now to consider the demographic characteristics of the people who inhabit the eight countries and some of their major similarities and differences. In an era in which increasing world population is a disturbing phenomenon, all eight nations exhibit growth rates (see Table 4–5) significantly below the global average. East Germany has actually demonstrated zero population growth. Further, with the exceptions of East Germany and Sweden these nations rank among the world's most populous countries. Once again the Soviet Union and the United States lead the way, with West Germany, Great Britain, Italy, and France clustering in the middle.

TABLE 4–5
Population Size and Growth Rate (estimates)

Country	Rank among the Eight	Population (1973) (millions)	Percent Average Annual Growth (1963–73)
Soviet Union	1	249.7	1.0
United States	2	210.4	1.1
West Germany	3	62.0	0.8
Great Britain	4	56.0	0.4
Italy	5	54.8	0.7
France	6	52.0	0.8
East Germany	7	17.0	0.0
Sweden	8	8.1	0.7

Source: U.S. Arms Control and Disarmament Agency, *World Military Expenditures and Arms Trade, 1963–1973* (Washington, D.C.: U.S. Government Printing Office, 1975).

The agenda and style of public policy-making within a nation are likely to be affected less by sheer population size than by where its inhabitants reside and what they do to earn their livelihoods. As argued in Chapter 2, the more urbanized a country and the higher the proportion of its population engaged in other than agricultural pursuits, the greater will be the need for its political system to deal with a wide range of public issues. In this light (see Table 4–6), it may be seen that Great Britain, West Germany, and the United States rank among the most urbanized nations, whereas France, Sweden, the Soviet Union, Italy, and East Germany, though above the global average, are considerably less dominated by large cities.

Figures showing the proportion of the male labor force engaged in agriculture (see Table 4–7) tend to be consistent with those for urbanization. Yet the former figures also reveal that East Germany and Sweden have reduced their farm sector considerably more than their urbanization ranking indicates and that the Soviet Union, France, and Italy stand out as countries with exceptionally large agricultural sectors. Although further reduction of the farm population has proceeded

TABLE 4–6
Urbanization

Country	World Rank (N = 109)	Percent of Population Living in Cities of 100,000 or More (1960)
Great Britain	3	71.6
West Germany	7	51.5
United States	8	50.5
France	16	34.0
Sweden	35	25.1
Soviet Union	36	24.8
Italy	39	24.2
East Germany	47	21.3

Source: Charles Taylor and Michael Hudson, *World Handbook of Political and Social Indicators*, 2d ed. (New Haven: Yale University Press, 1972), pp. 219–21. These data were collected under the direction of Kingsley Davis and published by International and Urban Research, Institute of International Studies, University of California, in *World Urbanization, 1950–1970*, vol. 1: *Basic Data for Cities, Countries, and Regions*, Population Monograph series, no. 4 (Berkeley: University of California Press, 1969).

TABLE 4–7
Distribution of Male Labor Force
(percentage in agriculture)

Country	World Rank (N = 106)	Percent in Agriculture
Soviet Union (1959)	73.5	34
France (1962)	77.5	25
Italy (1965)	80	24
East Germany (1961)	89.5	18
Sweden (1965)	89.5	18
United States (1965)	100	8
West Germany (1965)	100	8
Great Britain (1961)	104.5	5

Source: Charles Taylor and Michael Hudson, *World Handbook of Political and Social Indicators*, 2d ed. (New Haven: Yale University Press, 1972), pp. 332–34.

throughout the industrialized world during the past decade, the relative positions of the eight have changed little.

In sum, if we were to consider the factors urbanization and non-agricultural employment as agenda-setting determinants of public policy, we would expect to find the most pressing problems and experiences in Great Britain, the United States, and West Germany. However, beyond these broad-gauge indicators of urbanization are important sources of social cleavage which are likely to have substantial consequences. These divisions can vary with respect to their type, complexity, and intensity.

By *type* of division we have in mind these basic sources of cleavage in industrialized societies: religious affiliation, ethnic-racial distinctions, geographic or regional differences, and social class divisions.[2] By *complexity* we refer to the number of such cleavages, both within type and between type, that are present in any national population. We use *intensity* to mean the extent to which the divisions alienate various groups in society from one another and from the political system.

In regard to both the type and the complexity of cleavages the United States and the Soviet Union are, in some respects, similar. Starting from very different premises, national leaders in both countries tend to play down the importance of social class as a meaningful basis of cleavage within their countries. In the United States the rhetoric emphasizes and reinforces shared beliefs in individual social mobility and equality of opportunity as opposed to class solidarity or interclass hostility. The view expressed by Soviet representatives is that through the application of Marxist-Leninist principles their system has successfully eliminated major class divisions, so that today only two "nonantagonistic strata," workers and peasants, are said to exist.[3] In reality both the American and Soviet societies exhibit major disparities of wealth, power, and status. Although the Soviet regime maintains narrower gaps among income groups in comparison with the capitalist countries in this survey, it exceeds them in the maintenance of special privileges based on office and position.

When we examine the structure of the American and Soviet societies in relation to our other types of social cleavage, their similarity is, we believe, also evident. Both countries' populations exhibit highly complex divisions along ethnic, racial, religious, and regional lines. Further, in both the United States and the Soviet Union these cleavages are often

---

[2] Seymour Martin Lipset and Stein Rokkan, "Cleavage Structures, Party Systems, and Voter Alignments: An Introduction," in Lipset and Rokkan, eds., *Party Systems and Voter Alignments* (New York: Free Press, 1967), pp. 1–64.

[3] Paul Hollander, *Soviet and American Society: A Comparison* (New York: Oxford University Press, 1973), pp. 202–44.

associated with rather intense feelings and behavior patterns that undermine official attempts to promote a more united society and polity. Given the greater legitimacy that open social and political conflicts enjoy in the United States, expressions of solidarity and hostility are allowed to flower to a far greater extent than is the case in the USSR. But to say this is really only to argue that it is far easier to gauge the intensity of such sentiments in the United States than in the USSR.[4]

The situations in France, Italy, and Sweden vary considerably from the American-Russian pattern. In these Western European countries, differences in religious affiliation, race, ethnicity, and regional identification are somewhat less evident, their populations more homogeneous. We cannot ignore the manifestations of regionalist sentiment in Brittany, Corsica, and southern Italy or the clerical versus anticlerical conflicts in France and Italy. Yet as compared to the complex cleavages of the American and Soviet societies there exists a higher degree of religious, racial, and ethnic uniformity.

On the other hand, leading analysts of the French, Italian, and Swedish societies typically take pains to point out that social class distinctions are authentic bases of group solidarity and meaningful sources of political division.[5] People are highly conscious of belonging to distinct class groupings in these nations. In the mid-1960s it was argued by some that increasing prosperity and certain changes in the occupational structure of Western Europe were lessening interclass hostility and working-class alienation.[6] Yet of the three countries only Sweden appears to have made a major breakthrough in the reduction of interclass tensions.[7]

At present the United Kingdom is afflicted by serious old and new conflicts that challenge the unity of the state. Among the oldest are struggles between the religious communities of Northern Ireland and

---

[4] Walter Dean Burnham, "The United States: The Politics of Heterogeneity," in Richard Rose, ed., Electoral Behavior: A Comparative Handbook (New York: Free Press, 1974), pp. 653–720.

[5] Richard Rose, ed., Studies in British Politics (New York: St. Martin's Press, 1966); David Butler and Donald Stokes, Political Change in Britain (New York: St. Martin's Press, 1969); Stanley Hoffman, Decline or Renewal: France since the 1930's (New York: Viking Press, 1974); Joseph LaPalombara, "Italy: Fragmentation, Isolation, Alienation," in Lucien Pye and Sidney Verba, eds., Political Culture and Political Development (Princeton: Princeton University Press, 1965), pp. 282–329; Sidney Tarrow, Peasant Communism in Southern Italy (New Haven: Yale University Press, 1967).

[6] Ralf Dahrendorf, "Recent Changes in the Class Structure of European Societies"; and Seymour Martin Lipset, "The Changing Class Structure and Contemporary European Politics," both in Daedalus 93, no. 1 (Winter 1964): 225–67, 271–97.

[7] M. Donald Hancock, Sweden: The Politics of Postindustrial Change (Hinsdale, Ill.: Dryden Press, 1972).

revivals of nationalism in Scotland and Wales. These conflicts are compounded by continued hostility along social class lines and racial cleavages resulting from the white majority's reaction to the immigration of "coloured" persons from Commonwealth countries.

Generally, the character of social divisions in West Germany comes closer to the French, Italian, and Swedish pattern than to the American or Soviet pattern. That is, class distinctions are of central significance. At the same time, there is another type of cleavage, religious in nature, which is of greater importance in the Federal Republic than in the other continental European countries we have discussed. The nearly equal division of West Germany into Protestant and Catholic communities serves to set it apart. Political conflicts built around class and religion have been historically intense. But observers of postwar West Germany stress that much of the bitterness which previously surrounded these cleavages has been eliminated.[8]

The social divisions in the "other Germany," the German Democratic Republic, are somewhat elusive. Distinctions based on religion, ethnicity, and region seem minor—in terms of the homogeneity of its population East Germany approximates Sweden. So the matter really boils down to the issue of class. Here travelers from the West have noticed the existence of substantial disparities in occupational prestige and consumption style between the "new class" of engineers, scientists, economists, academicians, and industrial managers who run the thriving industrial system and the rest of the population. Occupation-related differences appear to be given even greater official recognition and political significance than in the Soviet Union.[9]

THE ECONOMIES: ORGANIZATION AND PLANNING

In evaluating the eight nations' economies, we shall explore major similarities and differences in their economic structures, level of technological sophistication, and economic performance. By economic organization we have in mind basic aspects of ownership and control. We also intend to explore the roles of the marketplace and planning institutions in determining production and the distribution of benefits. The overall pattern or economic system is itself the outcome of major public policy decisions. Yet it serves in turn to facilitate or limit sub-

---

[8] Ralf Dahrendorf, *Society and Democracy in Germany* (Garden City, N.Y.: Doubleday & Co., 1967), pp. 67–104; Alfred Grosser, *Germany in Our Time* (New York: Praeger Publishers, 1971), pp. 175–255; and Arnold Heidenheimer, *The Governments of Germany*, 3d ed. (New York: Thomas Y. Crowell, 1971), pp. 40–61.

[9] Jean Edward Smith, *Germany behind the Wall* (Boston: Little, Brown & Co., 1967), pp. 24–82; and John Dornberg, *The Other Germany* (Garden City, N.Y.: Doubleday & Co., 1968), pp. 201–63.

sequent choices. In Chapter 10 we discuss approaches to competition and worker participation in enterprise decision-making. Both of these issues take different forms, depending on the basic character of the economic system.

Although they display major variations the United States, Great Britain, France, Italy, West Germany, and Sweden each represents a mixed capitalist economy.[10] Large public or quasi-public sectors of production and distribution as well as efforts at governmental economic planning combine with private ownership and control over the bulk of the economy. Government regulation continues to grow even as the private sector and market forces determine most economic outcomes. Conversely, the economic systems of both the Soviet Union and East Germany are primarily socialist or state capitalist on the basis of the minimal roles of private enterprise and markets.[11]

In Western countries public enterprises take a variety of forms.[12] The state may treat such enterprises as part or an extension of the regular public administration as a ministry or department. Telephone, telegraph, and postal services are frequently organized in this fashion. Another approach, particularly favored in Britain, involves the organization of enterprises as public corporations. Direct control over institutions (for example, the British Broadcasting Company) is placed in the hands of governmentally appointed but semi-independent managerial boards. Advocates of the public corporation argue that it permits more flexible and efficient operation than would be possible under ministries. Still more removed from immediate national governmental control are the state holding company and the mixed enterprise. The former refers to broad, quasi-independent companies established by government which manage a variety of industries in different sectors of the economy. In mixed enterprises the state owns some of the firm's shares and achieves partial control over its management. Finally, such activities as water, gas, and street transportation are often left with local rather than national governmental authorities.

Despite certain common positions within the fields of communications, transport, energy, and metals, the five designated Western European systems vary considerably in the forms, scope, and importance of their public enterprise. Direct ministerial control is most

---

[10] Andrew Shonfield, *Modern Capitalism* (New York: Oxford University Press, 1965), pp. 66–67.

[11] John M. Montias, "A Classification of Communist Economic Systems," in Carmelo Mesa-Lago and Carl Beck, eds., *Comparative Socialist Systems: Essays on Politics and Economics* (Pittsburgh: University of Pittsburgh Center for International Studies, 1975), pp. 39–51.

[12] William Robson, *Nationalized Industry and Public Ownership* (London: George Allen & Unwin, 1960), pp. 17–32.

110   *Comparing Public Policies*

favored in France, while Italy leads in the use of state holding companies.[13]

The British epitomize the use of state monopolies in given fields. However, the areas of public ownership are considerably more diverse in the four continental Western European nations. The French government probably has the largest direct stake in the economy, and the Italian regime dominates an exceptionally important grouping of industrial and other sectors.[14] Despite its reputation for socialism the Swedish government maintains the smallest ownership role among the five.[15] It is followed by West Germany—one of the few Western European countries to divest itself of considerable public holdings in industry since 1945.[16]

The United States appears to stand by itself, with a minute public sector. Even broadcasting and the bulk of transport are in private hands in that country. Yet a substantial government role exists in such fields as passenger railroads, electric power, and land leasing, and public enterprise exists within the weapons, space, and nuclear energy fields.[17] If we include "private" firms dependent on government contracts, the American public sector may well be as large as that of many Western European countries.

Economic planning assumes some degree of governmental influence over the direction of such basic decisions as the level of investment, employment, and prices. It may involve direct government control over all such decisions in conformity with the regime's projections and objectives. The imperative planning used in Communist-ruled states endows the plan with the force of law. Another form, refined by the French after World War II, is indicative planning. This approach involves the determination of a series of targets (for example, full employment, a rapid growth rate, a balance in economic development among different regions of the country or among certain sectors of industry). The government then seeks to achieve these objectives through the consistent application of a variety of direct and indirect inducements, including subsidies, public investments, tax incentives, and the con-

---

[13] F. Ridley and J. Blondel, *Public Administration in France* (London: Routledge & Kegan Paul, 1964), pp. 233–65.

[14] Mario Enaudi et al., *Nationalization in France and Italy* (Ithaca, N.Y.: Cornell University Press, 1955); and Kevin Allen and M. C. MacLennan, *Regional Problems and Policies in Italy and France* (Beverly Hills, Calif.: Sage Publications, 1970).

[15] Martin Schnitzer, *The Economy of Sweden* (New York: Praeger Publishers, 1970), pp. 33–43.

[16] Centrum voor Economische Studien, *The Market Economy in Western European Integration* (Louvain: University of Louvain, 1965), pp. 51–53.

[17] Emmette Redord, *American Government and the Economy* (New York: Macmillan Co., 1965), pp. 593–613.

trol of access to credit. Finally, something less directive than the indicative approach may be viewed as planning by some governments and outside observers. This may involve efforts largely limited to the public sector or largely limited to forecasting.

Such approaches to planning are vital to our subsequent analysis because social, physical environmental, and other goals are often directly or indirectly linked to economic objectives. We will want to know whether, based on the record of the eight countries, any form of planning contributes to progress in such areas of national development.

The development of planning in most of the six mixed capitalist states has been rather limited. The strongest commitment has been made by France. French planning has been more comprehensive than that of the others in terms of such noneconomic goals as expanded social services and urban development. In the 1950s and the early 1960s French planners set specific targets for investment and output for particular industries and used considerable powers to encourage compliance by the private sector. However, by the late 1960s a less rigorous approach to planning was being utilized and France had moved closer to other Western European states in this regard.[18]

The Swedish, Italian, British, and West German commitments to economic planning have been more cautious and limited than the French. Sweden moved toward planning during the 1930s and has been creative in efforts to effect structural and regional balance in its economy. Yet, as noted by Lindbeck, "Economic planning in Sweden has been confined mainly to social policies, to institutional reform, and to the establishment of a publicly operated infrastructure, rather than to experiments with government managerial initiatives or detailed regulation of private enterprise."[19] Detailed input-output planning has been avoided.

For Italy, as for Britain, the introduction of economic planning dates from the 1960s. The Italian planning impulse derived from the desire to improve the quality and distribution of public services in the midst of rapid economic growth and to achieve greater regional balance in the economy. Before the 1960s, attempts at planning were partial and limited. The *Cassa per il Mezzogiorno* was a plan for the economic development of southern Italy, and the Vanoni Plan was little more than a statement of certain desirable economic and social objectives. Subsequently, planning machinery was created (1964) and five-year plans

---

[18] Malcolm MacLennan et al., *Economic Planning and Policies in Britain, France, and Germany* (New York: Praeger Publishers, 1968), p. 364.

[19] Assar Lindbeck, *Swedish Economic Policy* (Berkeley: University of California Press, 1974), p. 10.

were devised (1966–70 and 1971–75). Yet analysts have suggested that the Italian approach to planning was far too general and that it did not make adequate provision for specific implementing techniques.[20]

Only in 1962, with the creation of the National Economic Development Council, did the British seek to stimulate a higher rate of economic growth by means of planning.[21] The subsequent effort has been hindered by conflicts over the institutional location of a planning agency; whether to follow the advice of professional planners and economists as against that of spokesmen for competing interest groups; and the reluctance of organized labor to agree to wage restraint in the hope of greater growth.[22] The British could not proceed beyond devising forecasts and making recommendations for reforms.

West Germany long shared the basic aversion to economic planning that also characterized the United States. However, beginning in 1964 the West German government began to shift toward manipulation of aggregate investment and consumption without coercion of individual firms.[23] With the growth of medium-term planning of public expenditures and an advanced regional policy, the planning gap between France and West Germany has closed markedly during the past decade.

Among the mixed capitalist states in this survey the United States remains most reluctant to attempt significant planning. Not even federal government spending has been effectively programmed beyond a given year. Since the brief effort at Appalachian development in the 1960s little has come of regional policy or the structured reform of industrial sectors. However, considerable efforts at information gathering and projections have been made, and the concept of planning is slowing developing elite support.

Although similar, the East German and Soviet patterns of ownership and planning have diverged significantly. During the 1950s both East Germany and the Soviet Union utilized the Stalinist pattern of highly centralized party and government control over most economic enterprises and an imperative planning system that minimized enterprise-level autonomy in production and trade. The major difference during

---

[20] P. A. Allum, *Italy—Republic without Government?* (New York: W. W. Norton & Co., 1973), pp. 167–72; and Joseph LaPalombara, *Italy: The Politics of Planning* (Syracuse: Syracuse University Press, 1966).

[21] Shonfield, *Modern Capitalism*, pp. 88–120.

[22] Gerald Dorfman, *Wage Politics in Britain* (Ames: Iowa State University Press, 1973), pp. 98–115; and Jack Hayward, "The Politics of Planning in France and Britain," *Comparative Politics* 7 (January 1975): 285–98. Major progress in wage restraint was achieved early in 1976.

[23] Graham Hallett, *The Social Economy of West Germany* (New York: St. Martin's Press, 1973), pp. 75–77.

that decade was the East German toleration of a substantial role for private and mixed state-private firms.[24] The Soviet pattern of ownership had long precluded significant private roles except as a supplement to the agricultural system and for some personal services.

Since 1957 most of the Eastern European countries have experimented with important changes in organization and planning. Changes have come haltingly in most of these countries, and the Soviet Union has been among the most hesitant to adapt.[25] Yet even there the Khrushchev-sponsored 1957 regionalization of management has been succeeded by some increase in autonomy for groups of enterprises. These institutions now have fewer performance indicators set by central ministries and more control over their own resources. Yet with most changes in organization and planning emerging from compromises, many aspects of the former structure of centralized supply, pricing, and overall ministerial and planning agency responsibility have been retained in the Soviet Union.

East Germany, a state whose technical intelligentsia has more influence than that of the Soviet Union, has moved more consistently to alter its Stalinist economic system. Although not as bold as Hungary and the abortive Dubcek regime in Czechoslovakia, beginning in 1963 the German Democratic Republic did shift a considerable amount of control from central ministries to new combinations of enterprises. However, autonomy in such areas as investment was not coupled with a significant adaptation to market forces.[26] Further, any possible inference of movement away from socialism was met by the recent elimination of much of the private sector.

ECONOMIC CAPACITY AND TECHNOLOGY

Advances in technology and economic growth help determine whether a given country can and will provide particular services, effectively regulate and tax, or even consider certain policy issues. Though all are among the wealthier and technologically advanced countries of the world, the eight countries range over a wide spectrum in terms of technological advancement and wealth.

Measurements of gross national product (GNP), the value of all final goods and services produced over the course of a year, indicate the

---

[24] Marie Livigne, trans. T. G. Waywell, *The Socialist Economies of the Soviet Union and Europe* (White Plains, N.Y.: International Arts and Science Press, 1974), pp. 20–21.

[25] See Abraham Katz, *The Politics of Economic Reform in the Soviet Union* (New York: Praeger Publishers, 1972); and Karl W. Ryavec, *Implementation of Soviet Economic Reforms* (New York: Praeger Publishers, 1975).

[26] Jan Marczewski, trans. Noel Lindsay, *Crisis in Socialist Planning: Eastern Europe and the USSR* (New York: Praeger Publishers, 1974), p. 89.

total national output available for distribution among various societal groups and economic sectors. Table 4–8 reveals that the eight countries fall into four categories in terms of the overall size of their economies. The populous United States and Soviet Union, though still far from equal in output, rank well above the others. West Germany and France reflect dynamic growth over most of the past several decades and have left Great Britain behind. The British and Italians, both suffering from major economic difficulties in the 1970s, have markedly less economic resources at their disposal as compared to the two leading economic powers of the European Communities. Finally, the much smaller populations of Sweden and East Germany produce by far the smallest total output.

TABLE 4–8
Gross National Product (in constant 1973 dollars; ranked by 1974 per capita levels)

	Total (in millions)		Per Capita	
	1965	1974	1965	1974
1. Sweden	$ 39,000	$ 52,000	$5,040	$6,380
2. United States	954,000	1,270,000	4,920	5,980
3. West Germany	247,000	350,000	4,200	5,610
4. France	164,000	265,000	3,370	5,000
5. East Germany.......	36,900	54,300	2,170	3,210
6. Great Britain	140,000	175,000	2,580	3,110
7. Soviet Union	464,000	722,000	2,010	2,870
8. Italy	93,300	143,000	1,790	2,580

Source: U.S. Arms Control and Disarmament Agency, World Military Expenditures and Arms Transfers, 1965–1974 (Washington, D.C.: U.S. Government Printing Office, 1976), pp. 28–51.

Although total national product is highly relevant to overall national capabilities, per capita output has an even greater impact. Two broad groupings have emerged in regard to per capita wealth (see Table 4–8). Sweden, the United States, France, and West Germany, having reached the $5,000 per capita level, are among the most affluent countries in the world. The other four nations have much less capacity to provide high standards of living while also making major investments in such spheres as defense and the economic infrastructure.

GNP figures only reflect the potential ability of the eight nations to provide high standards of living. They do not tell us anything about the purposes to which the national products are put or the sources from which they derive: how much of the GNP comes from private consumption, how much from public consumption, how much from public or private investment? Nor can we tell from these data how evenly distributed the national wealth is — whether material abundance is enjoyed by a narrow stratum of the privileged or widely dispersed among the many. These fundamental policy themes will be explored as we investigate the extractive and distributive patterns of the political systems of the eight nations.

Technology is at the heart of economic development, though it must be harnessed to natural resources, capital, and other ingredients.[27] We shall explore here the relative capabilities of the eight to meet technological challenges, examining both the available human resources and the output of goods which require a high order of technological sophistication.

One indicator of the extent of a country's technological progress is the occupational distribution of its labor force. Tables 4–9 and 4–10 reveal that money, training, and manpower are most generously di-

TABLE 4–9
Scientists and Engineers Engaged in Research and Development (per 10,000 population)

1. Soviet Union	1973	44.4
2. United States	1973	25.0
3. West Germany	1972	16.2
4. Sweden	1971	12.2
5. France	1971	11.8
6. Great Britain	1969–70	7.9
7. Italy	1972	6.0

Source: *Unesco Statistical Yearbook, 1974* (Paris: Unesco Press, 1975), pp. 642–47.

TABLE 4–10
Expenditures for Research and Development (as percentage of GNP)

1. Soviet Union	1973	5.0%
2. United States	1973	2.5
3. West Germany	1972	2.3
4. Great Britain	1969–70	2.3
5. France	1971	1.8
6. Sweden	1971	1.5
7. Italy	1972	0.8

Source: *Unesco Statistical Yearbook, 1974* (Paris: Unesco Press, 1975), pp. 642–47.

---

[27] Daniel Bell, *The Coming of Post-Industrial Society* (New York: Basic Books, 1973); and Zbigniew Brzezinski, *Between Two Ages* (New York: Viking Press, 1970).

rected at research and development in the Soviet Union and the United States. The Soviet Union's figures are not fully comparable and should be interpreted in the light of the severe distortion produced by the exceptional emphasis given there to military and space technology and of that nation's inefficient use of trained manpower.[28] The United States has been able to provide a better balance in manpower and expenditure between the military and civilian sectors and seems to have been more efficient in deployment.

At the other extreme the figures indicate the weakness in Italian and British technical manpower development. However, even the leading Western European states lag significantly behind the two superpowers in this respect. If only civilian expenditure is considered, the American lead over Western Europe is reduced but not eliminated.[29]

Energy consumption reflects technological development insofar as a mechanized economy is more energy-intensive. Table 4–11 reveals the continued American lead in energy use (and misuse). The impressive development of East German industry is indicated by its second place ranking. East German industrialization and energy consumption exceed its level of affluence. France and the Soviet Union maintain relatively low levels of energy consumption, and Italy places in a low category all by itself in this measure of development.

A second indicator, perhaps the most symbolic, of the production and use of goods dependent on science and technology pertains to the

TABLE 4–11
Commercial Energy Consumption (in kilograms per capita; ranked according to 1974 usage)

	1964	1974
1. United States	8,867	11,901
2. East Germany	5,533	6,946
3. West Germany	4,331	6,002
4. Sweden	4,423	5,804
5. Great Britain	4,992	5,464
6. Soviet Union	3,452	5,252
7. France	3,009	4,342
8. Italy	1,664	3,104

Source: United Nations Department of Economic and Social Affairs, *Statistical Papers: World Energy Supplies, 1950–1974* (New York: United Nations, 1976), pp. 42–111.

---

[28] Michael Boretsky, "The Technological Basis of Soviet Military Power," in Joint Economic Committee, U.S. Congress, *Economic Performance and the Military Burden in the Soviet Union* (Washington, D.C.: U.S. Government Printing Office, 1970), pp. 187–231.

[29] *Reviews of National Science Policy: Netherlands* (Paris: OECD, 1973), p. 40.

electronic computer. As the data arrayed in Table 4–12 suggest, the United States is far and away the leader in computer use among the eight nations with which we are concerned. If we were to convert the figures to a per capita basis, the differences between the United States and the other countries would still be impressive.[30] With the explosion in computer use in the industrialized world since 1970, the order of countries may well have changed. Yet a substantial share of the new computers which have come into use since 1970 were manufactured by American firms or their Western European affiliates.[31]

TABLE 4–12
Computers in Use (1970)

1. United States	62,500
2. West Germany	6,100
3. Great Britain	5,900
4. Soviet Union	5,500
5. France	4,500
6. Italy	2,700
7. Sweden	820 (1972)
8. East Germany	500

Sources: Ivan Berenyi, "Computers in Eastern Europe," *Scientific American* 223, no. 4 (October 1970): 104. Copyright © by Scientific American, Inc. All rights reserved. The figure for Sweden was taken from U.S. Department of Commerce, *Computer Equipment: Global Market Survey* (Washington, D.C.: U.S. Government Printing Office, 1973), p. 102.

In summary we point to a less even pattern of development in the Soviet Union and East Germany as compared to the others. The former country has industrialized on a massive scale without the large-scale use of such dimensions of technology as computers and without achieving a high level of visible affluence. East Germany has not yet achieved Northern European standards of affluence but is impressive in its productive utilization of energy and trained manpower.

Among the six Western countries the United States maintains a substantial lead in the mobilization of trained manpower and the large-scale production of sophisticated technology. Although Sweden, West

---

[30] Bohdan Szuprowicz, "Eastern Europe's Thirst for Computer," *Computer Decisions* 5 (November 1973): 28.

[31] Bohdan Szuprowicz, "East Europe: Computer-Hungry Nations Eye the West," *Computer Decisions* 3 (December 1971): 15–19; and U.S. Department of Commerce, *Computer Equipment: Global Market Survey* (Washington, D.C.: U.S. Government Printing Office, 1973), p. 3.

Germany, and France have approached or exceeded the American standard of living they remain behind in these critical dimensions of national economic power.

INTERNATIONAL ROLES

As suggested in Chapter 3, the external environment produces a wide range of pressures on domestic policy-makers. These pressures, interacting with domestic factors, shape varying international economic and military-political roles. The Soviet Union and the United States have both stood out as strategic actors, yet Moscow has never been a major factor in international trade or finance. Neither economic capacity nor economic interests have pushed West Germany (or Japan) into the front rank of military powers.

Decision-makers in Washington and Moscow have chosen to have their nations take on vast worldwide responsibilities which involve penetration into the domestic affairs of other countries. Yet as measured by the public pronouncements of their representatives, the United States and the Soviet Union do not play identical international strategic roles.[32] Soviet leaders have long stressed their "proletarian internationalist" role as supporter of "anti-imperialist" and "popular liberation" forces. Since 1941, American leaders have committed their country to preserve the status quo both regionally and globally.[33] In practice Soviet policy has at almost every stage been marked by both great caution and opportunism. The United States, after paying a great price as intervenor in Korea and Indochina, now seems ready to limit at least the territorial scope of its military involvement.

In the economic sphere the Soviet Union and the United States operate in a world in which they must compete on increasingly equal terms with many states which have comparatively modest military capacities. Moscow continues to operate on the fringe of the North Atlantic–centered international financial system and depends on international commerce to a surprisingly small extent. Washington is adjusting in the mid-1970s to a position of reduced economic dominance and finds itself making more fundamental concessions to foreign economic pressures than in the 1945–70 period.

Immediately before World War II the unified German Reich, France, Britain, and Italy were all states with intercontinental concerns and

---

[32] K. J. Holsti, "National Role Conceptions in the Study of Foreign Policy," *International Studies Quarterly* 14, no. 3 (September 1970): 276.

[33] Henry Kissinger, *American Foreign Policy* (New York: W. W. Norton & Co., 1969); and Adam Ulam, *The Rivals: America and Russia since World War II* (New York: Viking Press, 1971).

aspirations. Since the war's conclusion Germany has been divided in two and each of the Western European states has lost all or most of its colonies. Although the division of Germany was at one time regarded by some as a temporary phenomenon, in the last several years the status quo has been given recognition by all the relevant parties and relations between the Federal Republic and the Democratic Republic have been partially normalized.

After long periods of cautious fence-mending within their respective economic and military groupings, both German states have satisfied a major part of their desires for respectability and influence. East Germany influenced the Soviet decision to invade Czechoslovakia in 1968. Beginning in 1969, West Germany initiated major steps toward the normalization of its relations with Eastern Europe while continuing to solidify its position as a leader of the European Communities and the mainstay of European trade and finance. It remains a firm ally of the United States in the European context. Yet, like other NATO states, the Bonn government showed during the 1973 Arab-Israeli War and the subsequent oil crisis that it could not be relied on to support American objectives in conflict with its own.

Italy's loss of empire and diminished global status was the unambiguous consequence of military defeat. Ostensibly victorious in World War II, Britain has had a much more difficult time adjusting to its reduced circumstances. Over the last several decades the British have had to decide whether or not, with sharply reduced relative economic resources, their interest is best served by the retention of a "special relationship" with the United States, a military presence east of Suez, and close ties to the globally distributed members of the Commonwealth. The alternatives included the establishment of closer ties with Europe and a further reduction of global commitments.[34] Britain took its most decisive step by joining the Communities in 1973, and it has also continued to retreat from extra-European responsibilities. However, its strong ties to Washington have not been sacrificed.

France, unlike West Germany, Italy, and Britain, has strongly resisted a role as subordinate ally to the United States. Under de Gaulle and his successors France has concentrated on forging an independent course in its international transactions. By resisting British membership in the European Communities, withdrawing from the military structure of NATO, developing an independent nuclear deterrent, and separating France from other Western countries in energy negotiations, French leaders have sought to gain the leading role in the European Communi-

---

[34] Ian Taylor, "The Dilemma of Great Britain," in Robert Jordan, ed., *Europe and the Superpowers* (Boston: Allyn & Bacon, 1971), pp. 170–92.

ties in competition with West Germany, to act as a third force vis-á-vis the United States and the Soviet Union, and to become something more than a European regional power.[35]

The watchwords of Swedish foreign policy are neutrality, mediation, and cooperation. Sweden is a nation which belongs neither to NATO and the European Communities nor to their Communist-bloc counterparts. Sweden's position in world affairs has been neutralist rather than passive.[36] It is heavily committed to its own defense and also participates in United Nations peacekeeping in such trouble spots as the Middle East. Sweden is also an active member of the European Free Trade Association (EFTA) and the Nordic Council.

POLICY-MAKING AND THE POLITICAL SYSTEM

It would be easy enough, though not very illuminating, to label the six Western nations in our analysis as democracies, while regarding East Germany and the Soviet Union as totalitarian. There are two principal reasons why such an approach would be unsatisfactory. First, by treating the United States, Great Britain, France, West Germany, Italy, and Sweden solely as democracies, we might be inclined to ignore substantial differences among their political systems. Second, to define the Russian and East German systems as totalitarian might lead us to disregard not only significant differences between the two but also to downplay the internal evolution each has undergone since the death of Stalin.

Yet we can assert that the main lines of political differences fall between the Western six and the Eastern two. At the root of these differences are the character of political participation and competition.[37] In addition, there are basic differences in the roles of interest groups and political parties in formulating and implementing policy.

Political Community and Culture: The Context of Policy-Making

The study of political culture has enriched our understanding of how and why people interpret their own political roles and evaluate political communities.[38] Although few people reflect a full-blown ideology, most

---

[35] Alfred Grosser, *French Foreign Policy under De Gaulle* (Boston: Little, Brown & Co., 1967); and Elliot Goodman, *The Fate of the Atlantic Community* (New York: Praeger Publishers, 1975).

[36] Nils Andren, "The Special Condition of the Baltic Subregion," in Jordan, *Europe and Superpowers*, pp. 193–228.

[37] Robert Dahl, *Polyarchy* (New Haven: Yale University Press, 1971), pp. 1–16.

[38] Gabriel Almond and Sidney Verba, *The Civic Culture* (Princeton: Princeton University Press, 1963), pp. 3–42; and Sidney Verba, "Comparative Political Culture," in Pye and Verba, *Political Culture*, pp. 512–60.

people bring some orientations to the political world. They may ignore, hate, or love their country, political institutions, and leaders. Each pattern may have major consequences for the quality of political life and public policy outcomes.

We shall concentrate here on the nature of public support for the political system and of public attitudes toward participation. These are among the important orientations given much attention in cross-national studies by political scientists. Are citizens loyal, alienated, or apathetic toward their political system? Do they believe themselves to be active participants who are able to affect the course of policy-making, or do they regard themselves as passive subjects of an uncontrollable governmental apparatus?

Available survey research data suggest to us that the political cultures of the United States, Great Britain, Sweden, and West Germany are primarily allegiant in character. Despite the existence of alienated subcultures of a variety of types in these countries and despite popular dissatisfaction with particular policies, officials, and institutions in these systems, the bulk of the evidence suggests popular endorsement of the existing political order. To make such an assertion about the British and Swedish publics may not be especially surprising.[39] But claiming the same allegiant status for Americans and West Germans requires some elaboration.

Much of the data pointing to the allegiant character of the American political culture was accumulated before the upheavals of the last decade.[40] After Vietnam, urban rioting, and Watergate, is it still accurate to identify Americans as allegiants? Rather astonishingly, the answer is yes. In spite of a sharp decline in the level of popular trust and confidence in our policy-making institutions, a substantial majority of Americans continue to hold the system in general in relatively high esteem.[41]

Until recently the dominant view of how West Germans perceived their political system was that they were essentially apathetic or indifferent toward it. Scarred by their previous experience with emotional

---

[39] For evidence on Sweden see Hancock, *Sweden,* pp. 61–88; and Kaj Bjork, "Individualism and Collectivism," in M. Donald Hancock and Gideon Sjoberg, eds., *Politics in the Post-Welfare State* (New York: Columbia University Press, 1972), pp. 246–56. For Britain see Richard Rose, "England: A Traditionally Modern Political Culture," in Pye and Verba, *Political Culture,* pp. 83–129; and Almond and Verba, *Civic Culture,* pp. 455–69.

[40] Donald Devine, *The Political Culture of the United States* (Boston: Little, Brown & Co., 1972).

[41] For a discussion of the extent and meaning of the decline in popular trust see Arthur Miller, "Political Issues and Trust in Government: 1964–1970"; and Jack Citrin, "Comment: The Political Relevance of Trust in Government," *American Political Science Review* 68 (September 1974): 951–72, 973–88. For data on the continued high level of support see William Watts and Lloyd Free, eds., *State of the Nation* (New York: Universe Books, 1973), pp. 237–41.

commitment to the Nazi regime, West Germans were said to be reluctant to trust any set of political arrangements.[42] However, current assessments point to a considerable change. Recent public opinion analyses suggest a growing popular allegiance to the Federal Republic's political order, based perhaps on the positive experiences of the postwar generations.[43]

Commentaries on French political culture consistently stress attitudes of mistrust and resentment. Observers emphasize the high degree to which the French mistrust one another as individuals and as members of different social classes organized to achieve conflicting political objectives.[44] The state, a remote higher authority to which all appeal for justice and equity, is also very suspect. Its powers must be carefully circumscribed lest it violate the basic interests of various French groups. The outcome of this pattern of intergroup and political system mistrust has been long periods of political stalemate, punctuated by occasional bouts of heroic and authoritarian decision-making. Yet this pattern may be changing in the post–de Gaulle era.

There is no evidence whatsoever of such a change in Italy. As Almond and Verba put it, "The picture of Italian political culture . . . is one of relatively unrelieved political alienation and of social isolation and distrust."[45] In their five-nation study of political culture in the United States, Great Britain, West Germany, Mexico, and Italy, these analysts discovered that a random sample of Italians were far less likely than comparable groups in the other countries to believe other individuals to be either trustworthy or cooperative. What is more, almost all observers of Italian politics agree that the substantial improvements in the country's economic conditions over the last several decades have failed to bring a parallel decline in political alienation and resentment.

Until the construction of the Berlin Wall in 1961, the most visible manifestation of how East Germans judged their system was their massive propensity to flee to the West. Although subsequent interviews with refugees from the German Democratic Republic disclosed their motives to be more economic than political, it seems fair to say that the country's political system was not the object of strong allegiance. However, more recent visitors from the West have noticed a

---

[42] Sidney Verba, "Germany: The Remaking of Political Culture," in Pye and Verba, *Political Culture*, pp. 130–70.

[43] David Conradt, "West Germany: A Remade Political Culture?" *Comparative Political Studies* 7 (July 1974): 227–37.

[44] See, for example, Michel Crozier, *The Bureaucratic Phenomenon* (Chicago: Phoenix Books, 1967); Laurence Wylie, *Village in the Vaucluse* (Cambridge, Mass.: Harvard University Press, 1967); and Stanley Hoffman et al., eds., *In Search of France* (New York: Harper & Row, 1963), pp. 1–117.

[45] Almond and Verba, *Civic Culture*, p. 402.

significant change in attitude.[46] Gains in economic prosperity and social services, backed by strong efforts to win over the minds of the younger generation, appear to have broadened the appeal of the regime and system.

Since Stalin's death in 1953 a system in which allegiance from the Soviet population was extracted predominantly through the threat and application of terror has been modified. Today the Soviet regime depends primarily on positive citizen reactions to steadily increasing material benefits and on appeals to pride in Soviet patriotism. With an effective near-monopoly of mass communications and a complex network of educational and socialization agencies, the regime has molded a citizenry that appears to offer more than ritualistic support to the political system and regime.[47]

Measured by such criteria as voter turnout and involvement in party political and governmental affairs, all eight political cultures probably deserve the designation participatory. But this observation does not tell us very much about the character or the quality of participation. In both East Germany and the Soviet Union popular involvement is frequently passive in nature; these are clearly cultures in which citizens are encouraged to take part in a great variety of officially sponsored activities. Yet the citizens' role is often that of approving spectators. On critical policy matters, citizens are expected to comprehend, ratify, and celebrate decisions made by the national political leadership. In regard to local and nonsensitive issues the widespread involvement may be more meaningful. Despite the passivity there have been largely successful efforts to draw individuals from all walks of life into the political system.

The patterns of participation in France and Italy exhibit certain parallels. First, as compared to other Western nations, personal identification with political parties is relatively limited.[48] Second, reflecting the alienation so widespread in both cultures, there is both a high level of electoral support for antiregime parties and movements and large-scale involvement in protest demonstrations and rioting.

In this connection the American culture displays certain anomalies. On the one hand, a comparatively large proportion of Americans believe that they have the ability to affect the course of public policy-

---

[46] Smith, Germany, pp. 3–69; Dornberg, Other Germany, pp. 227–63.

[47] Frederick Barghoorn, "Soviet Russia: Orthodoxy and Adaptiveness," in Pye and Verba, Political Culture, pp. 450–511. See also Roy Medvedev, On Socialist Democracy (New York: Alfred A. Knopf, 1975).

[48] Giuseppe Di Palma, Apathy and Participation (New York: Free Press, 1970), pp. 162–78; and Phillip Converse and Georges Dupeux, "Socialization into Apathy: France and America Compared," in Mattei Dogan and Richard Rose, eds., European Politics: A Reader (Boston: Little, Brown & Co., 1971), pp. 114–20.

making via involvement in conventional and largely peaceful forms of political expression. In other words a high proportion of Americans believe themselves to be effective participants in the political process. Yet turnout in national elections tends to be consistently lower than that in comparable Western European nations, and recently Americans have been even more likely than their counterparts in France and Italy to engage in protest demonstrations and politically significant rioting.[49] These contrasts may be explained in part by noting the existence of a variety of formal and informal barriers to conventional political expression by racial minorities and the poor.[50] The contrasts may also stem from the existence of cultural norms which are more tolerant of all kinds of violent behavior than are the cultural norms of comparable European societies.[51] We should also point out that the objects of political violence in America have tended to be particular policies and leaders and not the system as a whole.

If the American political culture may be said to exhibit a certain freewheeling, populist style along with certain restraints on lower-class participation, it is also probably fair to say that mass involvement in Britain and West Germany is affected by the strands of elitism and social deference which are present in these class-sensitive societies. And just as we have noted the anomalous character of American political culture, so too we must cite the paradoxical nature of these largely allegiant cultures. In Britain and the Federal Republic, unlike the United States, there exist political parties—Labour and Social Democratic—which facilitate the participation of the working-class population in political life. Yet these are also societies which, in contrast to the American society, restrict access to higher education to a thin stratum of their populations. Most citizens are apparently inclined to leave political decisions to an elite of well-educated civil servants and party politicians.

In Sweden this deference is certainly less marked. In fact the prevailing norms of Swedish political culture, which stress the importance of compromise and the peaceful accommodation of group differences, facilitate popular involvement in the political process. As Hancock writes, "The community values of modern Swedish political culture encompass national pride, a sense of individual political competence, and a pervasive moral commitment to sociopolitical activism."[52]

---

[49] Ted Gurr, "A Comparative Study of Civil Strife," in Hugh Graham and Gurr, eds., *Violence in America* (New York: New American Library, 1969), pp. 544–605.

[50] Peter Bachrach and Morton Baratz, *Power and Poverty: Theory and Practice* (New York: Oxford University Press, 1970).

[51] Alphonso Pinkney, *The American Way of Violence* (New York: Vintage Books, 1972), pp. 154–85.

[52] Hancock, *Sweden*, p. 45.

Interest Groups

Interest groups make demands on the political system as sponsors of particular governmental policies. Our focus is on those formal structures which Almond and Powell identify as associational and institutional.[53] Associational structures may represent workers, industrialists, religious denominations, or ethnic groups. Designed primarily for political articulation, such organizations can effectively represent bodies of people with no alternative organizational base. Institutional structures include corporations, churches, and governmental agencies. These are formal organizations with designated functions other than interest articulation. Yet their political input may outweigh that of the associations.

With respect to the milieu or context within which interest groups function, the style and effectiveness of these groups are likely to be determined by such factors as their own internal cohesion or fragmentation, the reputation they enjoy both in the society and with relevant decision-making bodies, and the structure of the policy-making institutions which may hear their cases.[54] Subsidiary to these factors are such issues as the extent to which interest groups are ideologically, functionally, or geographically fragmented. Is interest group activity in general or the activity of particular interest groups regarded as legitimate, appropriate, and authentic in the political system? Are policy-making institutions permeable to outside influence? How centralized and cohesive are these institutions?

Observers of the American political system have long regarded it as an interest group heaven. The heterogeneous society, capitalist economy, and dispersed policy-making authority at both the state and national levels have all fostered a powerful array of associational and institutionalized groups.[55] Interest groups penetrate all governmental structures, and sometimes they capture decision-making authority. Business, labor, and agricultural associations become clients of executive agencies that often join them as advocates before other decision-making bodies.[56] Yet institutional structures in both government and the private sector have in no sense been displaced by the strong associations.

---

[53] Gabriel Almond and G. Bingham Powell, *Comparative Politics: A Developmental Approach* (Boston: Little, Brown & Co., 1966), pp. 73–97.

[54] Harry Eckstein, *Pressure Group Politics* (Stanford, Calif.: Stanford University Press, 1960), pp. 15–39.

[55] David Truman, *The Governmental Process* (New York: Alfred A. Knopf, 1962); and Grant McConnell, *Private Power and American Democracy* (New York: Alfred A. Knopf, 1966).

[56] Theodore Lowi, *The End of Liberalism* (New York: W. W. Norton & Co., 1969); and Peter Woll, *Public Policy* (Cambridge, Mass.: Winthrop Publishers, 1974), pp. 53–87.

Although their ideological orientations are often quite apparent, most major interest groups in the United States are noted for their pragmatism and flexibility. Further, the fragmentation within the labor, business, and agriculture sectors is only partially due to differences over values and purposes. Sharper ideological lines have recently developed with the dramatic growth of consumer and environmental interest groups.

Business, labor, agricultural, and professional associations in Britain, Sweden, and West Germany are generally as active and effective as their American counterparts. There are, however, some differences in their methods of operation. Since legislative and judicial institutions are weaker in these systems than in the United States, associations evince a greater propensity to channel their demands to executive branch and national political party leaders.[57] Corresponding to the differences in governmental structure, British, Swedish, and West German associational interest groups tend to be far more centralized than are such interest groups in the United States.[58]

In addition to these differences in style and structure between British, Swedish, and West German interest groups and the American groups, there are substantial similarities. In all four systems the major associations are committed to the existing political order. Further, there is little ideological cleavage among associations seeking adherents in the same sphere of group activity. Moreover, there is a growing tendency for these groups to achieve formal representation (that is, on boards and committees) in governmental policy-making bodies relevant to their concerns and to enjoy the right of prior consultation, and in many instances the right to veto governmental decisions.

The situations in France and Italy are different in several respects. These differences are most visible in, though by no means restricted to, trade union organization. In both countries union organizations are divided along ideological lines: Communist, Socialist, Christian Democratic, and so on. In addition, unlike the objectives of their counterparts in the United States, Britain, Sweden, and West Germany, the objectives

---

[57] Henry Ehrmann, "Interest Groups and the Bureaucracy in Western Democracies," in Dogan and Rose, *European Politics*, pp. 333–53; J. Roland Pennock, "Agricultural Subsidies in Britain and America," in Richard Rose, ed., *Policy-Making in Britain* (New York: Free Press, 1969), pp. 199–200; Wolfgang Hirsch-Weber, "Some Remarks on Interest Groups in the German Federal Republic," and Gunnar Heckscher, "Interest Groups in Sweden: Their Political Role," both in Henry Ehrmann, ed., *Interest Groups on Four Continents* (Pittsburgh: University of Pittsburgh Press, 1958), pp. 96–116, 154–172; and Eric Jacobs, *European Trade Unionism* (New York: Holmes & Meier, Publishers, 1973).

[58] Nils Elvander, "Democracy and Large Organizations," in Hancock and Sjoberg, *Post-Welfare State*, p. 303; R. M. Punnett, *British Government and Politics* (New York: W. W. Norton & Co., 1971), p. 135; and Lewis Edinger, *Politics in Germany* (Boston: Little, Brown & Co., 1968), pp. 198–235.

of the French and Italian unions tend not to be restricted to issues of higher pay and better working conditions, but frequently encompass demands for the total reorganization of labor-management relations and the restructuring of basic governmental institutions. The Italian labor unions have come to exert an influence on government economic planning that is substantially greater than that of their French counterparts. This greater impact is based on the higher proportion of the Italian work force that is unionized and on the ability of the three major Italian labor federations to overcome their ideological differences sufficiently to coordinate bargaining with the government and employer groups.

Though the structure of government decision-making in both France and Italy is formally centralized, there are nevertheless observable differences in the environments within which interest groups operate in the two systems. In France, with its Rousseauist tradition of disdain for particular interests, symbolized by de Gaulle's observation that "in matters where the national interest is involved, the State does not give way," organized interest groups historically have been objects of popular and often well-deserved suspicion."[59] The impact of Catholic social thought in Italy, especially the Church's view that the state is just one of a variety of natural associations to which individuals appropriately belong, has helped create a somewhat more tolerant atmosphere.

Both Italian and French interest groups are closely connected to political parties, with control running in both directions.[60] Up to 1958, associational groups in both countries emphasized access to parties and legislatures. Since 1958 the two systems have gone in somewhat different directions. With the advent of the Fifth Republic, French interest groups were encouraged to bypass parties and legislatures and to seek influence in the departments and ministries through, among other things, representation on advisory committees.

Such Italian associational groups as those affiliated with the Church's Catholic Action and Coldiretti as well as big business's Confidustria, have the reputation of being exceedingly persuasive not only in their dealings with the public administration but also with certain political parties and parliament.[61] The Church itself is without question the dominant interest group in the Italian system, playing a role in political life unparalleled in France. Moreover, given the weakness, fragmenta-

---

[59] Philip Williams and Martin Harrison, *Politics and Society in de Gaulle's Republic* (Garden City, N.Y.: Doubleday & Co., 1971), p. 186.

[60] Gabriel Almond, "A Comparative Study of Interest Groups and the Political Process," in Harry Eckstein and David Apter, eds., *Comparative Politics* (New York: Free Press, 1963), p. 402.

[61] Joseph LaPalombara, *Interest Groups in Italian Politics* (Princeton: Princeton University Press, 1964).

tion, and instability of Italian governmental structures, institutional interest groups engage in a wide variety of lobbying activities. For instance, the heads of IRI and ENI, the state holding companies, have been known to purchase newspapers and parliamentarians in their efforts to have policies favorable to their interests enacted into law.

Although associational groups in East Germany and the Soviet Union are becoming increasingly visible sources of policy demands, they are still at an embryonic stage of development and are rarely treated as legitimate expressers of public sentiment.[62] Yet this does not mean that politics is monolithic in these countries. Bitter competition routinely takes place among major regime institutions and factions. Conflicts inevitably develop among representatives of the military establishment, the police forces, agriculture, and heavy and light industry, and among central and regional party and governmental power centers, over the allocation of scarce resources.[63]

In the Soviet Union there exists an apparently growing inclination for the leaders of these strategically placed institutional groups to articulate openly their demands concerning such matters as educational policy, economic planning reforms and priorities, and agricultural organization.[64] However, there is no necessary correspondence between the ability to voice demands and the capacity to influence policy.

Groups which in a Western setting would be regarded as private and associational in nature (for example, trade unions, farmers' organizations, professional associations) are, in the Soviet context, confined to highly controlled official "mass organizations." Although some of these organizations have been given responsibility for implementing certain state policies (for example, the unions administer social security programs), their ability to make demands on the system is slight as compared to that of their Western equivalents.

Conditions in East Germany are similar but not identical to those in the Soviet Union. Since the early 1960s, leaders of institutional groups and mass organizations have been much freer to articulate demands, particularly if these are couched in terms of making the system more

---

[62] Joel Schwartz and William Keech, "Group Influence and the Policy Process in the Soviet Union," *American Political Science Review* 52 (September 1968): 840–51; and James H. Wolfe, "Corporatism in German Political Life: Functional Representation in the GDR and Bavaria," in Martin O. Heisler, ed., *Politics in Europe* (New York: David McKay Co., 1974), pp. 323–40.

[63] Sidney Ploss, "Interest Groups," in Allen Kassof, ed., *Prospects for Soviet Society* (New York: Frederick A. Praeger, 1968), pp. 76–103.

[64] H. Gordon Skilling, "Group Conflict in Soviet Politics," in Skilling and Franklyn Griffiths, eds., *Interest Groups in Soviet Politics* (Princeton: Princeton University Press, 1971), pp. 379–415; and Phillip Stewart, "Soviet Interest Groups and the Policy Process: The Repeal of Production Education," *World Politics* 22 (October 1969): 29–50.

efficient and improving productivity. Further, the Lutheran church has acted as an interest group in such a way as to increase its independence from state control.[65]

Political Parties

Political parties may be distinguished from interest groups in that their primary activities involve winning public office, controlling policy-making institutions, and combining diverse interests. Parties may also be distinguished from power-wielding or power-seeking factions, prevalent throughout recorded history, by virtue of the fact that they consistently seek popular support and usually develop techniques and organizations for the mobilization of that support.[66]

All eight political systems included in our analysis have political parties, but the roles of these parties vary substantially. First, we should note that in the six Western systems the rules of the game are such as to allow open electoral competition among the parties, whereas this is not the case in either East Germany or the Soviet Union. The competitive systems may be further divided into those in which there is relatively frequent turnover in office, in which one party or coalition of parties regularly replaces the "in" party or parties in controlling the executive, and those in which one hegemonial or dominant party, either by itself or in coalition with others, usually forms the government.[67]

Italy and Sweden, disparate in so many ways, are similar here in that for decades each country's government was dominated by a single political party, the Christian Democrats and the Social Democrats, respectively. In both instances, however, significant changes have occurred recently. The 1976 elections resulted in the waning of the Christian Democrats' power in Italy, to the benefit of the Communists, so that today the party's continuation in office appears problematic. During the same year the Swedish Social Democrats were forced to relinquish office as a consequence of their electoral defeat. By contrast to these slow-changing systems, the United States, Great Britain, and now West Germany have parties which regularly alternate in controlling the execu-

---

[65] H. Gordon Skilling, *The Governments of Communist East Europe* (New York: Thomas Y. Crowell Co., 1966), pp. 125–30; and Smith, *Germany*, pp. 137–59.

[66] Maurice Duverger, *Political Parties* (New York: John Wiley & Sons, 1954), pp. xxiii–xxxvii; and Leon Epstein, *Political Parties in Western Democracies* (New York: Frederick A. Praeger, 1967), pp. 3–18.

[67] Joseph LaPalombara and Myron Weiner, "The Origin and Development of Political Parties," in LaPalombara and Weiner, eds., *Political Parties and Political Development* (Princeton: Princeton University Press, 1966), pp. 3–42.

tive. The French case is somewhat ambiguous because between 1958 and 1974 the Gaullist party, both under de Gaulle himself and under Pompidou, was clearly the dominant force.[68] However, recent elections and opinion surveys point to the end of Gaullist hegemony.

Although both the Soviet and East German systems prohibit open interparty competition for public office, the two systems are not identical. While in the USSR only the Communist party (CPSU) is allowed to function, the German Democratic Republic has several parties. In addition to the dominant Socialist Unity party (SED), itself an amalgamation of Communist and Socialist elements, there are also the Christian Democratic, Liberal, National Democratic, and Farmer's parties. By prior agreement each is allocated a given number of seats in the Volkskammer, the East German parliament, with the SED awarding itself the lion's share. The minor organizations tend to act more like interest groups than as full-fledged parties.[69]

The parties in any political system also vary in the level of interparty antagonism or polarization that they exhibit. In some countries the parties are bitterly divided, whereas in others they are relatively close and are consensually committed to the existing political order. Although the intensity of partisan hostility varies over time, the major parties in the political systems included in our analysis, except for the French and Italian, are not highly polarized. Either as the result of natural evolution (the United States, Britain, Sweden, and West Germany) or of authoritarian inducement (East Germany), the major parties do not normally regard one another with great mutual hostility and are not alienated from the systems in which they function.

Since the end of World War II, political parties in France and Italy have offered examples of intense interparty antagonism and system alienation. Particularly in Italy, but also in France, there are parties, on both the Left and Right of the ideological spectrum, which as a matter of principle oppose the existing regime and regard other contestants in electoral politics as incarnations of villainy.[70] The two large Communist parties in both countries have long played this role. Of late, however, the leaders of these parties have committed themselves to the support of democratic institutions and have sought popular front alliances with other parties on the Left in France and broad coalitions with diverse parties in Italy. Yet these developments have not reduced the level of antagonism directed at the Communists by parties of the Center and

---

[68] Jean Charlot, *The Gaullist Phenomenon* (New York: Praeger Publishers, 1971).

[69] David Childs, *East Germany* (New York: Frederick A. Praeger, 1969), pp. 104–23; Wolfe, "Corporatism," pp. 326–30.

[70] Giovanni Sartori, "European Political Parties: The Case of Polarized Pluralism," in LaPalombara and Weiner, *Political Parties*, pp. 137–76.

Right.[71] In France, with the disappearance of the Poujadists at the beginning of the Fifth Republic and with the resolution of the Algerian
issue in the early 1960s there are at present no significant forces on the
Right wishing to bring an end to the regime. However, the Italian system is still plagued by the presence of the neo-Fascist Italian Social
Movement.

The ability of any political party or of any coalition of such parties to
shape the course of public policy-making is largely determined by the
structure of the governmental institutions that the party seeks to direct,
by the party's competitive position vis-à-vis other parties and groups,
and by its internal discipline and cohesiveness.

Seen in this light, it is apparent that both the Soviet Union and East
Germany have party-dominated political systems. In both instances the
dominant parties, the CPSU and the SED, are highly disciplined,
strongly centralized, and ideologically coherent. Challenges to their
supremacy by other parties or groups (for example, the military) are not
tolerated. In the USSR, the Politburo of the party's Central Committee
is the chief policy-determining institution. Through various subordinate party organs, most notably the Secretariat, the Politburo directs
not only the activities of the party's mass membership but also directs
and oversees the implementation of policy by bureaus at all levels of
government and by every cultural, economic, and social institution.[72]

As in the Soviet Union, so too in East Germany the party leadership
(that is, the Politburo) is theoretically elected by a central committee
whose composition is, in turn, supposed to be determined by the party
congress. In fact, however, the distribution of power is the other way
around, with Politburo members coopting members of the latter bodies.
The similarity in structure and function between the CPSU and the SED
is not coincidental. It derives from the not totally voluntary inclination
of the East German party leadership to adopt practices judged appropriate by Moscow during the pre-1953 Stalinist era.[73] However, since
the 1960s the SED has gone further than the CPSU in coopting highly
educated technocrats and in refining cooperative relationships with
nonparty economists, planners, and other elites.

The role of parties in the American system represents the other extreme. Although obviously crucial in the competitive electoral process,

---

[71] Georgio Galli and Alfonso Prandi, *Patterns of Political Participation in Italy* (New
Haven: Yale University Press, 1970); and Frank Wilson, *The French Democratic Left:
1963–1969* (Stanford: Stanford University Press, 1971).

[72] Barghoorn, *Politics in the USSR*, pp. 213–57; and Merle Fainsod, *How Russia Is Ruled*
(Cambridge, Mass.: Harvard University Press, 1963), pp. 307–45.

[73] Arthur Hanhardt, Jr., *The German Democratic Republic* (Baltimore: Johns Hopkins
Press, 1968), pp. 77–105; and Heidenheimer, *Governments*, pp. 270–74.

neither the Democrats nor the Republicans dominate the pattern of policy-making. Internally the major American parties are notoriously weak, poorly disciplined, and decentralized. The national committees have next to nothing to do with the selection of the parties' presidential or congressional candidates, and even at the state and local levels party committees and conventions have, thanks to the primaries, only a moderate say in determining who the parties' candidates will be.[74]

Ideologically or programmatically the parties may best be viewed as open-house jamborees of conflicting tendencies, with national party platforms the result of endless compromises. Periodic efforts at reform, most notably in the Democratic party, evoke contradictory results. Efforts to make the parties more ideologically coherent are balanced by endeavors to make them more diverse in composition.

Although the structure of governmental institutions in the American system (that is, the separation of powers, checks and balances, and federalism) has been seen as facilitating interest group activity, it has the effect, conversely, of inhibiting party domination of policy-making.[75] An obvious example is the common situation of one party's winning the presidency while the other controls the Congress.

In Great Britain, Sweden, and West Germany the political parties play a substantially stronger role in the policy-making process. Although not devoid of intraparty factionalism, the mass parties in these systems generally exhibit greater internal discipline and centralized control than in America, the Christian Democratic Union in West Germany excepted. Further, the structural characteristics of the regimes act to enhance the role of parties in policy-making. In each system parliamentary and executive powers are fused rather than separated, the executive being chosen by and constitutionally responsible to parliament. In and of itself this practice provides incentives for a prime minister or a chancellor, who is also typically the majority party leader, to work out policy proposals congenial to his supporters in the legislature. Correlatively, ordinary parliamentarians, whose reelection and attainment of positions in the cabinet are likely to hinge on their degree of party loyalty, have incentives to go along with the party leadership.[76]

Beyond these factors of internal party discipline and governmental structure, which facilitate a strong party role in policy-making, competition among the parties may have something to do with the phenome-

---

[74] William Keefe, *Parties, Politics, and Public Policy in America* (New York: Holt, Rinehart & Winston, 1972).

[75] James Burns, *The Deadlock of Democracy* (Englewood Cliffs, N.J.: Prentice-Hall, 1963).

[76] R. T. McKenzie, *British Political Parties* (New York: Frederick A. Praeger, 1963); Gerhard Loewenberg, *Parliament in the German Political System* (Ithaca, N.Y.: Cornell University Press, 1967), pp. 131–218; and Hancock, *Sweden*, pp. 170–97.

non. In countries where extreme multipartyism is found and where there is no stable majority in parliament to support the executive, there is necessarily a need to organize interparty coalitions. If, as in Italy, the coalition parties are themselves internally divided, with parliamentarians from the majority coalition often voting against their own government, the result is likely to be highly unstable. A rapid turnover of cabinet governments accompanied by policy deadlock may ensue. When this occurs, the role of parties in the policy process may diminish.[77] This role may then be filled, if it is filled at all, by other forces, most notably by associational interest groups and elements in the public bureaucracy. Where disciplined parties with majority or near-majority support are able to form a cabinet alone, as in Britain and West Germany, these problems of cabinet instability do not arise.[78]

The installation of the Fifth French Republic in 1958 was itself testimony to the failure of political parties to resolve the major policy issue on the old regime's agenda: Algeria. As a consequence, and at de Gaulle's behest, a new constitution was written which implied a reduction of party influence on public policy-making. By providing for the resolution of major issues via popular referenda, by making membership in the cabinet incompatible with membership in the legislature, and by reducing the latter's capacity to make law, the new rules of the game have reduced the impact of parties. Given the fact that, the Communists excepted, French parties are weakly disciplined and frequently faction-ridden, it should come as no surprise that administrative technocrats rather than party politicians have tended to hold the significant posts in recent French governments.[79]

Political parties also vary in the extent of the support they receive from the electorate. As we noted in Chapter 2, voting is one means, albeit imperfect, by which citizens may register their policy preferences. At least in the six Western nations in which competitive elections are legitimate, the popular support enjoyed by the different parties over time is likely to reflect broad-gauge preferences about the direction and implementation of government decisions.

Assuming that left parties, given their natural have-not constituencies, tend to be more supportive of egalitarian social policies than do their center or rightist counterparts, then it might follow that countries in which the Left is consistently popular at the polls would also be those in which policy patterns would be most egalitarian.

---

[77] John Adams and Paolo Barile, *The Government of Republican Italy*, 3d ed. (Boston: Houghton Mifflin Co., 1972), pp. 168–69.

[78] Gerhard Loewenberg, "The Remaking of the German Party System," in Dogan and Rose, *European Politics*, pp. 259–80.

[79] Williams and Harrison, *Politics and Society*, pp. 275–302.

TABLE 4-13
Popular Support for Left Parties in National Elections, 1950–1972

Mean Percent of Left Vote	Left Parties	Elections Included*
1. Sweden 51.0	Social Democrats, Communists	1952, '56, '58, '60, '64, '68, '70
2. France. 46.6	Communists, Socialists, Radicals, Unified Socialists	1951, '56, '58, '62, '67, '68
3. United States. 46.3	Democrats, Progressives, Socialist Labor	1952, '56, '60, '64, '68, '72
4. Great Britain. 45.9	Labourites, Communists	1950, '51, '55, '59, '64, '66, '70
5. Italy. 45.0	Communists, Socialists, Social Democrats, Proletarian Socialists, Republicans	1953, '58, '63, '68, '72
6. West Germany 37.8	Social Democrats, Communists	1953, '57, '61, '65, '69, '72

* Except for those of the United States all the elections were for the lower chamber of the country's parliament. The figure for the United States was derived from presidential elections.
Source: The data were drawn from Thomas Mackie and Richard Rose, *The International Almanac of Electoral History* (New York: Free Press, 1974).

Table 4–13 ranks the six nations in our analysis which hold competitive elections regularly in terms of the average voting strength achieved by left parties in national elections since 1950. As may be seen, the average (mean) level of left support in France, the United States, Great Britain, and Italy is approximately the same, with a difference of only 1.6 percent separating France from Italy. Sweden and West Germany are the deviant cases. The former has an electorate with a leftist majority, as measured by the Social Democratic and Communist vote, whereas in West Germany the Left has been significantly weaker than in the other systems.

The meaning and impact of left voting require some explanation. First, as we have suggested, the ability of parties to shape policy varies from nation to nation. Thus policy outcomes in two countries whose left parties receive roughly the same level of electoral support (for example the United States and Great Britain) may differ, owing to the general role of political parties in policy-making. Second, there is obviously a difference between voting Democratic in the United States and voting Communist or Socialist in France and Italy. Parties in the six Western systems differ collectively with respect to their bent, or central tendency. In some systems the party spectrum is skewed to the left, whereas in others even the left parties may hold views which would make them appear centrist or even rightist by the standards of the former. At any rate we will see in subsequent chapters whether or not, or the extent to which, relative left voting strength is related to the degree of egalitarianism in public policy.

Finally, since the dominant parties in both the Soviet Union and East Germany are Communist, we would expect public policies in these political systems to be highly egalitarian in character. This expectation is reinforced by the fact that in both systems party elites are the crucial policy-makers. Yet these elites are confronted with problems of ruling and achieving specific goals that, to an extent that will be appraised in later chapters, point them toward conservatism.

The Political Executive

Formally, if not always in practice, public policies are made, implemented, and evaluated by authoritative governmental institutions. Thus the character of executive, legislative, bureaucratic, and judicial institutions and their relations with one another are likely to affect policy patterns.

Let us begin by inspecting executive arrangements. Great Britain, Sweden, West Germany, and Italy appear to cluster. In each regime we find a head of state, either a constitutional monarch or an indirectly elected president, whose role is largely ceremonial. The British and Swedish monarchs, like the West German and Italian presidents, are supposed to act as symbols of national unity in positions largely devoid of substantial political power. Day-to-day control over executive functions rests in the hands of a head of government—a prime minister, premier, or chancellor—and a cabinet. The head of government, either alone or with the cabinet, is responsible to parliament in the sense that continuation in office is dependent on the executive's ability to command majority support in that body. If such support is not forthcoming, the executive may be removed from office. In Britain and West Germany the executive is only responsible to the lower chamber of parliament. Since 1970 the Swedish parliament, the Riksdag, has become unicameral, with the executive accountable to it. In Italy the executive is responsible to both the Chamber of Deputies and the Senate.

The British, Swedish, and Italian executives are legally based on cabinet government, with the decision-making prerogative belonging collectively to the cabinet. And it is the cabinet as a whole which is responsible to the legislature. The prime minister is supposed to be simply a first among equals, although in practice, especially British practice, there may be a tendency for power to be increasingly concentrated in his hands.[80] Some observers of British politics emphasize the growing capacity of the prime minister to play a role in the system not terribly unlike that of the president in the United States.

In West Germany the chancellor alone is accountable to the Bundestag, the lower chamber. And the chancellor, both in theory and practice, is invested with executive authority. Cabinet ministers are the chancellor's subordinates, not his peers.[81]

Under the American system the roles of head of state and head of government are combined and placed in the hands of a popularly elected president. Aside from the Constitution's rarely employed impeachment provisions, the president's tenure in office is not dependent on majority congressional support. However, senatorial confirmation is necessary for all the individuals whom the president nominates to serve in his cabinet. As a collectivity the cabinet is an advisory body to the president whose involvement in policy deliberations depends on the organizational preferences of particular presidents rather than constitutional mandate.

Fifth Republic France has developed a dual executive which has been copied in various parts of the world. There is at once a popularly elected president with a fixed term, to whom significant powers have been entrusted, as well as a prime minister and cabinet accountable to the National Assembly. Since the prime minister is formally designated by the president and also apparently dismissable by him (the relevant constitutional provision is ambiguous), both he and the cabinet members he selects are, in effect, responsible to both parliament and the president. As the arrangements have worked out in practice, the prime minister and his cabinet have served as implementing agents for broad policy decisions made by the president. Though some have argued that a potential exists for deadlock if the president repeatedly designates prime ministers unacceptable to a majority of deputies, there has been far less governmental instability and cabinet turnover under the Fifth Republic than under the previous regime.[82]

Most Communist regimes seek to create an exaggerated appearance of diversified decision-making by granting great constitutional powers to the legislature and by providing for a plural executive and head of state. Such a situation prevails in both the Soviet Union and East Germany. With party dominance in policy-making, the state executives in

---

[80] On this theme see R. H. S. Crossman's "Introduction" to Walter Bagehot, *The English Constitution* (London: Fontana Library, 1963), pp. 1–57; and Richard Neustadt, "White House and Whitehall," and George Jones, "The Prime Minister's Power," both in Rose, *Policy-Making in Britain*, pp. 291–306, 307–28.

[81] Edinger, *Politics in Germany*, pp. 296–97.

[82] Henry Ehrmann, *Politics in France* (Boston: Little, Brown & Co., 1968), pp. 245–55.

both systems act primarily as implementing bodies. Within this context the Supreme Soviet of the USSR, the parliament, formally selects
the members of the Council of Ministers. The Presidium of the Supreme
Soviet, parliament's executive committee, is legally empowered to act
as a surrogate for the Supreme Soviet when the latter is not in session,
and the chairman of the Presidium performs the duties of ceremonial
head of state. In theory the Supreme Soviet and its Presidium can interpret laws, ratify treaties, declare war, proclaim martial law, and dismiss
and appoint ministers. In practice they mainly ratify decisions already
made by the party organs.

With the party's Politburo preempting many of the roles of a cabinet,
the government's Council of Ministers is basically limited to the economic sphere. Drawn from the central and republic ministries and coordinating bodies, the Council and its Presidium coordinate and implement party policy through the state administrative apparatus. The
Council's members are routinely selected as full or candidate members
of the party Politburo and Central Committee, in which they constitute
a power center second only to the party's own top staff.[83]

Analogously, the East German regime has a Council of State, similar
to the Supreme Soviet's Presidium, and a Council of Ministers. Both
are constitutionally accountable to the legislature, the Volkskammer
(People's Chamber). During the 1960s the German Democratic Republic's Council of State, unlike its Russian counterpart, took on important
executive responsibilities on behalf of the SED leadership.[84] One reflection of the Council of State's importance is the fact that it has been
chaired by the party's top leaders, the late Walter Ulbricht and his successor, Erich Honecker. As in the Soviet Union there is a good deal of
overlap in membership between the party elite and these state bodies.

Parliaments

Whatever else their virtues and representative functions, the current
ability of parliaments to set the course of public policy has been severely
questioned. Many have argued that even in liberal democratic settings
control over policy-making has passed from legislative leadership to
executive, bureaucratic, or party leadership. The reasons for this alleged
decline of parliaments include: the inability of most legislators to deal
with highly complex technical matters; an increased volume of demands placed on governments, resulting in parliamentary overload,

---

[83] David Lane, *Politics and Society in the USSR* (New York: Random House, 1971),
pp. 142–50.

[84] Grosser, *Germany,* pp. 263–68.

paralysis, and an inclination to grant sweeping authority to executive and administrative institutions; and the rise of disciplined mass political parties whose leaders consign individual parliamentarians to the role of unquestioning foot soldiers of the party.[85] We want to assess the contribution of parliaments to policy-making in the eight political systems with which we are concerned in the light of these contentions. But before we do, it seems necessary to describe some of the major structural attributes of the parliaments in these systems.

With the exception of the Swedish Riksdag, the parliaments of the Western regimes in our analysis are bicameral. Although the lower chambers of these bodies are popularly chosen, this is not always true for the upper houses. In Britain the House of Lords is largely composed of hereditary peers; the French Senate is selected by an electoral college of local governmental officials; and the West German Bundesrat, reflecting the regime's federal structure, is made up of representatives from the *Läender* (state governments). As an outgrowth of their popular selection, both the American and Italian Senates have constitutional powers equal to, if not greater than, their companion lower chambers. On the other hand, the British, French, and West German upper houses have more limited prerogatives.

With respect to internal structure, the Western parliaments, except for the British, have functionally specialized standing committees whose responsibility is to scrutinize legislation. Frequently their range of activities parallels that of particular executive departments (for example, committee on agriculture — ministry of agriculture). However, in the British House of Commons most standing committees are not specialized in this fashion, and the weight of standing committees in evaluating proposed legislation is less than that of standing committees in the other parliaments.[86]

In general the functional specialization of standing committees encourages their members to become experts in the particular spheres of activity with which they are concerned and thus provide their plenary bodies with informed advice about relevant legislation. In addition, the committees' expertise offers them the opportunity to play at least an oversight or watchdog role vis-à-vis the corresponding executive bureaucracies.

The capacity of parliamentary committees, standing or select, to play an autonomous legislative role is affected by the party organization in the chambers. In most cases political party groups or caucuses

---

[85] For a review of these arguments see Gerhard Loewenberg, ed., *Modern Parliament: Change or Decline?* (Chicago: Aldine-Atherton, 1971).

[86] Ivor Jennings, *Parliament*, 2d ed. (Cambridge, England: Cambridge University Press, 1961), pp. 268–79.

organize the parliament, designate its presiding officers, determine its order of business, and make committee assignments. Where party discipline is strong, as in Britain and West Germany, committee members tend to reflect the preferences of their respective party groups; where it is not, as in the U.S. Congress, the committees may act in a far more autonomous manner as relatively independent bastions of power. However, the U.S. House of Representatives moved somewhat closer to Western European patterns of party dominance in 1975.

The Soviet parliament, the Supreme Soviet, consists of two chambers, the Soviet of the Union, with districts based on population, and, as an expression of the country's federal structure, the Soviet of Nationalities. Elections to both bodies occur every four years on the basis of universal suffrage. Each has a variety of commissions which are formally empowered to evaluate proposed legislation and oversee the administration. In recent years the commissions have begun to play a useful, though subordinate, role in these areas. By contrast the East German Volkskammer is unicameral and has a multiparty group composition. Its 16 standing committees, constituted along functional lines, are not invariably chaired by SED deputies. But this should not be construed to mean that the committees exercise great autonomy in relation to the plenary body.

In comparing and weighing the capacity of these eight parliamentary institutions to affect public policy patterns, we should consider their ability to make laws and raise and spend money, two functions crucial to the policy process. Are decisions concerning these matters really made by the parliament, or does it merely ratify them?

The Soviet and East German institutions are easiest to deal with here. Despite constitutional rhetoric investing the Supreme Soviet and the Volkskammer with fundamental powers, observers invariably stress the fact that both function primarily to ratify and celebrate decisions made elsewhere, usually by the Communist party leadership. This impotence is exhibited by their habit of giving unanimous approval to government-sponsored measures and by their infrequent and brief plenary sessions.[87]

Among the six Western legislatures the U.S. Congress probably plays the strongest role in the policy process. This is true notwithstanding the president's constitutional independence and recent arguments suggesting the evolution of an "imperial" presidency, especially in the realm of foreign affairs. Congressional power in regard to the budgetary process is impressive. Unlike the members of most European parliaments, individual legislators are not prohibited from introducing their

[87] J. Blondel, *Comparative Legislatures* (Englewood Cliffs, N.J.: Prentice-Hall, 1973), pp. 57–74.

own bills dealing with money matters. In addition, both the House and the Senate have specialized standing committees which closely scrutinize proposed executive budgetary and taxation measures. These committees frequently alter executive proposals and are frequently consulted before the executive submits the legislation. Moreover, Congress has at its disposal an auditing agency, the General Accounting Office, which works to ensure that funds are spent in the ways which it intended. The GAO will also advise Congress on the efficiency and effectiveness of programs which Congress has authorized executive agencies to perform.[88] Although a significant number of bills submitted to Congress are actually drafted by executive agencies, it is nevertheless true that all executive programs, including efforts to restructure the executive branch itself, require congressional authorization.

The strong impact that Congress exerts on policy derives from several factors. In particular, the weakness of party discipline allows individual legislators and shifting coalitions of legislators to behave in a more independent fashion than is typical in Western European parliaments. Second, the powerful and amply staffed committees provide high levels of expertise independent of executive agencies. Finally, the Constitution grants Congress powers which at once place it at the heart of the policy process and insulate it from control and manipulation by the president.

In terms of their ability to influence public policy, the parliaments of Great Britain, France, Sweden, West Germany, and Italy stand somewhere between the American and the Soviet and East German cases. The parliamentary body whose powers have declined most precipitously in recent years has been the French. That decline is in large measure a consequence of the Fifth Republic's Constitution, which contains a number of provisions limiting parliamentary influence. Among the most important are the following: the domain of policy requiring legislative enactment has been severely reduced; the government, not parliament, controls the order of business; restrictions have been placed on the length of time parliament has to evaluate the budget; no private member has the right to introduce legislation to increase expenditures or reduce revenues; and the president has acquired an enhanced ability to dissolve parliament and call for new elections if parliament behaves in ways he disapproves.[89]

Although the British Parliament does not suffer the same kinds of

---

[88] Aaron Wildavsky, *The Politics of the Budgetary Process* (Boston: Little, Brown & Co., 1964); and Richard Fenno, Jr., "The House Appropriations Committee as a Political System," and John F. Manley, "The House Committee on Ways and Means," both in Raymond Wolfinger, ed., *Readings on Congress* (Englewood Cliffs, N.J.: Prentice Hall, 1971), pp. 132–57, 158–79.

[89] Philip Williams, *The French Parliament* (New York: Frederick A. Praeger, 1968).

constitutional restrictions as the French, its policy-making role is still less than that of the U.S. Congress. The principal but not the only reason for this situation is strong party discipline. Assuming that the government enjoys disciplined majority support in the House of Commons, as is almost always the case, any bill submitted by it will inevitably be enacted into law. Parliamentary individualism plays a role mainly on issues defined as moral. The House of Lords, where party-line voting is less salient, has only the right to delay legislation, not veto it. Beyond the party factor, parliamentary powers are attenuated by the prohibition on private members' introducing taxing and spending bills without previous executive approval and by the MPs' own reluctance to grant themselves adequate pay, staff, and research facilities.[90]

For reasons similar to the British developments, the West German and Swedish parliaments play relatively restricted roles in policy-making. Between 1949 and 1965 about 80 percent of the bills considered by the Bundestag were initially drafted in a federal ministry; most of these were enacted into law with only minor changes.[91] Bills introduced by private members rarely become law unless they obtain executive approval. However, unlike the House of Commons, the West German parliament handles the bulk of its legislative work, including budgetary matters, in committee. Although most of the Bundestag's committees do not exert anywhere near the influence of their U.S. counterparts, its Appropriations Committee does provide detailed scrutiny of executive requests and can alter the proposed allocation of funds.[92] Furthermore, the Bundesrat exercises significantly greater powers than the House of Lords, and is particularly influential on questions affecting Laender activities.

Despite its exclusive constitutional prerogative to tax and spend, the Swedish Riksdag is largely subordinate to cabinet control. Yet a good deal of Swedish public policy is formulated by and implemented upon the recommendation of various royal commissions. Roughly a hundred of these executive-appointed bodies are active in any one year. A significant percentage of the commissions' membership is drawn, on a multiparty basis, from among Riksdag deputies. Therefore, while the Riksdag's role in policy-making is limited by the factor of party government, individual parliamentarians do have a substantial impact.[93]

Cabinet instability as well as several unique institutional features

---

[90] Bernard Crick, *The Reform of Parliament* (Garden City, N.Y.: Anchor Books, 1965), pp. 58–71.

[91] Edinger, *Politics in Germany*, p. 302.

[92] Loewenberg, *Parliament in the German Political System*, pp. 374–75.

[93] Thomas Anton, "Policy-Making and Political Culture in Sweden," and Hans Meijer, "Bureaucracy and Policy Formation in Sweden," both in *Scandinavian Political Studies*, vol. 4 (New York: Columbia University Press, 1969), pp. 88–102, 103–16.

combine to make the Italian parliament a somewhat stronger policy-making institution than other Western European legislative bodies. Aside from budgetary matters, there are no prohibitions on private member legislation, and the evidence indicates that individual deputies and senators have been comparatively successful in getting their own proposals enacted.[94] Both the Chamber of Deputies and the Senate invest their standing committees with a good deal of authority. In fact, these committees can pass many bills on to the next chamber without the necessity of returning them to their plenary body for a vote. The most important bills are returned to the floor and enacted by secret vote. Theoretically this permits individual parliamentarians to insulate themselves from the commands of the party leadership. In practice, despite pronounced factionalism among the ruling Christian Democrats, party discipline is stronger in the Italian parliament than in the U.S. Congress. As a result the former's policy-making discretion is measurably less than the latter's.[95]

Executive Bureaucracies

If parliaments have undergone a decline in their capacity to affect the policy process, it is generally conceded that executive bureaucracies have come to play an enormous role. Not only are administrative institutions charged with the responsibility of implementing policy, but in many cases they have become involved in its formulation and evaluation as well. Thus the issue of bureaucratic control and responsiveness to external forces becomes crucial to our effort to assess administrative behavior in the eight nations with which we are concerned. We seek to discern the mechanisms by which the state administration is held accountable to other political institutions and the public at large. In this connection Fainsod suggests several patterns, among which are the representative bureaucracy and the party-state bureaucracy.[96] The former refers to instances in which bureaucracies are responsible, by and large, to the public via its elected representatives, while the latter obtains when bureaucracies are controlled by a single political party in an authoritarian setting. Clearly the party-state pattern applies to the Soviet and East German systems. Representative bureaucracies seem to

---

[94] Allum, *Italy*, p. 133.

[95] Dante Germino and Stefano Passigli, *The Government and Politics of Contemporary Italy* (New York: Harper & Row, 1968), pp. 61–67; and Raphael Zariski, *Italy: The Politics of Uneven Development* (Hinsdale, Ill.: Dryden Press, 1972), pp. 238–50.

[96] Merle Fainsod, "Bureaucracy and Modernization: The Russian Soviet Case," in Joseph LaPalombara, ed., *Bureaucracy and Political Development* (Princeton: Princeton University Press, 1963), pp. 233–67.

exist, with important variations, in the six Western nations in our analysis.

Each of the three branches of the U.S. federal government seeks to exert control over the executive bureaucracy. The president, whose constitutional responsibility is to see that the laws are faithfully executed, is the chief executive officer. He has at his disposal several techniques for achieving this objective. First, he has the ability, with the Senate's concurrence, to appoint the heads and immediate subordinates of the various departments and agencies. As compared to the executive branch in most of Western Europe, the American executive branch includes a large number of political appointees. Most of these are responsive to the president's wishes and are dismissable by him. Second, there exists a personal Office of the President, including the Office of Management and Budget, which is structured to maximize bureaucratic accountability to the president. Finally, the president has the capacity to issue directives requiring the various departments and agencies, except for such independent regulatory boards and commissions as the Federal Reserve Board, to act in accordance with his preferences, subject to the bounds of law.[97]

Both Congress, through its power to make law and appropriate funds, and the federal courts, through their capacity to review the constitutionality of legislation and administrative practice and to interpret congressional intent, also exert substantial control over the public bureaucracy. Since president, Congress, and courts frequently see the world in different ways and are responsible to different constituencies, the public administration is often pulled and tugged in different directions by these authorities. In many cases, however, this phenomenon encourages various federal bureaucracies and the interest groups on whose behalf they may act to appeal to another authority.[98]

In Britain the lines of political control are ostensibly more clearcut. The courts and Parliament exercise less supervision over the central administration than is true in the United States. The cabinet and prime minister, with support from the Treasury and Civil Service departments, clearly dominate the control process. For example, in the British system, unlike the American, no legislative enactment must precede sweeping administrative reorganization. On the other hand, top-level posts in the state administration, except the very highest, are staffed by permanent civil servants. This fact, coupled with the relatively short period of time that any one cabinet minister usually pre-

---

[97] James Davis, Jr., *The National Executive Branch* (New York: Free Press, 1970).

[98] Lewis Mainzer, *Political Bureaucracy* (Glenview, Ill.: Scott, Foresman & Co., 1973), pp. 68–117.

sides over a department before being shuttled to another slot, has led to accusations that it is the permanent bureaucrats and not elected politicians who really run things. Although on occasion a weak and indecisive minister may be dominated by the higher civil servants in his ministry, this is not generally the case. The record suggests that Administrative Class "mandarins" have faithfully followed the existing government policy preferences.[99]

At least one of the devices for controlling administrative practice in France, Italy, West Germany, and Sweden is common to all four countries. In each a hierarchy of administrative courts outside the normal criminal and civil judicial system has the ability to ensure that public agencies operate within the letter of the law. Individual citizens with particular grievances, as well as various public and private bodies, have access to these courts. Unlike the United States and Great Britain, where a citizen who feels himself wronged by an administrative act must ordinarily take his case before a regular court, in these countries citizens have standing in administrative tribunals which are staffed largely by judges expert in the workings of the bureaucracy.[100]

When it comes to executive or ministerial supervision, the French and Italian systems are similar in that the cabinet ministers in charge of the various departments have at their disposal their own personal *cabinets*, groups of appointees whose loyalties are to the ministers personally. These ministerial *cabinets* are supposed to see to it that the wishes of their supervisors are carried out by the bureaucracies.

While the West German system approximates British practice, with most administrative positions below the minister held by career civil servants, the Swedish arrangements are relatively distinctive. Although Sweden has a cabinet government with individual ministers who are responsible for reporting to the cabinet the policy concerns of their respective departments (for example, defense, social welfare, agriculture), these officers are not themselves in charge of the administrative implementation of policy. Instead, this responsibility is placed in the hands of the administrative boards of each department. These independent boards are composed of career civil servants, not politicians.[101] This configuration might lead us to believe the Swedish bureaucracy to be unaccountable for its actions, but nothing could be farther from the case. In addition to the previously mentioned ad-

---

[99] W. J. M. MacKenzie and J. W. Grove, *Central Administration in Britain* (London: Longmans Green & Co., 1957); and R. G. S. Brown, *The Administrative Process in Britain* (London: Methuen & Co., 1970).

[100] Brian Chapman, *The Profession of Government* (New York: Macmillan Co., 1959), pp. 206–44.

[101] Nils Andren, *Government and Politics in the Nordic Countries* (Stockholm: Almqvist and Wiksell, 1964), p. 163.

ministrative court apparatus, the Riksdag also appoints several *Ombudsmen;* these officials, with staff assistance, are responsible for investigating a myriad of complaints from citizens concerning the treatment they have received from government agencies. If fault is found, the *Ombudsmen* see to it that the offending bureaus correct their errors. Several other countries have experimented with such offices, including Great Britain and West Germany.[102] In the latter the Bundestag has established a military *Ombudsman* to investigate soldiers' complaints. Beyond this the Riksdag, to a somewhat greater extent than is true for most other Western European parliaments, shares control over the public administration's financial operations with the executive.

If a central concern of observers of recent Western bureaucratic developments is with the maintenance of political accountability, the problem in the Soviet Union and other Communist regimes, including the East German, is perceived as the reverse. Given the intense party control of the state administration, Western scholars have been inclined to think greater bureaucratic autonomy, in the name of professionalism and rationality, to be desirable. In the Soviet system not only is the state bureaucracy subject to central supervision by such organs as the party's Secretariat, but at each level of state administration a parallel party organization oversees the bureaucracy's application of party-formulated policy.[103] In an earlier era, when the educational attainments and levels of technological understanding of local party officials were not very impressive, this control pattern produced delay and inefficiency. However, since their capabilities are now greater, the local party leaders often intervene in the administrative process in ways, for example, coordinating activities among organizations, that assist state officials.

In East Germany as well as the Soviet Union control is exercised by party organs at every level and within each area. However, the central apparatus plays a key role. All important government decisions are transferred to the appropriate department of the Secretariat, and through it to the corresponding party organs in province, region, district, or city.[104] Moreover, the part organs in both Communist regimes, from the local up to the highest, are able to intervene in all state personnel matters. With their careers at stake, if no longer their lives, state officials usually comply with party directives.

Fundamentally, there are four ways in which a modern government

---

[102] Donald Rowat, "The Spread of the Ombudsman Idea," in Stanley Anderson, ed., *Ombudsman for American Government?* (Englewood Cliffs, N.J.: Prentice-Hall, 1968), pp. 7–36.

[103] Jerry Hough, *The Soviet Prefects: The Local Party Organs in Industrial Decision-Making* (Cambridge, Mass.: Harvard University Press, 1969), pp. 101–25.

[104] Skilling, *Communist East Europe,* pp. 147–48.

may seek to apply its policies to its citizens. First, it may create sets of functionally specialized field offices throughout the country, with each set operating independently of the others and with all being directed by central departments at the capital. Second, it may place authority to implement policy in the hands of legally separate, subnational governments, such as states or provinces. Third, it may establish general agents in the country's major geographic subdivisions, each of whom is responsible for seeing to it that local field offices and governmental units execute the central policy.[105] Finally, it may turn over to private organizations the authority to apply state policy.

The eight regimes we are reviewing exhibit different mixtures of these techniques. The American approach appears to be a combination of the first, second, and fourth procedures. Some policies (for example, social security, internal revenue) are applied through the field offices of national agencies, while others (for example, unemployment compensation) are administered by state governments.[106] In some spheres such essentially private institutions as the Farm Bureau Federation and chambers of commerce are able to implement national policies.

Field administration in France and Italy depends heavily on the third technique. Here prefects, appointees of the central government and formally subordinate to the minister of interior, oversee and coordinate the application of national policy by local governments and state field offices.[107] The West German arrangement is rather distinctive because the application of most national policy areas, aside from such obvious ones as defense and foreign policy, is done by the Laender governments.[108] In Britain policy application is performed either by field offices of the central administration or, increasingly, by subnational units, especially in Scotland, Wales, and Northern Ireland. Swedish practice is similar to the French and Italian since the government in Stockholm appoints governors for the 25 provinces into which the country is divided. These officials have the responsibility for seeing that national policies are faithfully applied by local governmental bodies. However, in Sweden these local bodies exercise greater discretionary authority than has been exercised, at least until very recently, by their counterparts in France and Italy.[109]

---

[105] Robert Fried, *The Italian Prefects* (New Haven: Yale University Press, 1963), pp. xvii–xix.

[106] Daniel Elazar, ed., *The Politics of American Federalism* (Lexington, Mass.: D. C. Heath, 1969).

[107] Fried, *Italian Prefects;* and Ridley and Blondel, *Public Administration,* pp. 85–122.

[108] Herbert Jacob, *German Administration since Bismarck* (New Haven: Yale University Press, 1963), pp. 152–97.

[109] Hancock, *Sweden,* pp. 90–91.

Policy application in the Soviet Union is affected by the state's formally federal character. The state bureaucracy includes three types of ministry — all-union, union republic, and republic, in descending order of centralization of structure. The most important domains of policy implementation are reserved to all-union ministries with headquarters in Moscow and branch offices throughout the country. Union republic ministries have their central offices in Moscow and apply policies through counterpart ministries located in each of the USSR's 15 republics. Although such matters as public health and education are handled by republic ministries accountable primarily to the governments of the republics in which they are situated, Moscow maintains substantial control through planning, budgetary, and party supervision.

Originally the 1949 East German Constitution provided for a regime with a federal structure, with state governments able to make and execute policy in all matters not "essential to the existence and development of the German people as a whole." Since then, however, the state governments have been replaced by regional units, all of whose activities are subject to strict central state and party supervision. It is the responsibility of subnational governments, local as well as regional, to assist the central authorities in executing policies concerning the maintenance of law and order, civil defense, public works, health, and welfare.[110] As in the Soviet Union, the most important policy domains are administered by the central ministries through field offices.

The Judiciary

It seems that the capacity of courts to fundamentally affect the policy process is determined by whether or not they possess the power of judicial review. In other words, do a nation's courts have the ability to hold unconstitutional, and hence unenforceable, any law or official action based on a law which they judge to be in conflict with the country's constitution?[111] To be sure, the judiciary may play a policy role even without the review prerogative, as, for example, the ability of administrative courts to control bureaucratic practice. Yet in regard to the determination and application of broad areas of public policy, those national courts which have the power of judicial review are much more influential than those which do not.

So far as the courts in the eight countries included in our analysis are concerned, judicial review exists in the United States, West Ger-

---

[110] Childs, *East Germany*, p. 96.

[111] Henry Abraham, *The Judicial Process*, 2d ed. (New York: Oxford University Press, 1968), p. 283.

many, Italy, and to a more limited extent, France. The courts of Great Britain, Sweden, the Soviet Union, and East Germany do not have this power.

Judicial review in the United States may be defined as decentralized because all federal courts of general jurisdiction (not merely the Supreme Court), as well as some state tribunals, have the power to rule on the constitutionality of national and state law. Conversely, in Italy and West Germany this judicial prerogative is centralized in the sense that it is only the single constitutional court in each system which may decide on constitutionality.[112]

The issue of constitutionality arises in the American judicial system only in the course of conventional civil and criminal proceedings. In Italy and West Germany a court may also decide while hearing a particular case that a constitutional question has been raised and will then submit the specific issue at stake to the country's constitutional court for a ruling. In addition to this procedure, and unlike American practice, in both countries regional and Läender governments enjoy the right of direct access to the constitutional courts.

In France the Fifth Republic's Constitution created a Constitutional Council. Access to this body is restricted exclusively to government authorities: the president of the Republic, the prime minister, and the presidents or a minimum of 60 members of the National Assembly or the Senate. What is more, the Council will rule only on the constitutionality of statutes or decrees before they are promulgated.

CONCLUSION

In this chapter we have sought to interpret the basic socioeconomic and political characteristics of the eight countries which are being compared in this book. A basic East-West line of division was confirmed in regard to political systems, one based on patterns of participation and competition. Important differences were also evident among the six Western states in regard to mass attitudes and various political institutions.

Except for planning and enterprise management, East-West lines did not dominate the socioeconomic comparisons to a similar degree. Area, population, resources, technology, and economic output varied independently of political lines. Perhaps most notable is the distinction between the four highly affluent nations (Sweden, the United

---

[112] Mauro Cappellitti, *Judicial Review in the Contemporary World* (Indianapolis: Bobbs-Merrill Co., 1971), pp. 45–68; Taylor Cole, "Three Constitutional Courts: A Comparison," in Eckstein and Apter, *Comparative Politics,* pp. 164–72; and Donald Kommers, "Comparative Judicial Review and Constitutional Politics," *World Politics* 27 (January 1975): 282–97.

States, West Germany, and France) and the rest, with per capita GNP in the latter at roughly half the level of the former. However, the Soviet Union's great size, abundance of trained workers, and vast natural resources give it advantages for the present and future that raise it out of any category of "have-nots."

It is our intention to devote most of the remainder of this book to comparisons of current policies in each of the eight countries and to relate observed similarities and differences to the patterns described in this and previous chapters. But first we shall explore the history of public policy in Europe and the United States since the rise of nation-states. We intend this to serve as a basis for better understanding of the contemporary patterns in the eight designated countries.

5 Patterns and Stages of Policy Development

The direction and pace of change in public policy cannot be understood by a study of the present and recent past alone. The study of public policy provides us with new reasons to turn back to the history of our entire European and Western heritage. We must try to comprehend how policies changed through the centuries and why earlier responses to problems succeeded or failed.

The history of public policy, an often neglected part of our Western heritage, deserves to be studied for its own sake. Yet it is also our intention to point out instances in which doctrines and practices of past centuries have influenced current policies.

History does not consistently favor any particular political persuasion. Conservative students of policy often contend that sudden shifts in policy fall victim to environmental and political constraints. They also suggest that policies which have allowed societies to survive and prosper should not be tampered with. Yet careful study of the history of public policy can also serve reformers and radicals. It can help dispel myths concerning the "good old days." Much past "progress" may have benefited only a small part of the society or may have been achieved at the expense of the physical environment. History can also demonstrate that allegedly newfangled ideas are at least as old as the "stop and frisk" police practices in 13th century Venice, the guaranteed minimum income in 18th century England, or the comprehensive regulation of commerce in medieval French towns. To know that prison reform and the liberalization of public assistance have ebbed and flowed for centuries is to know that reformers in most countries must make extraordinary efforts in order to alter underlying attitudes and that conservatives can appeal successfully to those traditional values. On the other hand, some trends, such as expanded social and political equality and opportunity, tend to develop an almost unstoppable momentum.

Types of Historical Influences

A given country is influenced in many different ways by its own historical experiences as well as by those of other nations. First, history establishes which policies are to be considered traditional and thereby protected against all but the most concentrated pressures for abandonment or change. Tradition, the respect given to the old and established ways, is one of the most powerful operative forces in most political systems. It even incorporates the "revolutionary traditions" of supposedly radical nations. In this book tradition is invoked to help explain the continuing use of military conscription on the European continent and its abandonment in Britain and the United States.

Government-owned hospitals are traditional in Sweden, as is private enterprise health care in the United States. In the industrialized West we find such differing traditions as free trade and protectionism, government investment in manufacturing and mining or its absence, public provision for the poor or their neglect, concern for at least some sectors of the physical environment or the abandonment of nature. Few, if any, of the eight survey countries can be termed highly traditional, at least not in relation to most of the developing world. Yet each carries forward some parts of its centuries-old heritage. Almost every nation seeks to perpetuate some practices and institutions, largely because time-tested ways make people comfortable and secure.

A second and closely related impact of historical experience is to provide constituencies for particular programs. Students of social insurance have found that the most generous programs tend to be found in the countries which established them earliest.[1] Rising num-

---

[1] Henry J. Aaron, "Social Security: International Comparisons," in Otto Eckstein, ed., *Studies in the Economics of Income Maintenance* (Washington, D.C.: Brookings Institution, 1967), pp. 15–17; and Harold L. Wilensky, *The Welfare State and Equality* (Berkeley: University of California Press, 1975), pp. 22–27.

bers of administrators and recipients benefit from the programs and seek their expansion. This process is also associated with the rise of the "military-industrial complex," composed of the beneficiaries of prior investment in national defense, and with the support base of such other programs as agricultural subsidies and high tariffs.

Some policies are carried forward with the help of inertia and routine. Especially when policies are complex, technical, or protected by vested bureaucratic interests, major changes may be avoided for decades or even generations. The policy area that best reflects this pattern is taxation.[2] Few countries start from scratch in constructing their tax systems. Rather, the present and future generally reflect the inequities and contradictions inherited from the past. Those who benefit from these characteristics help make sure that fundamental reform is avoided. Yet many who benefit little or not at all go along with what they are used to, ignorant about, or too fearful to change.

We have also discovered that each country tends to carry forward obsessions, or at least emphases, relating to particular national traumas. East and West Germany share the national nightmare of runaway inflation in the 1920s. The British, among others, have taken to heart the need to avoid the persistently high unemployment of the interwar period. These concerns may distort public policy in areas which call for the balancing of economic and other objectives.

Certain policies are rejected because they are associated with discredited or imposed political regimes. Few policies are aided when opponents label them Stalinist, neo-Nazi, Fascist, Watergate-tainted, or neocolonialist. In countries which have undergone revolutions or have freed themselves from foreign occupation, it is often enough to invoke the specter of the old regime to justify major change. West Germany rejected Nazi and Allied education policies; in the Soviet Union Nikita Khrushchev sought to establish some elements of "socialist legality" in place of aspects of Stalinist repression; the United States seeks to change election campaign practices associated with the Nixon Administration.

Finally, history survives through ideologies shaped in prior centuries to meet older needs. Few countries avoid invoking old doctrines to aid in solving today's problems. Marxism-Leninism and classical liberalism, for example, have accomplishments to their credit and may be flexible enough to assist present and future progress. Although many Western intellectuals and policy-makers view ideologies as poor guides to contemporary public policy, this view is not accepted by most

---

[2] Ira Sharkansky, *The Politics of Taxing and Spending* (Indianapolis: Bobbs-Merrill Co., 1969), pp. 51–52; and Aaron Wildavsky, *The Politics of the Budgetary Process* (Boston: Little, Brown & Co., 1964).

officials in Communist-ruled countries or by some Western Catholic, socialist, and conservative circles. Ideologies continue to affect public policy throughout the industrialized world.

Doctrines in History

This chapter is organized on the bases of chronology, dominant orientations to policy, and particular functional sectors of governmental outputs. The major policy orientations discussed include mercantilism, liberalism, regulated-welfare capitalism, fascism, communism, and democratic socialism. These policy orientations tend to stress one or two functional policy spheres. For example, mercantilism centers on government economic policy, and fascism is most closely identified with political processes. Yet no doctrine or government in any era could restrict its impact to a few spheres, and outputs have always had important secondary effects in sectors of society other than those at which they are directed.

We begin our history with the policies of the European nation-states which had emerged or were in the process of establishing an identity in the 16th and 17th centuries. We first trace the development of mercantilist economic and social policies in those nations and then proceed to discuss the rise of classical liberalism in 18th and 19th century Europe and the United States. The chapter concludes with an examination of the new social movements and doctrines that challenged liberalism and conservatism in the 19th and 20th centuries.

Attention is paid to contradictions within each of the major doctrines, the inconsistencies that resulted from competition among the various approaches, and the compromises forced by conditions and circumstances. It is not our intent to present a case for ideological determinism. Numerous other factors are cited to help explain national and regional policies that evolved over time. Further, the reader is cautioned against inferring that any one approach to policy or ideology held sway without challenge in any given period or region. We contend only that broad orientations to policy were often quite important for particular issues in particular countries at particular periods of time.

MERCANTILISM AND THE POLICIES OF THE RISING NATIONAL MONARCHIES

A new historical era began to emerge in Europe by the 14th century and took definite shape by the 16th. Major institutional developments included the growth of stronger monarchies in such newly unified nation-states as France and Spain, the lessening of the unifying role of the Roman Catholic church as a result of the Reformation, and the beginnings of larger industrial and trading companies. Political competition among the rising monarchies led to many policies which were later referred to as mercantilist.

It is a subject of controversy among economic historians whether mercantilism ever existed, and if it did, whether it should be viewed primarily as a policy tendency or as a body of ideas or preconceptions about social and economic life. D. C. Coleman is persuasive in arguing that efforts to refer to all policies employed in Europe between the 16th and the 18th century as mercantilist have left the concept with so many contradictory dimensions that "as a label for economic policy it is not simply misleading but actively confusing, a red-herring of historiography."[3]

Yet even Coleman acknowledges the existence of certain dominant policy trends in the era of nation-building and early industrialization. Some of these trends continue to influence contemporary policy patterns in much of Europe and elsewhere. This legacy derives from the "mercantilist core" of policy in that era and the peripheral, derivative, and contradictory policies of an epoch which was nowhere wholly ended by the rise of liberalism in the 18th and 19th centuries.

Each of the continental European countries in this study adopted some policies described as mercantilist and was influenced by the doctrinal assumptions of that approach. England, for reasons centering on its greater dependence on foreign trade, its weaker administrative structure, and its more independent entrepreneurs, was less inclined than other European countries to adopt key regulatory and tax policies associated with mercantilism. The United States, 13 separate colonies for most of the mercantilist era, was often more an object of such policies than a promulgator of them. The increased use of mercantilist colonial policies by England, notably in the third quarter of the 18th century, did much to bring on the American Revolution.

The essence of mercantilism has a highly contemporary ring. Emphasis is placed on the state as molder of economic and social policy in the interest of expanded political authority for the national monarchies. Private fortunes were made and fostered by mercantilist policies as various industrial, commercial, and agricultural interests were supported at the expense of other interests. Conflicts of interest within and among these sectors provided the mercantilist era with much of its variation and contradiction. Yet the financial, political, and military interests of the monarchies gave the policies of the epoch such coherence as they had.

---

[3] D. C. Coleman, "Eli Heckscher and the Idea of Mercantilism," in Coleman, ed., *Revisions in Mercantilism* (London: Methuen & Co., 1969), p. 117.

Extraction

Although mercantilism involved marked increases in regulation and protection, mobilization was the essence of the policy direction:

> The important thing was the ability to mobilize economic resources: to draw or direct men, capital, organizational skills, commercial connections, towards desired ends — whether for industrial or commercial expansion, for agricultural reconstruction or for war.[4]

Obligations of labor time to landlords generally declined after 1500, but commitments to the rising monarchs increased. Peter the Great of Russia can be viewed as a modern Pharaoh, drafting at the turn of the 18th century for a military establishment that reached 300,000 men, and also for road and canal projects, the construction of St. Petersburg, and other grandiose schemes. Western monarchs acted similarly in conscripting for the merchant marine and the armed forces, though generally not on the same scale for civil projects.

Levels and varieties of revenue-raising also owe much to mercantilist-era monarchs. In time of war the governments of 16th and 17th century Spain and France collected as much as 15 percent of the national income.[5] Added revenue allowed the state, especially in France, to come of age in the century after 1550. Although peasants and merchants tended to be the major targets of collections, an increasingly wide range of groups and classes was reached. The British pattern stood out for the inclusion of the landowning aristocracy as major taxpayers.[6]

Among the revenue sources that emerged as newly significant were the local taxes designated for poor relief, direct capitation taxes, the institutionalized sale of offices, and the profits from grants of government monopolies in industry and trade. The increased use of customs duties represented one of the most characteristic trade and fiscal policies of mercantilism.[7] Monarchs had to be inventive to circumvent customary limits on taxation that continued to be maintained by parliaments.

The ingenuity of the revenue-hungry rulers occasionally reflected eccentricity. Peter the Great taxed both varying religious beliefs and the wearing of beards. With foreign trade a lesser factor in Russia than in most other European countries, Peter and his successors depended

---

[4] Ralph Davis, *The Rise of the Atlantic Economies* (London: Weidenfeld and Nicholson, 1973), p. 89.

[5] John U. Nef, *Industry and Government in France and England, 1540–1640* (Philadelphia: American Philosophical Society, 1940), p. 128.

[6] Guido de Ruggiero, *The History of European Liberalism*, trans. R. G. Collingwood (Boston: Beacon Press, 1959), p. 9.

[7] Eli F. Heckscher, "Mercantilism," in Coleman, *Revisions*, p. 27.

more on internal taxes than did many other European monarchs. Participation in emerging industries, state monopolies on commodity trade, coin debasement, and a heavy direct capitation tax were other major sources of Russian revenue.

Distributions

The era of the rising national monarchies saw some significant innovations in government spending in support of the economy. But the resulting river improvements, canals, and roads were developed more for strategic and administrative purposes than for commercial ones.[8]

Governments did not hesitate to subsidize industry with such varied instruments as investment loans, contracts, operating subsidies, importation of skilled workers, and guaranteed monopolies. As in modern states, such attention was heavily oriented to the arms and heavy industry sectors that were closely tied to military needs. However, the structure and character of court and society also led to major state investments in luxury production. In the view of most students of this era, the subsidy and direct investment policies lacked coherence and economic rationality and were substantially negated by counter-expansionary regulations. This helps explain the quite limited amount of industrial progress in most mercantilist states. England, relatively less regulated and less dependent on direct state subsidies during most of the mercantilist era, stood out as an example of greater progress in industry and trade.

Other new areas of spending by the mercantilist monarchies included imperialist adventures, such contributions to the physical environment as street paving, and such social institutions as poorhouses and hospitals. Yet neither these nor the previously noted contributions to the economy displaced war, standing armies, court luxury, and basic administration as the staples of governmental budgets.

Social Distributions

Early public assistance emerged in response to economic dislocation and the widespread violence that was both anticipated and experienced, and because of a mercantilist preference for maximum employment of the poor in the interest of national productivity and low wages. The first national "Poor Law" system began in England in 1536 and was codified in 1598 and 1601. Only the most recent adaptations of the 20th century welfare state go beyond the principles of that

---

[8] Davis, *Rise*, pp. 294–95.

original system. Maurice Bruce describes the stated aims of the British Poor Law Act of 1930 as "that of 1598, suitably edited."[9] However, the similarity is less a tribute to the progressiveness of the Elizabethans than testimony to the regressiveness of recent generations. Based on a system of repression and control of the poor, Elizabethan policies added a critical aspect of local government distribution and established a system of local taxes, in the form of compulsory alms, to support the "welfare" grants. These distributions were designed to supplement the broad governmental concern for the supply and price of food and for the determination of wage rates. Under the Poor Law, the justices of the peace were to ensure work for the employable and means of subsistence for the unemployable. Sweden was among the states that moved in similar directions in the 16th and 17th centuries.[10]

Yet such steps toward public generosity were not very typical of this age. In post-Elizabethan England and contemporary France national supervision of poor relief was sporadic, and the emphasis shifted to control structures, including workhouses and "hospitals," for all poor people who were excessively mobile or otherwise inconvenient.[11] Seventeenth century France failed to establish the legal obligation of the parish to provide relief; was more aggressive than England in using police to control begging, vagrancy, and movement from locality to locality; and drafted the poor into public labor projects. France pioneered in locking up the poor and failed to develop even the basic legal structure of a distributive welfare system. For reasons centering on general historical backwardness Russia provided a negative example that emphasized private obligations within an increasingly rigid system of serfdom.

Education made some strides in the mercantilist era, though the gains were generally more on paper than consummated. National government was slower to intrude into the Church's prerogative in this sphere than in the area of welfare. Nonetheless, the history of national systems of education begins in the 16th century. Schools and universities were encouraged in England by legislation passed in 1547, and parts of Germany proclaimed compulsory elementary education in the 16th century.[12] Opportunity for elementary education became fairly

[9] Maurice Bruce, *The Coming of the Welfare State*, 4th ed. (London: B. T. Batsford, 1968), p. 32.

[10] Hugh Heclo, *Modern Social Politics in Britain and Sweden: From Relief to Income Maintenance* (New Haven: Yale University Press, 1974), pp. 49–51.

[11] See ibid., pp. 44–51; and Gaston V. Rimlinger, *Welfare Policy and Industrialization in Europe, America, and Russia* (New York: John Wiley & Sons, 1971), pp. 18–33.

[12] Robert Ulich, *The Education of Nations: A Comparison in Historical Perspective* (Cambridge, Mass.: Harvard University Press, 1967), pp. 78, 200–201; and David Landes, *The Unbound Prometheus: Technological Change and Industrial Development in Western Europe from 1790 to the Present* (Cambridge, England: Cambridge University Press, 1969), p. 342.

common in major Western European cities, though not for most of those who could not afford tuition. Public education was provided under legal sanction in Massachusetts and other American colonies from 1642. Although American education helped produce a literacy rate higher than that of any 18th century European country, "from any absolute point of view, colonial education was sporadic, seldom in skillful hands, and ill organized."[13]

Regulating the Economy

The economic regulation of the 16th to 18th centuries in Europe, another area of special attention, was marked by the conversion of medieval town and regional regulation to national patterns. The newly powerful monarchies sought to exercise maximum governmental control over economic processes except when economic freedom could be seen to serve interests of state. Mercantilist states closely regulated the conditions of production, consumption, and exchange with such varied tools as state enterprises, exchange controls, patents, and monopoly privileges. Efforts were also made to expand to national scope most of the medieval restraints on the freedom of labor, investment, and trade while simultaneously reducing local controls on national commerce.

The change was not so much in what was regulated as in who regulated. The Crown, most extensively in France, sent out its own officials and developed guilds as royal instruments. The policies of the French monarchs tended to be emulated throughout the Continent. Yet even in France the emerging administrative corps could not effectively enforce the minute regulations throughout the countryside. In such comparatively amateurish and decentralized governmental systems as the English, enforcement was substantially weaker and evasion was general. As 17th century French ministers, such as Jean-Baptiste Colbert, intensified the administration of mercantilist policies, the English were in the process of repealing many of their restraints on industrial development, while retaining quality controls in the interests of domestic and foreign consumers.

Similarities have been noted between mercantilist regulation and the forms of economic planning employed in the Soviet Union and the East European Communist-ruled states between 1929 and 1960. According to Bert Hoselitz, both the mercantilists and the Communist-ruled states operated systems of "horizontal planning" which involved

---

[13] J. C. Furnas, *The Americans: A Social History of the United States, 1587–1914* (New York: G. P. Putnam's Sons, 1969), p. 226.

a mass of specific rules for many minute transactions and forms of economic behavior.[14] Hoselitz is correct in suggesting that both the "model" mercantilist regulations, typically embodied in industrial codes, and the Stalinist planning system contained so much direct control of resource allocation and prices as to require constant violations of rules to avoid system breakdowns. Yet neither he nor any other authority on the mercantilist era has made a strong case for the existence of planning, as we ordinarily use that term, before 1800. The policies of even the most dedicated mercantilist regulators represented little more than a collection of political expedients. The continental policies of the 16th and 17th centuries did tend to place limits on the development of private industrial enterprise. Mercantilist monarchies did expand direct and indirect state interests in the founding and operation of numerous industries. However, as noted by David Landes, the 17th and 18th century continental European state "was incapable of planning economic development nationally or allocating resources efficiently."[15]

Social Regulation

The economic regulations of the mercantilist era were also strongly motivated by efforts to maximize social stability. The basic socioeconomic patterns varied substantially—from the disappearing or disintegrating serfdom in much of Western Europe to the growing serfdom of Russia and the slavery of the future United States.[16] Royal authority was used in England to protect the poor from loss of the right to work the land. In Russia it more often encouraged increases in the legal and customary bondage of serfs to landlords. Yet both the English and the Russian monarchies acted to assure that poor farmers would not pose a threat to domestic tranquillity.

Violent crime reached high levels by the 17th century, as indicated by the recording of more than one murder per day in Paris.[17] In response the French led Europe toward professionalization of the police function and such innovative programs as comprehensive weapons control and widespread urban street lighting.

Typical punishments for convicted criminals between 1500 and the

[14] Bert F. Hoselitz, "Economic Policy and Economic Development," in Hugh G. F. Aitken, ed., *The State and Economic Growth* (New York: Social Science Research Council, 1959), p. 347.

[15] Landes, *Unbound Prometheus*, p. 136.

[16] Alexander Gerschenkron, *Economic Backwardness in Historical Perspective* (Cambridge, Mass.: Harvard University Press, 1962), p. 154.

[17] Leon Bernard, *The Emerging City: Paris in the Age of Louis XIV* (Durham, N.C.: Duke University Press, 1970), p. 157.

late 1700s were fines, banishment, and corporal redress. Jails were still largely reserved for debtors.[18] Yet this was also an age when incredibly severe and gruesome penalties were inflicted on a national scale, perhaps most notably by Ivan and Peter of Russia and Henry VIII of England. These monarchs contributed to a new expansion of capital punishment that did not lose its momentum until after 1800.

The criminal law reflected the intense religious conflicts of the age, though the impact of religious values on economic and social welfare policy was in decline. Spain and England stressed intolerance of heresy and of other religions than that of the state. Almost everywhere punishment was prescribed for an extraordinary range of sexual and public behavior offenses. Much of the contemporary American approach to "victimless" crime has 17th century roots, as even the "liberal" Quaker criminal code of the 1682–1718 period included penalties for bigamy, gambling, profanity, and smoking in the street. Religious institutions also influenced the inclusion of witchcraft as a capital offense in several European countries as well as in the American colonies.

Protecting the Physical Environment

Our fragmentary knowledge of environmental policy in the mercantilist era suggests that as a by-product of economic and military policies the rural environment in most of Europe was both exploited and protected.[19] War and colonization could lead to both conservation and waste in a given state. Financial pressures threatened the extensive areas of protected royal land, resulting in the early deforestation of Spain during the Golden Age. Yet significant progress in forest protection took place in Switzerland, France, and other states. The Dutch pioneered land reclamation and landscaping, and such policies were actively fostered by the English monarchy in the 17th century. Max Nicholson views English policy in the 18th century as constituting a positive "landscape and land use revolution."[20] Yet the role of government in such efforts, quite significant in the continental states mentioned above, was modest in England.

Unfortunately, neither the development of the urban environment nor government urban policies merit a similarly positive evaluation.

---

[18] Harry E. Barnes, *The Repression of Crime: Studies in Historical Penology* (Montclair, N.J.: Patterson Smith, 1969; originally published 1926), p. 86.

[19] Lynton K. Caldwell, *In Defense of Earth: International Protection of the Biosphere* (Bloomington: Indiana University Press, 1972), pp. 109–10.

[20] Max Nicholson, *The Environmental Revolution: A Guide for the New Masters of the World* (Harmondsworth, England: Pelican, 1972), p. 169.

Certainly the era identified with ambitious baroque architecture and other urban aesthetic advances was not a total loss. Yet, as Lewis Mumford says, "With all its luxurious display, the baroque city will not bear close inspection in the matter of hygienic and sanitary standards: the typical medieval town was more salubrious."[21] The generally less congested American towns tended to fare better than did most of their European counterparts.

The Parisian reaction to urban pollution suggests that substantial effort, including use of the newly developed police, was made to deal with some environmental conditions when problems were recognized. However, as Leon Bernard notes, "Despite the endless prohibitions, householders continued to use their streets as sewers."[22] In 17th century Paris, though not London and many other places, public health efforts directed against plague proved quite effective. Yet the physical environment was allowed to deteriorate in many other ways even in Paris, a harbinger of a worse fate still to come.

The most significant changes in public policy in what we have cautiously termed the mercantilist era appear to have occurred in the areas of taxation, poor relief, and economic regulation. Twentieth century experience in each of these areas has been influenced by innovations made between the turn of the 16th century and the French Revolution.

LIBERALISM AND THE EMERGENCE OF THE INDUSTRIAL STATE

The old order of Europe was dramatically transformed between the mid-18th century and the onset of World War I. Much of the change took place in the name of liberalism and laissez-faire. Yet, just as the previous several centuries had only partially reflected mercantilist policies, the period between 1750 and 1914 was far from being a purely liberal era.

The contemporary reader may be puzzled by the use of the term *liberal* as a label for policies that date back 200 years. Classical or traditional liberalism, which represented the most significant new ideological force of the 18th century, is fundamentally different from mid-20th century American liberalism. The latter is identified with greater power for central government, increased public spending, expanded social programs, and greater regulation of business enterprises in the

---

[21] Lewis Mumford, *The Culture of Cities* (New York: Harcourt Brace Jovanovich, 1966; originally published 1936), p. 119.

[22] Bernard, *Emerging City*, pp. 205–6.

interest of consumers and the environment. Traditional liberalism emphasized the reduction and minimal renewal of governmental involvement with the economic and social systems.

The policy content of 19th century liberalism can be understood only in the context of its political support and of the historical and philosophic roots of its doctrine. These derive from the late 17th century English movement to challenge the power of the strong monarchy and from the simultaneous widespread European movement toward greater religious toleration. John Locke's emphasis on natural rights and social compact, various attacks on religious institutions and beliefs, and rationalist critiques of laws and political institutions were all manifestations of early liberal thinking. John Maynard Keynes contended that the men of the emerging Enlightenment promoted the individual in order to depose the strong monarch and the Church.[23] Actually, many religious people and monarchists also contributed to the emerging liberalism. Various intellectuals helped foster the greater valuation of equality, freedom of thought, pluralism, competition, freedom of enterprise, profit-making, wealth, and material success that underlay the emerging liberal ideology.[24]

Liberal doctrine and political power shifted into some additional directions in the second half of the 18th century. In France the Physiocrats Quesnay and Turgot gained ministerial power within the *ancien régime.*[25] The Physiocrats did not share the religious and political goals of the British liberals, but they did develop in theory and practice a program based on reducing the heavy agricultural tax burden together with restraints on the export of such crops as corn. They believed in the centrality of agriculture and in the benefits to be derived from expanding production there and not in industry. Yet they also proclaimed, and to a lesser extent acted on, a desire to free manufacturing and commerce from governmental restraint. Indeed, the Physiocrats probably originated the term *laissez-faire,* which was to become the watchword of those who sought to keep government out of economic affairs.[26]

As de Ruggiero has noted, "While the reformed economic life of agriculture found expression in the system of the physiocrats, that of

---

[23] John Maynard Keynes, *The End of Laissez-faire* (London: Hogarth Press, 1937, as reprinted by Wm. B. Brown Reprint Library), pp. 6–7.

[24] Maurice Duverger, *Modern Democracies: Economic Power versus Political Power,* trans. Charles L. Markmann (Hinsdale, Ill.: Dryden Press, 1974), p. 29; and Paul Hazard, *European Thought in the Eighteenth Century* (New Haven: Yale University Press, 1954), pp. 325–34.

[25] See Ronald L. Meek, *The Economics of Physiocracy* (Cambridge, Mass.: Harvard University Press, 1963).

[26] Keynes, *End of Laissez-faire,* p. 18.

industry was modelled upon the doctrines of Adam Smith."[27] In *The Wealth of Nations* (1776) Smith emphasized that economic man could serve his best interests and those of society when government allowed market factors to determine the patterns of production, employment, investment, distribution, and pricing. Not as much of an absolutist concerning laissez-faire as were some later popularizers of this creed, Smith left significant areas open to government intervention. These included the protection of individuals from the injustice and oppression inflicted by others, national security, and the construction and maintenance of public works and public institutions that were too expensive or too unprofitable to attract private capital. Yet future policy was influenced more by the thrust of Smith's critique of what he labeled mercantile policies than by his suggested exceptions to laissez-faire.

By 1815 English liberalism had extracted from what became known as classical economics the underpinning for an ideological commitment to the dismantling of surviving feudal or mercantilist policies that could be interpreted as paternalist, preferential, or restraining. English liberals successfully opposed policies that limited enclosure of land or freedom of investment, restricted labor mobility, provided subsidies or guarantees to the working population, and protected domestic production and consumption through export controls or import tariffs. Much of the legislation that was overturned had been regularly ignored or inadequately administered. The new element was that such policies could no longer be defended in principle in the context of changed priorities, values, and objectives.

Laissez-faire extended beyond these economic questions into social, environmental, and cultural matters. In none of these areas did laissez-faire doctrine hold the field to itself. Yet, as Arthur J. Taylor has said, "The principle was all-pervasive; it is to be found as much in the discussion of education as of free trade, in the consideration of public health as of railway amalgamation."[28]

The elimination of restraints and the concentration of government on facilitating a competitive market economy reflected the essence of 19th century liberalism. However, even the most doctrinaire advocates of laissez-faire conceded the need for government to promote systems of currency, credit, and communications; provide military and public security; limit corporate liability for debt or injury; enforce contracts; and support trade through diplomacy and force. As such, classical liberalism had activist aspects.

---

[27] de Ruggiero, *History of European Liberalism*, p. 48.

[28] Arthur J. Taylor, *Laissez-faire and State Intervention in Nineteenth-Century Britain* (London: Macmillan, 1972), p. 48.

The "Neo-Mercantilist" Alternatives

"Neo-mercantilism," a 19th century rival to traditional liberalism, involved the adaptation of mercantilist policies to new social and economic conditions while retaining a protectionist and regulative emphasis. This orientation was strongest wherever authoritarian regimes nurtured paternalist and protectionist policies. It was strongest in Germany during the birth of the new German state and in Russia during its unprecedented industrial boom, beginning in the 1880s. A limited version of this orientation was fostered in the United Kingdom by the Conservative party, especially in the 1870s under Benjamin Disraeli.

Russian governments of the late 19th and early 20th century created state dominance in industrial and transportation investment, forced national savings through taxation, and attracted foreign resources on a large scale. Those who view the policies of the Soviet Union as a major break with orthodox government roles should consider the following summary of czarist Russian policy by George Barr Carson, Jr.:

> From 1890 until the middle of 1917 the major decisions on the direction of the economy and the channeling of investment had been made in the last analysis by public authority. Government policy on the protective tariff, on the maintenance of the favorable trade balance (which broke down only with the outbreak of the war), on land and colonization, on railroad building and defense, was the determining factor.[29]

It cannot be said that Russia was totally unaffected by liberal stirrings between the American Revolution and World War I. Catherine the Great toyed with ideas of the French *philosophes* as early as the 1760s, took some measures to limit serfdom, and began a 50-year period of de facto abolition of capital punishment. The period between 1860 and 1880 brought the legal emancipation of all serfs and reforms of such basic institutions as the judiciary, the army, and the schools. Tariffs were periodically reduced, and the flow of foreign capital into Russia was encouraged. Factory labor conditions were allowed to decline to a state of cruelty and repression, with industrialists using arguments against governmental interference that paralleled those of Western liberalism.

Yet the dominant motivation of state policy remained essentially the same as in earlier centuries. The autocracy acted for the land-based nobility rather than for the small group of middle-class industrialists. Reforms were offered mainly to bolster the political and military

---

[29] George Barr Carson, Jr., "The State and Economic Development: Russia, 1890–1939," in Aitken, *State and Economic Growth*, p. 133.

strength of the state rather than to promote private enrichment. Labor regulations were usually enforced to a minimal extent, though laws offering many guarantees of limited hours, safety, and sanitation existed in Russia at an earlier stage of industrialization than had been the case in Western European states.

The policy model that can be synthesized from the experience of emerging 19th century Germany is highlighted by a quite strong government involvement in the promotion and regulation of industry and commerce, and by the pioneering of a labor protection and social insurance system. A degree of liberalism was fostered by the Napoleonic occupation, the emergence of strong private banking interests with a capacity to sponsor industry independently of the government, a drive for national unity that was fostered through intra-German trade liberalization, and the rise from the 1870s of a significant socialist movement which sometimes supported classical liberal goals. Yet preunification Germany was quite slow to free its labor force fully or to end the use of guilds as instruments of control, and resisted the idea of matching Britain in the removal of foreign trade protection. During the first half of the 19th century, German states went quite far in the direct sponsorship of mining, factories, and transportation. After unification in the 1860s, "the role of the state in Germany changed from one of active participation in the running of industry to one of more remote control."[30] However, domination of the economy shifted to bank-organized cartels rather than to a comparatively free and competitive private sector, and the government retained much of its direct holdings in economic enterprise.

The most significant German contribution to European public policy under its authoritarian governmental system was its pioneering efforts in social insurance, a direction followed soon after by the somewhat similar regime in Sweden.[31] Liberal and socialist preferences affected the major German social insurance legislation. Yet more important influences included the desire of the authoritarian regime to utilize social insurance as an instrument of social pacification in place of greater sharing of political power, and the inclination of the major bankers and industrialists to institutionalize what Gaston V. Rimlinger terms a "feudal patriarchal perspective" concerning the social relations of modern industry.[32] Eighteenth century Prussia pioneered in the development of compulsory primary education. In the 1880s Germany led the world in the enactment of health, accident, old-age, and invalidity

---

[30] Norman J. G. Pounds, "Economic Growth in Germany," in ibid., p. 98.

[31] For the relationship between German and Swedish social policies see Heclo, *Modern Social Politics*, pp. 179–85.

[32] Rimlinger, *Welfare Policy*, p. 109.

protection for workers. In contrast, no comparable national social programs were developed in the "liberal" United States until 1935. The
authoritarian orientation of German policy limited the further development of social insurance before 1914, and progress was not extensive
in such areas as safeguarding factory conditions or labor standards.
Able to choose among possible methods to gain worker support for his
regime, Bismarck chose selectively.

Disraeli's Conservative British administration was also devoted to
a hierarchic and organic social order. In his landmark legislative year
of 1875, Disraeli was able to give broad effect to his skepticism toward
liberal self-help and laissez-faire, setting new directions in housing,
sanitation, food and drug purity, and the legal rights of workers.[33]
Although British Conservatism drifted away from such orientations
between Disraeli's time and the 1930s, the thrust toward state activism
in social and economic policy was able to reassert itself very strongly
during the Great Depression under a Conservative-dominated National
government.

Some of the forces at work in Russia and Germany were also powerful in other European countries, especially after 1870. Economic nationalism brought pressures toward greater militarism, imperialism, and
protectionism. As Barry Supple states:

> To differing degrees in such countries as Germany, Britain, France and
> Belgium, economic nationalism took a far more restrictive turn as tariff
> barriers were raised and the intensified rivalry of the international econ-
> omy led to the nationalistic control of markets and the extension of
> exclusive empires. Meanwhile, the state moved to tackle the economic
> and social problems of growth, to salvage railways systems, to bolster
> weak sectors of the economy, and to ameliorate the increasingly apparent
> social tensions and problems of urban and industrial maturity, which
> demanded more welfare legislation and social reform.[34]

Such international economic pressures brought back some of the policy
orientations identified with mercantilism even in states where laissez-
faire had been quite influential.

France, mentioned by Supple as a bastion of economic nationalism
at the close of the 19th century, developed public policies that are
particularly difficult to characterize. With more varied political leadership than that of most European states, French politics reflected an
exceptional degree of ideological flux and division. The ascendancy of
industrialists was less evident in France than in some other Western

---

[33] Samuel H. Beer, *British Politics in the Collectivist Age* (New York: Alfred A. Knopf,
1965), pp. 263–70.

[34] © Barry Supple 1971, "The State and the Industrial Revolution 1700–1914," in *The
Fontana Economic History of Europe*, vol. 3, edited by Carlo Cipolla, p. 340.

European states. Paris saw an intense struggle between liberal and protectionist orientations. Although labor protection began even before the programs of Bismarck, implementation of these programs was very limited and social insurance was delayed.[35] Similarly, in France governmental promotion of industry was more direct than in Britain but more restrained than in Germany or Russia. The followers of Saint-Simon, many in power in the 1830s and 1840s, provided France with a body of thought inclined toward modern concepts of state planning. Yet for most of the second half of the 19th century the major force for French economic growth was the private investment banks.[36] Finally, although France periodically responded to opportunities to lower tariffs through bilateral agreements, French producers came to expect comparatively high tariff protection as well as a pattern of subsidies and tax preferences for selected sectors of the economy.[37]

Other Doctrines and Movements

The conservative forces of the 19th century had counterparts to the left of laissez-faire liberalism in all European countries and the United States. These elements ranged from violent outsiders to participants in the governmental process. Their goals varied from expanding the electoral franchise to eradicating such particular evils of industrialism as windowless houses and child labor to supporting fairly broad programs for reshaping the capitalist political economy. In the United Kingdom the leftist elements were personified by Chartists, Owenites, trade unionists, and both working- and middle-class radicals.[38] More consistently moderate elements emerged from the ranks of the utilitarians, religious humanists, and governmental administrators and investigators. Such forces never truly controlled the political process, but they could achieve substantial reforms as a result of the major political parties' competition for votes and fears of mass unrest. Radicalism managed to infiltrate the leadership of the British Liberal party, especially between 1885 and 1914. Both major parties were compelled to make some constructive response to subhuman social conditions at and away from places of employment once those conditions became public knowledge through disasters and investigatory reports.

American reform was sponsored by forces, including the Granger

---

[35] Rimlinger, *Welfare Policy*, pp. 60–62.

[36] Gerschenkron, *Economic Backwardness*, pp. 11–16.

[37] Landes, *Unbound Prometheus*, p. 400.

[38] See G. D. H. Cole and Raymond Postgate, *The Common People: 1746–1946*, 4th ed. (London: Methuen & Co., 1949).

and Progressive movements, which recognized a need to protect weak individuals and groups from the powers of such private organizations as corporations and banks. None of these movements explicitly challenged the foundations of the liberal economic order. Yet they altered the course of official liberalism during the first third of the present century.

By the 1880s interventionist liberalism was being propelled throughout Europe by the emerging power of trade union reformism and socialism. In Germany and France, fairly comprehensive programs of social and economic reform were fostered by rapidly growing socialist parties. The British trade union movement, distinctive in its avoidance of Marxist socialist ideology, had considerable political impact by the 1870s. The critical difference in Marxist socialism lay in its proposal of a radically new society based on public ownership of the means of production and a government dedicated to comprehensive economic planning and the provision of comprehensive social services. Yet Western European socialist parties tended to be more reformist than revolutionary in their programs once they became, as in Germany and France, major elements in their countries' political systems. As such, their pre-1914 influence tended to be directed primarily at reinforcing selected programs of reformist liberalism and paternalist conservatism.

Contending Doctrines and Policies, 1776–1914: Britain and the United States Emphasized

If liberalism dominated public policy development in any of the survey countries in the 19th century, this had to be in Great Britain or the United States. Yet some historians insist that any liberal ascendancy was short-lived in Britain and mutated in its North American version. In contrast, other historians insist on the essential victory of laissez-faire in those countries. Bruce notes, expressing the first view, "By the time that the old mercantilist restrictions, against which Adam Smith and others had inveighed, had finally been removed, new social restraints were being devised."[39] The economic historian Phyllis Deane takes this position even farther, contending that "as industrialization proceeded the state was intervening more deeply and more effectively in the economy than it had ever done before."[40] Henry W. Broude is more restrained in his summary of 19th century American economic intervention. Yet he concludes that "a survey of the many dimensions of economic participation open to political units in the nineteenth cen-

---

[39] Bruce, *Coming of the Welfare State*, p. 13.

[40] Phyllis Deane, *The First Industrial Revolution* (Cambridge, England: Cambridge University Press, 1967), pp. 214–15.

tury impresses one with the extensive functional range of these activities at all levels of government."[41]

In contrast, the case for laissez-faire is expressed in these terms by William Ashworth:

> In Britain in the mid-nineteenth century the functions of government, central and local, changed considerably, expanding in some directions, contracting in others. But on balance they probably became more restricted than they had ever previously been in any other state with a highly developed economy. Practical recognition was temporarily given to the view that "he governs best who governs least"; and, especially, reduces his participation in economic affairs to a minimum.[42]

The ascendancy of liberalism is asserted even more strongly with reference to the United States by Karl Polanyi: "For a century, labor, land, and money were traded in the [United] States with complete freedom, yet no measures of social protection were allegedly needed, and apart from customs tariffs, industrial life continued unhampered by government interference."[43]

The reader cannot depend on such summaries alone for an understanding of the Anglo-American experience in the 19th century. It is again necessary to analyze the specific content of public policies. We trace below particular areas of British and U.S. domestic policy between 1776 and 1914, comparing them with each other and with continental European practices.

Taxing and Spending. Laissez-faire in revenue-raising is indicated by low levels of overall taxation, the de-emphasis of revenue from export and import duties, fewer nuisance taxes on commerce, and minimal government borrowing. Laissez-faire in spending is reflected in low overall spending, balanced budgets, and priority for such allegedly basic areas of governmental activity as defense, routine administration, and internal security. New areas of public expenditure would be expected to be resisted, with budget items that facilitate private business receiving the highest priority among new programs.

The above is a generally valid description of British public finance in its most "liberal" period, between about 1825 and 1870.[44] Tariff

---

[41] Henry W. Broude, "The Role of the State in American Economic Development, 1820–1890," in Aitken, *State and Economic Growth*, p. 12.

[42] William Ashworth, *A Short History of the International Economy since 1850*, 2d ed. (London: Longman, 1962), p. 130.

[43] Karl Polanyi, *The Great Transformation: The Political and Economic Origins of Our Times* (Boston: Beacon Press, 1957), p. 201. It should be noted that this work generally emphasizes the growth of governmental activity in Europe.

[44] The following analysis is based on Stephen Dowell, *A History of Taxation and Taxes in England*, vol. 2 (London: Longmans Green, 1884; reprinted by Franklin Cass, 1965); and Sidney Buxton, *Finance and Politics: An Historical Study, 1789–1885*, vol. 2 (London: John Murray, 1888; reprinted by Augustus M. Kelley, 1966).

rates were lowered significantly during the middle four decades of the 19th century, though greater volume allowed tariff revenues to hold up. Peacetime revenue was derived increasingly from personal and corporate income and excises on nonessentials. Taxes tended to be a declining burden on national income between 1820 and 1870, though not thereafter. With the help of a continuous increase in the value of the pound, total government revenue grew from about £54 million in 1825 to only some £70 million in 1870.[45]

Further, the times did not require substantial borrowing. The relatively large national debt incurred during the wars of 1793–1815 was gradually reduced during the following century. The absence of other major wars helped in this regard, as did the reigning fiscal policy, which called for debt reduction after short periods of borrowing.

Such a tight revenue policy sustained very limited government spending. During most of the 19th century only unavoidable expenditures were included in British budgets.

Central government spending was concentrated on the armed services and the repayment of war debts. Less than 25 percent of the budget was allocated to domestic programs during the greater part of the 19th century. Most cultural, social, and economic programs grew slowly. Before 1850, no central government domestic spending item exceeded the modest costs of public works, parks, and buildings. Police costs did not "take off" until the 1850s, and education grants were not characterized by sustained growth until 1870. Even basic civic administration costs failed to grow until the 1840s.

The reasons for this frugality were numerous. Fiscal policy reflected laissez-faire ideology, the priority given to private consumption and investment over the provision of public services, and a tendency to encompass low public spending within the orbit of Victorian morality.[46]

Although the United Kingdom met most tests of laissez-faire liberalism in the areas of taxation and spending for the greater part of the 19th century, the rate of budget increases grew after 1870. Further, civil expenditures began to grow much faster than the rising defense sector, and by 1895 some 41 percent of total governmental allocations were directed toward social, economic, and environmental services. Although most of these expenditures were local, the central government share had grown at a faster rate. According to Peacock and Wiseman, a decisive change had taken root. The more generous concept of "taxable capacity" had largely replaced that of "retrenchment" in the

---

[45] Local taxes, based on property rates, constituted about 25 percent of total government revenue in 1890. Alan T. Peacock and Jack Wiseman, *The Growth of Public Expenditure in the United Kingdom* (Princeton: Princeton University Press, 1961), pp. 99, 190.

[46] George Dalton, *Economic Systems and Society: Capitalism, Communism, and the Third World* (Baltimore: Penguin Books, 1974), p. 49.

1880s, and the era of continuous expansion of government social programs had opened by the 1890s.[47]

While the last decades of the 19th century brought the beginning of the welfare state to the United Kingdom, those years did not see the fulfillment of that transformation. Peacetime government expenditure reached only between 12 and 13 percent of the gross national product before 1914, compared to more than twice that level in the 1920s and more than triple that level when the British welfare state became full-blown after World War II. Spending is only one indicator of the welfare state, yet it is probably the most valid single clue.

It would have been surprising if the new United States had followed the same fiscal policies as Britain between 1815 and 1914. America possessed a much younger industrial sector and a far more decentralized governmental system. Its heritage lacked most of the feudal and mercantilist restraints that the British reacted against; its social needs became evident more slowly; and its economic and environmental problems were submerged in the vision of plenty. Further, the long Civil War had a major impact on fiscal and economic policy.

America's variations from the patterns of British fiscal policy and laissez-faire-oriented liberalism were evident in its tariffs on imports. Despite some strong advocacy of freer trade the young republic was convinced at an early point that relatively high tariffs were needed to ensure industrial survival and high wage rates. One result was a federal revenue system that was dominated by customs receipts from before 1800 to 1910.[48] Alcohol and tobacco excises tended to take care of most other federal needs in that period, though a federal income tax contributed significantly to revenue in the decade of the Civil War.

Another major American break from laissez-faire was evident in what proved to be an excessive policy of borrowing for internal improvements, practiced by many state governments between the 1820s and the 1840s.[49] As a result of actual and imminent bankruptcy, state-level borrowing was sharply curtailed, beginning about 1840. Yet the practice of heavy governmental borrowing persisted at the local level.

American governmental spending varied from the British patterns in the greater scale of allocations for transportation and other internal improvements, bank investments, and education. The U.S. government followed the continental European pattern of investing in and guaranteeing railroad and canal development. However, after a surge in the

---

[47] Peacock and Wiseman, *Growth of Public Expenditure*, pp. 65–66.

[48] Bureau of the Census, U.S. Department of Commerce, *Historical Statistics of the United States: Colonial Times to 1957*, p. 712. Except for the years 1864–68, customs provided more revenue than did internal taxes during this period.

[49] Margaret G. Meyers, *A Financial History of the United States* (New York: Columbia University Press, 1970), pp. 143–46.

first quarter of the 19th century, direct federal spending and borrowing for such projects was largely replaced by state and local investment. Although education failed to become a major item in the federal budget until the 1960s, state and local education budgets outside the South reflected the high cost of free public elementary schools decades before British school spending counted for much. By 1900 public schools were the most costly governmental programs in the United States.[50]

Despite these variations from the laissez-faire ideal and British practice, American fiscal policy did not differ so very much from the British approach and may well be said to have been even more dedicated to the spirit of laissez-faire. In terms of revenue sources federal borrowing was minimal except during the Civil War, and great effort was made to pay off war debts.[51] Although post–Civil War taxation followed the conventional practice of finding a new plateau substantially higher than the prewar level, the new expenditures were applied mainly to the armed forces and debt payments. Total federal peacetime spending doubled between 1867 and 1916, but this increase was modest in relation to population growth and other pressures.

Although laissez-faire liberalism was shaken under Theodore Roosevelt and Woodrow Wilson during the decade before World War I, federal fiscal policy reflected great restraint until the early 1930s. Taxation and expenditure by all levels of American government in 1927 represented about the same proportion of gross national product as was reached by the British in 1890.[52]

Comparisons with a leading continental state reinforce the idea that both the British and U.S. fiscal policies had a laissez-faire tilt. As a percentage of GNP, in 1890–91 all levels of German government were spending half again as much as their British counterparts and twice as much as their U.S. counterparts.[53] Parallelly, progressive death duties and individual income taxes constituted twice as large a share of the German tax system as of the British in that year. The United States used such taxes only sporadically before World War I.

Social Distributions. As to the distribution of spending, the United States in 1929 was still a country in which the post office alone used 26.5 percent of the federal budget and in which less than 1 percent of that budget was allocated for social welfare and health. Elements of

---

[50] Bureau of the Census, *Historical Statistics,* p. 723.

[51] Ibid., p. 711. Direct investment in internal improvements was a policy of the federal government until the administration of Andrew Jackson, after which such investment was made by state and local governments.

[52] Richard A. Musgrave and Peggy B. Musgrave, *Public Finance in Theory and Practice* (New York: McGraw-Hill Book Co., 1973), p. 190.

[53] Richard A. Musgrave, *Fiscal Systems* (New Haven: Yale University Press, 1969), pp. 100–101.

welfarism were being nurtured by some state governments, but a federally based welfare state did not even begin to take shape until after the election of Franklin Roosevelt as president.

Most social services were antithetical to widely shared belief in many tenets of laissez-faire. The development of such programs as social insurance and the protection of labor from exploitation were opposed in theory and action by an ideological commitment to maximize the "natural" operation of the labor market. Laissez-faire advocates opposed any public program that gave a worker an alternative to seeking work, interfered with the setting of wages and working conditions, or provided decent living conditions to those who could no longer compete for employment or support their families. On the other hand, accelerating industrialization and urbanization produced changes in social and economic conditions that made new kinds of distributive governmental programs virtually inevitable.[54]

Laissez-faire influence is most clearly evident in the tendencies of British social legislation between 1825 and 1850 and in the decisive policy-making approach of the U.S. Supreme Court for most of the 1870–1936 period. Yet new protective social legislation was passed in the United Kingdom as early as the 1830s, and the U.S. Supreme Court would not have had a laissez-faire reputation if state and federal legislatures had not passed social and economic legislation for its review.

Britain's laissez-faire reputation is strongly associated with the 1834 Poor Law. This was a policy package that eliminated the remnants of the Speenhamland wage supplement system developed in 1795. It sought to eliminate "outdoor relief," meaning public assistance outside workhouses, for the presumably able-bodied poor. British public assistance policy was thereby directed toward greater repression and less assistance. This institutionalized an attitude of utter disdain for the poor which extended to the helpless as well as possible shirkers. As Bruce has said, "It was this attitude to the unfortunate which, taken together with the prison-like character of the workhouses, made the poor law an object of horror to the working classes in the nineteenth century."[55] The poor were undifferentially mixed together, and the central authority worked to ensure against the unlikely possibility of excessive local generosity. Early English liberalism required that public assistance be granted only in exchange for utter degradation. This was to ensure that all workers would compete for industrial wages regardless of how low these might be or how brutal the conditions in the workshops, factories, and mines.

[54] Harold L. Wilensky and Charles N. Lebeaux, *Industrial Society and Social Welfare* (New York: Free Press, 1965), especially pp. 49–114.

[55] Bruce, *Coming of the Welfare State*, p. 107.

Laissez-faire was also reflected in the slow British response to public needs in the areas of housing and education. The rapid growth of new factory towns brought conditions of urban living that were inferior to those experienced during the previous several centuries. The desire for young laborers represented a major force blocking even elementary education for working-class children. The "liberal" political response to industrialization left the United Kingdom well behind many Western European states in the provision of such basic services as public assistance, housing, and education.

A growing range of health and environmental programs emerged as early as the 1830s, and the Poor Law was gradually eased in terms of a lessening of repression, the reacceptance of "outdoor relief," and the differentiation of poverty groups. Yet it is evident that "Victorian collectivism" was to be found more in the limited rebirth of governmental regulation of economic life in the interest of workers and consumers than in direct distributions to the needy. Only between 1908 and 1911, a generation after Germany, did the United Kingdom adopt the beginnings of national programs to protect citizens against poverty in old age and against sickness. The British began earlier (1897) to develop workmen's compensation and were among the earlier providers of unemployment insurance. Yet the benefit levels were uniformly low before World War I and the programs can be interpreted as minimal responses to needs and pressures.

American social and cultural distributions have at virtually all stages of development differed significantly from continental paternalism and even from the British levels of responsiveness described above. It would not be correct to conclude that the American movement toward welfare state policies was retarded in all sectors. A major exception was the world leadership demonstrated by the United States after 1900 in the field of postelementary education. Yet one can generalize that the United States avoided most kinds of social distributions substantially longer than did most Western European states. Neither increased national wealth nor earlier democracy succeeded in pushing America very far toward social collectivism before the Great Depression of the 1930s, and only during the administration of Lyndon Johnson were contemporary Western European levels of social benefits even approached.

At the dawn of the New Deal workmen's compensation was one of the few available instruments of modern social distribution. Social insurance was still ahead, and the almshouse was still the major means of caring for the destitute. Private insurance companies and trade unions were able to make only small contributions toward filling the gaps.

Some of the reasons for the slow movement toward welfarism in the

United States were discussed in Chapter 4. These included the broader ideological consensus behind liberal values, the power of the American judiciary to impose the liberal ideology on other branches of government, the considerable political power of business and the medical profession, the weakness and ambiguity of organized labor, the reputation of government for inefficiency and corruption, and federalism.

These directly political factors sprang from or interacted with various nonpolitical or quasi-political influences on social policy. As claimed by Gaston Rimlinger, "The main difference between industrialized Europe and the United States was that here the tension could be successfully managed, for the time being, without the granting of social rights."[56] This tension may have been partly ameliorated in the 19th century by the availability of free land and seemingly unlimited resources in the West, and by the presumably more open avenues for class and income advancement. However, given the special problems generated by racial division and massive immigration, Rimlinger's formulation is debatable. For example, America's advantages were not enough to assure labor peace. Police and military power was used more often to suppress labor and urban unrest in the United States than in most European states.

Promoting and Regulating Companies. As noted above, late 18th and early 19th century liberalism centered on the elimination of outmoded feudal and mercantilist restraints on the processes and markets of commerce. Yet the spirit of laissez-faire was soon challenged more effectively in Britain in regulation than in extraction or distribution. Controls were not directed at basic aspects of business operation, such as production levels, wages, and prices. Rather, they focused on such particularly indefensible aspects of growing capitalism as the long workday, the absence of basic conditions for safety and health, adulteration of food, and the exploitation of women and children in production. By 1878 most sectors of production were covered by factory and public health laws.

Yet meaningful capability and the will to enforce such laws were slow to emerge. Unfortunately for the workers, one of the early areas of strong regulatory enforcement related to restraints on the actions of organized and unorganized labor. Parliament and the courts were quite inventive in defining criminal and civil combinations, conspiracy, and coercion after conceding at an early point the basic legality of trade unions. Railways and banks were among the few capitalist enterprises that were comparatively well regulated, with even "public utilities" weakly controlled.

The impact of such regulation was subordinate to that of govern-

---

[56] Rimlinger, *Welfare Policy*, p. 85.

ment policies designed to promote and facilitate business expansion. Unlike most continental European countries and the United States, the United Kingdom experienced no great need for direct state investment in domestic economic development. Adequate private capital existed for vast foreign and domestic investment. Yet, as elsewhere in Europe, business gained a good deal from governmental legalization of joint stock companies, high interest loans, and bankruptcy. Improved commercial law, patent regulation, and the centralization and regularization of banking and monetary systems were also among the critical contributions of government. Finally, the absence of direct subsidies at home was partially offset by the active imperialist role of British diplomacy and armed force, ostensibly in defense of open seas, secure markets, and needed raw materials.

Few of these facilitating interventions were widely viewed as challenging the basic perspectives of laissez-faire. As argued by Arthur J. Taylor, "Intervention was prompted not by any conviction of its innate desirability but by the inescapable need to meet pressing problems."[57] Political forces that were never truly dominant worked with frustrating slowness to secure the beginnings of needed regulation. They had some success in virtually every decade of the 19th century in areas in which the essence of capitalist economic freedom was not challenged.

As compared to the United Kingdom, the 19th century U.S. government tended toward a greater amount of direct promotion of business interests and noticeably less regulation. However, this statement must be modified by reference to the quite wide range of state government regulation in the United States during the first 70 years of the new republic.[58] Inspection programs reached major food items, construction materials, and gunpowder, and licensing was used on an even broader basis in some states. Labor protection had a significant start, particularly in New England. As compared to Britain, the young American republic had a greater fear of private corporate powers and a somewhat more proconsumer approach to the economic role of the state. This reflected the political weakness of private economic institutions at an early stage of industrialization and the relative weakness of ideological opposition to government economic intervention before the Civil War.

During the second half of the 19th century the United States declined to move rapidly to regulate its booming industry and transport while continuing to provide major inducements to private capitalists whose need for such assistance far exceeded that of the stronger British

---

[57] Taylor, *Laissez-faire and State Intervention*, p. 56.

[58] See Louis Hartz, *Economic Policy and Democratic Thought: Pennsylvania, 1776–1860* (Cambridge, Mass.: Harvard University Press, 1948); and Oscar Handlin and Mary Flug Handlin, *Commonwealth: A Study of the Role of Government in the American Economy: Massachusetts, 1774–1861* (New York: New York University Press, 1947).

companies. Although it was often sufficient in the United Kingdom to provide a charter for the private development of canals, railroads, and turnpikes, in the United States such development was routinely subsidized through large direct investments by national, state, and local governments. Less obvious subsidies included the services of public officials, free and near-free government land and materials, permission to import cheap labor, rights-of-way, mail contracts, tax exemptions, and military protection.[59] Farmers, ranchers, and developers also profited from cheap money and generous access to government land. Increasingly, larger developers gained privileged access to resources. Later, as the need for direct assistance decreased, high tariffs became increasingly important as aids to northern industry.

In contrast with these promotional aids, which were usually more than met the eye, legislation provided for little additional regulation of business. Actual control was even less as a result of the weak and corrupt administration of laws and of a federal judiciary that often sought to protect business from government. Transport, communications, money and banking, trusts, public utilities, and food were regulated in the 19th century. Yet, except for the antitrust laws, such regulatory legislation typically came considerably after the analogous developments in Britain. Regulatory agencies were very slow to emerge or to be given strong powers. The Interstate Commerce Commission was created to regulate railroads in 1887, and the Federal Reserve System for banking was established in 1913. Post–Civil War government regulation of business was substantial only in such limited areas as railroad rate discrimination and the operation of grain storage facilities. Morally stigmatized trades, such as prostitution and the production of alcoholic beverages, were amply restrained by legislation but not by enforcement.

The post–Civil War 14th Amendment to the Constitution, as interpreted by judges who were frequently recruited from the growing banks, railroads, and other corporations, provided a unique instrument for the delay of more meaningful regulation. This amendment was employed with greatest effect in limiting state regulation. Yet it brought judicial power to bear against "unreasonable" regulatory decisions at all levels and, in the name of freedom of contract and due process, it was used to prohibit or limit government licensing authority and direct government control over wages, hours, and prices. In a characteristic decision the Supreme Court ruled in 1905 that business could be regulated for reasons of health, morals, or safety, but not for the benefit of labor alone.

This did not prevent a gradual broadening of regulation over the

---

[59] Broude, "Role of the State," pp. 12–14.

increasingly corporate national economy. Yet it left almost all business units other than banks, railroads, and public utilities largely free from such control before 1914, and even decades after. To the end of the 19th century the wage and price system, the use of resources, the provision of capital, and other elements of the entrepreneurial function were kept within and held to be within the province of the private sector of the economy.[60] Limits of this nature were challenged during the administrations of Theodore Roosevelt and Woodrow Wilson in such major areas as banking, food and drug adulteration, antitrust violations, and the exploitation of labor. Yet America was still a far from regulated society in 1914.

Environmental Regulation. One of the most regrettable prices paid for industrial revolutions has been the physical damage inflicted on mankind and its environment. Social historians compete to characterize the crowdedness, pollution, disease, and other negative attributes of the new and expanding 19th century cities. Writing of England, Mumford argues that "a pitch of foulness and filth was reached that the lowest serf's cottage scarcely achieved in medieval Europe."[61] America, lacking a base of urban regulatory policy, also suffered in this regard. According to J. C. Furnas, "Advanced as America was with steamboats and manhood suffrage [in the 1840s], its sanitary practices looked medieval to alien eyes."[62] Yet the great expansions of industrialization, urbanization, and immigration were still decades ahead.

The mid-century rebirth of environmental regulation in Britain was slow to produce results. Both factory pollution and unsanitary homes were products of the private enterprise that was being assisted by the state. When housing regulations began to be imposed after 1850, as they later were in Germany and the United States, the net result was "to give the sanction of law, philanthropy, and municipal effort to a low grade urban environment."[63] Some recognized before 1830 the interdependence of all classes in the area of health and the fact that disease and pollution were related to the cost of labor and relief. Yet extensive studies by governmental agencies had to be publicized before regulatory measures were approved in such areas as housing design, sanitation, air and water pollution, immunization, and food adulteration, and distributive relief was begun in regard to such necessities as public housing, public baths, and parks. These measures, together with the creation of a substantial public health bureaucracy, made England a

---

[60] Ibid., p. 9.

[61] Mumford, *Culture of Cities*, p. 165.

[62] Furnas, *Americans*, p. 455.

[63] Mumford, *Culture of Cities*, p. 179.

somewhat healthier place to live in by 1900 as compared with 1830, though not for such large groups as pregnant women and young children.[64] In 1900 town planning and public housing were still minimal and the alleged need of industry to pollute was still widely accepted.

Although Americans helped pioneer such governmental interventions on behalf of urban environments as central parks and improved water systems, smoke and industrial wastes were less controlled in the new American industrial centers than in most of their European counterparts. Tenements filled with immigrants decayed in the absence of substantial state or local aid. No major federal government involvement with human settlements was initiated before the 1930s.[65]

Bad as the record was for protection of the urban environment during the 19th century, the policies toward rural areas were often worse. The United States was more prone than any other nation to act on a belief in inexhaustible resources. Yet few European governments seriously restricted the development and disposal of resources in the 19th century. German, Swiss, Russian, and French efforts at forest conservation and German river basin protection were among the positive examples of environmental protection. Max Nicholson considered the following English approach to have spread throughout the world:

> It was not so much a defeat as an abject surrender to the invasion of half-baked greedy materialism and to the ascendancy of barbarian values in aesthetics, in ecology, in economics and in social responsibility. It initiated a new Dark Age for the natural environment, and placed the bulk of available human ingenuity and resources at the disposal of developments disastrous to the trustee interests of those generations toward their descendants.[66]

Whereas the British were primarily guilty of failure to intercede in behalf of their traditionally protected countryside, America combined the absence of regulation with sustained official encouragement of resource exploitation throughout the 19th century. The private use of resources on public lands was authorized by such American legislation as the Mining Act of 1866 and by grants and leases to companies. As noted by Earl Finbar Murphy, in the United States "it has been conventional to regard the private use, appropriation, or pre-emption of public possessions as progressive, economical, and shrewd."[67]

---

[64] Bruce, *Coming of the Welfare State*, p. 136.

[65] *National Report on the Human Environment*, U.S. report at the United Nations Conference on the Human Environment, Stockholm, June 1972, p. 33.

[66] Nicholson, *Environmental Revolution*, p. 171.

[67] Earl Finbar Murphy, *Governing Nature* (Chicago: Quadrangle Books, 1967), p. 211.

Despite its lamentable record during the past century, it is arguable that the United States initiated the closing of the era of unplanned resource exploitation that it had come to epitomize. According to Nicholson, developments in the United States during the last 30 years of the 19th century "may be said, for the first time in any country, to have put conservation on the map as a serious public issue."[68] The immediate fruits of this interest were not very substantial. Yet during Theodore Roosevelt's administration programs multiplied in such fields as forestry and wilderness preservation, and Europe came to view the United States as a leader in at least a few areas of resource conservation. This was true despite the fact that most government conservationists were probably more interested in coordinating and rationalizing resource exploitation than in slowing it down.

Social Regulation. The strongest link between traditional liberalism and its contemporary manifestations is in the area of crime and punishment. Prison reform and the abolition of corporal and capital punishment were major liberal concerns in Europe and America even before 1800, as they are now. Between 1815 and 1914, prison sentences were shortened in the United Kingdom and the United States even as they almost entirely replaced corporal punishment and deportation. The number of capital crimes in Britain fell from a peak of hundreds at the beginning of this period to relatively few by the close.

Prison reforms were advocated during the 18th century by such authors as Beccaria and Montesquieu, and experiments in improved prisons proceeded before 1800 from Rome to Ghent. John Howard, Robert Peel, and Jeremy Bentham were among those who moved Britain toward greater enlightenment between 1775 and 1835. As a next step in this notably international movement, America became the world's leader in prison innovation, beginning in the 1820s.[69] For many decades afterward Europeans came to the United States to study "model prisons." Not all of the American innovations deserve to be described as reforms, since these innovations included isolation cells and other means of restricting communication. However, Americans also provided more constructive work for prisoners and pioneered in the use of the parole system.

It is difficult to select one country as least progressive in its treatment of individual defendants and convicts during the 19th century, but the French seem to stand out for the scope of their continued use of capital punishment and deportation to places like Devil's Island. Russia had a notable policy of internal exile, and only in the 1860s were rods,

---

[68] Nicholson, *Environmental Revolution*, p. 197.

[69] See J. J. Tobias, *Crime and Industrial Society in the Nineteenth Century* (New York: Schocken Books, 1967); and Barnes, *Repression of Crime*.

whips, cudgels, gauntlets, and branding irons formally abolished by a czar. Yet Alexander Solzhenitsyn portrays czarist incarceration as benevolent compared to later Soviet patterns.[70]

Another side of the repression and punishment was the increased ability of the 19th century industrial state to deal harshly with collective violence. Traditional food riots and tax revolts were supplemented by actions directed at such diverse targets as machinery, working conditions, and disfranchisement in Britain, and new immigrants, blacks, Civil War conscription, and economic deprivation in the United States.[71] National police systems throughout continental Europe and the first professional urban police organizations in America were largely responses to actual and threatened protests by working people and represented the emergence of an effective state monopoly of coercive power.

With some notable exceptions the British pattern of repression was substantially milder than the responses in America and in most continental European countries. Ben C. Roberts cites a change in Britain between 1783 and 1867 "from a conflict-ridden society in which mob violence was matched by the savage brutality of hangings and transportation for life to a society in which conflict was regulated by rules adopted voluntarily."[72] Nevertheless, British officials were capable of notable acts of violence at home, in Ireland, and throughout the Empire during the entire 19th century.

America, in contrast, was developing new forms of collective violence and new aspects of private and public repression throughout the 19th century. Civil war, Indian wars, immigration, frontier society, racial hatred, and the absence of governmental capacity or willingness to head off violence through reforms of working conditions all contributed to a situation in which private and public violence often dominated social, economic, and political relations. Among the most notable sources of 19th century American violence were unofficial repression by frontier and southern vigilantes and the antilabor and anti-Indian efforts of such governmental agencies as the Army and the National Guard. Like the Russian government in its response to pogroms in about the same era, the American government did little to inhibit vigilantes and private police forces. However, there was less repression of political dissent in America than in certain contemporary European

---

[70] Alexander Solzhenitsyn, The Gulag Archipelago, vol. 1 (New York: Harper & Row, 1974).

[71] See Cole and Postgate, Common People; and Hugh Davis Graham and Ted Robert Gurr, eds., Violence in America: Historical and Comparative Perspectives (New York: New American Library, 1969).

[72] Ben C. Roberts, "On the Origins and Resolution of English Working-Class Protest," in Graham and Gurr, ibid., p. 264.

states which were far more advanced in police intelligence and considerably more fearful that political and economic organizations would move toward revolution.

Conclusion: Liberal Influence

In summary, classical liberalism touched virtually every country in Europe and dominated British and American policy during the greater part of the 19th century. The United Kingdom was also strongly influenced by conservative paternalism and variations on radicalism. American liberalism took hold somewhat later and persisted substantially longer as the dominant strain of policy. It was not heavily challenged by paternalist conservatism, and the radical assaults tended to be less intense in the United States than in Great Britain.

Even in the most paternalist and neo-mercantilist European countries the levels of pre-1914 public finance and regulation seem quite modest in the perspective of the 1970s. A "revisionist" literature has emerged to challenge the idea of liberal ascendancy during the century before 1914.[73] It forces us to reject a purely laissez-faire model for all industrializing countries. Yet it does not require us to substitute a dominantly "collectivist" perspective in its place.

COLLECTIVIST TRENDS

"The Great War of 1914–18," says Barbara Tuchman, "lies like a band of scorched earth dividing that time from ours."[74] The next 30 years brought an unstable peace; socialist, Communist, fascist, and Nazi regimes; the Great Depression; Keynesian economics; World War II; the Cold War; and a nuclear balance of terror. These were some of the central economic, social, and political developments bridging the eras discussed thus far and current political settings and policies.

We noted earlier that the two world wars and the Great Depression that came between were enormous forces for policy change. Each of these events produced common needs and problems that had to be faced by industrial states regardless of their differing political systems. In some areas the situation created by these events seems to have determined policy, with neither the character of the regime nor ideology having a major impact. In other areas and crises the problems allowed for substantial variations in national policies.

Political patterns took increasingly varied forms after World War I.

---

[73] See Deane, *First Industrial Revolution;* and Polanyi, *Great Transformation.*
[74] Barbara W. Tuchman, *The Proud Tower* (New York: Macmillan Co., 1966), p. xv.

That conflict helped bring the Bolsheviks to power in Russia in 1917. War-related political and economic difficulties and the fear of another such war helped produce a fascist regime in Italy in 1922, Hitler's National Socialist variation on fascism in Germany in 1933, and democratic socialist governments in post–World War I Britain, Sweden, and France.

World War I also directly produced intensive pressures toward increased regulation, extraction, and distribution. Most industrialized states responded by making greater changes in their policy postures than had taken place during the previous several decades. Some of the changes produced by great wars and the reasons for those changes were discussed in Chapter 3 in relation to World War II. Most of the same tendencies also developed between 1914 and 1918, with the difference that in some nations, especially the United States, a will was expressed after World War I to return to the "normalcy" of prewar policy. Yet even in the United States that could not be consistently achieved. In 1922 America was taxing and spending at a dollar level three times that of 1913. The share of the British gross national product represented by government spending doubled to a 1922 level of 27.8 percent. These figures reflected a major growth in governmental assumption of responsibility for the public welfare and the stability of the economy in both states as compared to the prewar era. Yet the gaps between British and American programs remained as great as before the war.

If one label can be applied to domestic policy in Europe and North America since 1914 it would be *collectivist*. This term suggests the opposite of individualism and laissez-faire. Various collectivist policies were developed during previous centuries, and such policies seem to have dominated the scene in many eras. Yet this is a somewhat illusory impression. Earlier levels of governmental nonmilitary spending and regulatory effort rarely approached the recent patterns. The present century has offered us far more comprehensive models of collectivism than existed earlier, including National Socialist Germany and the Soviet Union. Perhaps more significant, a far greater degree of collectivist welfarism, income redistribution, and limits on the private control of property became the standard pattern of policy in virtually all states accepted today as liberal and democratic.

By 1914 the age of traditional liberalism was fading even in those European states, such as Britain, where its ascendancy had been most evident. The major economic, social, and political events of the following several decades eliminated many of the lingering supports for individualist policies and minimal government roles. The United States stood out as a country where the rhetoric of classical liberalism largely retained its position of dominance. Yet this only delayed collectivist policies and resulted in having such programs packaged and justified in ways compatible with traditional liberal (now labeled conservative) ideology.

Fascism, Nazism, and Stalinism

As noted above, the most obvious movement toward collectivism was in such systems as Mussolini's Fascist Italy, Hitler's National Socialist (Nazi) Germany, and Stalin's "Communist" Soviet Union. These regimes stood out a generation ago for political repression, disrespect for the forms and processes of liberal democracy, and the uses of mass mobilization. It became common to refer to such systems, particularly those of Hitler and Stalin, as totalitarian.

The concept totalitarianism has been applied in several different ways, none of which goes deeply or broadly into the character of the domestic policies of the given regimes. Such expounders of the concept as Carl Friedrich and Zbigniew Brzezinski did suggest that totalitarian regimes possess a unique degree of control over society, particularly over the economy and the mass media, and that their pattern of control over individuals and groups is "terroristic."[75] The policy content of totalitarianism is less apparent in the pathbreaking work of Hannah Arendt, who posited few specific policies linking totalitarian regimes other than imperialism and terror.[76]

Policy was not given broad treatment in such works mainly because these authors were intent on finding common features of the various regimes. If they had paid more attention to the specific social, economic, and cultural policies of the "totalitarian" regimes they might have found more major variations among them.

Theorists of totalitarianism have also minimized major discontinuities in the development of these regimes. The Soviet system has been influenced by a far more coherent ideology than existed in Nazi Germany or Fascist Italy. Marxist-Leninist doctrine allows the Soviet regime to present itself as legitimately moving through stages of development from capitalism to socialism to communism, having allegedly progressed by 1936 to the socialist stage. Between 1917 and 1953 this system was transformed under Lenin and Stalin in the face of such pressures as wars, external threats, domestic economic difficulties, and changes in political leadership. It evolved at least five distinct policy

---

[75] Carl J. Friedrich and Zbigniew K. Brzezinski, *Totalitarian Dictatorship and Autocracy* (New York: Praeger Publishers, 1961), pp. 9–10.

[76] Hannah Arendt, *The Origins of Totalitarianism*, 2d ed. (New York: Harcourt, Brace and Co., 1958).

patterns—the desperate measures of War Communism (1918–20); the relatively liberal New Economic Policy (1921–28); the forced draft social and economic revolution accompanied by full-scale terror that took place between 1929 and 1939; the relaxation of several major aspects of social control combined with continued exceptional mass mobilization during World War II; and the reimposition of most elements of prewar social and political repression during the eight years between the end of the war and Stalin's death in 1953. The contrast that stands out most dramatically is between the 20s, with substantial levels of cultural freedom, individualist agriculture, and capitalist commerce, among other relatively liberal features, and the unparalleled level of cultural and economic controls imposed after 1928. Only after 1953 did the Soviet Union achieve higher levels of cultural autonomy and "socialist legality."

Somewhat comparable variations can be found in the Nazi tendency to sharply intensify societal mobilization, repression, and economic controls after 1939, as compared to the previous patterns. Similarly, Italian Fascist controls tended to intensify over time, with particularly strong impetus stemming first from the Great Depression and then from the need to conform to Nazi objectives, beginning in 1938.

Like mercantilism, the original conceptions of totalitarianism have been challenged by "revisionist" arguments.[77] The challengers have stressed such aspects of these regimes as the existence of some mass and elite autonomy from regime control and the limited efficacy of certain cultural, social, and economic controls. Further, some of the challengers emphasize the tendency of contemporary liberal democratic regimes to move in many of the same directions as the designated totalitarian systems in crucial aspects of structure and policy. In this section we will compare the allegedly totalitarian systems to one another and to their leading democratic counterparts.

Objectives

Interwar public policy reflected the fact that European states were part of the same unstable security system. As noted in Chapter 3, the Great Depression brought similar economic, political, and social pressures to all capitalist societies. Only in a few areas were there basically different liberal democratic, Nazi, democratic socialist, or Italian Fascist ways to cope with these pressures or with the problems that would

---

[77] See Chalmers Johnson, ed., *Change in Communist Systems* (Stanford: Stanford University Press, 1970; Carl J. Friedrich et al., *Totalitarianism in Perspective: Three Views* (New York: Praeger Publishers, 1969); and Herbert Marcuse, *One-Dimensional Man* (Boston: Beacon Press, 1964).

come during World War II. Yet there were many variations in emphasis that reflected in part the ideological orientations, the levels of morality, and the political constituencies of the various regimes.

Policies were designed to achieve such regime objectives as economic stability, recovery, and growth; income and wealth redistribution; political popularity and support; and military preparedness. No one regime monopolized or fully rejected any of these goals. Between the wars most major industrial states increased the share of national income absorbed by government. They acted to augment cash transfers and other forms of relief, social insurance, arms manufactures, and direct subsidies for industry and agriculture. Each regime increased welfarism and regulation after the Great Depression finally discredited old-fashioned laissez-faire. On the other hand, before 1945 no regime considered the welfare state to be the central aspect of its policies.

The Stalinist regime sought to achieve certain objectives that were significantly different from those of all the other states in our study. The Soviet leadership was interested in attaining a uniquely rapid pace of industrialization. Stalin had no substantial capitalist class to favor or deprive, though he was troubled at the beginning of his reign by the independence of some peasant producers. He was determined to sharply increase the provision for education in order to raise the industrial, agricultural, and military capacities of the population. His regime attempted, and largely achieved, one of the most rapid broad-scale economic and social revolutions in world history and simultaneously converted the Soviet Union into the strongest European military power.

The Nazi and Fascist regimes, in contrast, combined objectives of economic stabilization and development with goals for the social order. Both utilized the rhetoric of social revolution, but neither instituted major programs designed to accelerate movement across the lines of social class or sectors of employment. The Nazis, as men of the lower and middle classes, did seek to blur the impacts of traditional class and occupational biases. Yet, like the Italian Fascists, after seizing power they largely forgot their earlier pledges to redistribute income and wealth. It can be argued that the basic purpose of Nazi-Fascist authoritarianism and regulation was to ensure that no such redistribution would be imposed by working-class organizations and parties. The Nazi and Fascist regimes sought to provide sufficient distributions to ensure the willing political support of large sections of the working classes. Their immediate objectives during the 1930s were to restore economic stability, as measured by production and jobs, to increase self-sufficiency in raw materials, and subsequently, to dramatically bolster the military-related industries in anticipation of war.

The objectives of the European democracies and the United States were in accord with those of the German and Italian regimes in many areas. Even before Keynesian economics became dominant, there was general agreement concerning desirable levels of stability and growth in such sectors as employment, finance, trade, and productivity. Most industrializing nations in that era also concurred on the need to protect environmental values only when this was compatible with increased production. Except for land reclamation, this period was no better for the physical environment than for economies. The democratic regimes did tend to offer more resistance to the diversion of resources to armaments. Among them, the democratic socialist administrations in Sweden and France were pledged to the redistribution of income and the achievement of other aspects of social justice. Yet these variations in stated goals among the democracies rarely produced comparable differences in policies.

Regulation: Political, Social, Cultural

The strongest case for the existence of distinct totalitarian policies can be offered in regard to political repression and terror. Like their more authoritarian counterparts most liberal democracies used repression against striking and demonstrating workers and other citizens during the interwar era of major economic and social stress. The French and British employed brutal measures against strikers, and the U.S. government even attacked demonstrating war veterans. In each of the liberal democracies, new aspects of control over vaguely designated "subversives" were frequently legislated and enforced. All governments became more personalist and executive-dominated and gained new levels of control over many aspects of the lives of all citizens. Yet despite all of this few could deny that Germany and the Soviet Union developed a qualitatively different level of political repression and an unheard-of degree of raw terror before and during World War II. Further, neither these regimes nor Fascist Italy gave workers, political dissenters, and others new economic and political rights comparable to those developed in the Western democracies during that period.

The Nazi and Stalinist regimes both created comprehensive systems of mass arrests, deportations, and death that destroyed possible political opposition, reinforced other aspects of control, and won favor from those who benefited materially or psychologically from the removal of the victims.[78] Yet the destruction of millions of lives in both Germany

---

[78] See Raoul Hilberg, *The Destruction of the European Jews* (Chicago: Quadrangle Books, 1961); Hannah Arendt, *Eichmann in Jerusalem* (New York: Viking Press, 1963); Solzhenitsyn, *Gulag Archipelago*; and Robert Conquest, *The Great Terror* (New York: Macmillan Co., 1968).

and the Soviet Union was less pragmatic than irrational and self-propelling. Although no qualitative difference exists in their respective abuse of humanity, there were differences in their approaches. The German holocaust was different from the Stalinist in that it tended to focus on defined political, national, and religious groups in contrast to the dominant randomness of the Soviet effort. Hitler did not achieve the level of political intimidation of the average citizen that resulted from the techniques of the Soviet secret police. Yet he outdid Stalin in the crime of genocide, the physical destruction of a particular national or religious group.

The terror complemented a broader pattern of disrespect for law as a means to regulate social, economic, and political behavior. In both Germany and the Soviet Union the basic legitimacy of law was challenged and subordinated to political authority and arbitrary processes. Both regimes intensified the punishment of criminal law violations and weakened many kinds of private property rights. Yet neither found it necessary to eliminate every aspect of the preexisting legal order. In both countries horrendous concepts were written into law, including Nazi racialism and Stalinist guilt by association.

This common denominator of terror and subjugation of law does not fully apply to Mussolini's Italy. The Italian Fascists operated a system of police repression that was closer to such earlier authoritarian regimes as czarist Russia than to the interwar regimes in Germany or the Soviet Union. Before World War II the victims of the Mussolini regime numbered "only" in the tens of thousands and few lost their lives. This regime cooperated with Nazi efforts to round up Jews and others during the war, but it did not differ from many occupation regimes in that respect. The authoritarian and arbitrary quality of the legal order contributed to the relative successes of the regime's efforts against the Mafia in Sicily as well as in explicitly political cases. Yet, as noted by Edward Tannenbaum, "Although the courts had to enforce the rather harsh Fascist conception of law and order and most judges joined the party, they managed to preserve a good deal of their professional integrity."[79]

Political repression and terror are closely associated with penetration of the mass media, popular culture, intellectual life, and religion. With some regrettable exceptions these were all areas in which the liberal democracies tended to make progress toward the original — and continuing — ideals of liberalism during the interwar period. Few organizational controls were used except in education, and even programs to sustain the arts during the Depression, as in the United States, usually allowed for broad toleration of varied political perspectives.

---

[79] Edward R. Tannenbaum, *The Fascist Experience* (New York: Basic Books, 1972), p. 72.

Paris and pre-1933 Berlin may have been freer than Boston in some aspects of cultural policy, yet America enjoyed its traditional advantage in religious toleration. Schools were among the well-policed institutions in all of these countries, but the criteria for judgment and control were more often moralistic than specifically political.

The parallels among the allegedly totalitarian regimes in such areas of control as communications and culture are quite evident. The Stalinist regime was most comprehensive and intense in such sectors, and Nazi Germany was close behind. Mussolini's Italy was, again, much more moderate than either of these regimes in its methods and policies, but more controlled than the liberal democracies.

Both the Nazi and Stalinist regimes were intent on securing complete control over the mass media and employed complex systems to accomplish this task. Differences existed, as in the Nazis' toleration of an autonomous Catholic press for a time and their continuation of some preexisting newspapers and editors. These differences can be explained in part by Hitler's need to move gradually in regard to some respectable sectors of society and by his recognition of the value of non-Nazi endorsement of his policies.[80] Both regimes applied their controls to all personnel and media involved in the expression of art, ideas, and information, depending on regime monopolies, precensorship, and guild-like organizations which could exclude persons from such careers. Under Nazism and Stalinism the decision that a person or his work was unacceptable could quite possibly constitute a ticket to a concentration camp or a labor camp. As to education, purges of faculty members and students were widespread in both systems and teaching that challenged the official approach to a wide range of subjects was not tolerated. Further, positive evidence of political loyalty was expected as a condition of holding a teaching position.

The prescribed truths differed in important ways. The Nazis emphasized racism and militarism, whereas the Stalinist regime officially rejected these teachings and concentrated instead on Stalin's own peculiar perspectives on philosophy, economics, natural science, and other disciplines.[81] On the other hand, these regimes were similar in their predisposition toward atheism, nationalism, and puritanism in social norms, and their opposition to abstract and experimental forms of expression.

Mussolini's regime was disposed toward many of these same policies in such sectors as art, education, religion, and communications, but

---

[80] Karl Bracher, *The German Dictatorship*, trans. Jean Steinberg (New York: Praeger Publishers, 1970), p. 255.

[81] See Roy A. Medvedev, *Let History Judge*, trans. Colleen Taylor (New York: Alfred A. Knopf, 1972), chap. 14.

it did not approach the scope or intensity of the Nazi and Stalinist approaches to any of these areas. The Italian regime's presence was exerted in all spheres, and the participants in each sphere had to contend with limits placed on their activities. Yet they did not face effective systematic controls in many areas and they enjoyed substantial toleration in both the forms and the substance of expression. Substantial autonomy of the Catholic church was confirmed by the Lateran Accords of 1929.[82] Tannenbaum insists that Fascism had little direct effect on Italian university life.[83] This was a regime that acted as if it were too insecure to seriously attempt totalitarian controls in areas that carried enormous weight with domestic intellectuals and foreign observers.

Economic Regulation

The regulatory approaches of authoritarian and democratic European and North American governments were more similar to one another in the economic sphere. In terms of industry, agriculture, finance, and trade, each of the leading capitalist states recognized the need to use government to shift industry further toward planning and cooperation in order to reduce wasteful competition, excess capacity, and duplicated investment. In the view of several authorities the result was new "corporative" controls in democratic and fascist countries alike.[84] Indeed, in the view of some leading commentators the American New Deal administration, with its Agricultural Adjustment Act, National Recovery Administration, and improved regulation of the securities industry, attempted to go farther in that direction than did any of its fascist counterparts.[85]

In a recent updating of his list of totalitarian features Carl Friedrich insists that totalitarian regimes are all marked by monopolistic control over all organizations, including economic ones, "thus involving a centrally-planned economy."[86] Friedrich and Brzezinski recognized earlier that the Stalinist and Fascist-Nazi regimes had industrial arrangements that differed in such basic ways as the control of profits, the positions occupied by former owners and decision-makers, and the formal autonomy of private institutions. Yet they argued that the Stalinists, Fascists, and Nazis alike had made increased production a central theme of their

---

[82] A much more limited degree of autonomy was afforded by Stalin to the Russian Orthodox Church during World War II.

[83] Tannenbaum, *Fascist Experience*, p. 169.

[84] Donald Winch, *Economics and Policy: A Historical Study* (London: Hodder & Stoughton, 1969), p. 231.

[85] Duverger, *Modern Democracies*, p. 106.

[86] Friedrich et al., *Totalitarianism*, p. 126.

action programs and in having "penetrated and subordinated the industrial machine, labor, and agriculture to the requirements of the regime."[87]

Such views have not been effectively challenged in regard to the Stalinist regime but have been strongly criticized insofar as the Hitler and Mussolini regimes are concerned. The Stalinist regime implemented a revolution in collectivized agriculture, completed Lenin's program for the nationalization of industry, and expanded a highly centralized and rigid system that approached financial and production planning in a comprehensive way.[88] Virtually all of industry was organized and directed by central government agencies which were in turn supervised by Communist party and police organs.

The central agencies failed to provide complete control over the economy. During the 1930s Stalin fostered a feverish pace of economic development that was inherently incompatible with rational planning. Political terror, war, and natural calamities also shattered the planning system. As a result, extralegal manipulation at the enterprise level was critical to the continuity and progress of the forced draft economic development. Nevertheless, the system was a model of enormous regime control over enterprises, labor, and almost all other economic processes.

German Nazism and Italian Fascism also involved increased political control of the economies that went beyond the patterns of any pre-1930 "liberal" state. Each developed versions of the "corporative" state in which labor-management relations were strictly controlled by the government, business cartels were encouraged, labor mobility and wages restricted, prices frozen, and the allocation of raw materials and trade in finished products were increasingly controlled. Efforts were made to increase government ownership of industry, mainly as a means to save sagging sectors in Italy at the peak of the Great Depression and, in Germany, to accelerate investment in military-related fields. Official plans were promulgated, most notably the 1936 German Four-Year Plan. Autonomous labor unions were ended in Germany, and only a cautious remnant was able to survive in Italy under Catholic church sponsorship.

Despite these policies and the great capacity of the Nazi regime to use technology to accomplish economic ends it appears that economic control in both the Hitler and Mussolini regimes tended to be closer to the contemporary levels of the Western democracies than to the Soviet Union. In both Italy and Germany public ownership remained limited,

---

[87] Friedrich and Brzezinski, *Totalitarian Dictatorship*, p. 211.

[88] See Harry Schwartz, *Russia's Soviet Economy*, 2d ed. (Englewood Cliffs, N.J.: Prentice-Hall, 1954); and Maurice Dobb, *Soviet Economic Development since 1917* (New York: International Publishers, 1948).

no developed planning system existed before World War II, and labor mobility and wages were only partially controlled. As Landes notes, "It was only after the defeat at Stalingrad, when it was too late to win, that the [Nazi] regime faced up to the need for total resource mobilization and began to make effective use of its powers to plan and direct industrial activity."[89] Wartime Germany fell behind its principal enemies in materials rationing, the deployment of labor, and numerous other areas in which a totalitarian regime could have been expected to set the pace. Italian economic controls were even less effective, reflecting a level of intensity that was much greater in theory than in fact.[90] The managers of private corporations, less infiltrated by political personnel than in Germany, retained most of their powers. Even the formal structure of the Italian corporative state was largely abandoned before 1939. It is true that both the Nazi and Fascist regimes actively sought to control their economies and that neither recognized any "liberal" restraints on such efforts. Yet both systems were characterized by an absence of consistent economic goals, shortages of expertise in planning and management, and modest levels of concern for economic problems at the highest political levels. As a result, neither Nazism nor Italian Fascism created a genuine model of a supercontrolled economy.

Distributions

A popular view of Depression-era distributions is that the totalitarian regimes concentrated on arms whereas the democracies promoted social welfare. Although there is some truth to this dichotomy, it is quite inadequate and is distorted in favor of the democracies.

Social welfare distributions did become somewhat broader in scope and somewhat more generous in the leading democracies than in the alleged totalitarian systems. Yet for several reasons the two sets of states did not diverge dramatically in this sphere. Germany already had a relatively advanced social welfare program built into its law, bureaucracies, and public expectations. Paternalist traditions also had deep roots in Russia and Italy. Perhaps more significant, each of the authoritarian regimes recognized that public assistance and social insurance could be shaped to support labor discipline and accelerated productivity. To achieve these goals, social benefits were made contingent on long duration of employment and certain classes of employees were provided with much greater benefits. Further, the three "totalitarian"

---

[89] Landes, *Unbound Prometheus*, p. 413. See also Albert Speer, *Inside the Third Reich* (New York: Macmillan Co., 1970).

[90] Tannenbaum, *Fascist Experience*, chap. 4; and S. J. Woolf, ed., *The Nature of Fascism*, part 3 (New York: Random House, 1969).

regimes emphasized social benefits that promoted larger families, these benefits including family allowances and maternity bonuses. The Soviet Union moved in the 1930s to institute diverse programs with grossly inadequate levels of funding. Italy increased its social benefits very slowly, and Nazi Germany matched increases with some cutbacks in social insurance benefits.

Yet these mediocre records do not contrast sharply with those of the major industrial democracies. Although the United States was forced to spend large sums on direct public assistance during the Great Depression, the national programs of social insurance begun during that decade involved very low benefit levels and narrow coverage of the population. Britain did little more than further nationalize its unemployment insurance program after the sharp expansion of its social programs in the aftermath of the 1914–18 war. Bruce wrote from the perspective of 1939 Britain that "looking back we see the nation, in most matters of social policy, feeling its way forward then, slowly and painfully—too slowly and painfully for the dispossessed—towards a wider sense of social responsibility."[91] Beginning in 1928 France took steps to catch up with Britain and Germany in health and old-age insurance, but it continued to give such programs a low priority.

Higher education was one sector of distributive policy in which Nazi Germany was quite distinguishable from all other major industrial states. The number of students in German universities fell more than 50 percent during the 1930s, and such educational opportunities were particularly restricted for women.[92] Fascist Italy took some steps in the same directions during the 1920s, but allowed its universities to grow rapidly in the 1930s. Apparently, such restrictive policies were primarily practical efforts to relieve the oversupply of graduates. Yet the reductions were also a result of Nazi disruption of the universities.

In contrast to the trends under Nazism the Stalinist system consistently championed higher education for both sexes and administered a "frenzied educational drive."[93] American spending on higher education grew much more slowly during the Depression than during the previous several decades since other social welfare needs provided greater competition for scarce resources. Yet the broad American commitment to maximum periods of mass education was maintained at a level beyond that of any Western European state and helped set the stage for the later Soviet-American competition for leadership in the extension of public higher education.

---

[91] Bruce, *Coming of the Welfare State,* pp. 289–90.

[92] Richard Grunberger, *The 12-Year Reich* (New York: Holt, Rinehart & Winston, 1972), p. 353.

[93] Schwartz, *Russia's Soviet Economy,* p. 522.

The dissimilar approaches taken to female educational opportunity extended to many other areas of government policy. World War I had contributed to the achievement of female suffrage and had opened up many new kinds of jobs for women. Genuine economic opportunities for women were most actively promoted in the Soviet Union. This was most widely opposed, mainly in support of a traditional view of women's role, in the fascist states. The Depression also brought some pressures to decrease female economic opportunity in the democratic systems, though World War II provided fresh opportunities to break new ground.

It would be extraordinary if the vast differences between the democracies and the alleged totalitarian systems in the scope of repression and terror were not reflected in budget distributions. The data confirm our expectations. Labor camps could be profitable, but they and other trappings of the police state had to be capitalized and staffed. The German Ministry of Interior was able to increase its allotments from ninth place among the Nazi ministries in 1934 to a position second only to the military by 1939.[94] As in the Stalinist system, internal security costs were also incurred by numerous agencies other than the Ministry of Interior. The total budgetary costs of Stalinist and Nazi repression and terror can only be estimated, yet were certainly enormous in relation to any nation's previous distributions for such purposes. Despite growing concern for internal security in the major democracies before World War II this sector tended to obtain a declining share of total government spending in those states.

Was governmental pump priming in the various sectors of agriculture and industry, including armaments, a totalitarian monopoly before 1939? The answer to this question is that the Soviet economic distributions were basically different from all the others due to the vastly greater public sector, but that the fascist patterns of help to producers differed from those of the democracies largely in degree — in the amount of subsidies — rather than in kind.

The essential distributive component of the Soviet socioeconomic revolution that began in 1929 was the very heavy priority placed on investment in industry over investment in agriculture and on construction materials, machines, metals, and sources of energy over consumer products. Although inadequate investment levels did not alone determine the continued relative lags in agricultural productivity, this was a contributing factor. Consumer products excluded, the rapid progress in industry was notably broad. This investment program, more than any other aspect of Soviet policy between 1929 and 1941, allowed the USSR to rise from a mediocre ranking in major industrial indicators and arma-

---

[94] David Schoenbaum, *Hitler's Social Revolution* (Garden City, N.Y.: Doubleday & Co., 1966), p. 161.

ments production to one of outproducing Germany by 1943. This success made the Stalinist priorities quite difficult to challenge even after Stalin's death. Many Western scholars have sought to reveal exaggerations in the claimed Soviet industrial achievement, yet even their more conservative figures on industrial growth during the 1930s leave the Soviet Union with one of the fastest rates of industrial growth in world history.[95] This growth provided the base from which Moscow later moved toward quantitative parity with the United States and created major pressures for post-1945 American and Western European acceleration of progress in many areas of technology and productivity.

Governmental investments grew in each of the countries under discussion in such areas as public works, agriculture, and subsidies of companies. Expanded public works were used early and heavily to create jobs in such disparate states as Sweden, the United States, and Germany. Likewise, subsidies to agriculture became major policy instruments to promote stability in that sector in both the United States and Nazi Germany. Fascist Italy and the United States utilized similar structures for pumping needed capital into financially hard-pressed corporations early in the Depression.

The critical factor of rearmament is subject to varying perspectives. The Nazi regime began its concerted effort to achieve arms primacy in Europe only in 1936 and was not nearly as productive in this sphere on the eve or at the peak of the war as some foreign analysts feared. On the other hand, Hitler's regime distinguished itself from its democratic rivals by directing a larger proportion of industrial subsidies to the military-related industries. Further, its armed forces were given a rapidly increasing share of the sharply rising total governmental resources. The major democracies did increase spending considerably through most of the 1930s after some retrenchment during the previous decade. The British, for example, increased their defense budget by more than 300 percent between 1930 and 1938.[96] Yet the decisive trend remained the substantially faster rate of growth of the military sector in Germany and the Soviet Union during this period. Consequently, they were in a position to play the largest roles in the coming war in Europe, especially in terms of manpower.

Extraction: Conscription

Labor conscription and tax policies were extraordinarily intensive in the Soviet Union in the 1930s, but less consistently severe in Italy and Germany. All three regimes employed historically high military con-

---

[95] See Abram Bergson, ed., *Soviet Economic Growth* (Evanston, Ill.: Row, Peterson, 1953).

[96] Peacock and Wiseman, *Growth of Public Expenditure*, p. 170.

scription, but not record rates.[97] Germany and Russia led the major European countries in peacetime use of the draft (as a proportion of population), though Italy trailed slightly behind France in this respect. Britain and the United States, following traditional peacetime approaches, avoided military conscription until each was on the eve of entering World War II.

Forced mobilization of civilian labor was also resorted to in the Soviet Union, Germany, and Italy. In the first two countries, concentration camp systems constituted industrial empires. The three regimes mobilized particular groups, including youth, for such projects as harvesting and land reclamation. One major distinction was the Nazi and Fascist hesitancy to involuntarily mobilize women as compared with the full equality of women in Stalin's civilian labor programs. Further, there were no Nazi or Fascist labor programs equivalent to Stalin's collectivization of agriculture or to the extraordinary restraints on labor mobility operating in the Soviet Union.

The British and American governments avoided any civilian labor drafts during the interwar years. Yet Britain showed its capacity to institute industrial conscription during both world wars and the United States made part of its relief effort contingent on participation in public service labor, while continuing to support the legal structure of extraordinarily exploitative tenant and migrant farming.

Extraction: Taxation

The analysis of taxation alone would not reveal the basic variations in the designated countries' prewar and World War II approaches to revenue-raising. The massive Soviet effort at resource mobilization involved low wages, food expropriated from producers, high retail prices, excessive currency distribution, and compulsory bond purchases in addition to a new tax structure which punished consumers. The outcome of these policies was a significant decline in overall consumer purchasing power while investment funds climbed.

Nazi Germany was less inclined toward such forced material extractions but outdid Moscow in a few areas, including forced bond sales. Like Mussolini's Italy, Hitler's regime put the greater burden on the lower classes through a tax system that was increasingly tipped toward indirect taxes. Yet German corporate and individual income taxes were also increased in order to sustain booming expenditures.

Such democratic capitalist regimes as the British and the American were notably light on extractions of revenue during most of the inter-

---

[97] James M. McConnell, "European Experience with Volunteer and Conscript Forces," *Studies Prepared for the President's Commission on an All-Volunteer Armed Force*, vol. 2, part 3, study 2 (Washington, D.C.: U.S. Government Printing Office, 1970), p. 5.

war period. Britain's taxes and public spending fell slightly as a proportion of gross national product from the early 1920s until its arms program began in earnest in 1938.[98] The comparable ratio rose appreciably in the United States, but this was due as much to the poor performance of the total economy after 1929 as to the modest spending increases approved under the New Deal. The Roosevelt Administration was notable for its break with American restraint on the use of borrowing to sustain the federal budget. Beginning in 1931, budget deficits became a normal part of federal fiscal policy in peacetime, the national debt rising by about 250 percent between 1930 and 1940.

Conclusions: Interwar Collectivism

Our comparison of the alleged totalitarian regimes with various European democracies and the United States emphasized major differences in control over the political process and cultural sectors and pointed out considerable variations in spending on the military and police sectors. However, even in these spheres the Italian Fascist regime tended to occupy a middle ground. In most aspects of economic policy the differences were not great except as between all of the capitalist systems and the Soviet Union. Social distributions did not tend to respond very much to macropolitical variables.

Collectivism did advance substantially during the interwar years and, to an even greater extent, during World War II. Yet this advance did not show up nearly as much in regard to public welfare as in economic regulation during this period of economic and political crisis.

Fascist Italy and Nazi Germany were brought down by the cataclysm that they did so much to create. Stalin's system survived, and it intensified most of its policy orientations during the eight postwar years of that dictator's life. After the war Western Europe became more homogeneous in its political orientation, often synthesizing elements of liberalism and democratic socialist collectivism.

The rise and fall of the Nazi and Fascist regimes gave old-fashioned liberalism a boost, especially in regulatory matters. Some postwar Western states, particularly West Germany and the United States, were eager to separate themselves from the extremes of collectivism represented by those regimes and the surviving Soviet system. However, democratic socialism was quite strong in most of the remaining Western European states at the close of World War II and no general retreat from collectivism took place. On the contrary, the war intensified the movement toward the welfare state as well as toward new levels of planning and regulation. The Soviet Union resumed many of its more extreme pre-

---

[98] Peacock and Wiseman, *Growth of Public Expenditure*, pp. 190–91.

war policies until the death of Stalin in 1953 and the emergence of Khrushchev as an inconsistent liberalizing force.

Was there a totalitarian era and, if there was, is it now merely a legacy of the past? We have indicated our skepticism of the totalitarian model as an analytic or descriptive tool. The alleged totalitarian systems often faced problems similar to those of democratic countries and frequently developed policies that were close to those of the Western democracies. What made Nazism and Stalinism unique were the terrors that destroyed tens of millions of people and the scope of cultural penetration. Even in these areas Italian Fascism tended to be a rather half-baked version. The Stalinist system was easily the most ambitious, and the Nazi regime the most capable of putting its policies into effect.

The legacies of Nazism and Fascism have taken various forms in the successor regimes. In some areas, as in Italian criminal law, Fascist-made policies remained operative for decades. In West German education, the rejection of the Nazi approach has reinforced a return to a pre-Nazi traditionalism. Such elements of constitutional structure as parliamentary power and federalism have profited from the negative example set by Nazism.

The heritage is less clear in the Soviet Union. Stalin died, and Khrushchev undertook a partial anti-Stalin campaign. But "Stalin's heirs" continue to exercise power at all levels of Soviet society.[99] The "cult of personality" and the terror are in disrepute, and "socialist legality" is praised, but many of the basic Stalinist policies have not undergone major change. Since Khrushchev's ouster in 1964, evolutionary reforms in such sectors as industrial administration and social welfare have been combined with renewed repression of dissident groups. No firm or broad attack on Stalinism has been sustained.

CONCLUSION: PATTERNS AND STAGES

The reader has been taken on a long journey through doctrines, policies, and eras. It has been our intention to provide a long-term perspective for the analysis of contemporary policy. We have found that a strong case can be made for the traditional character of broad governmental involvement in societal, and especially economic, affairs. This involvement developed in the Middle Ages and grew into national policies with the emerging European monarchies. However, mercantilist regulation and promotion of the economy were often not implemented effectively, and true planned regulation did not develop until the present century.

---

[99] "Stalin's Heirs" was the title of a poem written by Yevgenii Yevtushenko. "Neo-Stalinism" is discussed in Roy A. Medvedev, *On Socialist Democracy* (New York: Alfred A. Knopf, 1975), pp. 48–65, 318–32.

In such areas as public assistance, the negative and limited scope of mercantilist and classical liberal orientations have cast a pall over movement toward a genuine welfare state up to the present. The idea of a minimal government obligation to aid the poor emerged at the local level in mercantilist monarchies. Restrictions on such assistance were later refined under the banner of liberalism, especially in Britain and the United States. The contemporary welfare state depended on a break from the attitudes of classical liberalism and an expansion of the approaches of conservative paternalism.

Although the physical environment was victimized by classical liberal influences, present-day protection requires a return to some older attitudes toward limiting individual and corporate abuses. Centuries-old sources of pollution have been combined with the results of recent technology, urbanization, and industrial growth. Unfortunately, few effective approaches to pollution control were bequeathed to our generation.

Political rights have grown considerably in the leading democracies during the past several centuries. Yet the world has experienced in this century two political regimes which rank as the most destructive of lives and liberties of any in history. The present world society functions very much in the shadow of Nazism and Stalinism, the latter only partially supplanted.

In addition to providing background information, the present chapter has approached the question of the relationship between doctrines and policy. One finding is that pure tests of such correlations are difficult to make because doctrines have often competed with one another. In no country did a single body of mercantilist or classical liberal ideas reign alone.

Even when a single approach — or even an ideology — achieved a degree of dominance, policy reacted to other forces and the need for pragmatic adjustments. Thus regulations gradually emerged in the liberal United States of the late 19th century and Stalin shifted course on several occasions regarding such issues as organized religion.

Nonetheless, we believe that we have established that doctrines mattered in every era discussed. European and North American social, economic, and cultural policies often moved in identifiable patterns and cycles. Ideas have provided some cohesion and direction to the development of policy trends.

We have also identified the fact that certain currents flow regardless of regimes or ideologies. The welfare state and economic regulation have been expanded and intensified by nearly all recent governments. Common problems resulting from transnational technological, economic, and military development require policy responses that often defy labeling as communist, socialist, or liberal.

6 Distributions: The Welfare State

While doubtful about the benefits of many governmental regulations and most extractions, the average citizen appreciates many public distributions of goods and services. In this and the following chapter we are interested in the patterns of such allocations in the eight chosen nations.

One such pattern, the welfare state, involves policies and programs designed to place at least a safety net under most residents. This net ensures that people will not be compelled to do without food, shelter, health care, or other basic human needs. The welfare state gradually developed as a structure of programs sustained by bureaucracies and their clienteles. New needs began to be satisfied, and increasingly higher standards were set for most of the core provisions.

Analysts of contemporary public policy offer varying assessments concerning the degree to which welfare objectives have been achieved. Some believe that the welfare state has stalled or stagnated in the face of such pressures as mass resistance to higher taxes, high defense spending, and concentration on industrial growth and profits.[1] Others write positively concerning major break-throughs in programs and levels of expenditure.

Proponents of still another view suggest that the welfare state has been developed largely in terms of what we call outputs, but not in regard to outcomes. These contemporary critics of the welfare state, largely but not exclusively conservative, reflect broad public disillusionment with contemporary society and place much of the blame on government for the shortcomings.[2]

Just as the whole range of policies — distributive, extractive, and regulative — is involved with the welfare state, so all of these policies contribute to the contemporary military-industrial state. We mean by this the development of large and well-equipped military units, backed by a strong industrial capacity that can be readily converted to additional production for aggression or defense. Burdensome tax increases and compulsory military service usually become necessary. A strong military emphasis may distort economic and social life through the diversion of human, financial, and other resources into the defense sector. It may involve concentration on the production of "heavy" industrial goods, violations of individual rights in deference to national security, and an affinity for shifting resources to foreign trouble spots. It is a phenomenon of contemporary life that is often condemned and is usually defended only as an unpleasant necessity.

New forces and pressures can be viewed as taking public policy in the most highly developed countries beyond the confines of the military-industrial and welfare states. Among these factors are affluence, the satisfaction of basic welfare goals, mass higher education, occupational shifts from manufacturing to services, and new technological capabilities in fields ranging from communications to medicine. Post-industrialism has been discussed thus far by social scientists principally in relation to such developments and only marginally in terms of politics and public policy.[3] But an agenda of new policy issues is emerging, propelled by a broadened and intensified interest in the physical environment, equality for women and national minorities, privacy and personal freedom, expanded participation in politics and openness in governmental processes, new social services relating to culture and

---

[1] James O'Connór, The Fiscal Crisis of the State (New York: St. Martin's Press, 1973); and Bruce R. Russett, What Price Vigilance? (New Haven: Yale University Press, 1970).

[2] Roger A. Freeman, The Growth of American Government (Stanford, Calif.: Hoover Institution Press, 1975).

[3] The shortage of policy discussion in this literature is emphasized in Samuel Huntington, "Postindustrial Politics: How Benign Will It Be?" Comparative Politics 6, no. 2 (January 1974): 163–91. See also M. Donald Hancock and Gideon Sjoberg, eds., Politics in the Post-Welfare State (New York: Columbia University Press, 1972); and Daniel Bell, The Coming of Post-Industrial Society (New York: Basic Books, 1973).

leisure, the promotion of alternative life-styles, and lifetime education and training. New issues are continually added to this list, as political concerns inevitably respond to social, technological, and economic developments.

Such an agenda of new issues coexists with continuing national security and social welfare concerns. We will seek to explore in these chapters the comparative impacts of the older and newer spheres of public policy in each of the eight countries, especially as they affect distributive programs and priorities.

Public Goods and Grants

This chapter is focused on efforts by government to distribute goods and services. The goods include cash, food, and housing; education, health care, and transportation are among the services. In practice, a contemporary industrial state tends to provide an enormous range of goods and services.

In order to categorize such goods and services and move toward a theory of their allocation, economists have developed the concept of public (or collective) goods as well as that of the "grants economy."[4] Neither concept has yet led very far toward a theory of how goods and services are allocated or the criteria for choice. Yet both can contribute to shaping our view of what distinguishes governmental "gifts."

Initial writings on public goods by Paul Samuelson, Richard Musgrave, and others focused on those goods and services provided by government that were deemed "pure" in that their benefits are not easily viewed as divisible among the sectors of the community and are seen as being consumed equally by all people. The goods and services included in the provision of national security through military power were often suggested as models of the pure public good. Such goods and services cannot be effectively supplied without government involvement, and individuals cannot effectively determine the personal benefits derived from them.

Revisions of public goods theory place more attention on "quasi-collective" goods that differ from pure goods in that "the consumption of units by one person must decrease the availability of units for others in the group."[5] Most such goods turn out to be supplied only in part by

---

[4] For a summary of the theory of public goods see John G. Head, *Public Goods and Public Welfare* (Durham, N.C.: Duke University Press, 1974); for an introduction to the grants economy approach see Kenneth E. Boulding, *The Economy of Love and Fear: A Preface to Grants Economics* (Belmont, Calif.: Wadsworth Publishing Co., 1973).

[5] James M. Buchanan, *Public Finance in Democratic Process* (Chapel Hill: University of North Carolina Press, 1967), p. 18.

government and to be consumed in a manner that is not indivisible. Both the private sector and the public sector can supply health, education, and housing. The provision of these goods and services benefits some individuals more than others but also serves public interests.

The concept of "grants economics" has emerged during the past decade in response to a growing view that the theory of public goods constitutes a futile effort to force the framework of exchange economics, derived from analysis of the marketplace, onto the operations of public finance. According to Kenneth E. Boulding, governmental programs are not the stuff of a trip to the marketplace at all. Rather, they constitute gifts and tribute that are provided out of a mixture of love and fear. Such grants, viewed as widespread in private relationships, are seen as central to government distributions. As such, the public is acting like a parent in relation to its children when it establishes priorities. It creates through public officials "a system of related one-way transfers rather than a system of exchange."[6]

Such grants are deemed to be implicit as well as explicit. Implicit grants include transfers that result from the application of what we term extractive and regulative policies. Taxes and business regulations offer material benefits and losses to those affected by them that often exceed gains and losses from budgeted expenditures.

Thus we are offered a conceptual basis for approaching the study of the governmental supply of goods and services. It is the study of public goods, more or less "pure," and of grants, varyingly explicit and implicit. For a given individual the outcome is the sum of his or her costs and benefits, with extractions, regulations, and distributions all contributing to the result. For some goods the recipient may be what the economists call a "free rider," enjoying without cost. For others he or she may be paying more than a fair share, often without an accurate idea of the actual costs.

Distribution and Redistribution

The politics of the distribution of goods and services may increase or decrease inequalities among classes, national and religious groups, races, sexes, age groups, and regions in a particular country. The political scientists Theodore J. Lowi and T. Alexander Smith term redistributive those policies with the potential to reallocate major values among broad categories of people.[7] Some policies, including income taxation

---

[6] Boulding, *Economy of Love and Fear*, p. 6.

[7] Theodore J. Lowi, "American Business, Public Policy, Case-Studies, and Political Theory," *World Politics* 16 (July 1964): 677–715; and T. Alexander Smith, *The Comparative Policy Process* (Santa Barbara, Calif.: ABC-CLIO, 1975).

and public assistance, are distinguished from such decisions as are involved in patronage and pork barrel programs. The latter, termed distributive policies, are viewed as being dispensed through isolated and discrete actions that result in gainers but not losers. Lowi includes among distributive policies public works projects, defense procurement, and the "traditional" tariff.

Separating different kinds of distributions (and extractions) in this manner, Lowi and Smith are able to formulate an interesting framework for analyzing policy processes. They contend that distributive and redistributive politics involve fundamentally different processes, patterns of structural interactions, and styles. Although their initial formulations have been challenged,[8] the distinction between distributive and redistributive processes appears to have some value for the analysis of political systems at work.

However, the same distinction appears to be of limited value for the present effort to distinguish basic patterns of governmental allocation of goods and services. As acknowledged by Lowi, redistributive processes often fail to produce actual redistribution. Conversely, the sum of the "isolated" decisions of pork barrel distributions may produce substantial reallocation of resources among classes or regions. Consequently, we will consider as distributions all programs designed to provide or implicitly offering benefits through the expenditure budgets of government.

The Choices

The politics of distribution involves numerous basic kinds of choices. Private and public investment and consumption, civilian and military sectors, and various regions and classes all compete for allocations. Intensive competition also proceeds within such broad categories for whatever resources are available. Education may well compete with health, and the army with the navy.

Modern fiscal and monetary policy requires choices to be made prior to the dividing of collective resources. Government must be responsive to the stability and growth of economic systems as well as to gaps in the provision of public goods and services. In some situations, as when high unemployment and recession are present without high inflation, macroeconomic policy will call for an increased money supply, lower interest rates for borrowing, and more funds for job-intensive and pro-

---

[8] See Barry S. Rundquist and John A. Ferejohn, "Observations on a Distributive Theory of Public Policy: Two American Expenditure Programs Compared," in Craig Liske, William Loehr, and John McCamant, eds., *Comparative Public Policy: Issues, Theories, and Methods* (Beverly Hills, Calif.: Sage Publications, 1975), pp. 87–108.

duction-intensive sectors. When inflation or international balance-of-payments deficits constitute major concerns, pressures for decreased government expenditures may well overwhelm calls for easy money and enlarged programs. However, the principal macroeconomic illnesses tend to come in combinations that defy simple medication.

States differ substantially in their sensitivity to particular economic problems. Britain has a reputation for concern about unemployment and has been under great pressure to adjust to balance-of-payment problems throughout much of the post-1945 period. West Germany, reflecting its experience with devastating inflation in the interwar period, is considered to be exceptionally alert to price trends. Yet all advanced industrial states assert a major concern for economic growth, inflation, unemployment, and balance-of-payments equilibrium.

Most industrial states have recently become more concerned about evaluating social and physical environmental impacts of policy, trends that have broadened earlier economic and political emphases.[9] Nonetheless, the exceptionally difficult economic problems of the 1970s have been a force for retaining "economic primacy" in North American and Western European budget policy. The Communist-ruled states in our survey have established an even more economic-centered orientation than operates in the West, with an overwhelming emphasis on industrial growth.

The Welfare State

The military-industrial and welfare states are competitive but not necessarily mutually exclusive. Although military budgets have followed somewhat erratic patterns since 1945, direct public benefits to individuals and families have grown steadily. The welfare state, though failing to accomplish some of its minimal goals in most countries in our survey, has advanced in each since 1945.

The nature of the welfare state has varied from decade to decade and from country to country. We have shown in Chapter 5 that elements of the welfare state existed in Europe as early as the 16th century. Yet Wilensky's conception of its essence, "government-protected minimum standards of income, nutrition, health, housing, and education, assured to every citizen as a political right, not as charity," was not fully accepted in industrial states until after 1945.[10] Since that date minimal welfare standards have been adopted as part of the Universal Declara-

---

[9] Governmental Statistical Services, *Social Trends*, no. 4, 1973 (London: H.M.S.O., 1973); and Office of Management and Budget, *Social Indicators, 1973* (Washington, D.C.: U.S. Government Printing Office, 1973).

[10] Harold L. Wilensky, *The Welfare State and Equality* (Berkeley: University of California Press, 1975), p. 1.

tion of Human Rights (United Nations, 1948) and through various conventions of the International Labor Organization.

Although no dramatic events have spurred the expansion of the welfare state since World War II, this direction of public policy has advanced steadily in scope of services, inclusion of larger parts of the population, and levels of benefits. New goals of equal opportunity have emerged, and the 1942 Beveridge conception of minimum fixed benefits has been replaced in some countries by policies designed to redistribute income and provide benefits that approach or exceed average wage levels.

Although each of the eight countries in this survey can plausibly be termed a welfare state each differs in its degree of progress from minimal to high standards of benefits. Most have not yet approached the extent of educational opportunity in the few states which have virtually universal secondary education. Health and housing are provided by an extremely wide variety of mixes of public and private resources. And although destitution has not been eliminated in any of these states, some have come much closer to winning their "war against poverty" than have others.

The welfare state is presented here in terms of income maintenance and health services. Along with education these areas involve the largest expenditures of funds and manpower. Certain other welfare programs, including recreation, are viewed as belonging to an essentially postwelfare conception of national responsibility. Education, viewed as an area that contributes to warfare, welfare, and post-industrial priorities, is discussed under the last of these headings in Chapter 7.

INCOME MAINTENANCE

The origins and core of the contemporary welfare state lie in the concept of income maintenance. The Universal Declaration of Human Rights affirms "the [individual's] right to security in the event of unemployment, sickness, disability, widowhood, old age or other lack of livelihood in circumstances beyond his control."[11] This social security can be provided by public expenditures, tax allowances, and mandatory obligations on employers.[12] The three main means by which the state distributes benefits through expenditures are: (1) *public assistance:* normally paid from general taxation; generally limited to those who apply and pass a means test that establishes individual need; (2)

---

[11] Article 25, 1948.

[12] P. R. Kaim-Caudle, *Comparative Social Policy and Social Security: A Ten Country Study* (London: Martin Robertson, 1973), pp. 6–13.

social insurance: generally given only to those who have contributed or on whose behalf contributions have been made; paid from insurance-type contributions alone or in combination with governmental funds; and (3) universal benefits: given to residents or citizens because they fall into such defined categories as children, mothers, or the elderly; require neither contributions nor means tests and are usually financed from general taxation.

Although developed in the order in which they have been presented, the three forms of income maintenance continue to supplement one another in most advanced welfare states. It is argued that such nations "seem to be working towards an overall pattern of social security consisting of a basic universal benefit, supplemented by a wage-related, actuarially calculated, insurance benefit for the better off; and for the relatively poor and underprivileged, by an assistance scheme which emphasizes needs rather than means, and which attempts to meet the individual's needs with services as well as cash allowances."[13]

No single measurement can categorize the income maintenance programs of the eight designated countries. A broad assessment should consider overall levels of funding, the scope of particular programs, and evidence of leadership toward efficient and equitable services.

No one country embodies all the social security features that are being emulated and developed by other countries. The attributes of efficiency and progressiveness constitute movement toward:

1. Universal consolidated coverage. Such frequently ignored groups as farm, self-employed, migrant, casual, and household workers are being incorporated into social insurance plans. Separate plans for various occupation groups are being eliminated or coordinated.
2. Social assistance becoming more firmly based on legal entitlement and the arbitrary and humiliating character of its administration being reduced.
3. Social insurance benefits increasing in relation to poverty levels, average wages, and the wage record of the recipient. Minimum benefits are being raised to reduce dependence on social assistance.
4. Earners of higher incomes gaining the opportunity to secure larger, earnings-based benefits.
5. Benefits being automatically reviewed and increased in order to keep up with higher prices, wages, and salaries.
6. More rational integration of tax policy, private pensions, and all kinds of social security distributions to ensure that increased bene-

---

[13] Barbara N. Rodgers, John Greve, and John S. Morgan, Comparative Social Administration, 2d ed. (London: George Allen & Unwin, 1971), pp. 236–37.

fits in one program are not taken back by lost eligibility for another.

7. Reduction or elimination of discrimination between the sexes in eligibility and benefits.

8. Variation in benefits to fit various levels of actual financial need, including adjustment for the number and age of dependents.

9. Extension of the duration of preretirement insurance benefits so as to reduce the need for public assistance in cases of extended unemployment or disability.

10. Broadening of social insurance coverage to include protection for unemployment, maternity, and accidents occurring outside the place of employment.

11. Assistance for the working poor that does not create an excessive employment disincentive.

12. Providing levels of benefits for preretirement income losses that are unrelated to the cause of disability or unemployment.

13. Implementing extensive programs to promote employment, including job training, public employment, regional aid, promotion of labor mobility, and controls on layoffs of workers.

The standard statistical presentations of "social security" expenditures combine health and income maintenance data in such a way as to obscure the levels of government spending in the two areas. With this caveat in mind, the reader will find the eight survey countries ranked in Table 6–1 in order of their 1966 levels of social security spending as a percentage of GNP. The nine members of the European Communities are ranked in Table 6–2 according to their 1972 ranking. The two tables differ regarding the definition of social security and GNP. (While factor price GNP—also known as national income—measures the cost of producing goods and services, market price GNP measures the economy's

TABLE 6–1
Social Security Spending as Percentage of GNP at Factor Cost

	1949	1955	1961	1966	1968	1970
West Germany	13.7	17.4	18.0	19.6	23.1	22.6
France	11.0	16.0	16.1	18.3	21.4	20.9
Sweden	9.1	11.6	12.9	17.5	–	–
Italy	8.2	11.2	12.8	17.5	21.1	21.1
East Germany	–	–	–	16.4	17.1	–
United Kingdom	10.6	19.9	12.6	14.4	17.1	–
Soviet Union	–	8.1	9.6	10.1	–	–
United States	4.4	5.4	7.7	7.9	–	–

Sources: Data from International Labor Office, *The Cost of Social Security, 1964–66* (Geneva, 1972), pp. 317–23; European Communities Statistical Office, *Sozialkonten, 1962–70* (Luxembourg, 1972), pp. 18–19; Bundesministerium für innerdeutsche Beziehungen, *Bericht des Bundesregierung und Materialien zur Lage der Nation, 1971* (Bonn: 1971), p. 397; as compiled in Harold L. Wilensky, *The Welfare State and Equality* (Berkeley: University of California Press, 1975), pp. 30–31. Copyright © 1975 by Harold L. Wilensky; reprinted by permission of the University of California Press.

TABLE 6–2
Social Security Expenditure as Percentage of GNP at Market Prices in
European Communities Member States

	1962	1966	1968	1970	1972
Netherlands	12.2	16.5	17.5	18.6	20.6
Denmark	–	–	–	19.4	20.4
Italy	11.9	15.9	16.4	16.5	20.4
West Germany	14.5	16.0	17.2	17.4	18.7
Luxembourg	13.9	16.1	17.3	15.9	18.6
Belgium	13.4	15.1	16.5	16.0	17.1
France	13.1	15.5	15.9	15.9	16.4
United Kingdom	–	–	–	13.7	14.0
Ireland	–	–	–	10.6	11.0

Source: Statistical Office of the European Communities, *Basic Statistics of the Community, 1973–1974* (Brussels, 1975), p. 91.

total output of goods and services, valued at current market prices paid by the ultimate consumer.)

Mixing these and other statistics with authoritative assessments of our other major bases of evaluation, we conclude that the eight survey countries fall into four sets of two in regard to the overall standards of their income maintenance programs. The leaders, Sweden and West Germany, are followed fairly closely by France and Italy. Britain and East Germany failed to keep up with the strong pace of development of the top four and constitute a third set. Finally, the United States and the Soviet Union retain some of the most glaring gaps to be found in the social security systems of highly industrialized nations.

Sweden and West Germany

The leadership of Sweden and West Germany is based on factors extending beyond total expenditures for social security. The incomplete available data presented in Table 6–1 indicate that France, Italy, and East Germany have rivaled these countries in such distributions. As late as 1972 Italy continued to match the rapid growth of the Swedish and West German systems.

No state's social programs have been more highly praised than Sweden's. Martin Schnitzer found there "the most comprehensive set of welfare measures of any country in the world."[14] He and others have claimed for Sweden unparalleled success in resolving problems of un-

---

[14] Martin Schnitzer, *The Economy of Sweden* (New York: Praeger Publishers, 1970), p. 16. For a much less effusive view of the standards of Sweden's distributions see Albert H. Rosenthal, *The Social Programs of Sweden* (Minneapolis: University of Minnesota Press, 1967).

employment, poverty, and income inequality through tax, social security, and employment policies.

First with a national pension program for all citizens, Sweden today has exceptional retirement benefits. Its earnings-related supplementary pension, added to a foundational basic grant, is designed to provide the majority of retirees with 60 percent of the annual earned income averaged during the 15 best years before retirement. Unemployment and disability insurance was upgraded in 1974 to provide 90 percent of regular earnings for the average worker. On the basis of somewhat lower earlier benefit levels Wilensky found Sweden's expenditures per recipient in "a class of its own—tops by every measure we can devise."[15]

The avante-garde character of the Swedish welfare system is reflected in its recent addition of paternity benefits to its outstanding range of aids to mothers and babies. Further, the active program for combating unemployment through training, relocation, and other means is second to none in expenditure and commitment.[16]

West Germany's social security system also stands out for its innovations and well-rounded character. The Bonn government leads in relating benefit levels to increases in wages and productivity, "dynamic" insurance that allows recipients to profit from strong economic growth together with the active work force. West Germans also enjoy a unique allocation of full pay for the first six weeks of employment disability. One authority claims that the 1969 Wage Payment Continuation Act "placed the incapacitated worker in Germany in a financial position unequalled anywhere in the world."[17] Citizens of West Germany became accustomed to fairly adequate pension levels before other Western European retirement programs exceeded minimum standards. They have also come to expect an exceptional program of assistance in securing employment.

The consistently high standards of Bonn's social insurance offerings are reflected in the conclusions of a comparative analysis of six programs in ten countries (which excluded Sweden, France, and Italy).[18] West Germany's programs ranked as one of the two most progressive in regard to employment injury, temporary disability, old-age, and unem-

---

[15] Wilensky, *Welfare State*, p. 17.

[16] See Santosh Mukherjee, *Making Labour Markets Work* (London: Political and Economic Planning, 1972).

[17] Kaim-Caudle, *Comparative Social Policy*, p. 125. For further information see *Survey of Social Security in the Federal Republic of Germany* (Bonn: Federal Minister of Labour and Social Affairs, 1972).

[18] Kaim-Caudle, *Comparative Social Policy*, pp. 300–306. The other nations surveyed were Austria, Ireland, Britain, Denmark, the Netherlands, Canada, New Zealand, Australia, and the United States.

ployment protection. This survey extended to such factors as criteria for eligibility, the duration of benefits, and benefit levels.

Although leaders, these countries have not been without problems and shortcomings in social security policy. Sweden was not strong in pensions until after its supplementary program was developed, beginning in 1960.[19] With augmented benefits enacted so recently, many Swedes reaching retirement age in the 1960s and 1970s do not reap full superannuation benefits. West Germany continues to suffer from excessive administrative fragmentation, with separate funds for various categories of citizens. Bonn has also been late in providing assured coverage for farmers and other self-employed persons, and has only recently raised its family allowances to a level near those of its neighbors.

France and Italy

As will be evident in regard to numerous other areas of policy, France and Italy maintain major similarities in their social security systems. Both cover high proportions of their citizens and provide protection against a wide range of conditions. Among the ways in which they differ from Sweden and Germany are greater variations in the standards of the various programs and greater administrative fragmentation and complexity.

French and Italian families receive family allowances that are among the world's largest.[20] In France the allowances are linked to an outstanding network of family-oriented benefits in cash and services.[21] Such programs go far toward assuring adequate resources for the families of low-paid workers. On the other hand, some observers believe that the existence of high allowances encourages the payment of relatively low minimum incomes in these countries.

France has long maintained such weaknesses in its social security programs as relatively low retirement pensions, sharp limits on survivor rights, and the omission of statutory unemployment insurance. Improvements have been made in these areas in recent years, especially since the election of President Giscard d'Estaing in 1974. In 1975 the unemployment protection gap was largely closed. However, the pension program remains fragmented and includes difficult eligibility requirements for full benefits.

Italy inherited from the Fascist era the most complex and, probably,

---

[19] Hugh Heclo, *Modern Social Politics in Britain and Sweden* (New Haven: Yale University Press, 1974), pp. 227–53.

[20] For a comparison of OECD countries see *Revenue Statistics of O.E.C.D. Member Countries, 1965–1972* (Paris: OECD, 1975), p. 220.

[21] See Rodgers, Greve, and Morgan, *Comparative Social Administration*, pp. 65–70, 313–38.

least efficient social security system in Western Europe. Although Italy's benefits tend to be somewhat more generous than those of France in relation to average wages, unemployment insurance has also been a weak area in Italy. Although limited by continued cabinet instability, progress has recently been made in the reorganization of program administration, movement toward wage-related benefits, and increased minimum pensions to complement the high maximum levels.[22]

Britain and East Germany

The countries that make up our third set constitute an odd couple by most standards. Both are about average for Europe in income maintenance benefits. They have opted for more restrictive programs than those of the leaders in continental Western Europe.

East Germany has been strongly affected by both the pre-1945 German traditions of social security and the need to harmonize with the Soviet Union's approaches.[23] The result is an impressive program with near-universal coverage of population and risks. With a probirth policy akin to that of France, the German Democratic Republic has strong maternity and child allowance programs. The close association achieved between income maintenance and economic productivity policies produces strengths and weaknesses. As in other Communist-ruled countries, the greatest benefits go to the active working population through sickness and disability benefits. The reverse of this generosity is reflected in the exceptionally meager provision (10 percent of earnings as basic benefit) for the unemployed. Further, old-age pensions fall substantially behind those of West Germany even as a proportion of average earnings.[24] Until 1971 little effort was made to meet the larger pension needs of higher paid workers. The inequalities embodied in the system of special pensions paid to a substantial number of highly valued citizens have been continued.

The British welfare state is often viewed by North Americans as an all-encompassing system that is overburdening the economy of the United Kingdom. Yet many British authorities contend, and few deny, that the country so closely identified with the welfare state has fallen years behind much of continental Europe in benefit levels and other

---

[22] *Report on the Development of the Social Situation in the Community in 1973* (Brussels: Commission, European Communities, 1974), p. 171; and *Social and Labour Bulletin*, vol. 2, September 1975 (Geneva: ILO), pp. 303–4.

[23] For comparisons between East and West German social security systems see Martin Schnitzer, *East and West Germany: A Comparative Economic Analysis* (New York: Praeger Publishers, 1972), especially pp. 416–27; and Stanley Radcliffe, *25 Years On* (London: George G. Harrap, 1972), pp. 171–230.

[24] Schnitzer, *East and West Germany*, p. 417.

policies.[25] The United Kingdom has been termed an "irresponsible society" by Richard Titmuss and "the unpaternal state" by Andrew Shonfield.[26]

The social security programs of the 1940s, identified with William Beveridge, constituted an achievement as limited in certain ways as it was progressive in others. National insurance was limited by its non-compulsory treatment of married women employees, benefits below subsistence levels, the absence of earnings-related benefits as a basis for the security of better paid workers, and token acceptance of family allowances.[27] Despite these shortcomings Britain was a leader in social insurance in the late 1940s, providing most citizens with protection against a broad range of risks.

This initial effort was followed by what Shonfield described as "a failure to consolidate and to build further on foundations that had been established in Britain in advance of other European countries."[28] Unlike the leading providers of social insurance, the British have only belatedly and on a limited scale adjusted earnings-related benefits that extend the "flat-rate" distributions designed to provide uniform minimum standards. Further, social insurance benefits continue to be deeply entangled with the tax system as well as public assistance. Increased insurance benefits are frequently "clawed back" by Britain's income tax, and public assistance is required to bring large numbers of social insurance beneficiaries up to minimum income levels.

No other nation studies social security and argues about alternative approaches more than the British. Unfortunately, this interest long contributed to a virtual stalemate in this policy area. Various plans were endorsed by one major party or the other and then scrapped before initiation or implementation. Few major shortcomings of the 40s' system were effectively alleviated during the 1950s and 1960s. A significant breakthrough appears to have been made by the Labour government that took office in 1974. Progressive and expensive steps were taken to incorporate married women into the compulsory schemes, raise pensions by as much as 70 percent, and integrate several of the programs that were previously administered separately. However, the Wilson government's decision to continue the emphasis on flat-rate benefits

---

[25] See Sir John Walley, *Social Security—Another British Failure* (London: Charles Knight & Co., 1972); J. C. Kincaid, *Poverty and Equality in Britain* (Baltimore: Penguin Books, 1973); and A. B. Atkinson, *Poverty in Britain and the Reform of Social Security* (Cambridge, England: Cambridge University Press, 1969).

[26] Richard M. Titmuss, *Essays on the Welfare State*, 2d ed. (Boston: Beacon Press, 1963), p. 243; and Andrew Shonfield, *Modern Capitalism* (New York: Oxford University Press, 1969), p. 112.

[27] Heclo, *Modern Social Politics*, pp. 253–59.

[28] Shonfield, *Modern Capitalism*, p. 91.

left unresolved the insufficiency of benefits for higher-paid workers and many short-term beneficiaries. Britain is moving hesitantly to develop a wage-related benefits system and to routinize procedures for benefit increases. Although its relative commitment to income maintenance has recently increased considerably, Britain remains substantially behind many of its European Communities neighbors in the evolution of social security.

The United States and the Soviet Union

The designation superpower has been earned by the United States and the Soviet Union largely as a result of their military achievements and capabilities. In contrast, both have lagged behind most industrialized countries in the provision of cash and in-kind benefits to their people. Of the countries in our survey these nations have been the last to provide many basic programs and remain short of a number of international standards for benefits, eligibility, and coverage.

The United States operates clearly inadequate programs for short-term income loss and assistance to families, whereas its largest program, for retirement and survivors' pensions, reflects higher standards. Improving more in benefit levels than in other aspects of program structure, American income maintenance expenditures (including related health and medical programs) rose from 7.5 percent of GNP in 1965 to 12.2 percent in 1973.[29] Yet no major overhaul of social programs was implemented during this period.

The long-standing deficiencies in American public assistance and short-term social insurance are numerous and serious. At the heart of the matter are state-administered programs that vary between the scandalous and the barely adequate in their benefits and methods of operation. In 1973, under the Aid to Families with Dependent Children (AFDC) program, the maximum cash grant to a family of four with no earned income ranged from $60 in Mississippi to $364 in Michigan. Wilensky repeated in 1975 what he had originally written a decade earlier: "Our support of national welfare programs is halting; our administration of services for the less privileged is mean."[30] A public assistance crisis was declared by President Nixon in 1969. Yet, says Gilbert Steiner, "Low benefit amounts, great variations among the states in assistance payments, and increasing costs and increasing num-

---

[29] Alfred M. Skolnik and Sophie R. Dales, "Social Welfare Expenditures, Fiscal Year 1974," *Social Security Bulletin* 38, no. 1 (January 1975): 12. These figures are only roughly comparable with those in Tables 6–1 and 6–2.

[30] Wilensky, *Welfare State*, p. 32.

bers of recipients (especially deserted and unmarried mothers) despite both high employment and extensions of social security coverage could have been officially labeled 'crises' at least as early as 1965."[31] To this list can be added the often irrational gaps in provision for families with unemployable or unemployed fathers and for those without children, the large disparities in cash grants offered to the various categories of recipients, and the heavy penalties against earnings by beneficiaries of most programs.

Short-term social insurance benefits have also been criticized by close observers. Ranking programs operating in wealthy countries in 1969, Kaim-Caudle found those in the United States to be among the all-around worst two of ten for employment injury, temporary disability, invalidity, and unemployment.[32] For family endowment, the United States stood out as the only major industrial country not providing benefits through social insurance or universal grants. American social insurance has also been plagued by the absence of national uniformity and by inadequate minimal levels. The major losers are persons who must suddenly discontinue active employment. Such people have long been subjected to low benefits, great difficulty in meeting eligibility requirements, and short benefit duration. Americans involved in maternity or long-term unemployment receive treatment from social insurance that is farthest behind contemporary Western European standards.

Although the United States had become by the mid-1960s "a specialist in pensions," this reflected as much the relative weakness of the other schemes as the strength of retirement and survivorship programs.[33] Pensioners enjoy the advantages of supportive federal administration and coverage of 90 percent of the employed population, both factors contrasting with state-run social insurance. However, Old Age and Survivors Insurance (OASI) has suffered until recently from low benefits resulting from dependence on quite limited employer and employee contributions. Further, until 1974 the gaps in cash provisions had to be filled by widely varying state public assistance programs.

Although not given a needed full renovation, the American income maintenance system has progressed during the past decade. Major recent improvements include the establishment of uniform federal assistance to the aged, blind, and totally disabled; automatic price-related increases for OASI pensions; federally funded extensions of unemploy-

---

[31] Gilbert Steiner, *The State of Welfare* (Washington, D.C.: Brookings Institution, 1971), pp. 77–78.

[32] Kaim-Caudle, *Comparative Social Policy*, pp. 290–312.

[33] Wilensky, *Welfare State*, p. 105.

ment payments; the beginnings of aid to the working poor through tax credits; and the slight reduction of penalties against increased earnings by public assistance and social insurance recipients.[34]

Perhaps the most significant of these changes has been the creation of large and expensive programs for medical services and food purchases. Medicare and Medicaid will be discussed below in relation to health programs. Food stamps have largely replaced commodity food surplus distributions as a major supplement to the incomes of poor and lower-middle-income households. In the less generous states food stamps provide greater assistance to AFDC recipients than do the basic cash grants. This program greatly reduces benefit disparities in state-administered programs and potentially reaches needy people who are not eligible for categorical public assistance programs. However, the poor need more cash income, and the increased dependence on in-kind assistance is in many ways a throwback to the earliest forms of poor relief.

The income maintenance system of the Soviet Union followed a course similar to that of the United States. Both countries molded infant systems in the 1930s, starved them through most of the 40s and 50s, and subsequently developed more mature and complete programs that left intact unfortunate legacies of the past.

The Stalinist regime built its industrial and military might very much at the expense of social security beneficiaries. The same low pension maximums established in 1932 were still in force in 1956; public assistance remained erratic and meager; and most shorter-term benefits were closely tied to long and continuous employment records.[35] A pattern of widely varying benefits to distinct categories of workers was developed. The unemployed, the most poorly paid, the many collective farmers, and most retirees and invalids were all treated extremely badly under a system dedicated almost exclusively to sustaining those actively employed in industry and, especially, an economic, academic, and political elite. As noted by Rimlinger in 1971, "It is fair to say that only within the last ten years or so has their system paid serious attention to those who are no longer producers."[36]

The most important post-Stalinist reforms were approved in 1956 and 1964. Under the first, basic pensions were increased by 55 to 100 percent, making retirement a real possibility for much of the population for the first time. By the late 1950s most covered workers could

---

[34] See Barry M. Blechman et al., *Setting National Priorities: The 1975 Budget* (Washington, D.C.: Brookings Institution, 1974), pp. 182–206.

[35] Bernice Q. Madison, *Social Welfare in the Soviet Union* (Stanford, Calif.: Stanford University Press, 1968), pp. 57–62.

[36] Gaston V. Rimlinger, *Welfare Policy and Industrialization in Europe, America, and Russia* (New York: John Wiley & Sons, 1971), p. 299.

anticipate pensions equal to 50 to 100 percent of basic preretirement earnings, though later adjustments reduced the highest ratios to about 65 percent.[37] Maternity and disability allowances were also liberalized. A 1964 law enacted the first genuine social insurance program for collective farmers.

Notwithstanding these major advances, the Soviet income maintenance system remains progressive only by Moscow's own standards. The relatively high basic old-age pension is offered at a low retirement age and provides substantial postretirement employment income to many. However, the maximum benefits are modest, most invalidity and survivors' pensions remain at the minimal subsistence level, and the system is short on such supplements as superannuation programs and private pensions. Public assistance is less well developed than in any other country in this survey, and unemployment benefits cover only retraining and resettlement. Despite Moscow's strong pronatalist orientation, family allowances remain much more restrictive than in most other European states.

HEALTH SERVICES

Health services are integrally linked with income maintenance at the nucleus of the welfare state. Welfare and health overlap in disability, maternity, and invalidity benefits as well as medical insurance. Injury and illness are central risks to individual security and trigger the need for comprehensive services. Reciprocally, no society can achieve high levels of health without first overcoming widespread poverty.

International standards are no more precise for health services than for income maintenance. Health spending levels tell us little about actual services because most of the expenditure goes to facilities and care providers rather than directly to the patient. Experts often disagree about the value of large numbers of hospital beds as well as the comparative virtues of comprehensive health services and national health insurance systems.

Authorities describe as progressive systems that are able to keep costs from spiraling, to provide services for all residents without reference to income or physical location, to plan the development of services and facilities on a national or regional basis, to integrate direct medical services with public health education and control over the physical environment, to promote medical screenings and other prevention programs, to maintain high standards of initial and continuing medical training, to supply hospital beds and health professionals in sufficient

---

[37] Robert J. Osborn, *Soviet Social Policies* (Homewood, Ill.: Dorsey Press, 1970), pp. 73–74.

quantity, to maintain facilities at a modern standard with appropriate new technology, to offer patients free choice of physicians, and to maintain the morale of both medical personnel and clients.

This list compels trade-offs and makes perfection a virtually unattainable goal. Most of the items involve considerable expenditure, but excessive costs tend to detract from availability or force a burden on the taxpayers. Planning may conflict with patient choice, and high standards for personnel may affect both costs and availability. No system is likely to be all things to all people.

The evaluation of medical delivery systems must be undertaken with the understanding that government can provide care but cannot assure good health. Just as police services cannot assure low crime rates and good teachers cannot guarantee knowledgeable students, physicians cannot assure a long-lived population. Health care providers are only one factor in a chain of influences that improve or impair national health standards. As Anderson points out, mortality comparisons "do not reflect the inferiority or superiority of any of the systems but rather a measure of how well each system does, given the social and cultural conditions and priorities it has to work with."[38] After considering the "life-style" factors that place the United States behind Sweden in mortality rates, Victor R. Fuchs concludes, "Given our present state of knowledge, even the most lavish use of medical care probably would not bring the U.S. rate more than a small step closer to the Swedish rate."[39] Yet these same authors, as well as most other observers, view accessibility and affordability of health services as major ends that justify substantial exertions by modern societies.

A given country can maximize its efforts to provide health care but cannot be certain that it is on the right track in terms of the relationship between particular investments and measurements of the quality of health of the residents. Brian Abel-Smith contends: "Once one accepts the citizen's right to receive medical care as a broad philosophy underlying a century or more of European history, the considerable difference in financing systems among the different countries becomes matters primarily of detail."[40] Similarly, few significant relationships have been established between health quality and the organization of the system, the number of health care providers, or the number of hospital beds.

The indicators used most commonly to measure health results in-

---

[38] Odin W. Anderson, *Health Care: Can There Be Equity? The United States, Sweden, and England* (New York: John Wiley & Sons, 1972), p. 147.

[39] Victor R. Fuchs, *Who Shall Live?* (New York: Basic Books, 1974), p. 46.

[40] Brian Abel-Smith, "The History of Medical Care," in E. W. Martin, ed., *Comparative Development in Social Welfare* (London: George Allen & Unwin, 1972), p. 231.

clude life expectancy, infant and maternal mortality, and workdays lost due to illness. Cross-national studies by the World Health Organization (WHO) and other researchers have found that among highly industrialized countries mortality rates correlate weakly with ratios of hospital beds and physicians and most strongly with patterns of education, work, consumption, and overall levels of modernization and development.[41]

The eight countries in our survey differ little in life expectancy but do vary considerably in infant mortality (see Tables 6–3 and 6–4). The assembled data suggest that, with the possible exception of France, progress in life expectancy has been quite slow during the postwar period in each of the eight countries. By the late 1960s these industrial states had drawn closer to one another and were having difficulty extending male expectancy to age 70 and female expectancy to 75. The most apparent shortcomings involved Soviet and American males.

In contrast, a highly significant variation continues to exist in infant mortality, with the extremes represented by Sweden and Italy.

TABLE 6–3
Expectation of Life at Birth, by Sex (ranked by 1965–1969 levels for males)

		1950–54	1955–59	1960–64	1965–69
1. Sweden	M	70.4	71.2	71.6	71.8
	F	73.2	74.6	75.5	76.6
2. England, Wales	M	66.9	67.9	68.2	68.6
	F	72.1	73.5	74.2	74.9
3. France	M	64.9	66.6	68.0	68.4
	F	70.8	73.1	74.9	75.9
4. East Germany	M	–	66.2	67.3	68.1
	F	–	70.8	72.3	73.2
5. West Germany	M	65.2	66.3	67.1	67.5
	F	69.5	71.3	72.8	73.6
6. Italy	M	–	66.2	67.1	–
	F	–	70.7	72.4	–
7. United States	M	66.0	66.7	66.8	66.8
	F	71.9	73.1	73.6	74.1
8. Soviet Union	M	–	–	–	65*
	F	–	–	–	74*

* 1970–71.

Sources: *World Health Statistics Report 27*, no. 10, (1974): 698; for the Soviet Union, *Sovet ekonomicheskoi vzaimopomoshchi, Statisticheskii ezhegodnik stran-chlenov, 1973* (Moscow, 1973), p. 9.

---

[41] Bui-Dang-Ha Doan, "World Trends in Medical Manpower, 1950–70," *World Health Statistics Reports* 27, no. 2 (1974): 93–94; and "Health Trends and Prospects, 1950–2000," *World Health Statistics Reports* 27, no. 10 (1974): 688. In addition, it has been found that high socioeconomic development can contribute negatively to health through linkage with poor nutrition, lack of exercise, pollution, and other factors.

TABLE 6-4
Infant Mortality per 1,000 Live-Born (ranked by 1972 ratios)

	1950-54	1955-59	1960-64	1965-69	1972
1. Sweden	20.0	17.0	15.4	12.9	13.3
2. France	46.2	33.9	25.5	20.2	16.0
3. England, Wales	27.9	23.2	21.2	18.6	17.2
4. East Germany	59.9	45.2	33.8	22.4	17.7
5. United States	28.1	26.4	25.3	22.7	18.5
6. West Germany	49.3	37.3	29.3	23.2	22.7
7. Soviet Union	75.0	–	–	26	24.7
8. Italy	61.0	48.7	40.7	33.3	27.0

Source: World Health Statistics Report 27, no. 10 (1974): 654–57, 678, 699.

Each of our states had made substantial progress since 1965, but the most dramatic advances came in East Germany and the Soviet Union.

The laggards in infant mortality, Italy and the Soviet Union, were in 1971 leaders in the provision of physicians on a per capita basis. Both of these countries also compare well with most others in our survey in the provision of hospital beds (see Tables 6–5 and 6–6).

Of course, the quantity of physicians and the number of hospital beds are only two of the many factors that are involved in health care delivery. The quality of care and facilities also matters, though no precise measurement of either of these determinants is available.[42] The total expenditure for health services might be expected to correlate closely with the combined quantity and quality of medical services. Yet expenditures are greatly affected by the levels of income for care providers, the excess capacity of facilities, and other barriers to direct benefits.

TABLE 6-5
Physicians per 10,000
Population, 1971

Soviet Union	26.4
Italy	18.4
West Germany	17.8
East Germany	16.4
United States	16.1
Sweden	13.9
France	13.9
England, Wales	12.7

Source: World Health Statistics Annual, 1971, vol. 3, "Health Personnel and Hospital Establishments" (Geneva: World Health Organization, 1975), p. 49.

TABLE 6-6
Hospital Beds per 10,000
Population, 1971

Sweden	149.4
West Germany	112.6
Soviet Union	111.3
East Germany	110.2
Italy	105.8
France	103.9
England, Wales	91.2
United States	75.1

Source: World Health Statistics Annual, 1971, vol. 3, "Health Personnel and Hospital Establishments" (Geneva: World Health Organization, 1975), pp. 172–76.

[42] Ibid., pp. 93–94.

In Table 6-7 we note the results of major efforts by the World Health Organization and the U.S. Social Security Administration to collect comparable statistics on national health care expenditures. We see from these data that the United States and Sweden lead our group of nations in combined public and private spending. United States outlays have been particularly high for physician services, as doctors in that country earn approximately three times as much as their British counterparts. Although Sweden's high expenditures have been primarily associated with the exceptional provision of hospital places, progress is being made there to supplement this with a high physician ratio. Fully comparable figures for East Germany, the Soviet Union, and Italy are not available; however, other evidence suggests that the expenditures of Italy and East Germany are close to those of West Germany and France, whereas those of the Soviet Union are lower than those of the United Kingdom.[43]

TABLE 6-7
Total Expenditure for Health Services as Percent of GNP

	Year	Percent of GNP	Year	Percent of GNP
United States............	1961–62	5.8	1969	6.8
Sweden	1962	5.4	1969	6.7
West Germany.........	1961	4.5	1969	5.7
France................	1963	4.4	1969	5.7
United Kingdom	1961–62	4.2	1969	4.8

Sources: For 1969 data and West Germany in 1961: *Social Security Bulletin* (Washington, D.C.) 36, no. 3 (March 1973): 39; for the original compilation of 1961–63 data: Brian Abel-Smith, *An International Study of Health Expenditure*, Public Health Papers, no. 32 (Geneva: World Health Organization, 1967).

We do not equate low expenditures with poor service. On the contrary, the Soviet Union and Britain stand out for the comprehensiveness of their health services. They have maintained comparatively low costs through such devices as low payment of staff at most levels and, particularly in the Soviet case, highly integrated and carefully planned services.[44]

The countries in our survey vary significantly in the organization and financing of health services. Major differences in the organization of health care exist among industrialized countries in these respects:

---

[43] Frederick L. Pryor, *Public Expenditures in Communist and Capitalist Nations* (Homewood, Ill.: Richard D. Irwin, 1968), p. 168; and Committee on Ways and Means, U.S. House of Representatives, *National Health Insurance Resource Book*, part 3, "Health Financing and Delivery Systems of Selected Foreign Nations" (Washington, D.C.: U.S. Government Printing Office, 1974), p. 403.

[44] See John Fry, *Medicine in Three Societies* (New York: American Elsevier Publishing Co., 1970), pp. 11, 95, 101.

whether or not a sharp separation is maintained between hospital-based and first-contact physicians; whether physicians are paid in direct relationship to services rendered, by salary, or according to the number of registered patients; the degree of central and regional planning and coordination; the amount of preventive medicine; the extent of hospital outpatient and polyclinic facilities; whether or not free choice of physicians is maintained; the extent of quality checks; the balance between the services provided to various age groups and categories of patients; and the relative provision of services to rural areas. In toto, we seek to discover how closely each country's health care services approach an integrated system for the direct provision of all services, that is, a genuine national health delivery system.

Differences in the financing of health services are linked as closely to tax policies as to distributions. What is at stake is whether individuals pay for their health care through general taxes, social insurance contributions, private health insurance, or direct private payment. This is not a pure choice of one approach, as each country in our study uses more than one source. What is most significant for us here is the effect of such payment methods on service costs, quality control, and the availability of services.

It seems useful to divide the eight countries into three categories in order to illustrate some broad patterns of similarities and differences. One group consists of the nations which most closely approach a comprehensive system for direct government provision of health services. These nations are East Germany, the Soviet Union, and Great Britain. Another group, which includes West Germany, France, Italy, and Sweden, relies on near-universal systems of compulsory health insurance operated through a network of partially autonomous public agencies. Finally, the United States stands out for the dominance of private health insurance and private direct payment and the greater autonomy of its physicians and hospitals.

National Health Services

The three officially designated national health services rely primarily on resources obtained from general taxes and minimize fee-for-service payment of physicians and hospitals. East Germany and the Soviet Union pay all physicians as salaried employees in state-owned facilities. They also provide separate hospital staffs, multispecialty polyclinics to supplement hospital use, superior services to industry, well-developed preventive care and public education programs, and high levels of planning and integration. Their principal weaknesses include the absence of free choice of physicians and a degree of isolation from Western medical developments. In the Soviet case we should also note continued problems with rural services, a mass education approach to initial medical training, the probable overuse of hospitals, the modest quality of the facilities, and an ideology-related minimization of mental health services.[45] Almost certainly, medical care is one of the stronger public services in both the Soviet Union and East Germany. With costs kept at moderate levels, medical services are effectively extended across income groups.

Among the significant differences between the British National Health Service (NHS) and the Eastern European systems is the use by NHS of "capitation payments"—income based on the number of patients on the rosters of individual physicians—as a factor in the remuneration of general practitioners. Yet the British physician, like his Eastern European counterparts, has no incentive to overtreat his patients. Although maintaining generally high professional standards and exceptional coverage of the population on a geographic and income basis, Britain is less than outstanding in a number of areas in which a national service could be expected to excel. Reflecting a tendency evident in many spheres, British health planning can be termed "piecemeal and unco-ordinated."[46] Although Britain's hospital system is fairly well integrated, little progress has been made in preventive screening, public health education, reducing an apparent overuse of hospitals, and increasing coordination between hospital services and other programs.[47] On the other hand, the British have retained a largely free choice of first-contact physicians.

In terms of overall assessments, one can pick and choose from evaluators who range from extreme critics to those who regard the British service as the best in the world. It is clear that the system is meeting increasing pressures rooted in the government's unwillingness and/or inability to spend generously for facilities and salaries.[48] Hospital construction and remodeling proceeds haltingly. With junior physicians and other health personnel denied adequate wages, British doctors are emigrating at a high rate and labor unrest has mushroomed. Yet, as D. Stark Murray argues, "In no feature do the U.K. services lag seriously behind any other country and on an overall average the nation gets a fairly comprehensive service, a fairly evenly distributed service and an above average level of medical skill."[49]

---

[45] Ibid., pp. 2, 113.

[46] Ibid., p. 144.

[47] R. F. Bridgman and M. I. Roemer, *Hospital Legislation and Hospital Systems*, Public Health Papers, no. 50 (Geneva: World Health Organization, 1973), p. 150.

[48] See Donald Gould, "Sickness in the Health Service," *New Statesman*, September 12, 1975, pp. 301–3.

[49] D. Stark Murray, *Blueprint for Health* (New York: Schocken Books, 1974), p. 34.

National Health Insurance Systems

The four continental Western European states appear at first sight to maintain quite similar systems for financing and delivering health care.[50] A Western European pattern can be said to include near-universal employment-based health insurance administered by semi-autonomous public agencies, a lesser degree of central government control over hospitals and other elements in the system than in the national health services, and a substantial degree of "free enterprise" for at least those private physicians who function outside hospitals.

These similarities tend, however, to obscure many basic factors that distinguish the Swedish, West German, French, and Italian systems from one another. For one, the amount of government regulation and sponsorship of health services varies widely. Involvement by the Swedish government is so extensive that several observers regard its system as a virtual national health service. The unique features of the Swedish system include reliance on general tax revenue for hospital services and public provision of relatively extensive nonhospital physician services. In contrast, the French government provides minimal subsidies to operate the health system, thereby forcing the contributory sickness funds to pay for construction and preventive programs as well as other basic services. In West Germany the majority of hospital beds are in private hands.

Although various mixtures of central and regional governments have been increasing their already considerable control over the health care system in each of these countries, legal traditions and the differences in government and sick fund roles have influenced the levels of integration and the development of various programs. Again, Sweden leads our survey group, and probably all other countries, in the overall hospital system and in such particular elements as mental health services.[51] Neither West Germany, France, nor Italy are considered well-integrated systems. France and Italy have been considering conversion of their systems into some form of national health service. West German government planning has not been able to overcome exceptionally wasteful uses of health resources.

The health insurance systems of the four continental Western Euro-

---

[50] For discussions of these systems see Jozef Van Langendonck, "The European Experience in Social Health Insurance," *Social Security Bulletin* 36, no. 7 (July 1973): 21–30; Joseph G. Simanis, *National Health Systems in Eight Countries* (Washington, D.C.: Social Security Administration, 1975); Bridgman and Roemer, *Hospital Legislation;* Anderson, *Health Care;* and Derick H. Pulcher, *A Study of Some Aspects of Medical Care Systems in Industrialized Countries* (Geneva: International Labor Office, 1975).

[51] Michael O'Donnell, "Health," in Richard Mayne, ed., *Europe Tomorrow* (London: Wm. Collins Sons & Co., 1972), p. 91.

pean states vary in such aspects as diversity of schemes within a given country, methods of payments for services, and freedom of choice for physicians and insured persons. Each system retains strong vestiges of its origins in 19th century private sickness funds. This has contributed to slow progress toward universal coverage, equal protection, and effective cost control in all four countries.

In each country the health insurance administrative structure is linked with other social insurance programs and maintains aspects of autonomy or representation by relevant health interests. West Germany has the most diverse and autonomous structure, with almost 2,000 funds organized on occupational and regional lines; France and Italy maintain separate occupational schemes; and Sweden has developed the most unified system among this group of countries. A diversity of programs within a given country has tended to result in patterns of inequality in cost and benefits. A movement toward "national solidarity," under way in many Western European countries, is aimed at the elimination of multiple programs and gaps in coverage. The West Germans are now the least coercive in regard to participation, leaving self-employed and high-salary persons to join funds on a voluntary basis. Sweden has an advanced position in its extension of coverage to all residents. However, each of the four countries extends full medical benefits to the unemployed and others who are not called upon to make contributions.

The insurance system may take an active or a passive role in the arrangement of services and payments. The West German and Italian funds have been among the most active in guaranteeing to their subscribers access to comprehensive care. In these countries the insured person can also rely on his or her fund for direct payment of fees. Sweden's system lacks the tradition of prearranged services, but in 1974 moved toward a direct payment system. France retains the reimbursement approach, which is rarely popular with patients, and its funds do not assure access to services.

One of the most significant variations in health insurance relates to noncovered medical costs that must be paid by the individual. Here also the advantage is held by the Italian and West German patients, who are virtually as immune from residual costs as they would be in most national health service systems. In contrast, Swedish and French insurance normally requires the patient to pay for a significant proportion of service costs, including part of physician fees. In France patients must pay for approximately 30 percent of total health care costs out of their own resources or through supplemental private insurance, a pattern that leads many to view the French system as quite incomplete in providing financial protection. It should be noted that in all health care systems the patients are responsible for a major part of some costs, most commonly for drugs, appliances, and dental services. Even in the Soviet Union private payments constitute a substantial fraction of total health care costs.

Finally, among the four Western European systems the free choice of physicians is sharply limited only in Sweden. This has resulted from the heavy concentration of services in hospitals and polyclinics and the relatively small number of physicians in private practice.[52] However, no evidence exists that comprehensive national health insurance inherently precludes free choice in physician care, and each of the other three states provides considerable patient choice.

Thus the Western European health insurance systems involve a complicated set of trade-offs in the provision of medical care. Sweden's very high levels of planning and universal coverage are achieved at the cost of patient choice. France allows more choice but offers a less efficient service system and provides less financial protection to the patient. The reader can begin to evaluate these systems by ordering his or her own priorities for a health care system.

The United States: A Nonsystem?

Among the group of eight the United States stands out for the absence of a comprehensive health service or public health insurance system for a majority of residents. In addition, many agree with Anderson that its health services are "certainly a 'nonsystem' in a bureaucratic and administrative sense."[53]

The highest standards are reflected in the education of medical professionals and the support of research, and the United States ranks high in modernity of facilities and sophistication of technology. The costs of its programs, $104.2 billion in 1974,[54] certainly do not reflect a niggardly approach to the provision of health services.

Yet almost every aspect of the financing and delivery of American health services has been subjected to extensive criticism. The analysis of hospital utilization has already resulted in a substantial start toward coordination by a growing governmental health bureaucracy. However, the absence of alternative facilities still leads to overuse of hospital inpatient services and the lack of adequate supervision apparently contributes to the overemployment of surgery.

Much farther from resolution are problems resulting from the autonomy of physicians and the lack of assurance that health care is available to residents regardless of location or ability to pay. The United

[52] Joseph L. Andrews, Jr., "Medical Care in Sweden," *Journal of the American Medical Association,* March 19, 1973, pp. 1369–75.

[53] Anderson, *Health Care,* p. 178.

[54] Nancy L. Worthington, "National Health Expenditures, 1929–74," *Social Security Bulletin* 38, no. 2 (February 1975): 6.

States maintains weak quality standards for rural medical practice. Further, inadequate controls are maintained in regard to the number and quality of practitioners in the various medical specialties. The most critical problem is widespread inability to pay the costs of the world's most expensive medical care. The 1965 breakthrough that brought Medicare and Medicaid for the aged, those on categorical public assistance, and some other groups was a step in the right direction but nothing approaching a complete solution. Medicare protection is limited, and desperate situations continue for the near-poor, the unemployed, and almost all families that face a prolonged hospitalization. Indeed, the limited benefits in most private health insurance contracts make any hospitalization a major risk to family financial health. Military and veterans' programs extend broad protection, but even here services are not always available. In 1974 government at all levels was paying less than 37 percent of American health costs.[55] This left an estimated residual of $67 billion to be covered by private health insurance and direct individual payment. Good private insurance policies were paying approximately 80 percent of hospital charges and 40 percent of physicians' charges, mainly those for surgery. However, more than 30 percent of the population had no such insurance protection, and as late as 1969, individuals were paying more than one third of the total cost of medical care outside the insurance system.[56] This problem was compounded by sharply increasing charges by physicians and hospitals, which were accelerated by increased demand for services, inflation in other sectors, and an extraordinary rise in medical malpractice insurance premiums.

At this writing the federal government's response to this crisis has been stalled. It appears that cautious encouragement of some experiments in health delivery will be accompanied by modest steps toward protection against "catastrophic" risks. The experiments include health maintenance organizations, providing prepaid planned services to a designated clientele, and expanded peer review by which physicians check on the quality and economy of the care provided by their colleagues. The last is being used in existing government-sponsored programs and can be expected to be included in any future system of national health insurance.

DETERMINANTS OF WELFARE PROGRAMS

Social scientists have been determined to discover the basis for national variations in welfare. In no areas of public policy have policy determinants been analyzed more carefully than in health and welfare,

---

[55] Ibid.

[56] Anderson, *Health Care*, pp. 113–16.

and particularly income maintenance. Those who have explored this field have employed advanced quantitative methods as well as more traditional approaches. We will attempt here to summarize and evaluate some of their assertions and findings.

The effort to assess particular factors must be considered in the context of the broader debate between the supporters of socioeconomic forces and the supporters of directly political influences. In regard to welfarism, virtually every authority concedes that socioeconomic factors are important. Yet major differences arise in assessing particular forces. Much attention has been given to indicators of per capita national income and wealth. These show that rising levels of affluence have conflicting impacts on social insurance. More resources are made available for income security, but the need for some programs may be reduced and, especially in regard to public assistance, a "welfare backlash" may be generated. Income maintenance expenditures will tend to rise as a given country gets richer. Yet, as is evident from the experience of the United States, wealth may retard the development of welfarism in a comparative context. Expenditures on social security were inversely related to per capita GNP in the ten-country Kaim-Caudle study.[57] In his 14-country analysis Pryor found no significant relationship between per capita GNP and the ratio of public expenditures for health or welfare to GNP.[58] Yet, looking at a much broader sample of countries that included both less developed states and more developed states, Wilensky determined that per capita GNP was one of the three most significant variables influencing social security spending levels as a fraction of GNP.[59] These findings are not inconsistent with one another once the complex dynamics of the affluence factor is fully understood.

Among demographic variables considerable attention has been given to the proportions of the population that are old and very young. The postretirement population is the major beneficiary of pensions and receives a large share of public assistance and health insurance allocations. Children may be given disproportionate benefits through child allowances and health care. Whereas the USSR leads the Communist-ruled states in proportions of "preproductive" dependents, the German Democratic Republic has an exceptionally high share of old people.[60] Although the retirement population has been expanding in each of the Western states, among the capitalist countries in our survey the aged

---

[57] Kaim-Caudle, *Comparative Social Policy*, pp. 54–56.

[58] This refers to a time-fixed "cross-section analysis." Pryor, *Public Expenditures*, pp. 180–81.

[59] Wilensky, *Welfare State*, p. 22.

[60] United Nations, Department of Economic and Social Affairs, *World Economic Survey, 1973* (New York: 1974), p. 50.

constitute the largest share of the population in Britain and the smallest in the United States.[61] Aaron rejected the independent influence of age distribution,[62] but in his more comprehensive and recent analysis Wilensky singled out this factor as having the most significant correlation with social security expenditure of all those tested.[63]

In comparison with such socioeconomic factors Wilensky found that the correlations between social security effort and political variables were weak. In this he was reaffirming a contention made by many analysts of social policy in the American states and by other cross-national researchers. Yet Wilensky does not fully discount political variables, and others would go farther than he does in recognizing their significance. Heclo, a leading supporter of political factors, argues:

> Socioeconomic development is not the end but the beginning of social policy choice. . . . The distinction, in terms of Aristotle's classification of causes, is between a material cause — socioeconomic factors as the underlying conditions calling forth a policy response — and an efficient cause — political factors as the energizing agents by which specific responses have been made.[64]

Wilensky and Pryor both recognize that a leading factor in health and income maintenance variations is the age of the social insurance system itself. Yet this is hardly a purely socioeconomic factor. The start of particular programs has been linked with such political factors as the political mobilization of workers through unionization, bureaucratization, and the breakdown of ideological resistance. Wilensky also gives considerable weight to such essentially political factors as the visibility and perceived fairness of the tax system and the degree of government centralization. The middle class is viewed as providing maximum support to social security when taxes are least visible and seem fairly allocated. More centralized political systems tend to move earlier and with greater resources than do governmental systems which have decentralized control of revenue.

Among political factors much attention has been given to the role of ideology. Viewed as a value system, ideology is at the center of the assessment presented by Rimlinger and is regarded as significant by the majority of the leading writers on the welfare state. Noting the lag in social insurance in the United States, Rimlinger asserts, "The country's liberal heritage is still an important factor, making it difficult to

---

[61] Ibid., p. 35.

[62] Henry Aaron, "Social Security: International Comparisons," in Otto Eckstein, ed., *Studies in the Economics of Income Maintenance* (Washington, D.C.: Brookings Institution, 1967), pp. 32–33.

[63] Wilensky, *Welfare State*, p. 22.

[64] Heclo, *Modern Social Politics*, p. 288.

follow the European precedents in this modern interpretation of social rights."[65] He and others have noted the ideological support for egalitarian benefits in Britain, the limited compulsory coverage of the population in West Germany, and the close linkage between labor productivity and welfare in the Soviet Union. Most of the strong advocates of "ideological determinism" employ no quantitative evidence. Wilensky is one of the few scholars who have attempted to quantify ideological values by means of content analysis. He concludes that the differences among countries in basic welfare-related values are far smaller than is normally acknowledged and that many leading countries ignore ideological orientations when putting welfare policies into practice. Arguing that a "success ideology" competes with collectivist orientations in every major nation, Wilensky concludes that "it is a mistake to peg 'individualistic' values and beliefs as American or capitalist, and 'collectivist' as European or socialist."[66] Wilensky's indicators of values and beliefs are much less convincing than those he employs for wealth or political centralization. He asserts that his regression analyses demonstrate clearly and consistently that ideology has no effect on welfarism. Yet one must reject most of the existing literature to accept this conclusion.

International emulation is widely recognized as a contributor to the shaping of particular programs as well as the setting of expenditure levels. The long history of study missions and other forms of direct borrowing is described by Heclo. The strong impact of particularly close relationships among four pairs of peoples and governments in Europe, the Commonwealth, and North America is stressed by Kaim-Caudle.[67] He found that while expenditure levels in the paired countries showed "some similarity," there was a marked closeness in the organization of social security services and the character of particular schemes between such countries as Austria and West Germany or Ireland and Britain.

Only moderate emphasis has been placed on the effects of particular structures and roles within the national political systems. Heidenheimer and Heclo have both stressed the roles of government bureaucracies in policy formulation, and the former has also emphasized the level of organization of such service-providers as physicians.[68]

---

[65] Rimlinger, Welfare Policy, p. 244.

[66] Wilensky, Welfare State, p. 39.

[67] Kaim-Caudle, Comparative Social Policy, pp. 306–10.

[68] Heclo, Modern Social Politics; Arnold J. Heidenheimer, "The Politics of Public Education, Health, and Welfare in the U.S.A. and Western Europe," British Journal of Political Science 3 (July 1973): 315–40; and Heidenheimer, Hugh Heclo, and Carolyn Teich Adams, Comparative Public Policy: The Politics of Public Choice in Europe and America (New York: St. Martin's Press, 1975).

Piven and Cloward credit what political scientists term anomic interest articulation for the recent growth of American public assistance. In their view, "the contemporary relief explosion was a response to the civil disorder caused by rapid economic change — in this case, the modernization of Southern agriculture."[69] However, such developments as the American urban riots of the 1960s were not common in other developed political systems. Greater applicability seems warranted for Heclo's conclusion that, "forced to choose one group among all the separate political factors as most consistently important . . . , the bureaucracies of Britain and Sweden loom predominant in the policies studied."[70] He cites the steadier and more intensive influence of the bureaucrats as compared to party or legislative leaders, and stresses that the power of the administrators has been exerted both positively and negatively.

Looking more broadly at political systems, recent analysis has not sustained earlier speculations that the welfare state fares better in certain authoritarian systems than in democratic ones. Pryor, comparing Communist-ruled and Western states, found no statistically significant variation between his sets for welfare or health after accounting for socioeconomic differences.[71] Without discounting these factors, his study of 1956 and 1962 data showed that the "centrally planned economies" did register higher spending ratios for health and lower spending ratios for welfare. Using a larger sample, Wilensky and Cutright separately confirm the weakness of the authoritarian-democratic variable, though the latter concludes that "political representativeness" has a subordinate impact on the development of social security programs.[72]

Finally, it is recognized that welfare policies and budgets are everywhere affected by other policy objectives. Considerations ranging from defense posture to economic growth and stability have been viewed as shaping the limits and directions of health and income maintenance policies.

The empirical findings of Russett and Wilensky suggest that the impacts on welfare of wars and defense spending vary considerably in relation to the scale of the war and defense establishment and from country to country. In none of the countries analyzed by Russett is the

---

[69] Frances Fox Piven and Richard A. Cloward, *Regulating the Poor* (New York: Random House, 1971), p. 196.

[70] Heclo, *Modern Social Politics*, p. 301.

[71] Pryor, *Public Expenditures*, p. 285.

[72] Wilensky, *Welfare State*, p. 115; and Phillips Cutright, "Political Structure, Economic Development, and National Social Security Programs," *American Journal of Sociology* 70 (March 1965), pp. 537–50.

welfare state the primary victim of high or rising militarization. Personal consumption and economic investment are generally the main losers. Yet Russett finds that for the United States, "at all but the highest levels of defense spending achieved in World War II, the inverse relationship is very steep, with small increases in military needs having a very marked dampening effect on welfare costs."[73] For health care the relationship to the requirements of national defense is computed to be less powerful but still important in the United States. Countries with somewhat lower defense burdens, such as Britain and France, are viewed as better able to prevent military expenditures from limiting social programs. As confirmed by Wilensky, the welfare state gives way to military priorities during major international crises and in countries both at the periphery and at the center of such events. On the other hand, countries which are determined to have moderate-sized military budgets can do so without substantial verifiable effect on their rates of increase of welfare and health programs. Unfortunately, the Cold War arms race has not had the positive impact on support for equality and social justice that was produced by the world wars.

Although the effects are not as well documented for economic stabilization and industrial growth priorities as for military factors, these are also important. Miller and Rein state, "The basic economic policies of a nation, the so-called macro policies dealing with the rate of growth and inflation, must have redistribution as a primary objective if sizable redistribution is to occur and survive."[74] Yet redistribution is only now being affirmed as a policy objective in a few countries, and nowhere is it given primacy over efforts to achieve high rates of industrial growth with minimal unemployment and inflation. Fortunately, social security is increasingly recognized as a major tool of economic stabilization policy.

Social security is also subordinated to the growth of profits and industrial output in all countries in our survey. This is most explicit in the Communist-ruled states, yet no government seeks to make social security benefits so generous that the able-bodied will reject available employment. The extreme nature of Soviet policy in this regard is evident from the absence of unemployment benefits, the long delays in the provision of adequate pensions, and the penalties assessed for records of job turnover. However, Western countries commonly deny unemployment benefits to striking workers, and the linkage between employment goals and welfare is now almost as close in the United States as in the Soviet Union.

---

[73] Russett, *What Price Vigilance?*, p. 151.
[74] S. M. Miller and Martin Rein, "Can Income Redistribution Work?" *Social Policy* 6, no. 1 (May–June 1975): 15.

CONCLUSION

Welfare and health have emerged as the core of distributive policies in each of the industrialized countries. The welfare state is not a pre-planned policy package, but rather the result of many evolutionary refinements made during the past century. The redistribution of income is rarely put forth as the central objective of welfare state policy. Instead, the main objectives are the minimization of income loss and the development of human resources.

These goals are met to a high and steadily increasing degree, as many major industrial countries expend an amount equal to 20 percent or more of their GNP on income maintenance and health. In most Western countries a large part of the "poverty gap" is overcome through income transfers. However, the countries surveyed here show substantial variations in their provision for the poor and others who lose their source of income or their health. Although all of these countries shared certain elements of progress in this field, the United States and the Soviet Union were latecomers which have been reluctant to expand their programs. Less basic differences separated the other six countries in the survey, these differences tending to be most evident in the structure of particular plans.

In these industrial countries the actual medical services and facilities were rather similar, though not their cost. Only modest differences in results were evident, and most authorities were reluctant to credit or blame the health delivery systems for the observed variations. Major differences were observed in the availability of rural health care. However, only the United States was failing to serve most of its citizens equally, regardless of ability to pay.

The factors that influence variations in welfare programs are numerous and complex in their impacts. Although socioeconomic variables, such as national wealth and age distribution, are influential, such political factors as the sources of revenue for the system, value systems, the organization of service-providers, bureaucratic initiative, political centralization, and the imperatives of military-industrial development are also viewed as significant.

The welfare state goes well beyond income maintenance and health care. It also involves taxation, education, housing, regional development, employment, and numerous other policy areas. As such, it involves far more than 20 percent of GNP and takes up the bulk of most national budgets. Taxation will be discussed in Chapter 8 as a major aspect of extraction. In the following chapter some aspects of education will be related to the emerging post-industrial state.

7 Distributions: Military-Industrial and Post-Industrial

The welfare state has not displaced militarization as a major public priority throughout the world. Numerous spheres of international politics continue to be influenced by the relative military power of competing states and alliances. In most advanced industrial countries, large military commitments continue to affect allocations for civilian needs and pleasures. Designed to make each country more secure, such commitments often restrict freedom and contribute to world and regional conditions that threaten mankind.

Whereas militarization is all too clear a fact of modern times, post-industrialism suffers from lack of consensus about its definition and scope, and even regarding its very existence. The idea has been presented that those countries most advanced in socioeconomic terms have progressed beyond a dominant concern for welfarism and industrialization. Such nations as Sweden and the United States are viewed as having shaped new patterns of class and occupation, new centers of power, and new personal and group aspirations. They are seen as having created the need to set and the capability to achieve new public priorities based on higher standards of affluence, democracy, equality, social justice, and aesthetics.

Many of the claimed ends of post-industrialism are discussed in later chapters. These include economic planning, pollution control, women's rights, and worker participation in enterprise management. Here we focus on the distribution of educational opportunities, especially such advanced trends as the movement toward universal and comprehensive secondary schooling and the development of multipurpose systems of mass higher education.

Both military- and post-industrial developments will be reviewed in this chapter. They are interrelated in several key aspects and can be viewed both as alternatives to the welfare state and as complements to its priorities.

THE MILITARY-INDUSTRIAL STATE

One choice of priority for public spending and programs is to sustain the private and governmental organizations that are viewed as the major sources of profits, employment, and power in contemporary states. Galbraith, taking a broad view of this development, argues that governments place excessive emphasis on the needs of an industrial "planning system." Focusing on the United States, he contends that in the post-1945 era "public expenditures were set at a permanently high level and extensively concentrated on military and other technical artifacts or on military or industrial development."[1] It would be impossible to present accurate comparisons of government support to industry in each of the chosen states. Such support takes diverse forms and involves explicit and implicit benefits and costs. We concentrate here on the military dimension of government priorities in these countries.

Policy decisions concerning the military emphasize the mobilization and allocation of resources. The necessary extraction of manpower and taxes is dealt with in Chapter 8. Here we stress variations in the levels of public spending on the military.

Numerous decisions have strong impacts on defense spending levels. Governments decide whether to seek capability to influence events around the world, compete in the nuclear arms race, participate in wars either by proxy or with their own manpower, depend on the protection of an ally, or place an umbrella over their friends. Our eight countries include two superpowers which have taken strong leadership positions in military affairs, two countries with nuclear weapons and extraregional aspirations (Britain and France), and four countries with

---

[1] John Kenneth Galbraith, *Economics and the Public Purpose* (Boston: Houghton Mifflin Co., 1973), p. 177.

only conventional weaponry and limited military aspirations. Between 1945 and 1970 the United States stood out from even the Soviet Union in its capability of and inclination toward direct military involvement far from its borders.

We look first at the impact of military expenditures generally, without reference to particular countries. Ours is a highly dangerous and extraordinary wasteful world in which governments spend roughly as much on preparations for armed conflict as on education and health care combined.[2] Such an allocation of money, commodities, and manpower may be justified in particular countries as providing necessary levels of security against domestic and external threats. However, from a global perspective it does not seem possible to justify such a diversion of resources.

It is not impossible to find domestic benefits from military programs. Education and training may be promoted, certain industries and regions stimulated, and technological improvements produced for the civilian sector. Yet the commitment of hundreds of billions of dollars to military programs has generally negative overall effects on economic development, environmental quality, social stability, social services, and consumption.[3]

The extent to which military spending burdens a given nation varies greatly. For most of the post-1945 period and until quite recently the rate of military spending in proportion to gross national product was much higher in the industrial countries of Europe and North America than in developing nations.[4] Further, the Soviet Union and the United States have long outstripped all or most of their NATO and Warsaw Pact allies in terms of military effort. Led by suddenly wealthier oil-exporting nations and inflamed by regional conflicts, some developing states have recently caught up with the richer ones in relative militarization. However, the Soviet Union and the United States continue to contribute disproportionately to the military expenditures of their respective major alliances and to place a heavy burden on their alternative spending areas. To quote the verdict of the Stockholm International Peace Research Institute (SIPRI):

---

[2] Report of the Secretary-General, *Economic and Social Consequences of the Armaments Race and Its Extremely Harmful Effects on World Peace and Security* (New York: United Nations, October 22, 1971), p. 16.

[3] See Addendum to ibid., November 12, 1971; Joint Economic Committee, U.S. Congress, *Economic Performance and the Military Burden in the Soviet Union* (Washington, D.C.: U.S. Government Printing Office, 1970); and Adam Yarmolinsky, *The Military Establishment* (New York: Harper & Row, 1971).

[4] The leading sources of comprehensive data concerning military expenditures are *World Armaments and Disarmament, SIPRI Yearbook* (Stockholm: Almqvist and Wiksell, annual, Stockholm International Peace Research Institute); and U.S. Arms Control and Disarmament Agency, *World Military Expenditures and Arms Trade* (Washington, D.C.: U.S. Government Printing Office, annual). They differ most significantly in regard to estimates of Soviet expenditures, the U.S. government estimates being higher.

The United States and the Soviet Union are in a class of their own and essentially determine the military-technological environment for the rest of the world. Other countries accommodate themselves to this environment as their financial and technical resources permit.[5]

The U.S.-USSR combined share of world military expenditure has remained between 60 and 70 percent during the past quarter century, although their share of the world gross national product has been substantially less than 50 percent.[6]

TABLE 7-1
Military Expenditure as a Percentage of Gross Domestic Product

	1952	1955	1960	1962	1965	1970	1972
United States	13.6	10.0	8.9	9.3	7.5	7.8	6.6
France	8.6	6.4	6.4	6.0	5.2	4.1	3.7
West Germany	5.8	4.1	4.0	4.8	4.3	3.3	3.5
Italy	4.5	3.7	3.3	3.2	3.3	2.7	3.1
United Kingdom	10.0	8.2	6.5	6.4	6.0	4.9	5.4
Sweden	4.4	4.8	4.0	4.1	4.2	3.6	3.5
East Germany: 1*	−	2.7 (1958)	−	3.7	3.4	6.1	6.5
2†	−	6.0 (1956)	−	3.9	−	−	−
Soviet Union: 1‡	13.4	11.4	6.4	7.7	6.6	6.2	5.7
2§	−	−	−	22.5	18.1	16.5	14.8
3†	−	12.3 (1956)	−	9.4	−	−	−
4‖	14.7	13.2	9.6	12.2 (1963)	10.6	−	−

* East German figures are computed as a percentage of net material product. Data after 1967 are offered as "rough estimates," and price changes are viewed as making data after 1968 not strictly comparable with those for preceding years.
† Calculations of Frederick L. Pryor: ratios of defense expenditure to factor price GNP.
‡ Reflects official Soviet defense budget figures as a percentage of net material product.
§ SIPRI estimates of the dollar equivalent of Soviet military expenditure as a percentage of official Soviet estimates of Soviet national income.
‖ Defense share of expenditure composition of Soviet GNP.
Sources: For East Germany (2) and Soviet Union (3): Frederick L. Pryor, *Public Expenditures in Communist and Capitalist Nations* (Homewood, Ill.: Richard D. Irwin, 1968), p. 91; for Soviet Union (4): Stanley F. Cohen, "The Economic Burden of Soviet Defense Outlays," in Joint Economic Committee, *Economic Performance and the Military Burden in the Soviet Union* (Washington, D.C.: U.S. Government Printing Office, 1970), p. 169; all other data: *SIPRI Yearbook, 1974*, pp. 156–57, 208–12.

An overall pattern of declining emphasis on military expenditures in the most advanced industrial states is evident from the data in Table 7–1. In some cases such spending has declined in absolute terms. Of the eight states in our survey only East Germany has diverted an increasing share of its domestic product to the defense sector in the course of the 20-year period covered by the table. During the 1950s France and Britain joined the superpowers in diverting a comparatively large share

---

[5] *SIPRI Yearbook, 1974*, p. 142.

[6] Ibid., p. 143; *World Military Expenditures, 1963–1973*, pp. 14, 56, 61; and George Modelski, *World Power Concentrations: Typologies, Data, Explanatory Framework* (Morristown, N.J.: General Learning Press, 1974).

of resources to the military, but they have since reduced their commitment to levels closer to those of their European NATO allies. Sweden, West Germany, and Italy have consistently maintained their military burden at levels significantly lower than those of the superpowers.

In making these comparisons, one confronts the exceptional difficulties involved in developing accurate data for the Communist-ruled states. As the official defense budgets of these states are clearly less inclusive than those of their Western counterparts, experts proceed to estimate hidden budget items. A review of this literature does not generate a great deal of confidence in the accuracy of such calculations.[7] Many of the estimates are made on the basis of incomplete data and crude formulas. The substantial variations in the conclusions are suggested by an analysis of the ratios appearing in Table 7–1.

After comparing a variety of sources, we conclude that the Soviet defense expenditures/GNP ratios offered by Frederick L. Pryor and Stanley F. Cohen are most consistent with budget and deployment evidence (see Table 7–1, USSR, lines 3 and 4). The two complete series of SIPRI projections can be viewed as extreme minimum and maximum estimates. A review of post-1965 data from SIPRI and the U.S. Arms Control and Disarmament Agency suggests that the Soviet commitment probably leveled off at somewhere between 9 and 12 percent of GNP.

East Germany presents the additional problem of calculating its contribution to the large Soviet military presence on its territory. The Soviet Union's distrust of Germans and its desire to emphasize its own forces in Central Europe resulted in a notably low East German defense effort through 1967. After that year a substantial change resulted from such influences as the invasion of Czechoslovakia, new pricing policies, and increased East German contributions to the Soviet military presence. As a result, East Germany probably now maintains a defense burden that is at least average for the Warsaw Pact and higher than that of most middle-level powers in Europe.

Comparing the Warsaw Pact and NATO states as a whole, the pattern appears to be one of fairly close matching of military burdens from the 1950s through 1967. In relation to the 1956 and 1962 data, Pryor found that "the economic system does not appear to play a significant role."[8] However, after 1967 NATO defense spending began to decline after adjustment for inflation whereas Warsaw Pact programs increased substantially.[9] As a result, by the mid-1970s a substantially greater burden

---

[7] See William T. Lee, "The 'Politico-Military-Industrial Complex' of the U.S.S.R.," *Journal of International Affairs* 26, no. 1 (1972): 73–86; *SIPRI Yearbook, 1974*, pp. 172–204; Frederick A. Pryor, *Public Expenditures, in Communist and Capitalist Nations* (Homewood, Ill.: Richard D. Irwin, 1968), pp. 84–127; and Franklyn D. Holzman, *Financial Checks on Soviet Defense Expenditures* (Lexington, Mass.: Lexington Books, 1975).

[8] Pryor, *Public Expenditures*, p. 126.

[9] *World Military Expenditures, 1963–1973*, p. 15.

was probably being felt in those Eastern European countries as compared to the NATO states.

Causes of High Defense Spending

Having reviewed indicators of the extent of the chosen states' militarization, we can proceed to some vital questions of cause and effect. Why have the United States and the Soviet Union exceeded the arms burden of all or most of their allies? There are many possible explanations for high levels of militarization. Among those which have received substantial expert support are the following: (1) In an arms race, events that increase tensions and competition for qualitative and quantitative advantage make the prime competitors carry on their rivalry at ever higher levels. (2) Within a given alliance system the theory of public goods operates to encourage smaller allies to rely on the contributions of powerful alliance leaders. (3) Nations develop "military-industrial complexes" that provide domestic political support for continuing and increasing defense allocations. (4) The monetary costs of various elements of the military sector increase faster than do most civilian goods and services.

These are not the only possibilities that have been discussed in the literature. Many of the same factors that influence civilian allocations may have similar impacts on defense, including rates of national income growth. Yet the enumerated factors help make the defense sector unique.

The arms race factor gains support from Pryor's finding that the United States and the Soviet Union developed similar trends in military spending. Each of the superpowers is viewed as responding to common circumstances which included periodic changes in the expenditure and deployment patterns of the other.[10] This view is also supported by the fact that defense spending does not follow the incremental and regular patterns typical of other budget sectors. Military spending has fallen in real terms during certain periods, and increases by the leading powers have tended to come during particular crises. The sharpest increases since 1945 took place between 1949 and 1952 (Korea and the establishment of NATO), in the early 1960s (Berlin and Cuban crises), and from 1965 to 1967 (Vietnam). Notably, increases in these periods were not limited to the countries directly involved in the given wars and crises.

The mid-1970s appear to be a time of searching for ways to reduce the arms burden. However, this now requires success in highly complex negotiations for manpower reductions and ceilings on the deployment of nuclear weapons systems.

---

[10] Pryor, *Public Expenditures*, pp. 112–14.

The "free rider" phenomenon has been applied to military alliances by several leading economic and political theorists. As Bruce Russett says, "For so long as the smaller state is neither coerced by the big one nor offered special incentives, and unless the threat to the small state is very grave indeed—as in actual wartime—the small nation is likely to regard the big country's armed forces as a substitute for its own."[11]

Russett's analysis of various military alliances around the world provides evidence that countries with small national incomes do not consistently allocate smaller proportions to defense than do their larger allies. Yet the expected patterns were observed in NATO and the Warsaw Pact during the 1960s. He concludes, "The widened gap between the superpowers' defense ratios and the average for their European allies means that in continuing a policy of armed confrontation both America and Russia have become increasingly isolated from their pact members."[12] However, our data suggest that the gap has been narrowed in both alliances in recent years.

It has been suggested that such nonaligned states as Sweden tend to act as though they had the same protection from the United States and NATO as they would have if they were bloc members. However, Sweden has been more defense-oriented than have most nonaligned European states.

The attribution of high defense spending to the military-industrial complex has been more widely supported than any other explanation since President Dwight Eisenhower warned against the power of the complex in his 1961 "farewell address."[13] The essence of this argument is that once the defense sector is well established it generates virtually unstoppable pressures to maintain and expand itself. A military-industrial complex may have as its base the uniformed and civilian employees of the defense ministry and the workers and management of the institutions involved in military-oriented research and production. However, the supporters of the defense sector may reach out to a very broad public that benefits from defense contracts and payrolls or provides support based on ideological considerations.

Most critically, such a broad constituency may develop direct control over vital structures and processes involved in policy-making. Support may be evident in parliaments and political parties as well as in-

---

[11] Russett, *What Price Vigilance?* (New Haven: Yale University Press, 1970), p. 93.

[12] Ibid., p. 116.

[13] See the special issue of the *Journal of International Affairs* entitled "The Military-Industrial Complex: USSR/USA," vol. 26, no. 1 (1972); Yarmolinsky, *Military Establishment;* Russett, *What Price Vigilance?* and Seymour Melman, ed., *The War Economy of the United States* (New York: St. Martin's Press, 1971).

terest groups and executive departments. Public opinion can be won over through sustained indoctrination via the mass media.

The concept of the military-industrial complex is viewed here as quite valid and useful for analysis of the Soviet Union and the United States but as much less relevant to the policy processes of the other states in our survey. If we compare the role of such an entity in the two leading powers, it appears that the Soviet version has come to have a stronger hold. This conclusion is partly based on the American government's reduction of its armed forces and military expenditures (in constant prices) in the post-Vietnam period while Moscow has failed to follow suit. It is also supported by a series of budget-cutting and program-reduction votes in Congress and parallel positions taken by Democratic party bodies since the late 1960s.

This is not to suggest that the Soviet and American patterns are altogether different. It was difficult to find substantial opposition to major increases in U.S. military programs in the first half of the 1960s. In contrast, Nikita Khrushchev apparently made some progress in limiting the demands of what he termed the "metal eaters" in the late 50s and early 60s.

The major differences include the broader base of military and defense production support within the Soviet government and the greater autonomy and access to political power of Soviet military leaders. This is compensated for in the United States by such phenomena as the extremely close relations between the Pentagon and key congressional committees and the support given by individual congressmen to military programs affecting their districts. On balance, the Soviet structure seems to be more durable.

Such a support base is much less potent in countries which have not built up major systems of military-related research and defense production. To the extent that the allies of the two superpowers depend on their protectors for such goods, they need not confront domestic producers.

Britain and France stand out among the European middle powers in the scope of their weapons production. This is highlighted by their status as nuclear powers. In addition, they lead this group of states in volume of arms exports. Sweden and West Germany rank a few steps behind in arms production and export capability (the former being viewed in relation to its small population). Italy and East Germany appear to be relatively small weapons producers that are quite dependent on arms imports.

Finally, the costs of weapons systems and manpower play an important role in determining patterns of military spending and greatly influence government decisions about whether to compete in various areas. Inflation in the defense sector has far exceeded that in national economies as a whole. For example, the 1972 U.S. F-15 aircraft cost almost 20 times as much as the F-84 produced 26 years earlier.[14]

To a great extent the superpowers have priced most other states out of the competition for production of the most sophisticated weapons systems. They can achieve economies of scale that other states cannot approach. This compels other countries to buy certain systems from the superpowers and thus helps the superpowers subsidize their arms production. However, due to the expense of intercontinental missiles and the preference of the superpowers for such weapons systems, these remain superpower monopolies and increase the gap in military burdens between the superpowers and their allies.

Personnel costs also contribute to differences in military expenditures, but not to the same extent as weapons development. The movement away from conscription and toward a closer relationship between military and civilian pay has increased personnel costs in each of the eight states. Although the effects have been lessened by the tendency to decrease the size of the armed forces, most major states have increased the share of personnel costs in their defense budgets during the past decade.

Results

Though military programs may reap benefits in such areas as education and technical spin-offs, their central value is security. Have the leading industrial states bought greater security with their record peacetime military allocations? At a lower level of abstraction, have they acquired the capability that they sought from their defense allocations?

It is possible to argue that the peoples of Europe and North America have become more secure from external threats. The main evidence of security is the absence of large-scale armed conflict on these continents. None of the countries in our survey have been invaded since 1945, and a case can be made that a nuclear stalemate and relatively equal conventional capability have contributed to this outcome. From this viewpoint it is argued that a nation does increase its security when it raises itself out of a position of inferiority or creates a capability to inflict unacceptable damage to a potential adversary.

However, this is not the whole picture. As Russett notes, allocations to defense that are combined with slowed growth in critical areas of physical and human resources development can reduce a nation's abil-

---

[14] As calculated in constant (1962) prices. *SIPRI Yearbook, 1974,* p. 137. For further information on U.S. costs see Barry M. Blechman et al., *Setting National Priorities: The 1976 Budget* (Washington, D.C.: Brookings Institution, 1975), pp. 85–152.

ity to defend itself.[15] Others stress the risk factor in the arms race and the politics of brinkmanship. The world is probably in greater danger from major war through accident, individual irrationality, or uncontrollable crisis developments now than ever before. Finally, some of the billions that have gone to defense have done no more than create perceptions of warlike aims and promote escalation of the arms race. Such spending can in no sense be viewed as increasing security.

The survey states have made many policy decisions designed to maximize the value obtained from their particular defense budgets and to fulfill their respective military doctrines. Have some states obtained more capability than others in relation to their budget and resource input?

Some factors that relate to this question seem virtually indisputable. First, states that use low-paid draftees instead of volunteers can save as much as 1.5 percent of GNP. This has been a particularly large source of savings for the Soviet Union and France. Second, nations with larger defense industries can save considerably on "economies of scale" in unit production costs for equipment. For this reason and because of the noncomparability of nuclear and nonnuclear weapons, the middle powers cannot hope to match the great powers on a dollar-for-dollar basis. The very small nuclear capacities of Britain and France appear to be among the most uneconomical of investments, especially considering their high vulnerability.

The question of capability in relation to input probably cannot be answered very satisfactorily. Military capability involves more than the purchase of trained manpower and sophisticated equipment. It is affected by a wide range of factors that include energy and raw material reserves and high public morale. Consequently, very diverse kinds of government distributions may affect military capability.

Tables 7–2 and 7–3 compare the eight survey countries in regard to major indicators of military power. It is important to recognize that such measures are necessarily crude because of the breadth of particular categories. "Major surface combat vessels" includes both multibillion dollar aircraft carriers and mere frigates. The figures given therefore tend to minimize the differentials in the military capability of the two superpowers, the middle group, and the weakest countries. Of the nonsuperpowers, only France and Britain have invested in missiles and nuclear weapons. These countries have linked their modest nuclear weapons programs with the development of respectable navies, thereby setting themselves apart from the lesser powers in this category as well.

---

[15] Russett, *What Price Vigilance?* p. 179.

TABLE 7–2
Comparisons of Military Manpower, 1973 (ranked by total armed forces as percent of military-age males)

	Armed Forces: Regulars and Conscripts	Paramilitary Forces	Trained Reservists*	Armed Forces as Percentage of Military- Age Males
1. Soviet Union.........	3,425,000	300,000	3,000,000	6.8
2. United States	2,252,900	–	927,400	5.8
3. Sweden	93,100	–	557,000	5.8
4. France..............	503,600	85,000	540,000	5.0
5. East Germany	132,000	80,000	250,000	4.1
6. West Germany.......	475,000	20,000	625,000	4.0
7. Italy................	427,500	80,700	545,000	3.9
8. United Kingdom	361,500	–	435,000	3.3

* The definition of trained reservist varies from country to country.

Source: International Institute for Strategic Studies, *The Military Balance, 1973–1974* (London, 1973), p. 77.

TABLE 7–3
Inventories of Major Weapons Systems, July 1973 (ranked by total systems)

	Intercontinental Ballistic Missiles (ICBM)	Submarine- Launched Ballistic Missiles (SLBM)	Intermediate- and Medium- Range Bal- listic Missiles	Major Surface Combat Ships	Combat Aircraft, Air Force Only
1. Soviet Union	1,527	628	600	212	8,250
2. United States	1,054	656	0	221	5,750
3. United Kingdom	0	64	0	78	500
4. France	0	32	18	47	500
5. West Germany	0	0	0	17	456
6. Sweden	0	0	0	13	600*
7. Italy................	0	0	0	21	330
8. East Germany.........	0	0	0	0	320

* The Swedish total includes a considerable number of aircraft that would not be retained in the air forces of the other countries surveyed.

Source: International Institute for Strategic Studies, *The Military Balance, 1973–1974* (London, 1973).

The relationship between the two rival superpowers involves what appears to be a dramatic shift in the power of the Soviet Union since the mid-1960s. Up to that time the United States matched the Soviet Union in manpower and held major qualitative and quantitative advantages in most aspects of nuclear warfare capability. By 1975 Moscow was deploying three times as much army manpower as that of the United States, maintaining four times as many tanks and more submarines and surface vessels, and had a greater number of intercontinental missiles. Washington, in turn, retained major quantitative advantages in most major categories of aircraft, in aircraft carriers, and probably most significantly in missile warheads. Most observers granted the United States continuing, but declining, advantages in the technical quality of critical weapons systems.[16] A situation of clear American superiority in most theaters of possible warfare had been replaced within a decade by overall rough parity and a dramatically enlarged area in which Soviet power could be deployed on a competitive or superior scale. Moscow had apparently bought more power than Washington since 1960.

Moscow has attempted to manipulate statistics in such ways as to appear to be outstripping its principal rival with less involvement of resources. Prices, wages, and budget data all go into the deceptive accounting. Yet artificially low prices in military-related items cannot mask the cost of manpower and resources that could be used for other purposes. Low or nonexistent turnover taxes collected on defense goods, low conscript wages, and military budgets hidden under headings for science or national economy do not really make defense cheap for Moscow. Undoubtedly, catching up and keeping up with the United States have been enormous burdens for the Soviet Union. No economies have kept Moscow from having to divert to defense a substantially greater share of its resources as compared to the United States in such areas as research and development. The Soviet Union may still be getting somewhat more value than is the United States for its investment in defense, but the difference is probably not great.

Finally, we address the relationship of military allocations and the overall interests of the corporate structure and economic development. Although high military spending may promote particular companies, governmental organizations, and regions, it is generally a drag on the total industrial sector and on the economy as a whole. Stanley F. Cohn provides evidence that the Soviet Union's defense budget has harmed many other areas of Soviet economic investment, including basic industry.[17] Similarly, Russett found that in the United States "proportionately . . . investment is much harder hit by an expansion of the military establishment than is consumption."[18] Although Britain and France have been able to maintain investment levels during periods of high defense spending they have not disproved the idea that defense spending has a generally negative impact on investment and economic growth.[19] Clearly a military-industrial state may well re-

---

[16] See International Institute for Strategic Studies, The Military Balance, 1973–1974 (London, 1973), and subsequent editions; and SIPRI Yearbook, 1974, especially chaps. 4, 6.

[17] "The Economic Burden of Soviet Defense Outlays," in Joint Economic Committee, Economic Performance and the Military Burden in the Soviet Union, pp. 170–71.

[18] Russett, What Price Vigilance? p. 144.

[19] It should be acknowledged that economic growth is a product of dozens of factors. See Edward F. Denison, Why Growth Rates Differ (Washington, D.C.: Brookings Institution, 1967).

flect a shortsighted pattern of allocations even in relation to the interests of many of its chief supporters.

POST-INDUSTRIALISM

New public policy issues and priorities continue to result from important changes in the social, economic, and technological structure of advanced societies. Post-industrial trends, as suggested by Daniel Bell,[20] include unprecedented affluence, leisure, and the emergence of a dominantly service economy. The professional and technical classes establish preeminence because of their access to theoretical and applied knowledge that sustains complex planning. Government establishes control over the direction of science, and the university challenges the corporation as a center for technological advances and input into social policy.[21] Increased bureaucratization develops together with growing consciousness of its excesses and dangers.

Indeed, a new critical consciousness may be the decisive intervening factor of the age.[22] We say intervening because such consciousness is viewed as the product of socioeconomic and technological change and as the catalyst for a new political agenda.

The development of a revised set of political priorities has not been given a great deal of attention in the literature of post-industrialism. Huntington comments on the apolitical character of the initial discussion by Bell, Brzezinski, and others.[23] His own contribution emphasizes revised patterns of power and process, giving special attention to the rise of the mass media and new mass movements as challengers to the bureaucracies.

Yet post-industrial politics is already producing new priorities as well as new structures and processes. These priorities fit into our framework as distributions, extractions, and regulations. The proposed extractions include new efforts to use the tax system to redistribute income, as with negative income and wealth taxation. Long-term military service based on compulsion and sacrifice is becoming impossible to sustain.

Conventional approaches to the regulation of individuals and groups

---

[20] Daniel Bell, *The Coming of Post-Industrial Society* (New York: Basic Books, 1973).

[21] This summary of the sources and structural elements of post-industrial society reflects the views of Zbigniew Brzezinski, *Between Two Ages: America's Role in the Technetronic Age* (New York: Viking Press, 1970), and Alex Inkeles, "The Emerging Social Structure of the World," *World Politics* 27 (July 1975), pp. 467–595, as well as those of Bell.

[22] See Herbert Marcuse, *One-Dimensional Man* (Boston: Beacon Press, 1964); and M. Donald Hancock and Gideon Sjoberg, eds., *Politics in the Post-Welfare State* (New York: Columbia University Press, 1972).

[23] Samuel P. Huntington, "Postindustrial Politics: How Benign Will It Be?" *Comparative Politics* 6, no. 2 (January 1974): 163–91.

are increasingly rejected, as official and unofficial wards of society demand emancipation and equality. Students, homosexuals, the aged, women, prisoners, and mental patients are all involved in this movement to reform ineffective or repressive practices. Contemporaneously, new priorities are being established in the regulation of public institutions and private enterprises, priorities which emphasize revised standards of public health, safety, aesthetics, and morality. Post-industrial constituencies have been developed by environmentalists, consumerists, and civil libertarians at levels of intensity never before approached. Frontier issues for regulation include control over "progress" in genetics, the sustaining of life, and behavior modification.[24] The stakes in these issues are enormous for individual human beings and for the human species as a whole.

A greater sensitivity to tax and regulatory issues in the most advanced societies does not mean that distributions have become irrelevant. At one level the welfare state must be improved to meet earlier standards. As one observer argues, "Post-welfare politics is emerging while the controversies of welfare politics continue in full force."[25] On another plane post-industrial society takes a broader view of the necessary range of distributions, placing more emphasis on those not counted as either guns or butter. The new distributions tend to be more closely related to nonmaterial values. Further, higher qualitative standards are being used to evaluate services.

Bell distinguishes industrial and post-industrial societies largely in relation to distributions. He stresses the point as follows:

> If an industrial society is defined by the quantity of goods as marking a standard of living, the post-industrial society is defined by the quality of life as measured by the services and amenities—health, education, recreation, and the arts—which are now deemed desirable and possible for everyone.[26]

This perspective may seem to blur distinctions between the welfare state and post-industrial priorities. Yet it is evident that the welfare state in most "advanced" countries developed within a somewhat narrow framework, one that was limited both in the sphere of education and in such "frill" areas as recreation and the arts.

For Galbraith some post-industrial priorities are still weakly established, though the most advanced parts of Western Europe are viewed as ahead of the United States in a number of newly critical areas. In his

---

[24] See Alvin Toffler, *Future Shock* (New York: Random House, 1970); and B. F. Skinner, *Beyond Freedom and Dignity* (New York: Alfred A. Knopf, 1971).

[25] John Milton Cooper, Jr., "Neo-Progressivism and 'Slack-Water Politics,' " in Hancock and Sjoberg, *Post-Welfare State,* p. 51.

[26] Bell, *Post-Industrial Society,* p. 127.

view America stresses distributions to the "planning system"—including national defense, industrial research and development, support to technical education, and the building of interstate highways.[27] Others see such expenditures and the "planning system" as basic elements of post-industrial society. Yet Galbraith continues to reflect concern for the paucity of certain public expenditures, concentrating on such targets as the arts and the varied needs of the larger cities.

Post-industrial distributions may be deemed to include those that sustain the planning system as well as those associated with the quality of life. In the 1960s European writers like Servan-Schreiber emphasized the gaps in management training, market size, and technological level that separated such countries as France from the United States.[28] Galbraith presents as a mirror image of "the American challenge" the relative backwardness of cultural life, urban renewal, and transport in the United States.

Post-Industrialism as a Mirage

An academic backlash has recently assaulted the proposal that countries with advanced economies have emerged into a new and "higher" stage of development beyond industrialization and welfarism. This is not surprising in the light of the inflation, unemployment, slowed economic growth, and resource shortages that have left a deep mark on Western life in the mid-1970s. Several alleged manifestations of post-industrial politics have faded, including student protests and the particular mixture of ideas termed New Leftism. In some advanced states, progress toward affluence and leisure has slowed while old institutions cling to power.

Such countertrends are real and must be given weight together with evidence in support of rushing futurism. We simply cannot know whether Europe and North America will overcome existing shortages and strains and reestablish patterns of growth and stability. We must revise the image of post-industrial politics to include the need to adapt to expensive and politically controlled energy, food, and other critical resources. We must also recognize that post-industrial politics will proceed together with the continued politics of welfare and defense. A whole new political agenda will not take shape all at once in any coun-

---

[27] Galbraith, *Economics and the Public Purpose*, p. 285.

[28] Jean-Jacques Servan-Schreiber, *The American Challenge*, trans. Ronald Steel (New York: Atheneum, 1968). Such themes are also emphasized in Soviet commentaries. See Robbin Laird, "Post-Industrial Society: East and West," *Survey* 21, no. 4 (Autumn 1975): 13–14.

try, and emulative processes will often proceed slowly. Yet the new concerns identified as post-industrial are also genuine, and many will occupy us for decades or longer.

Convergence

Discussion of the elements of post-industrialism inevitably brings to the fore the question of whether trends in knowledge, social structure, abundance, and values are part of a growing "convergence" of all developed economies and politics. Many theorists of post-industrialism comment on this question, offering sharply differing conclusions.

The case for convergence is based on the spread from Scandinavia and North America of most of the basic elements of socioeconomic structure and priorities noted by Bell and Brzezinski. As applied to Soviet and American developments, the convergence thesis emphasizes bureaucracy, planning, militarization, education, and even the closer relationships between government and enterprises. Those who have perceived or projected considerable bridging of differences include Pitirim Sorokim, C. Wright Mills, Herbert Marcuse, and Jan Tinbergen. Perhaps the best-known vision of convergence is that of the dissident Soviet physicist-publicist Andrei Sakharov. He anticipates that "in the fourth stage, the socialist convergence will reduce differences in social structure, promote intellectual freedom, science, and economic progress, and lead to the creation of a world government and the smoothing of national contradictions (1980–2000)."[29]

Supporters of convergence constitute a formidable body of social thinkers. Yet the critics of this idea now seem to be dominant. Their criticism begins with the argument that similarities in such foundational spheres as social structure and technology are overstated by the theorists of convergence. As Hancock points out, even Sweden and the United States differ considerably in terms of post-industrial characteristics. In his view Sweden remains the more highly stratified society, though manifesting modern values to a greater extent.[30] Brzezinski and Sakharov agree that the technological lag of the Soviet Union in relation to the United States is great and may be increasing.

The rejection of convergence is probably most virulent in mainstream Soviet writing. Soviet journals are filled with references to a "scientific-technological revolution" that is viewed as accelerating

---

[29] "Progress, Coexistence, and Intellectual Freedom," June 1968, in Harrison Salisbury, ed., *Sakharov Speaks* (New York: Alfred A. Knopf, 1974), p. 109.

[30] M. Donald Hancock, "The United States, Europe, and Post-Industrial Society," *Comparative Politics* 4, no. 1 (October 1971): 139–40.

historical progress.[31] Yet in the official Soviet view such advantages of socialism as effective long-range planning will allow countries like the Soviet Union to adapt to new technological developments without substantial social disruption while the West flounders and fragments.

Several leading American views on the possibilities of convergence in post-industrial society are almost as cautious as the official Soviet line. For Inkeles, all of the processes identified as post-industrial "are, . . . subject to countervailing and contradictory trends which greatly mute the force of the tendency toward the emergence of a uniform world culture."[32] Bell agrees with the Soviet writers who insist that societies differ in the way they relate their political systems to social structure and culture. He notes that "there can be socialist post-industrial societies as there could be capitalist, just as both the Soviet Union and the United States, though separated along the axis of property, are both industrial societies."[33]

Conclusion: Post-Industrialism and Convergence

Our investigation of post-industrial society and convergence leads us to conclude that both concepts remain highly controversial and that readers must form their own opinions based on conflicting evidence. We lean to the idea that changes in social structure, technological and bureaucratic capability, and values have been of sufficient magnitude to compel a new framework for public policy in at least a few advanced societies. Emulatory processes are rapidly spreading many of these new elements and the political issues created by them. This new public policy embraces such diverse questions as life-sustaining medical devices, women's liberation, pollution control, and lifetime continuing education. Such issues do not fall under the other categories of welfare state and military-industrial politics, though the lines are not always clear-cut.

Post-industrial politics operates contemporaneously with welfarism and militarization, and is generally subordinate to either or both in even the most advanced countries. Post-industrial issues and priorities are only in the process of emerging, though the agenda is already fairly crowded. National leadership varies from one issue to another, with West Germany in an advanced position in at least one area—worker participation in management—and relatively backward in many areas

---

[31] This literature is reviewed in Laird, "Post-Industrial Society"; and Donald R. Kelley, "The Soviet Debate on Convergence of American and Soviet Systems," *Polity* 6, no. 2 (Winter 1973): 174–96.

[32] Inkeles, "Emerging Social Structure," p. 495.

[33] Bell, *Post-Industrial Society*, p. 114.

of education. Sweden is generally viewed as holding a leadership position in such diverse areas as women's liberation and mental health care. The United States is most closely identified with the structural underpinning of post-industrialism and has been the place of origin for many of the mass movements and mass media phenomena that characterize it.

The question of East-West convergence seems far more difficult to assess than that of whether post-industrialism is emerging. It is perhaps useful to separate the components of politics for the purpose of evaluation. The strongest case for convergence appears to lie in the existence and impending emergence of common problems requiring political response. Communist rule has exempted Eastern Europe from few of the major problems that increasingly concern the West. Among such issues that do not appear significant in the East are pornography and school discipline. However, East and West share such problems as pollution, the expansion of education, excessive bureaucracy, the loss of privacy, and adjustment to the rapid development of technology. New concessions to consumerism in most of Eastern Europe suggest that the remaining differences in the political agendas of East and West may be further reduced.

These similar problems are handled through significantly different political processes but result in Eastern European public policies that are not consistently at variance with trends in the West. The differences in process factors involve both values and structures. The direction of the new value systems proclaimed in Communist-ruled countries differs from the "critical consciousness" emerging in the most affluent Western states. Although much of such critical consciousness may be submerged in the highly controlled Communist political system, the sum of evidence suggests that support of advanced conceptions of human rights, opposition to industrial pollution, and other key post-industrial orientations are limited to relatively narrow elites in most Communist-ruled countries. This is closely linked with the limited development of autonomous groups capable of articulating demands in such areas. As a result, Communist political processes are normally left under the control of competing entrenched bureaucracies with minimal post-industrial orientations.[34] Other elites and the amorphous masses must strive for inputs into this process with minimal concentration of power and minimal publicity.

The fact that the policy outputs and outcomes of the Communist-ruled systems are often similar to those of the West is partly to be explained by the often limited and negative effects of liberal democratic

---

[34] See Cynthia Enloe, *The Politics of Pollution in a Comparative Perspective* (New York: David McKay Co., 1975), pp. 190–220.

and social democratic attitudes as well as interest group pluralism in many Western countries. It also suggests that socioeconomic and technological imperatives are at work which political systems cannot affect decisively.

Education in Post-Industrial Society

Education is an integral part of the welfare, military-industrial, and post-industrial states. Much of elementary and secondary training can be linked to the welfare state. This is justified by the relationship between basic education and the ability to get and keep a job and to claim benefits from government. The modern conception of the welfare state, as developed in North America and most of Europe, includes universal, compulsory, and free elementary and early secondary schooling.

The military-industrial state is no less dependent on education. This was directly underscored when the United States responded to Soviet triumphs in space in the late 1950s by reevaluating its secondary school programs and expanding federal assistance to higher education under the rubric of the National Defense Education Act. The warfare state requires a broad base of researchers, technicians, engineers, and production workers as well as uniformed personnel adaptable to sophisticated training. High defense expenditures may have a depressing effect on education spending in some countries. Yet the education sector has continued to expand independently of defense trends in most of the countries studied by Russett.[35] Association with military and industrial goals helps produce exceptional commitments to education in most advanced societies. This connection is made more often in the Soviet Union and other Communist-ruled states than in most advanced Western states. Yet many Western states are giving increasing attention to manpower development.

The positive association between education and industrial growth is apparently genuine. Denison has employed quantitative analysis to establish that between 1950 and 1962 increased education raised the quality of labor more and contributed more to the growth rate of real national income in the United States than in Northwest Europe.[36]

Yet education may be more closely related to the emerging post-industrial agenda than to welfare or warfare. Education, and most directly higher education, can be viewed as a major source both of the "technocratic" forces and of the consciousness that has led to resistance to and the redirection of public policy in post-industrial society.

---

[35] Russett, *What Price Vigilance?* p. 176.
[36] Denison, *Why Growth Rates Differ*, pp. 103–6.

Brzezinski, seeking to spell out the central place of education in post-industrial society, contends that in the technetronic society:

1. Education is universal, advanced training is available to almost all who have the basic talents, and there is far greater emphasis on quality selection.
2. The educational process becomes lengthier and is increasingly reliant on audiovisual aids, and the flow of new knowledge necessitates more and more frequent refresher studies.
3. Plutocratic preeminence is challenged by the political leadership, which is itself increasingly permeated by individuals possessing special skills and intellectual talents. Thus knowledge becomes a tool of power and the effective mobilization of talent becomes an important way to acquire power.
4. The university becomes an intensely involved "think tank," the source of much sustained political planning and social innovation.[37]

In setting out this approach, Brzezinski builds on Bell's foundation. Bell conceives of post-industrial society as one in which knowledge is the dominant resource, the university and research institutes are the social loci, scientists and researchers are the dominant figures, and education is a central means of access to power.[38]

Neither Bell nor Brzezinski places great emphasis on the educational system as the source of critical consciousness. The latter is openly scornful of countercultural orientations, especially those placed under the rubric of the New Left. However, New Left theorists like Marcuse are not alone in viewing the university as a source of dissident views. As Galbraith has noted:

> The universities . . . are a source of both dissident and supporting attitudes. Their emphasis on personality makes their members congenitally suspicious or skeptical of the purposes of the planning system. But the formal pedagogy, notably in economics but also in political science, strongly upholds them.[39]

The Emerging Consensus on Education Goals. An impressively broad area of agreement has emerged, especially among policy-makers in Western Europe and North America, concerning educational opportunity, structure, and purposes. This growing consensus has been influenced by conferences, study missions, and other activities of such international organizations as the Organization for Economic Coopera-

---

[37] Brzezinski, *Between Two Ages*, pp. 12–13.

[38] Bell, *Post-Industrial Society*, p. 359.

[39] Galbraith, *Economics and the Public Purpose*, p. 220. For Marcuse's position see *Counter-Revolution and Revolt* (Boston: Beacon Press, 1972), p. 32.

tion and Development (OECD) and the United Nations Educational, Scientific, and Cultural Organization (UNESCO).

Such external pressures have reinforced even more significant internal factors that have promoted trends that can be summarized under the rubrics democratization and modernization.[40] Among the major domestic forces that have been observed are changing levels of family aspiration, rapid job and technological obsolescence, a growing need for subprofessionals with substantial education and training, and a lack of confidence in the fairness and effectiveness of older patterns. Both elites and average citizens have moved toward greater appreciation of the potential economic, political, and cultural benefits of expanded and modernized education. With conservatism often entrenched among teachers and educational administrators, political leaders have often acted as catalysts for more rapid change. However, in a number of countries the major pressures for change have come from within the educational establishment.

In some instances exponents of the emerging consensus have referred directly to post-industrial trends. In 1972 an OECD study group called for educational systems "designed for a society that has reached such levels of material prosperity and psychic maturity that it can no longer define its goals in the fairly simple terms of material accumulation."[41]

The particular directions of the democratization and modernization program are drawn from the experience of numerous countries. The major models appear to include the United States, the Soviet Union, and Sweden. Other states, including Great Britain, have contributed models for such particular programs as adult higher education.

The core of the prescription for change endorsed by OECD and UNESCO representatives is a program for increasing exposure to formal education, especially by groups now facing patterns of discrimination. The affected groups include children of working-class and rural families, women, the physically and mentally handicapped, and national and racial minorities. The varied sources of discrimination that make effective change difficult include financial, psychological, and pedagogic barriers operating within and outside the formal educational system. Expanded educational opportunity is to be provided in the preadult period and, as permanent education, throughout adult life. Outmoded methods of evaluation and choice are to be eliminated in favor of methods that delay critical occupational and educational decisions

---

[40] For an attempt to encompass most of the major trends under the heading democratization see A. le Gall et al., *Present Problems in the Democratization of Secondary and Higher Education* (Paris: UNESCO, 1973).

[41] *Reviews of National Policies for Education: Germany* (Paris: OECD, 1972), p. 53.

until the upper secondary or higher education years and that leave maximum flexibility for second chances and new directions.

The primary structure related to expanded opportunity is the comprehensive middle and secondary school that delays or minimizes the "tracking" of students into separate paths of life. Other widely recommended structural adaptations are widespread preprimary programs and the universalization of secondary schooling. Higher education is expected to expand in direct proportion to the growth of secondary programs that include preparation for the diverse universities and institutes.[42] Growth at the secondary and higher education levels and in adult programs is assumed to require a high level of long-range planning for facilities and instructors.

The qualitative dimension of educational change is at least as closely related to post-industrial change as is the quantitative element. The critical question here is the purpose of education. The traditional emphasis on learning facts, discipline, and basic orientations to employment has been redirected and broadened to include the encouragement of participation, criticism, tolerance, and inquiry. Vocational goals are increasingly defined in relation to dynamic technological and employment patterns. A growing appreciation of citizen and cultural education has accompanied the changing definition of vocational training. The idea that education should coexist or alternate with employment throughout careers has led to suggestions for creative processes for reaching employed adults. Encouragement has been given to a common core of secondary studies as a reinforcement to open opportunity, and higher education has been called upon to diversify types of institutions while avoiding excessive specialization.

The emphasis placed here on consensus should be supplemented with reference to continuing outposts of traditionalism in even the most "progressive" countries and the continued domination of these outposts in several major European systems. A long-standing debate centers on the extent and pace of educational reform. The proponents of reform have been bolstered by much of the evidence on cross-national academic attainment gathered and analyzed during the past decade under the auspices of the International Association for the Evaluation of Education Achievement (IEA).[43] In the view of Torsten Husén, a Swedish educator, the extensive testing of students from numerous countries confirms his belief that comprehensive secondary education allows elite students to perform as well as their counterparts in tradi-

---

[42] Conference of Ministers of Education of European Member States of UNESCO on Access to Higher Education, *Access to Higher Education in Europe* (Paris: UNESCO, 1968), p. 83; and *The Educational Situation in OECD Countries* (Paris: OECD, 1974).

[43] See Alan C. Purves and Daniel U. Levine, eds., *Educational Policy and International Achievement* (Berkeley, Calif.: McCutchan Publishing Co., 1975).

tionally tracked systems, while the other students gain measurably from their longer exposure to academic programs.[44] Yet many still regard comprehensive schools as inconsistent with perceived variations in inherent academic ability and social environments. They see elitist and alternative schools as too valuable to eliminate and see virtue in having secondary schools emulate higher education in the pursuit of divergence in program and standards.[45]

Despite the remaining disagreement we will evaluate the eight national educational systems in the light of the standards and goals set out in most OECD and UNESCO proclamations. Although we recognize that education is inherently difficult to evaluate objectively, these standards do offer a basis for comparison.

Quantitative Leaders: The United States, Sweden, and the Soviet Union. To lead in education is not to be free from major problems and shortcomings. Illustrations of the latter include the growing waste in American inner-city secondary schools, continued elitism in selection for higher education in Sweden, and as viewed by numerous subjective observers, the unwillingness of Soviet teachers to instill attitudes and skills that encourage criticism of subject matter and society.

Nonetheless, the United States, Sweden, and the Soviet Union clearly lead in the objective evidence of democratization presented below in Tables 7-4 through 7-7, and they have each been applauded for significant innovations on behalf of comprehensive, continuing, and flexible education. They outspend the other countries in our survey and provide the broadest opportunities for higher education.

In contrast to the long-term lead of the United States in the democratization of education, the superior quantitative levels of Swedish and Soviet education have been reached largely during the past few decades. Even before World War II the majority of American teenagers graduated from high school. Today more than three quarters achieve this objective, and the majority of the graduates proceed to some form of postsecondary experience.[46] Evidence of quantitative progress is evident in regard to females, and American blacks now enroll in higher education at rates that exceed most European rates for majority communities. Only in the 1960s did most European countries reach the pre-1940 levels of American school participation.[47] With spending for private schooling added to the U.S. commitment to public education the total reached 8.0 percent of GNP in 1971 before leveling off.

---

[44] Ibid., pp. 117–46.

[45] See comments by Martin Trow in ibid., pp. 146–52.

[46] U.S. Department of Health, Education, and Welfare, *Progress of Education in the United States of America, 1972–73 and 1973–74* (Washington, D.C.: U.S. Government Printing Office, 1975), p. 6.

[47] Arnold J. Heidenheimer, "The Politics of Public Education, Health, and Welfare in the U.S.A. and Western Europe," *British Journal of Political Science* 3, part 3 (July 1973): 320.

TABLE 7–4

**Public Expenditure on Education as Percentage of GNP
(ranked by 1972 ratios)**

	1972	1965	1955
1. Sweden*.................	7.9*	6.2	4.14
2. Soviet Union†............	7.6	7.3†	—
3. United States	6.5	5.3	3.35
4. United Kingdom	5.9	5.1	2.67
5. East Germany†...........	5.7	5.2	—
6. Italy.....................	5.2	—	2.98
7. France..................	—	4.55	2.87
8. West Germany	4.5 (1971)	3.4	2.17

* Percent of gross domestic product at market prices.
† Percent of net material product.
Sources: For 1955: *Reviews of National Policies for Education: France*
(Paris: OECD, 1971), p. 48; all others: *Unesco Statistical Yearbook, 1974*
(Paris: Unesco Press, 1975), pp. 466–90.

TABLE 7–5

Median Educational Attainment of 25–34 Age Group

	Year	Median Years of Schooling
1. Sweden	1970	12.75
2. United States	1970	12.54
	1960	12.23
3. East Germany........	1971	11.88
4. Soviet Union	1970	10.09 (age group 20–29)
	1959	7.52
5. West Germany	1970	6.98
6. France................	1962	5.01
7. Italy..................	1961	4.05

Source: *Unesco Statistical Yearbook, 1974* (Paris: Unesco Press, 1975),
pp. 53–82.

TABLE 7–6

**Full-Time Enrollment Rates for Various Age Groups in OECD Countries
(percentage of age group enrolled; ranked by 15–18 ratio)**

	Year	Age 15	Age 18	Ages 15–18	Age 21
1. United States	1970	97.7%	53.8%	82.9%	28.3%*
2. Sweden	1972	96.7	40.8	68.1	17.9
3. France	1970	80.5	29.1	54.3	15.6
4. United Kingdom........	1970	73.0	17.6	39.4	12.4†
5. Italy	1966	42.1	20.2	30.8	7.0
6. West Germany..........	1969	54.9	15.7	30.5	9.5‡

* Estimate.
† Age 20.
‡ In 1968.
Source: *The Educational Situation in OECD Countries* (Paris: OECD, 1974), pp. 27, 34.

TABLE 7-7

Gross Enrollment Ratios for Various Age Groups, All Students, and Females, 1972 (ranked by third-level ratios)

		Second Level (Age)	Third Level (20–24)
1. United States	M–F	96 (13–17)	51.48
	F	–	45.01
2. Sweden	M–F	74 (13–19)	22.39
	F	74	19.16
3. Soviet Union	M–F	67 (15–17)	22.25
	F	–	22.52
4. Italy	M–F	64 (11–18)	20.11
	F	59	15.68
5. West Germany...........	M–F	70 (11–18)	17.13
	F	66	–
6. France	M–F	81 (11–17)	16.99
	F	84	–
7. East Germany (1970)......	M–F	61 (15–18)	15.04
	F	–	10.92
8. United Kingdom	M–F	76 (11–17)	15.00
	F	77	11.00

Sources: *UNESCO Statistical Yearbook, 1974* (Paris: UNESCO, 1975), pp. 138–53; for East Germany: *UNESCO Statistical Yearbook, 1972*, p. 110.

As noted by Coombs, "The United States has thus become an 'educational society,' with education its largest industry."[48] Remarkable aspects of this evolution include the paucity of national planning and the modest level of financial aid and other supports for participation by low-income families in America's educational system. Key contributing factors include public confidence in the capacity of education to provide high-income employment and to cure social problems ranging from crime to poverty. In a broader sense mass education has been sustained by the American emphasis on equal opportunity.

The Soviet Union symbolizes and leads the strong commitment to educational opportunity maintained in all Communist-ruled states, but has only recently made available educational resources on a scale rivaling that of the United States. Only in the 1970s have Soviet comprehensive secondary schools been extended to a ten-year program. The Soviet Union's higher education system, though extensive, provides for fewer places in regular day programs than are sought by those eligible for admission. Yet the Soviet Union has the largest correspondence, evening, and adult vocational programs in the world. Soviet citizens apparently engage in part-time studies at a higher rate than do those of any other major country. The Soviet Union's financial incentives to students are unsurpassed among our survey countries, and a genuine effort is made to insure that no academic talent is left undeveloped.

---

[48] Philip H. Coombs, *The World Educational Crisis* (New York: Oxford University Press, 1968), p. 20.

Regional and urban-rural variations remain significant, and family status remains highly relevant to higher education recruitment. Yet progress on these fronts has been substantial and is continuing.

Sweden has also moved rapidly since the 1950s to expand educational opportunity. By 1970 Sweden's 25–34 age group had obtained almost double the years of schooling received by their parents and had surpassed their American contemporaries in some measures (see Table 7–5). Since 1950 Swedish higher education has expanded from modest levels to the leading position in Western Europe. This pattern has been fueled by a comparable expansion of upper secondary enrollment. Early childhood programs have lagged, and only modest success has been achieved in overcoming higher education bias based on class and sex. Sweden's "comprehensive" secondary education continues to allow considerable tracking at the upper levels. Yet commitments to remedy such shortcomings have been made.

Since one of the major responsibilities of contemporary education is the production of scientists and engineers to spur national technological development, it is interesting to note the lead of the Soviet Union and the United States in this regard (see Table 7–8). Although military goals are responsible for a major part of this lead in both cases, particularly that of the Soviet Union, it is impressive that the two countries are so far ahead of most of Western Europe.

TABLE 7–8
Scientists and Engineers Engaged in Research and Development (per 10,000 population)

	Year	Number
1. Soviet Union	1973	44.4
2. United States	1973	25.0
3. West Germany	1972	16.2
4. Sweden	1971	12.2
5. France	1971	11.8
6. United Kingdom	1969–70	7.9
7. Italy	1972	6.0

Source: UNESCO Statistical Yearbook, 1974 (Paris: UNESCO, 1975), pp. 642–47.

As to the qualitative and structural dimensions of education, Sweden, the United States, and the Soviet Union differ little in proclaimed goals but register some significant variations in implemented programs. Common rhetoric is reflected in the recent statement of the Soviet Minister of Education that "in order to learn something a pupil must now have a much more independent and creative approach to his studies and a teacher must direct his or her entire educational work towards shaping the intellectual potential of the pupil's personality."[49] Differences in stated objectives include the much greater Soviet concentration on technological training, the planned integration of Soviet education with vocations, and the lesser commitment of Sweden to common programs at the upper secondary level. The United States has minimized the planning of relationships between educational places and expected employment needs but shares the Soviet approach to common secondary school programs.

In terms of results Soviet officials have been criticized for slowness in adapting teaching methods and goals and for the inaccuracy of their projections of needed places in particular fields.[50] Yet their record is good in the technological training given priority as well as the development of lifetime orientations to reading and continuing education.

Sweden and the United States both scored well in comparisons of their secondary school students with those in less comprehensive systems. Based on the Swedish record in IEA math and science tests, and to a lesser extent that of the United States, Husén concludes that "the comprehensive or retentive system provides a broader range of opportunities and a better utilization and development of talent."[51] The superior Swedish results probably relate to a carryover of traditional elitist standards and to a much more homogeneous population as compared to that of the United States. All the superior aspects of the Swedish welfare system can also be expected to contribute to Swedish achievements in education. However, this must be balanced with the lesser educational opportunity available to lower social classes in Sweden as compared to the United States or the Soviet Union.

The Lagging and the Aspiring. The five other states of our survey, four in the European Communities and one from the CMEA group, are more representative of Europe than are the countries discussed above. Each has struggled with limited economic resources and divisions within its elites to move toward a democratic and modernized educational system.

Progress has been most limited in West Germany, where little change has occurred in the structure of secondary schools, and inequalities on such grounds as sex, family status, location, and religion have not yet been targeted for elimination. OECD experts contended in 1972 that there were very few people in Germany "who can accept a

---

[49] Mikhail Prokofiev, "New Stage in Development of Education in USSR," *Soviet News* (London), February 24, 1976, p. 66.

[50] Barbara B. Burn, *Higher Education in Nine Countries* (New York: McGraw-Hill Book Co., 1971), pp. 299–300.

[51] Torsten Husén, "Implications of the IEA Findings for the Philosophy of Comprehensive Education," in Purves and Levine, *Educational Policy*, p. 139.

system such as the Swedes are now putting into operation, whereby a child goes from kindergarten to university entrance without entrance or learning examinations at the doors of the primary, secondary, or higher schools; or who can envisage a system in which children become partners in the educational enterprise with their teachers."[52] In the view of these experts OECD-endorsed structural and qualitative reform "simply does not appear to be practical politics in the Germany of the 1970s."[53] Although higher education has been expanded considerably, West Germany has sustained an educational system rooted in the Weimar regime and the 19th century. The system operates at or near the bottom in Europe in terms of school financing, teacher-student ratios in primary grades, and early selection of occupational and academic tracks. Its unique feature of on-the-job vocational and technical training for most teenagers is now widely criticized as inadequate.

A more balanced assessment can be made for educational trends in East Germany, Britain, France, and Italy. Of these, East Germany probably most closely approaches the leaders in educational opportunity. Though behind the Soviet Union in higher education enrollments, it has moved to near-universal secondary programs before its mentor. Its overwhelming emphasis on "education for the polytechnic society" is based on intellectual and child development goals that differ in crucial ways from those endorsed by OECD and UNESCO. Yet East Germany has created a model for the integration of vocational and general education within a unified basic program.[54]

The pressures that have raised the levels of educational opportunity in the leading countries have also penetrated Britain, France, and Italy. Since at least 1955 each has demonstrated a strong will to expand secondary and higher education and to raise levels of median educational attainment. Between 1955 and 1972 each generated impressive increases in educational spending (see Table 7–4) and had proportionate increases in postcompulsory enrollments. Quantitative progress has been particularly impressive in France, where upper secondary and higher education opportunities have increased too rapidly in relation to the available facilities. Yet even this progress leaves large gaps between this group of states and such quantitative leaders as the United States, Sweden, and the Soviet Union. Several independent European economists recently asserted that lack of higher education opportunity constitutes one of the three main barriers to social equality in Western

---

[52] *Reviews of National Policies for Education: Germany*, p. 54.

[53] Ibid.

[54] See Thomas A. Baylis, *The Technical Intelligentsia and the East German Elite* (Berkeley: University of California Press, 1974); and Arthur Hearndon, *Education in the Two Germanies* (Boulder, Colo.: Westview Press, 1976).

Europe.[55] They emphasized the continuing class barriers, noting "the extraordinary distortion between the share of the social categories in the active population and the participation of their children in higher education."[56] Such inequalities are still deeply embedded in the secondary as well as the higher schools of most member states of the European Communities.

The major Western European states are finding problems of structure and quality even more difficult to resolve than those of numbers. An extreme case is the subsecondary training level of many Italian primary school teachers. In many other Western European countries most teachers are trained outside universities. Pedagogic reform has been proposed in each of the survey countries, but few observers have noted or expect broad efforts toward individualization and creative teaching outside Scandinavia and Britain.[57]

Except for Britain, the major member countries of the European Communities have limited their secondary school reforms to the lower grades. Although Britain has moved with some hesitation to establish common upper secondary facilities, France and Italy have concentrated on movement toward comprehensive schools at the lower secondary levels. Complementary structural efforts at democratization and talent-searching have often proved to be little more than paper programs. For example, the French "guidance cycles" in the first years of secondary school have not produced the claimed flexibility among educational tracks. In fact, such barriers as examinations and separate curricula have tended to perpetuate multitrack education in most of Western Europe.

Differences in opportunity are less extreme at the higher education level than for secondary programs because such countries as France and West Germany allow most graduates of academic secondary schools to proceed to the next level. Such systems tend to perpetuate societies divided between those with higher education and those without academic work at even the secondary level. Even now the financial barriers against higher education for those outside the highest strata remain strong in France, West Germany, and Italy. In contrast, East Germany and Britain provide assistance for most university entrants.

France and West Germany have faced the most dramatic crises of student rebellion against the structures and processes of their higher edu-

---

[55] The other two are the systems for financial credit and for the taxation of inheritance. Sir Alec Cairncross et al., *Economic Policy for the European Community* (New York: Holmes & Meier, Publishers, 1974), pp. 176–78.

[56] Ibid., p. 176.

[57] Alain Drouard, "Education," in Richard Mayne, ed., *Europe Tomorrow* (London: Wm. Collins Sons & Co., 1972), p. 215.

cation institutions. This is more a product of the fossilization of these patterns than of the more highly developed critical consciousness of French and German students. The governments of both countries have attempted to be responsive to the new demands, with the emphasis on increased federal involvement in West Germany and on decentralization in France. Yet long-standing traditions and prerogatives have proved difficult to change.

Conclusion: Education and Post-Industrialism. We are far too aware of shortcomings in American education to flatly state that the open U.S. system represents a model for all post-industrial states. It is reassuring that leading interpreters of IEA tests have indicated that the best students in countries with long-term comprehensive schools perform as well as do their counterparts in systems which segregate the best academic performers and that the average and below-average students in such comprehensive schools gain from their longer exposure to formal education. We are also impressed with the ability of long-term comprehensive schools to prepare a much larger proportion of their youth for needed scientific and technical careers.

On the other hand, the freedom of choice that has characterized much of education in the United States and Sweden can lead to statistically verified declines in critical academic skills, most notably composition and foreign languages. Further, the American pattern has moved increasingly toward a narrow vocational orientation that seems to have little in common with the broad goals of post-industrial education.

Education today must try to reach numerous objectives that tend to be competitive if not mutually inconsistent. We ask it to provide personnel who can fuel and develop a highly technical society while also being capable of criticizing its distortions. We seek universal education in societies with large socioeconomic variations, while demanding that all traditional academic standards be maintained. Quality is also challenged by such new goals as the development of personality and citizenship.

Although variations in the levels of expenditure for education are smaller than the variations for most other public distributions, we have discovered major differences among our survey countries regarding approaches to educational opportunity, structure, and processes. These differences can be explained in part by their level of economic development and the proportion of school-age children in their populations.[58] Yet the most meaningful factors appear to be the structures and attitudes inherited from earlier generations, the commitment of recent po-

---

[58] Pryor, *Public Expenditures,* p. 225.

litical regimes to reform, and the inclination of key interest groups and bureaucratic strongholds to promote or resist change.[59]

No country has expanded opportunity or developed other major innovations without major resistance from teachers, administrators, and politicians who regard change as threatening to their prerogatives or to educational standards. The United States, the Soviet Union, and East Germany have each had a comparatively clean slate on which to create relatively democratic and comprehensive educational systems. Sweden was able to overcome traditional elements with a carefully orchestrated campaign to minimize resistance. The balance of forces appears to be much more difficult to contend with in France, Italy, Britain, and West Germany, though only in the last has momentum for reform been stalled.

Militarization and world role have certainly contributed much to the momentum for educational expansion and scientific-technical direction in the Soviet Union and the United States. As to Western Europe, it is possible that international emulation, spurred by the European Communities and other agencies, may combine with a growing awareness of education's role in technological lag to close the existing gaps.

It seems likely that education will expand regardless of the direction of post-industrial society. In all probability it will expand in several directions at once. It will meet more of the basic vocational and technical needs of advanced economies, seek to produce more broadly developed citizens, and extend its services from cradle to grave. It will be the source of more problems as a result of its fostering of technology, and it will breed some solutions as a result of increased criticism and planning.

CONCLUSIONS: DISTRIBUTIONS

Each of the eight states has set its own priorities regarding the distribution of public goods and services. An overall picture emerges of a choice between a typical Western European pattern of high income maintenance and low education allocations and a reverse pattern for the United States and the Soviet Union. Further, the two superpowers have combined high military expenditures with their strong quantitative commitment to education. Sweden, sharing emerging post-industrial status with the United States, combines an American-level commitment to education with a leadership role in income maintenance programs. Finally, East Germany reflects a significant variation from the Soviet

---

[59] See Arnold J. Heidenheimer, Hugh Heclo, and Carolyn Teich Adams, *Comparative Public Policy: The Politics of Public Choice in Europe and America* (New York: St. Martin's Press, 1975), pp. 44–68, 130–57.

pattern, with less military allocations and stronger income maintenance.

Funding levels are less closely associated with service levels in health services than in most other areas. Among the eight the most highly developed health delivery systems are the Swedish, British, East German, and Soviet. The U.S. nonsystem matches the structural weakness of its income maintenance programs.

We offer the following summaries of the priorities set by the eight states:

East Germany: Limited consumer goods are combined with a strongly balanced set of public goods and services. It does not lead in any area, but is in the top four in overall commitment to health services, education, and defense. Income maintenance remains somewhat weak.

France: Income maintenance rather generous, and education has progressed to a quantitative level between that of the "post-industrial" leaders and the Western European laggards. The military's share of resources has fallen considerably, and there are still serious gaps in the health delivery and insurance programs.

Great Britain: Has managed, with much strain, to maintain a rather balanced set of public distributions. However, its leadership positions in the military area and income maintenance have been given up and its health delivery system is facing a crisis of resources. Education has been strong compared to most of Western Europe, but even this area appears about to face some retrenchment.

Italy: Rather generous in income maintenance, but a laggard in the present company in regard to military and educational allocations. The health delivery system is not among the best coordinated.

Soviet Union: A quantitative leader in military and educational distributions. However, its well-organized health service system appears to be somewhat underfunded and its income maintenance programs are rather incomplete.

Sweden: A strong welfare and emerging post-industrial state that holds a leadership position in income maintenance, health care delivery, and education while maintaining a respectable military establishment for such a small country.

United States: Very strong in the military field and in its quantitative commitment to education. Lack of sound organization reduces the benefits from very high total health expenditures (public and private) and a rapidly growing income maintenance commitment.

West Germany: A leader in income maintenance but modest in military allocations, in need of better coordination of health services, and a notable laggard in secondary education.

8 Extraction: The Military Draft and Taxation

We term extractive those public policies designed to mobilize and allocate the costs and burdens of government finance and service. Masochists aside, we assume that ordinarily few people enjoy being compelled to undertake military service for extended periods or to have their disposable income measurably reduced by tax collections. Yet the distributive policies discussed in the previous chapters, whether they point toward the welfare, warfare, or post-industrial state, are made possible by resources mobilized primarily from within the given societies.

Although this chapter concentrates on extraction, the reader should be aware that no sharp line separates the extractive process from the distributive process. It can be argued that these are basically separate functions, one representing the taking and the other the giving of valued goods and services. However, a closer investigation of the specific means of extraction and distribution does not allow for such a clear separation.

Most significantly, modern tax systems are rife with *tax subsidies* or *tax expenditures*.[1] These

---

[1] Stanley S. Surrey, *Pathways to Tax Reform* (Cambridge, Mass.: Harvard University Press, 1973).

terms refer to reductions in the tax liability of individuals and firms to compensate for the economic responsibilities of these taxpayers or to promote particular kinds of private expenditure or behavior. Taxes may be reduced to encourage private investment in machinery or housing, philanthropy, and dozens of other government-approved purposes. The state does not usually send a check to the benefited individual or organization, but what it does provide amounts to a refund on taxes that would have been paid in the absence of the tax subsidies or expenditures.

The distributive character of this process is best seen from the vantage point of the government authority that debates how it will promote needed housing, exports, or machinery. On many occasions the officials will not even consider direct subsidies through the expenditure budget. Direct spending is often blocked by competing pressures and may lack precedent. In contrast, the tradition of tax subsidy may be well established and the opposition to this approach less vigilant. Sometimes a debate proceeds between advocates of direct and tax expenditure. The major significance of the policy decision is that for most tax expenditures recipients benefit in proportion to their tax bracket, whereas greater equity usually results from direct spending. A great deal of truth applies to the statement that the wealthier sectors of capitalist societies tend to receive their subsidies through the tax system while the poorer sectors depend on official budget distributions. The extent to which higher rates paid by the rich on their total taxable resources alter the effects of this pattern will be discussed below.

The main point of the present discussion is that taxes can best be analyzed together with expenditures. It is the combined effect of what government takes and gives that determines whether each of us is ahead or behind. Only by combining the two can we estimate whether welfare state or post-industrial distributions are worth the price that is extracted.

Indeed, such a discussion as this cannot avoid altogether the interaction of regulation and extraction. Taxes are often used to regulate designated vices as well as trade, investment, and other aspects of economic life. In turn, the tax system depends on the coercive capability of the state.

Forms of Extraction

Extraction has been defined as the mobilization of resources from the population. These resources include cash, commodities, and services. Extractive processes include the conscription of civilian and military services, fees for government services, taxation, the expropriation of property, borrowing (deferred taxation), the promotion of inflated national currencies, and the manipulation and control of prices and incomes. Each government may choose a different mix of these forms of extraction. The determining factors are as varied as those applicable to the other major governmental functions. Since industrialized nations require increasingly regularized, large, and growing public resources, taxation must be central to their extractions. Yet all of the alternative forms of extraction continue to be employed either routinely or in special circumstances. An unpopular war, such as the U.S. commitment to South Vietnam, may be financed largely through borrowing. Governments may promote or maintain inflation, realizing that it can serve to increase income from many kinds of taxes. A given generation of taxpayers is often attracted to the option of deferring its tax burden to the next generation through bonded debt. A "user pays" philosophy can increase the pattern of charging fees for certain public services. Although this generally results in reduced access to such services, this may be a desired outcome. Finally, a sector of the population may be called upon to pay forced loans or to give up property without adequate compensation.

Each of these forms of governmental resource appropriation can be developed in ways that are burdensome and unfair to greater or lesser degrees. Various extractions require major sacrifices from individuals and have an enormous impact on society. President John Kennedy, responding to complaints from recalled military reservists, noted that the allocation of burdens was inherently unfair. Most, if not all, systems of taxation and military conscription are badly in need of reform, radical reconstruction, or abolition.

CONSCRIPTION

Obligatory civilian labor, now most common in Communist-ruled Asia, remains in Europe and North America in such forms as required work for designated lawbreakers and, less regularly, government's price for aiding the poor and unemployed. To varying extents military draftees and striking workers have been employed as involuntary laborers on civilian projects. Further, the practice of requiring civilian services to the state in exchange for higher education has been spreading in the West as well as in Communist-ruled systems.

Yet conscription to secure military manpower is now the most widely used form of extraction of human services. This is not a new area of mobilization, having been employed widely for much of the past 600 years. Yet it is more modern than such other forms as compulsory service in agriculture and public works, which have tended to fade away in Europe in recent centuries. Some aspects of contemporary

Soviet and other Eastern European systems of agricultural service are legacies of those traditions.

Economists have chosen to reject any sharp distinction between conscription and taxation. The U.S. President's Commission on an All-Volunteer Armed Force emphasized in its 1970 report that the then-existing American system of military conscription, like all other drafts that had ever been employed, constituted a tax in kind.[2] Military conscription is a tax paid by the minority of the adult population which is actually drafted, is induced to enlist by draft pressure, or assumes less financially rewarding work to avoid conscription. The draftee's acceptance of less compensation reduces the tax burden of the general taxpayers. The latter are spared the need to pay the level of compensation that would ensure an adequate quantity and quality of military manpower without compulsion. The individual draftee can consider himself to be paying in taxes the difference between his military compensation and the salary and benefits that he would have demanded as a free seller of his labor services. In the mid-1960s this tax annually cost the average American draftee or draft-induced volunteer an estimated $3,600, for a national total of $2 billion per year.[3] Such financial penalties are augmented by the distortions imposed on personal choices regarding family formation and education as well as the casualty rates in wartime.

Conscripts have dominated continental European armies, in peace and war, for the bulk of the period since the French Revolution and especially since the Franco-Prussian War of 1870–71. Of the major powers, Germany and Russia have most consistently conscripted most of their active forces.[4] With multinational linkages of emulation and reaction operating strongly in this policy area, few continental European countries have felt that they have had an alternative to massive conscription during the past century.

Two major countries that have dominant traditions of conscription only in wartime are the United Kingdom and the United States. The traditional British opposition to conscription has been less consistent than the American, with impressment for service going as far back as the Hundred Years' War in the 14th century and the navy and militia employing peacetime compulsion as late as the early 19th century. Yet the voluntary principle was well respected for 100 years after Waterloo,

---

[2] *The Report of the President's Commission on an All-Volunteer Armed Force* (Washington, D.C.: U.S. Government Printing Office, February 1970), p. 13.

[3] *Ibid.* This is based on Larry A. Sjaastad and Ronald W. Hansen, "The Conscription Tax: An Empirical Analysis," in *Studies Prepared for the President's Commission on an All-Volunteer Armed Force*, vol. 2 (Washington, D.C.: U.S. Government Printing Office, 1970).

[4] James M. McConnell, "European Experience with Volunteer and Conscript Forces," in *ibid.*, part 3, study 2, p. 6.

leaving the British quite reluctant to impose conscription even at the peak of World War I or on the eve of World War II.

The United States, having, like Britain, a geographic situation that allowed it to reject a large standing army, traditionally limited compulsion in peacetime to service in the home militia. Before World War I conscription was used only during the Civil War, and no American draftees were sent abroad before 1917.

The traditional Anglo-American opposition to peacetime conscription was set aside during a substantial part of the Cold War era, as only the two restrained German states, of our designated eight, avoided conscription for all or most of the period between 1945 and 1960. Britain again broke away from this pattern in 1960, returning to an all-volunteer force, and the United States followed suit in 1973 in connection with post–Vietnam War reductions in its armed forces. Subsequent to 1960 the two German states resumed their traditional conscription and none of the continental states in our survey forswore military conscription in response to the Anglo-American initiatives.

It is not nearly enough to know whether or not a given country had conscription in a given year. Other basic considerations include the proportion of military and total manpower conscripted or influenced to enlist, the terms of required service, and the financial and other sacrifices enforced.

The terms of required service have recently been shortened to such an extent that in several countries the draft can be more accurately termed involuntary military training rather than service. In 1974 required service did not exceed 15 months in the armies or air forces of any major Western European state. This contrasted with two-year terms in the Soviet Union and its bloc allies other than East Germany, which was content with 18 months. Yet even the higher Soviet term represents a marked reduction from its traditional and even recent levels. Short terms of service, even when connected with long periods of reserve obligation, are expensive to the countries involved in that they require greater resources to be employed for training. The trend to reduced service terms can be viewed as a response to popular pressures in each of these countries. Presumably, these pressures were most intense in the traditionally volunteer-oriented Britain and United States.

The burden of conscription can perhaps best be seen from the proportions of total available manpower being conscripted shown in Table 8–1. McConnell includes reservists and youths in premilitary training as fractions of conscriptees on the basis of his own formula. His data exclude the years of major warfare that resulted in enlarged conscription.

TABLE 8-1

Average Annual Full-Time Peacetime Conscripts per Million Population, by Ten-Year Periods

Period	Britain	France	Germany/GFR	Russia/Soviet Union	Italy
1866-75	0	4,489	12,060	9,219	9,111
1876-85	0	13,606	10,818	9,725	9,239
1886-95	0	16,202	10,430	11,078	8,951
1896-1905	0	14,586	8,709	9,542	9,298
1906-15	0	14,419	7,589	9,222	9,750
1916-25	0	11,006	0	7,511	7,549
1926-35	0	7,658	462	7,650	9,325
1936-45	698	12,591	15,441	14,009	12,091
1946-55	5,378	5,050	0	30,348	4,291
1956-65	1,709	5,000	2,020	16,984	5,810

Source: James M. McConnell, "European Experience with Volunteer and Conscript Forces," in *Studies Prepared for the President's Commission on an All-Volunteer Armed Force*, part 3, study 2 (Washington, D.C.: U.S. Government Printing Office, 1970), p. 5.

The McConnell data suggest that while the Soviet Union and Britain expanded the use of conscription in the post-1945 period as compared with interwar levels, the draft has been resorted to at a reduced rate in recent decades in France, West Germany, and Italy. Although Britain resorted to a peacetime draft for the first time during the present century it employed the draft at a rate below continental prewar norms.

The American postwar draft had an exceptionally uneven pattern. Between 1951 and 1966 it directly provided as little as 13 percent and as much as 41 percent of an annual procurement of 600,000–900,000 men.[5] During the postwar period American annual draft calls averaged as follows:[6]

1948–55: 252,000.

1956–65: 122,200.

1966–71: 271,800.

Both the earliest and latest time spans were dominated by substantial wartime recruitment. The lower "interwar" figure represents a level of use significantly below even that of Britain. The peak level, reached during the Korean War, was still low by historic European standards. The American system, more than any other, sought to conscript only a minority of eligible candidates. This "selective service" contrasts with

[5] Colonel Samuel H. Hays, "A Military View of Selective Service," in Sol Tax, ed., *The Draft: A Handbook of Facts and Alternatives* (Chicago: University of Chicago Press, 1967), p. 7.

[6] Our computations are from data in Ryan C. Amacher et al., *The Economics of the Military Draft* (Morristown, N.J.: General Learning Press, 1973), p. 11.

the more or less "universal service" found in most other conscripting states.

Yet the proportion of official draftees fails to provide an adequate picture of the use of conscription in such a selective service system. The United States consistently produced a high proportion of draft-induced "volunteer" enlistments. Department of Defense attitude surveys of enlistees suggest that draftees and draft-induced personnel constituted almost half of total first-term personnel in 1965 and significantly more than half near the peak of the Vietnam War.[7] On the other hand, America had a huge pool of draft-age potential manpower that grew rapidly through most of the post-1945 period. As a result, even with this expanded view of the proportion of the population reached by conscription, the individual American male was more likely to avoid conscription than were most of his European counterparts.

Most of these statistics refer to a period ending in 1965 and are not fully indicative of present-day conditions. The most obvious change since 1965, other than the end of the American draft, has been in the continued reduction of total military personnel in an age of increased mechanization and firepower. This overall reduction has allowed Britain and the United States to return to and maintain all-volunteer armed forces. For most of the other nations it has allowed some movement from universal to selective service. As this trend develops, the conscription system, as in the American postwar versions, becomes generally less equitable. The military increases its ability to discriminate according to occupation, education, family status, intelligence, skills, and other factors. A smaller proportion of taxpayers are compelled to pay the conscription tax, and the draft becomes easier to evade.

Are one's chances of being drafted affected by the side of the Cold War barriers in which one lives? The armed forces of the Warsaw Pact countries do tend to comprise a larger proportion of military-age males than is comprised by the armed forces of NATO members. Yet the 1974 proportions were an average of 5.64 percent for Warsaw Pact countries as opposed to 5.1 percent for NATO members, and such Eastern European states as East Germany, Hungary, Poland, and Rumania were all below the NATO average. Further, analysis of the Swedish and Swiss experience suggests that one is as likely to be called to service under a policy of "armed neutralism" as in most of the aligned states.

The factors that have major impact on the proportion of manpower recruited include population size, bloc role, foreign military commitments, and location. Smaller countries tend to recruit and conscript at higher rates than do larger ones; bloc leaders, such as the Soviet Union and the United States, exceed average levels in their alliances; and geographi-

---

[7] *Report of the President's Commission,* p. 51.

cally peripheral states, such as Britain, have recruited at lower rates than most others. The United States was able to abandon the draft despite its bloc leader role largely because of its location and the size of its available manpower. The reduction of foreign commitments and the ability to maintain expensive technological substitutes for military manpower are also significant contributing factors. Soviet youths, in contrast, pay a heavy price in conscription because of their country's location between China and Europe, the long borders, and a military strategy that continues to involve a high manpower factor.[8] A substantial substitution effect has operated to place hundreds of thousands of Soviet and American troops, among others, on the soil of European states, especially East and West Germany. This may have contributed to a reduced need for recruitment in the receiving states.

The financial sacrifice of the conscript varies from state to state. France and the Soviet Union have been notably frugal in their compensation. Recent estimates suggest that in-kind benefits are meager and cash pay incredibly low in both of these countries. Soviet draftees, according to recent data, were receiving three rubles per month in cash, and French conscripts were paid less than the equivalent of one dollar per day until 1975.[9] At such long-fixed levels the "conscript tax" grew rapidly in both countries, increasing by a factor of almost 20 in the Soviet Union between 1950 and 1972 to an estimated average of over $700 per year per recruit.[10] French draftees, with much more highly paid alternative employment, were paying a much higher conscription tax. France and the Soviet Union also stand out among the high-population countries in Europe in maintaining the largest armed forces in proportion to their military-age manpower.[11] It may be that the availability of cheap conscripts encourages the expansion of military manpower.

One new factor that may have major effects on the pay and working conditions of conscripts is unionization. Military unions have already had a dramatic effect on the Dutch military, producing industrylike benefits and a marked reduction in controls on personal behavior. Such unions have already begun to spread through Western Europe.

Although American conscripts have long been regarded as the best-compensated, this has often been overstated. United States military

---

[8] Nevertheless, the number of Soviet draftees fell from a level of about 3,500,000 between 1952 and 1955 to a level of about 2,000,000 between 1965 and 1968. Earl R. Brubaker, "The Opportunity Costs of Soviet Military Conscripts," in Joint Economic Committee, U.S. Congress, *Soviet Economic Prospects for the Seventies* (Washington, D.C.: U.S. Government Printing Office, 1973), p. 167.

[9] Although French conscripts' pay was tripled in 1975, it still remained low by Western European standards. The Soviet ruble has recently been valued at (U.S.) $1.10.

[10] Brubaker, "Opportunity Costs," p. 174.

[11] *The Military Balance, 1974–75* (London: International Institute for Strategic Studies, 1975), p. 82.

pay, including the value of quarters, food, and clothing, equaled only 58–70 percent of the average American manufacturing wage earnings between 1945 and 1965.[12] Although this compensation gap is reduced if all active duty and veteran benefits are considered, the presidential commission on the draft concluded that the civilian-military pay gap remained significant despite these additional benefits. Only with the subsequent assistance of pressure from civilian federal employees and the effort to move toward an all-volunteer military did American military pay approach or exceed average civilian levels.

American draftees had an advantage over several of their European counterparts in that they were compensated at a level of equality with volunteers. Significantly lower pay for draftees is common, as in the post-1945 French and British systems. Such differences accentuate the taxation aspect of conscription.

Conscription: Conclusion

Military conscription is no longer implemented in Britain and the United States, and the conscription programs in the major continental European states are becoming more selective, better paying, and shorter in duration. Yet it cannot be said that the end of military conscription is in sight. At present the states in our survey are reacting to a general relaxation in their relations. The drafting and signing of a de facto European peace treaty between 1970 and 1975 were combined with steps toward Soviet-American détente. Yet the Soviet forces continue to reflect rising global aspirations for influence as well as tense relations with China. The Mediterranean area is increasingly unstable, and the Middle East explosive. The politics of energy and food threatens to flow over into violence. The military draft will continue to respond both to rises and falls in world and regional tensions and to domestic social and political currents.

TAXATION

Although governments may or may not need to conscript for military service, there can be little doubt that compulsion is necessary to provide the enormous amounts of money spent by modern states. Many Western European and North American governments are attempting to expand the share of revenue received through user charges for such services as higher education, museums, and the mail. However, other governments are consciously seeking to move in the opposite direction by expanding the scope of "free" services. Dependence on fees

---

[12] *Report of the President's Commission,* p. 124.

usually limits the distribution of such services and may result in less equitable allocations of burdens.

To the extent that fees and taxes are not sufficient to meet obligations, governments must resort to deficit spending paid from reserves, borrowing, and the additional printing of currency. Such financing schemes are increasingly viewed in Western industrial states as legitimate means to stimulate investment and employment as well as to finance wars. Since the world wars of this century, less conservative approaches to borrowing and accumulated national debt have been taken. However, even the comparatively huge levels of borrowing in such states as the United States, Britain, and Italy in the mid-1970s are small compared to the role of taxation in financing those states. All industrial states are compelled to obtain most of their needed revenue from compulsory assessments identifiable as taxes.

It is certainly possible for contemporary governments to create systems of taxation which, compared to those now employed in most developed states, come closer to paying for desired expenditures, can be collected more efficiently, and take from people in closer relationship to their ability to pay. Yet no consistent trend points to balanced budgets, efficiency, or progressivity.

In fact, governments do not consider such values to the extent that the reader might expect. Other priorities are often given precedence when fiscal policy is determined. The U.S. Office of Management and Budget suggests the following purposes of a budget that records intended taxing, borrowing, and spending:

> It is an economic document that reflects the taxing and spending policies of the Government for promoting economic growth, high employment, relative price stability, and strengthening of the nation's balance-of-payments position. It proposes an allocation of resources between the private and public sectors, within the public sector, and—through its effect on consumption and investment decisions and the distribution of income—within the private sector.[13]

In addition to development and stabilization of the economic system, fiscal policy often seeks to assist areas of social and cultural life, the physical environment, and the political process itself. Taxes have been used to encourage and discourage marriage, large families, churches, pollution, and political campaign contributions, among other things.[14] In the view of Richard and Peggy Musgrave, the role of the budget in

---

[13] Office of Management and Budget, *Special Analyses: Budget of the United States Government, Fiscal Year 1974* (Washington, D.C.: U.S. Government Printing Office, 1973), p. 7.

[14] For a critique of such policies see William F. Buckley, *Four Reforms* (New York: G. P. Putnam's Sons, 1973), pp. 49–50.

the modern welfare state, especially its tax aspect, "places the public budget at the hub of the social system."[15]

Given these multiple purposes, it is not surprising that tax systems are typically incoherent and contradictory. The tax exemption that encourages investment may, at least in the short run, make the distribution of income and wealth less equitable. In a given state some taxes encourage employment and others discourage it.

However, many factors other than conflicting goals contribute to the complexity, inefficiency, and inequity of most tax systems. In most developed states tax policies tend to appear quite beneficial to the majority of the population while actually serving special interests or privileged minorities. A progressive income tax, ostensibly costing the higher-income sector a large proportion of its earnings, will typically involve enough deductions and exemptions to convert the high nominal rates into modest burdens on the rich. Taxes on purchases and social insurance contributions, in contrast, are not perceived by the lower-income groups as the discriminatory burdens that they almost always are.

Such "fiscal illusions" were cataloged by the Italian scholar Amilcare Puviani at the beginning of this century and have been related to contemporary tax issues by Buchanan.[16] According to Puviani, the average citizen is unable to clearly distinguish the additional costs of indirect taxes on goods and services, or taxes "shifted" to him by the formally designated taxpayer. Further, the taxpayer can be persuaded to pay more if the variety of taxes is increased. Modern tax instruments that may promote such illusions include the withholding of income tax and the proposition that social security funds constitute insurance rather than income transfer schemes.

Several leading analysts have focused on the political context of tax policy-making as a major source of inequity. Reviewing such processes in the United States, Stern emphasizes the negative impacts of campaign contributions, the stacking of tax-writing congressional committees, secrecy, and the complexity of the revenue laws themselves.[17] Each of these elements is seen as contributing to the inability of tax reformers to make major inroads against the advocates of the large corporations and wealthy individuals. Yet one cannot develop a cross-national critique based on legislative power. Most of the countries in our survey leave little room for parliamentary tax-writing. Yet the out-

---

[15] Richard A. Musgrave and Peggy B. Musgrave, *Public Finance in Theory and Practice* (New York: McGraw-Hill Book Co., 1973), p. 101.

[16] James M. Buchanan, *Public Finance in Democratic Process* (Chapel Hill: University of North Carolina Press, 1967), chap. 10.

[17] Philip M. Stern, *The Rape of the Taxpayer* (New York: Random House, 1973), pp. 381–97.

comes that emerge from the civil service- and minister-dominated politics of revenue in such countries as Britain or France are even less progressive.[18] Legislative versus bureaucratic dominance may provide a distinction without a difference. Both may be similarly impervious to the influence of the largely unorganized mass of taxpayers. Secrecy, complexity, inertia, routine, tradition, and incrementalism seem to combine in most political systems to slow change and make retrogression possible. Incrementalism allows decision-makers to accept as unchallengeable those policies already in force. As Sharkansky notes, "In the taxing field, incremental decision-making appears in the tendency of legislators and administrators to pay nothing more than lip service to the notion of 'thorough overhaul.' "[19]

Other major influences on tax policy are the extent of socialization of the economy, of governmental centralization, and of operative international ties. Each of these factors will be explored within the context of the following discussion of tax burdens, rates, and structures.

Who Pays the Most Taxes?

It is probable that no public opinion survey has ever discovered that a community considers itself undertaxed. The press rarely provides comparative tax data that may suggest that one country is better off than another, and the public is most likely to compare present taxes with the lower levels that it remembers paying some years earlier. Further, most people are less aware of the services purchased by their taxes than of the pain involved in paying them.

As noted above, the total tax burdens on the populations of developed states vary considerably. These differences are extremely important, heavily influencing the allocation of resources between the public and private sectors of economies, the degree of redistribution of income and wealth, and the ability of governments to fund various programs.

A major problem is the validity of various measures of tax burdens. Differing tax systems make comparison of Eastern European tax levels with those of Western Europe and the United States quite difficult. Indeed, the Soviet Union officially proclaims itself to be almost tax-free. Although this is categorically untrue, the Soviet Union and other Communist-ruled states are able to manipulate revenue sources in ways not available to the Western states. As a result, meaningful comparisons of tax burdens are virtually impossible across East-West lines.

---

[18] See Sir Herbert Brittain, *The British Budgetary System* (London: George Allen & Unwin, 1959); and Guy Lord, *The French Budgetary Process* (Berkeley: University of California Press, 1973).

[19] Ira Sharkansky, *The Politics of Taxing and Spending* (Indianapolis: Bobbs-Merrill Co., 1969), p. 51.

Comparing Public Policies

TABLE 8-2
Total Tax Revenue as Percentage of Gross National Product and
Rank among OECD Countries

	1965		1972	
	Percent	Rank	Percent	Rank
Sweden	36.10	1	43.89	3
West Germany............	32.65	6	35.97	6
France	36.05	2	35.80	7
United Kingdom..........	30.61	10	34.73	10
Italy	28.95	12	31.07	13
United States............	24.88	16	28.06	15

Source: Adapted from *Revenue Statistics of OECD Member Countries, 1965–1972* (Paris:ʹOECD, 1975), p. 74.

State Budget Revenues in Percentage of National Income (net material product)

Soviet Union	53.4 (1965 – Birman)	54.1 (1970 – Birman)
East Germany*	66.2 (1965 – Schnitzer)	62.3 (1969 – Schnitzer)

* Figures are for total governmental expenditures (rather than tax revenues) as percentage of national income.
Sources: Martin Schnitzer, *East and West Germany: A Comparative Economic Analysis* (New York: Praeger Publishers, 1972), p. 260; A. Birman, "The USSR State Budget in the Perspective of Economic Development," *Voprosy ekonomiki*, 1973, no. 9, as translated in *Problems of Economics*, vol. 16, no. 11 (March 1974), pp. 74–87.

The wide range of tax burdens in industrial countries is indicated (see Table 8–2) by the finding that the Swedish load, the highest in our sample of six Western countries, was half again as great as that of the United States in 1965 and 1972. Despite a lower per capita income in 1972 Swedes paid a per capita tax bill of $2,231 as compared to the American rate of $1,568 (see Table 8–3).

In relation to total tax burdens the 23 capitalist and mostly industrialized OECD states fell into three groups, based on their total tax revenues as a percentage of GNP. The first group, with 1972 percentages over 37, included Sweden, three other Scandinavian states, and

TABLE 8-3
Tax Revenue in Dollars per Capita

	1965	1972
1. Sweden................	$1,012	$2,231
2. United States...........	892	1,568
3. West Germany	641	1,501
4. France	760	1,413
5. United Kingdom........	564	959
6. Italy	328	676

Source: *Revenue Statistics of OECD Member Countries, 1965–1972* (Paris: OECD, 1975), p. 86.

three of the smaller Western European states. Each of the other leading states of Western Europe fell within the middle range of 31–37 percent. The United States was one of ten OECD states, characteristically highly developed non-European or less developed European, under 31 percent. Between 1965 and 1972 the first group rose to the new plateau of 37–45.7 percent, leaving behind other developed European states which they closely paralleled up to 1965.

The dollar-equivalent per capita tax figures indicate that increases have varied considerably, taxes having more than doubled in Sweden, West Germany, and Italy in this seven-year period, while increasing at slower rates in France, the United States, and the United Kingdom. Differing rates of inflation greatly affected growth patterns, but national choices also played a role.

Onerous tax burdens seem to be linked to small population, high per capita income, and certain patterns of emulation (especially Scandinavian, Benelux, and European Communities). Insofar as medical care, social insurance, public assistance, and defense spending levels tend to vary considerably from country to country, these disparities can be viewed as the primary expenditure source of the differing total tax burdens.[20]

The major problems that emerge when tax obligations in Communist states are compared with those in advanced Western states include differing ideas of what constitutes a tax. Using 1964 figures, Richard Musgrave calculates Soviet total government receipts as 50.6 percent of GNP but the proportion of taxes to GNP as only 39.3 percent.[21] The best available figure for East Germany is revenues of 63.2 percent of national income, the latter concept representing a significantly smaller total than gross national product.[22] Because Communist-ruled states can manipulate most budget figures much more easily than can advanced capitalist countries, the level of reported taxes means little. In Eastern European states the bulk of the national product passes through either government-owned enterprises or government budgets. Yet not all of this amount should properly be called taxation. Official Soviet and East German summaries contend that only direct assessments on the population are actually taxes, and these produce less than 10 percent of all government revenue in the Soviet Union. We can safely reject this con-

---

[20] See Mary Garin-Painter, "Public Expenditure Trends in OECD Countries," *Occasional Studies* (Paris: OECD, July 1970), 43–56.

[21] Richard A. Musgrave, *Fiscal Systems* (New Haven: Yale University Press, 1969), pp. 43, 45.

[22] Martin Schnitzer, *East and West Germany: A Comparative Economic Analysis* (New York: Praeger Publishers, 1972), pp. 260–62. The East German proportion is higher than that of the Soviet Union partly because the former and not the latter counts as state revenue a share of enterprise profits that is spent directly by the enterprise.

tention, but cannot cite a figure for total taxation that fully corresponds to Western usage and financial realities.

A higher proportion of national income passes through the state budget in Communist-ruled states due to their inclusion of most capital formation in government budgets, their practice of recouping "excess profits" through taxes on consumption and direct levies on enterprises, and their greater use of taxation as a tool for economic planning and control.[23] On the other hand, the gap between these states and the most highly taxed Western European systems is not as great as might be expected. The reasons for this will be more evident after we take a closer look at the tax systems of our eight states.

What Differences Exist in the Use of Various Taxes?

The states in our sample vary much more in the structure of their tax systems than in their total tax receipts. Here we focus on the choice of certain taxes and kinds of taxes over others.

Varying tax structures have implications for numerous aspects of economic, social, and political life. The differences affect economic stability as well as growth.[24] Here we stress the impact of differing tax mixes on the national distribution of income and wealth.

Some taxes are progressive in their impacts, whereas others are proportional or regressive. A *progressive* tax assesses people with high incomes or levels of wealth at higher rates than are applied to the less prosperous. A *proportional* tax charges all or most people at the same rate; the tax bill of the privileged is greater, but wealthier people are generally better able to afford a proportional tax than are poorer persons paying at the same rate. Finally, a *regressive* tax, the opposite of a progressive one, assesses poorer persons at a higher rate than is paid by wealthier taxpayers.

It is exceptionally difficult to measure all such tax impacts because of such factors as the difference between the *nominal* tax rates, those that are officially stated, and the *effective* rates, those that are actually paid after deductions, exemptions, and other intervening factors. Another major problem is the ability of some taxpayers to *shift* certain taxes, that is, to pass on part or all of their tax bill to consumers, employees, or other ultimate payers.

Direct taxes, imposed on the income or wealth of individuals and households, tend to be progressive. *Indirect* taxes, imposed on such kinds of economic activity as the production and distribution of goods and services, can be expected to be shifted in whole or part to other

---

[23] Musgrave, *Fiscal Systems*, p. 45.

[24] See Bent Hansen, *Fiscal Policy in Seven Countries, 1955–1965* (Paris: OECD, 1969).

parties, including consumers and employees, and are most often proportional or regressive. Further, taxes paid as contributions to social insurance programs tend to have a regressive impact.

Yet no type of tax has to be progressive or regressive. An excess of deductions and exemptions can convert an income tax into a proportional or regressive device. By eliminating necessary commodities bought disproportionately by the poor, a sales tax can be made proportional or even progressive. Nonetheless, the patterns noted here are the generally expected outcomes of each of these kinds of taxes. Such expectations, often created in ignorance of effective impacts, generally constitute the bases of tax policy-making.

The post-1945 North American and European state is financed, as indicated in Tables 8–4 and 8–5, by four basic tax sources. These are personal income, corporate income, the purchases of goods and services, and social insurance contributions. Among our eight, only Britain and the United States also tap immovable property as a major source.

No significant trend toward generally progressive or regressive taxes emerges from an analysis of revenue collections in 1965 and 1972. Among the major categories of taxes, only the generally regressive social security taxes provided an increased share of the total revenue collected in our six Western states. Yet the biggest drop in that period was in the share of the generally regressive taxes on goods and services,

TABLE 8–4
Percentage of Total Tax Revenues Received from Major Categories of Taxes, 1965 and 1972

	Years	Goods and Services	Social Security	Net Wealth and Immovable Property	Personal Income	Corporation-Enterprise Income
France...............	1965	36.02	37.21	1.74	10.11	5.10
	1972	34.85	40.45	1.30	11.08	5.94
West Germany	1965	30.00	29.36	3.76	25.05	7.55
	1972	27.00	33.73	2.47	28.06	4.67
Italy.................	1965	37.18	34.17	1.74	11.13	6.89
	1972	32.50	39.08	1.03	12.72	7.43
Sweden	1965	30.22	15.60	0.93	44.71	6.07
	1972	28.60	20.33	0.57	42.11	3.94
United Kingdom	1965	30.87	15.40	11.22	31.12	5.69
	1972	26.36	15.56	11.14	32.09	7.10
United States	1965	19.22	16.40	13.58	30.53	15.81
	1972	17.24	20.48	13.22	33.61	11.19
Soviet Union..........	1965	39.11	5.50	–	7.25	31.55
	1972	31.75	5.30	–	8.45	34.25

Sources: *Revenue Statistics of OECD Member Countries, 1965–1972* (Paris: OECD, 1975), pp. 76–82; *United Nations Statistical Yearbook, 1973* (New York, 1974), p. 708; and *Narodnoye Khoziaistvo SSSR, 1973* (Moscow, 1974), p. 481. The authors were unable to find any comparably organized figures for East German tax receipts.

TABLE 8–5
Summary Ratings of 1972 Tax Ratings of 1972 Tax Revenues as Percentage of GNP as
Compared to Average of OECD States

	Goods and Services	Personal Income	Social Security	Corporate-Enterprise Income	Net Wealth and Immovable Property
France	High	Very low	Very high	Average	Very low
West Germany	Average	Average	Very high	Low	Low
Italy	Average	Very low	Very high	Average	Very low
Sweden	High	Very high	Average	Low	Very low
United Kingdom	Average	High	Low	Average	Very high
United States	Very low	Average	Low	High	Very high
Soviet Union	Very high	Very low	Very low	Very high	Very low

Criteria: Very high—more than 50 percent above OECD average.
High—20–50 percent above OECD average.
Average—20 percent above to 20 percent below OECD average.
Low—20–50 percent below OECD average.
Very low—more than 50 percent below OECD average.
Sources: Computed by the authors from *Revenue Statistics of OECD Member Countries, 1965–1972* (Paris: OECD, 1975), pp. 76–82; and *United Nations Statistical Yearbook, 1973* (New York, 1974), p. 708.

these almost balancing out the presumed negative effect of the social security tax increases. The leading generally progressive taxes declined slightly as factors in the combined Western tax systems. Yet this left the overall situation as one of only very slight shifting away from nominally progressive taxes.

We also seek to show in Tables 8–4 and 8–5 the use of particular kinds of taxes in each of the designated countries. It is not surprising that each state varies in its ranking from tax to tax. Generally, a low burden from one kind of assessment is made up with a heavier burden from another. Even the most heavily taxed nations in our study, namely Sweden, the Soviet Union, and East Germany, employ certain kinds of taxes quite moderately. Reciprocally, a relatively low-tax country like the United States has maintained several quite heavy specific taxes, including those on corporate income and real property.

Of all the tax categories noted in Table 8–4, those applied to personal income and net wealth (but not property) are least subject to the shifting of burdens and, partly for this reason, best lend themselves to progressive impacts. Such taxes play a large role in the United States, Britain, West Germany, and especially, Sweden. France, Italy, the Soviet Union, and East Germany assess personal income to a much smaller extent.

Indeed, Soviet spokesmen have invoked Marxist-Leninist ideology in behalf of the elimination of taxes on personal income. This is rather surprising in the light of the inclusion of progressive income taxes as a major theme of Marx's *Communist Manifesto*, but can be understood in part by recognizing that post-1945 Soviet income taxes have been paid disproportionately by people not employed in fully socialized enterprises. Consequently, further reduction of nonsocialized enterprise will eliminate much of the existing income tax burden. The Soviet Union and other Communist-ruled states prefer to extract from the ordinary worker through tightly regulated maximum pay, managed prices, and taxes on consumption.

Taxes on wealth are generally considered the most progressive of assessments. In fact, they are often attacked as being confiscatory. With this in mind, it is quite surprising that the United States stands out as the leading taxer of "net wealth and immovable property" among the OECD states. Only Britain, Canada, and Ireland approach the American level. Yet a major distinction exists between taxes on net wealth and the Anglo-Saxon custom of leveling heavy taxes on property. Much of the taxes on property is shiftable to others, particularly to tenants and consumers. Taxes on other net wealth, though less shiftable than property assessments, are often subject to avoidance through subterfuge. As of 1974, nine European states, including West Germany and Sweden, assessed taxes on accumulated wealth. Such taxes do not require that the wealth be transferred through gifts or inheritance in order to be assessed.

Up to this time such wealth taxes have been modest in their impacts. Maximum rates of 1 percent in West Germany and 2.5 percent in Sweden suggest that these taxes are viewed principally as supplements to the income tax and as contributors to the morale of nonpaying low-income persons.[25] However, the principal threat of taxes on wealth to the rich is the ease with which the rates can be increased when such a tax is in effect. As part of a serious effort to raise substantial new revenue, the British government has been moving in recent years to establish a wealth tax at a rate above that of Sweden.

As noted earlier, taxes are strongly affected by processes of international emulation, reaction, and penetration. These processes have lessened the variations among our six Western states in the uses of payroll, corporate profit, general consumption, and customs taxes and have also contributed to the similarities in the tax systems of our two Communist-ruled countries.

Harmonization has advanced in the European Communities in regard to assessments on the use of goods and services.[26] Through the Communities structures, the complex pattern of taxes imposed at vari-

---

[25] "Survey of European Wealth Taxes," *European Taxation,* vol. 14, no. 11, November 1974 (Amsterdam: International Bureau of Fiscal Documentation), pp. 374–78.

[26] See Carl S. Shoup, ed., *Fiscal Harmonization in Common Markets,* vol. 2: *Practice* (New York: Columbia University Press, 1967); and "Tax Harmonization in the E.E.C.: A Status Report," *European Taxation,* vol. 14, no. 8, August 1974, pp. 272–80.

ous stages of production and sales has been largely replaced by similar systems of value added taxes (VAT). For reasons of conformity and the intrinsic benefits of VAT, such non-Community states as Sweden have also adopted value-added taxes. For a while the Nixon Administration moved toward this approach, but its effort was aborted. The United States continues to stand out as a relatively light taxer of consumption.

The American system can also be singled out for its emphasis on corporate earnings taxes. However, though the United States collects from business at twice the rate of most Western European states, it does not approach the use of the enterprise profits tax in the Communist-ruled states. Indeed, while the United States has recently shifted away from business taxes, the Soviet enterprise assessment has contemporaneously become the leading source of that country's revenue. The current effort by the European Communities structures to harmonize corporate taxation does not seem to be directed at increasing the quite small role of such taxation in the member states.

The relationship between social insurance distributions and contributions is not as close as might be expected. Public assistance and family allowances are most commonly funded from general tax revenue rather than social security "contributions." The fact that Italy and France are exceptions to this pattern in regard to family allowances goes far to explain the high contribution burden in those countries. Health insurance and direct services are frequently subsidized. This helps explain the relatively low contribution burden in Sweden, the United Kingdom, and the Soviet Union. Some Western European states, including France, Italy, and West Germany, collect social security contributions at roughly twice the American rate. In recent years social security taxes have risen more sharply in the United States and Sweden than in the other four Western states in this study. Yet it does not appear likely that the United States or Sweden will soon approach the French, Italian, or West German emphasis on social insurance contributions.

In conclusion it can be seen that tax structures vary to such an extent that only those of Italy and France, on the one hand, and the Soviet Union and East Germany, on the other, are quite closely paired. The former have seemingly regressive patterns based on consumption and social security taxes, while the two Communist-ruled states depend on revenues from consumption and enterprise profits. The United States, emphasizing personal income taxes and de-emphasizing consumption assessments, could be expected to have highly progressive tax impacts. Nonetheless, a good deal more than the choice of taxes affects tax equity. We now proceed to look at one of the measures of how various taxes are assessed, this being the nominal rates applied.

How High Are the Tax Rates?

The actual tax bill that one pays is a product of *nominal*, or stated, rates modified by exemptions, deductions, shifting, illegal avoidance, and other intervening factors. Variations in nominal rates may or may not correlate with the *effective* rates paid by different categories of taxpayers. Such variations should be taken as only a starting point for the analysis of the effective rates and the redistributional outcomes of particular taxes.

For example, despite a 50 percent nominal rate on corporate profits in Britain in 1973, the manufacturing sector managed to pay at a mere 14 percent effective rate during that year.[27] In this case, the reduction was based primarily on a very generous system of deducting investment costs. Nominal rates may also be affected by the exclusion of a large part of income, consumption, profits, or payrolls from any tax burden; by variations in the steepness of rate progression; and by the multiplicity of incentives maintained for broader social or economic purposes. Nominal federal tax rates in the United States were modified in 1976 by an estimated $91 billion in tax expenditures, allocated much as the 1973 tax expenditures shown in Figure 8–1.

FIGURE 8–1

U.S. Federal Government Fiscal Year 1973 Tax Expenditures by Function

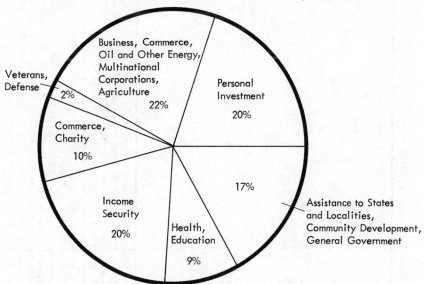

[27] *Economist* (London), March 15, 1975, p. 111.

TABLE 8–6
Basic Nominal Tax Rates in Effect in 1972

	Social Security (percent of taxable payroll)		Income (percent of taxable income or profits)		Consumption (percent of value-added or sales—standard rate of main tax)
	By employer	By employee	Households (single persons)	Resident Companies or Enterprises (retained profit)	
France	39	7	3–63 1973: 5–60	50 1973: 59	VAT: 23 1973: 20
West Germany	14	14	19–53[a] 1973: 22–56	49–51[a] 1973: 56	VAT: 11
Italy	47	7	2–65 maximum surcharge: 30	25–40	Turnover: 4 (cascading) 1974 VAT: 16
Sweden	14	6	29–82[b]	54.4	VAT: 17.75
United Kingdom	6	6	30–75[c]	40–50 1974: 52	Purchase tax: 13.75 1973 VAT: 10
United States	5	5	14–70[d]	22–48	State sales: 2–6
Soviet Union	4.4–9.0	0	1968: 4.1–52.6[e]	63[f]	1970 turnover: 33
East Germany	10	10	16–90[g]	Private corporation income: 16–95 Profits share: 35–70	Turnover: 3 (cascading)

[a] Exclusive of 3 percent supplementary levy.
[b] Local income tax with proportional rates between 19 percent and 28 percent was deductible against national tax of 10 to 54 percent.
[c] Excludes investment income surcharge of 15 percent.
[d] Maximum rate of 50 percent on "earned" income.
[e] Limited to maximum of 13 percent for wage and salary earnings.
[f] Effective tax rate on total enterprise and organization profits.
[g] Excluding surcharge on highest incomes.

Sources: *Revenue Statistics of OECD Member Countries, 1965–1972* (Paris: OECD, 1975), p. 225; U.S. Department of Health, Education, and Welfare, *Social Security throughout the World, 1973* (Washington, D.C.: U.S. Government Printing Office, 1973), pp. 112–13; *European Taxation*, vol. 14, no. 8, pp. 272–80; vol. 12, nos. 5–6, pp. 112–73; Martin Schnitzer, *Income Distribution: A Comparative Study* (New York: Praeger Publishers, 1974), pp. 149–55; Schnitzer, *East and West Germany: A Comparative Economic Analysis* (New York: Praeger Publishers, 1972), pp. 273–81; European Communities, *Inventory of Taxes* (Brussels, 1972); and *The New British System of Taxation* (London: Central Office of Information, 1973).

TABLE 8–7
Average and Marginal Personal Income Tax Rates Paid by Average Production Worker, 1972

	Single Man		Married Couple with Two Children	
	Average Rate	Marginal Rate	Average Rate	Marginal Rate
France	7	14	–	7
West Germany..........	16	28	7	16
Italy	8	17	7	16
Sweden	33	58	27	58
United Kingdom........	20	31	11	30
United States	19	29	10	23
East Germany (1971)	18	22.5	8.9*	30*

* Tax rates for husband, wife, and three children.
Sources: *Revenue Statistics of OECD Member Countries, 1965–1972* (Paris: OECD, 1975), p. 222; for East Germany: Deutscher Bundestag, *Materialen zum Bericht zur Lage der Nation 1971* (Bonn – Bad Godesberg: Dr. Hans Verlag, 1971), pp. 338–39, as found in Martin Schnitzer, *Income Distribution: A Comparative Study* (New York: Praeger Publishers, 1974), p. 153.

An enormous amount of income is exempted or taxed at reduced rates due to its source or to its subsequent private use. The former includes capital gains and public welfare grants; the latter, income used for such purposes as investment, the payment of other taxes and interest, and philanthropy.

In Tables 8–6 and 8–7 we record the nominal rates of various major taxes in effect in 1972 and data relating to the average and marginal rates of income tax liability for an "average production worker" in each of the countries in our survey except the Soviet Union.[28] Only with such data can we approach the question of how harshly certain taxes are imposed.

One of the most notable examples of low nominal tax rates is the unique situation of the Soviet wage and salary employee, who pays no social security tax from his paycheck and whose income taxes come to no more than 13 percent. Another is the exceptionally high nominal income tax levels in Sweden and the United Kingdom, which are often criticized as virtually confiscatory by taxpayers in those countries.

Although corporate and enterprise profits are taxed at rather similar nominal rates in the eight countries, the rates on consumption and payrolls are strikingly variant. The greatest variation in consumption taxes is between the United States, where the people of several states pay no general tax at all, and the Soviet Union, whose residents pay separate turnover taxes, the state's share of retail prices, that average as much as 30 percent. French and Italian employers must pay payroll taxes for social security at a rate six or seven times the contribution

---

[28] The term *average* refers to average income, and data is presented for an average single male worker and his counterpart with a spouse and two children.

of employers in the Soviet Union, the United States, or Great Britain.

Interpreting Table 8–7, we must first make clear the distinction between the *marginal rate,* the rate—determined by the taxpayer's "bracket"—which is paid on the most highly taxed part of the taxpayer's income, and the *average rate,* the tax liability expressed as a percentage of total taxable income. The OECD data in this table incorporated only a portion of the possible exemptions and deductions, and are thus not fully valid as indications of effective tax rates.[29] Yet these statistics do provide us with valuable information for assessing both nominal and effective rates as applied to the average production worker.

From these statistics and only partially comparable Soviet data we learn that effective income tax rates applied to average workers closely parallel a given country's overall level of dependence on this source of revenue. France, Italy, and the Soviet Union are notably easy on their average worker, and Sweden stands out for its exceptionally high rates. Most Europeans and Americans would consider the 58 percent marginal rate extraordinarily high, especially as it is not modified for greater family responsibilities. Taxpayers in the United States and Great Britain were paying at similar average rates, though the higher British marginal rates reflected the much steeper levies applied to higher incomes in that country.

Although the U.S. and British taxes on corporate and personal income show great variance between the effective and the nominal rates, the differences are much smaller in Sweden and the Soviet Union. Legal deductions and exemptions may, but do not necessarily, convert such taxes from progressive into regressive instruments of policy. As for other taxes, nominal rates are generally a much more meaningful indicator of actual obligations in relation to consumption and payroll taxes than to income and death duties. However, the former set of taxes is quite subject to the shifting of burdens to other parties.

Efficiency and Tax Avoidance

Both military conscription and taxation depend on a high level of underlying support for the given political system and on an effective threat of punishment. The history of taxpaying has been one of very high levels of avoidance that goes beyond the use of legalized loopholes, exemptions, and deductions.

Illegal tax avoidance relates directly to the taxation perceived by

---

[29] One particularly important distorting factor is the variation among countries that provide family allowances partly or completely through the tax system and those that provide the allowances only through distributions.

individuals and companies as proper and their judgment of the consequences of false reporting. Policy choices by government include whether or not to invite avoidance by setting exceedingly high rates and maintaining inefficient collection systems, and alternative patterns of investigating, prosecuting, and punishing offenders. Some countries, including a few in our survey, seem to allow tax avoidance as an additional benefit to privileged strata. Yet even in these states, most notably France and Italy, old patterns seem to be changing and the shortcomings in the collection systems are now probably associated more closely with administrative inefficiencies than with policy intent. Other states, most notably West Germany and the United States, have developed some of the most advanced systems of tax control and have used these to generate high levels of tax-reporting compliance. To some degree this has been a necessary consequence of the heavy dependence on more easily avoidable direct taxes in those states.

Central and Local Taxation

The relative capability and power of central and local government units is determined as much by ability to raise revenue as by any other factor. A provincial or city government that depends on a central government for "grants-in aid" or receives most of its funds as part of the central government budget will usually have difficulty in standing up to the central government. On the other hand, local government is stronger, when, through constitutional mandate or custom, it maintains control over large and growing revenue sources.

Tax autonomy for local government units both reflects and determines the character of federal or unitary patterns in the various states. The largest proportional tax collecting by local governments exists in the federal states in our study: West Germany, the United States, and the Soviet Union. In viewing these patterns, it must also be recognized that the high level of autonomy in tax matters enjoyed by the American states and the West German Länder is not shared by the republics of the Soviet Union.

Both federal and unitary states in our survey have faced major problems in trying to provide adequate financing for local government.[30] Both the tax system and budget distributions play major roles in the provision of adequate and equitable regional revenues. Several states, including West Germany and the Soviet Union, have utilized formulas for sharing particular taxes as a means of achieving greater equality among regional units.

---

[30] See John M. Echols, "Politics, Budgets, and Regional Equality in Communist and Capitalist Systems," *Comparative Political Studies* 8, no. 3 (October 1975): 259–92.

Because local governments tend to have tax structures different from those used by the central government, there may be major variations in tax equity. The tax structures of state and local government in the United States, weighted toward sales and property assessments, are significantly less progressive than the federal structure. However, much smaller variations in equity exist between the local and central revenue systems of Sweden and the Soviet Union.

FRONTIER ISSUES IN TAXATION

Tax policy is exceptionally resistant to abrupt change. Yet some very substantial shifts have occurred during recent decades. In most of the leading Western industrial states the post-1945 generation has been the first to pay roughly as much in social insurance taxes as through any other form of taxes, and only since World War II has the personal income tax become a major burden for the majority of taxpayers in most industrialized states.

Because the 1970s have thus far been a period of economic retrenchment, tax reform has been placed high on the political agenda in many industrialized countries. More is being demanded from tax systems — they are being altered to provide frequently conflicting medicine for inflation, recession, pollution, energy shortages, run-away public assistance programs, and other societal ills. Although tax policy has always involved a multiplicity of goals, a definite expansion of its problem-solving roles is in progress. This has frequently involved the use of taxes for new purposes of regulation and distribution.

The Negative Income Tax and Income Support

If the income tax is administered in a relatively efficient manner and public assistance programs are notoriously inefficient and irrational, why not adapt the income tax to provide income support? This is a question that has been asked in a number of countries, but particularly in those in which public assistance programs play an exceptionally large role in the social welfare system.

The American dependent-exemption and public assistance programs have generally been viewed as less satisfactory than the family allowance distributions employed in the other industrialized states in our study group. Family allowance programs provide benefits to a larger sector of the population than do such American programs as Aid to Families with Dependent Children, and do not result in a comparable employment disincentive.

The negative income tax idea extends the principle of progressive taxation, converting its low-income exemption into an entitlement for support from the government. Individuals and families become eligible for payments which represent the difference between their own earnings and a previously established benefit ceiling.[31]

In 1975 the U.S. government took a substantial step toward a negative income tax by approving and funding a "refundable earned income credit." Working taxpayers with children became eligible to receive a tax credit of up to $400, the maximum benefit going to families with incomes of $4,000 and lesser benefits going to families with incomes below $4,000 and between $4,000 and $8,000. The supporters of this program described it as an answer to the regressive impact of the growing social security tax. Yet this tax credit could well become something approximating a negative income tax if the credit were increased by a substantial multiple of $400.

Tax credit plans have also been proposed by the British cabinet and have been discussed in other states. However, most states do not feel pressed to replace existing distributive programs with a negative income tax.

Taxes and Business Investment

Every industrial state seeks to influence the timing, size, and direction of business investment. During the past several decades numerous states have developed new ways to use taxation as a major device for achieving these objectives.

Perhaps the most sophisticated application of taxes in relation to investment is being used in Sweden.[32] To restrict investment generally or in particular sectors during periods of strong economic activity Sweden has taxed investment capital and has exempted up to 40 percent of company profits from taxation. The "tax" on exempted profits, kept as an investment reserve, is employed at a later time that is subject to the approval of the authorities. The government can at any time increase total investment by more than 10 percent through release of these funds.

Among the anticipated advantages for the Swedish economy are the lessened need to raise interest rates on money and the high degree of assurance that investments are made when and where this is desired by the government. The investment reserve is used in conjunction with direct spending on public works, government contracts, and other fiscal and monetary measures.

---

[31] See Barry M. Blechman et al., *Setting National Priorities: The 1975 Budget* (Washington, D.C.: Brookings Institution, 1974), pp. 199–206.

[32] Assar Lindbeck, *Swedish Economic Policy* (Berkeley: University of California Press, 1974), pp. 97–102, 130–38; and Martin Schnitzer, *The Economy of Sweden* (New York: Praeger Publishers, 1970), pp. 85–114.

Other Western states are adopting versions of the investment reserve. The French variation ties the tax-exempt share of profits to the amount of profits shared with employees.[33] In West Germany an investment reserve is created through deposits of tax revenue by the federal and *Länder* governments instead of by private companies.[34] The other capitalist states in our survey generally use more conventional approaches in applying their tax systems to the control and stimulation of business investment, particularly variations in rates and rules for deducting the depreciation of investments.

Although the East European Communist regimes have not found it necessary to develop investment reserves to counter economic cycles they have devoted considerable attention to distributions of investment funds between individual enterprises and the governmental tax collector.[35] With profits increasing, the enterprises are instructed to provide slowly increasing revenues to the state budget while simultaneously keeping an increasing share of the profits in their own hands. These funds are utilized for immediate reinvestment as well as for wages and social overhead.

Taxes and Inflation

Basic Keynesian and post-Keynesian fiscal policy was conceived more as a tool for reducing unemployment than as a restraint on price inflation. Yet tax policy has been brought to bear on the latter problem, and with some new twists in recent years.

Standard Keynesian policy provides for increased tax rates during times of full employment and for decreased rates when unemployment is high. Such actions are designed to affect demand for goods and services, and can be expected to help employment at the expense of increased price inflation, or vice versa. Substantial deficit budgets designed to fight unemployment require governments to resort to equivalent borrowing. This raises costs for borrowing money as well as for other goods and services. Reciprocally, government budget surpluses can lead to decreased prices at the risk of decreases in demand, jobs, and economic growth.

Increases and decreases in indirect taxes can have important impacts on the cost of goods and services to the consumer. Such direct taxes as those on personal income may penalize taxpayers by taking increasing proportions of salaries while the taxpayers' inflated paycheck represents lower real income even before taxes are considered.

One of the newest uses of taxation as a device to combat inflation was

---

[33] "France: Budget 1974," *European Taxation*, vol. 13, no. 10 (October 1973), p. 351.

[34] Martin Schnitzer, *East and West Germany*, pp. 101–6.

[35] See Musgrave, *Fiscal Systems*, pp. 54–62.

established in France in 1975. Large French companies have been made subject to an additional tax, effectively a fine, when the cost of their products exceeds a national norm.[36] The British Liberal party has proposed a tax on excessive wage increases, but this has not been supported by the government. However, it seems likely that taxes will continue to be part of the search for inflation control.

Taxing Pollution and Energy Use

Solutions to industrial pollution and energy shortages require both enormous capital investment and regulations. Increasingly, tax systems are being employed as supporting tools.

Taxation in the form of assessments against discharges of effluent into rivers was a long-established policy tool in prewar Germany. Today such assessments are being introduced in France and other European states as a major policy tool for water management.[37]

Many leading economists favor the assessment approach over alternative regulative, direct subsidy, or tax subsidy methods.[38] This approach has been endorsed by the European Communities as a "polluter pays" policy that serves both equity and efficiency in the assignment of costs of pollution.

The approach has been applied primarily to waterways, though it has also been considered as a means for controlling atmospheric, noise, and other forms of pollution. The United States, though choosing to use subsidies through tax credits and depreciation allowances for pollution-control technology in its approach to water pollution abatement, developed some of the first plans to apply pollution charges to atmospheric sulfur emissions and certain other pollution problems.[39]

Taxes have been developed as means to reduce energy usage. New and increased taxes have been designed to make petroleum products more expensive to the consumer. Taxes on large cars and engines have been increased in much of Western Europe to encourage the purchase of small cars. In Britain, which has long maintained lower gasoline taxes than many other European countries, road users were financing more than 10 percent of the central government budget in 1974.[40]

The basic justification for pollution taxes is that they constitute a charge to help pay for the very real costs inflicted on society by the

---

[36] *Economist*, March 29, 1975, p. 106.

[37] Allen V. Kneese and Blair T. Bower, *Managing Water Quality: Economics, Technology, Institutions* (Baltimore: Johns Hopkins Press, 1968), chaps. 12, 13. See further discussion in Chapter 10.

[38] *Ibid.*; and Musgrave and Musgrave, *Public Finance*, chap. 29.

[39] Musgrave and Musgrave, *Public Finance*, p. 700.

[40] *Economist*, November 16, 1974, p. 103.

parties responsible for pollution. The major difficulty is the need to avoid licensing an unacceptable level of continuing environmental contamination.

The benefits of energy use taxes lie in conservation, improved balances of international payments, national security, and the availability of salvaged energy for more valuable purposes. The major weakness of the tax mechanism as a means of achieving these ends is the probable inequity of the burden. Taxes are generally imposed as an alternative to rationing, a technique that is usually less efficient but can be designed to affect rich and poor alike. Higher taxes on energy use may price such basic needs as home heating and such widespread aspects of the Western life-style as automobile driving out of the reach of the average citizen.

Other Frontier Areas

These uses of taxation as a policy instrument, involving as they do major areas of social, economic, and environmental life, should be viewed as mere illustrations of the many new areas in which taxation is being employed. For example, tax credits and deductions are now being used to fund American presidential campaigns and tax subsidies have been the foundation of vital regional development policies in several states.

No one country has pioneered all of these policy developments. Sweden, the United States, France, and West Germany have each been quite innovative in applying the revenue system to national social, economic, and environmental problems.

TAXES AND INCOME REDISTRIBUTION

Do taxes, like the sum total of direct distributions of governmental goods and services, contribute to the redistribution of income in our sample states? Many studies have been undertaken to answer this question. These have all faced certain unresolvable problems, including inadequate knowledge of tax-shifting patterns, so that none of the studies can offer highly accurate cross-country comparisons of the overall impacts of tax systems.

With these cautions in mind we note that authorities commonly describe the redistributional impact of the Soviet and East German tax systems as somewhat regressive. Reported impacts in the Western states in our study vary within a rather narrow range between small increases and small decreases in equality of income. We focus here on the distribution of income among income groups rather than on intragroup distributions based on family size or age.

For the most part, personal income taxes do provide progressive outcomes, and such taxes as those on consumption and payrolls do tend to be regressive. Disputes over shifting patterns make it very difficult to assess the impacts of such other taxes as those on corporation income and property.[41] However, the overall progressive impact of the personal income tax is considerably less in some states than in others, and such an indirect assessment as the West German value-added tax has been evaluated as at least somewhat progressive in its impact.[42]

Although few authorities feel that they have sufficient information to be certain, the case against contemporary tax systems as instruments promoting equality seems overwhelming. Martin Schnitzer refers to the East German system as one which "may be proportional or even regressive."[43] An official study revealed that "the French post-tax distribution of wages and salaries was more unequal than the pretax."[44]

Although more progressive outcomes have been found in some of the states with greater dependence on personal income taxes, the differences do not appear to be very great. Among our eight states this tax is stressed most in Sweden, Britain, and the United States.

Two of the most comprehensive studies of the effects of the U.S. tax system lend little support to progressive redistribution. Richard and Peggy Musgrave conclude that, largely because of regressive state and local taxes and excessive use of tax expenditures by the most wealthy, the distribution of 1968 aftertax income was only very slightly more equal than that of income before tax.[45] An even more sophisticated study by Pechman and Okner states, "In summary, the U.S. tax system is essentially proportional for the vast majority of families and therefore has little effect on the distribution of income."[46] Analyses of British taxes indicate that a very slight overall redistributive effect in the late 1950s was succeeded during the 1960s by a tax system with virtually no redistributional effects.[47]

Of the eight states only Sweden offers evidence of substantial pro-

---

[41] See Joseph A. Pechman and Benjamin A. Okner, *Who Bears the Tax Burden?* (Washington, D.C.: Brookings Institution, 1974), pp. 57–62.

[42] Schnitzer, *Income Redistribution* (New York: Praeger Publishers, 1974), p. 121.

[43] Schnitzer, *East and West Germany*, p. 276.

[44] Stu'y by Alain Fouon, Georges Hatchuel, and Pierre Kende cited in S. M. Miller and Martin Rein, "Can Income Redistribution Work?" *Social Policy* 6, no. 1 (May–June 1975): 9.

[45] Musgrave and Musgrave, *Public Finance*, p. 656.

[46] Pechman and Okner, *Who Bears the Tax Burden?* p. 10.

[47] J. L. Nicholson, *Redistribution of Income in the United Kingdom* (London: Bowes and Bowes, 1964); and J. C. Kincaid, *Poverty and Equality in Britain: A Study of Social Security and Taxation* (Baltimore: Penguin Books, 1973).

gressive redistribution of income through taxation. Schnitzer, analyzing 1970 data, notes that the Swedish combination of highly progressive effective personal income tax rates and moderate payroll taxes does provide significant income redistribution.[48] Assar Lindbeck evaluated research by Mats Hellstrom and determined that Swedish taxes before 1971 had a "considerable" impact on reducing inequalities at the higher levels of income and that the 1971 changes in tax rates were contributing to increased equalization within the large middle class.[49] Among Western states Sweden has probably made the most explicit commitment in principle to the promotion of income redistribution and stands out in its use of the tax system to that end.

CONCLUSIONS

Contrasting trends are evident for the military draft and taxation. Among the countries in this survey conscription has been ended in two states and has been eased in terms of duration and implicit tax cost in most of the others. In contrast, taxes continue to rise as a proportion of gross national product and show few signs of becoming more equitable.

These generalizations do not preclude major, even fundamental, variations in the tax systems of such developed states as the chosen eight. Differences of considerable magnitude have existed throughout the post-1945 era, as in earlier decades, in regard to every aspect of tax policy, from the total tax burden to the distribution of costs among sectors of the population. Our designated states have also differed substantially in their dependence on particular kinds of taxes, the sharing of taxes between central and local government, and the use of the tax system as a means of providing subsidies and incentives to foster economic, cultural, social, and physical environmental goals.

Major variations have persisted despite such meaningful processes of multinational penetration, emulation, and reaction as the Sovietization of East European tax policies, the effort within the European Communities to achieve "harmonization" in areas of taxation that affect business competition, and the tendency to adjust taxes to the multinational corporations' ability to avoid payments and move to greener tax pastures. European tax systems, and those of developed states generally, have tended to become increasingly similar in recent years. Yet substantial differences persist even among nations with close political and economic ties.

The level of taxation is influenced by such diverse factors as the

---

[48] Schnitzer, *Income Redistribution*, pp. 80–88.
[49] Lindbeck, *Swedish Economic Policy*, pp. 200–204.

size of the socialized sector of the economy and the demand for collective goods and services. Incrementalism contributes a good deal to year-to-year increases, but great events periodically move budgets to new plateaus of taxation and spending.

Inequities have many parents and continue to be nurtured in most countries. Among the principal factors are conflicting policy goals, uneven patterns of representation and access to decision-makers, the complexity of tax law, and the opportunities for masking regressive practices in progressive garb.

Yet some nations do enforce tax laws that are far more equitable than those of other nations. Sweden's taxes are exceptional in both their equitableness and their burdensomeness. Communist-ruled states in Eastern Europe, having other instruments available for promoting income equality, rarely use their revenue laws for progressive purposes. Yet this is not unusual for industrial states — most do not minimize income inequality through taxes.

9 Regulating and Protecting Civil Liberties and Rights

Students of psychology and sociology learn that the conduct of individuals may be shaped and regulated by a wide variety of forces and institutions. In this chapter we are concerned with aspects of human behavior that are subject to legal control by the state and are often maintained through the threat of force. Moreover, our interest is not in how the state preserves domestic tranquillity or inculcates loyalty but rather in the rights of man in an era characterized by extensive state activity.

What rights ought individuals and groups to be able to assert in dealings with their state and society? Instead of taking an excursion through several millennia of Western philosophy, we prefer to direct our attention to a more immediate source, namely the Universal Declaration of Human Rights, a document adopted and promulgated by the United Nations General Assembly in December 1948.[1]

The rights embodied in the Declaration may

---

[1] *Human Rights: A Compilation of International Instruments of the United Nations* (New York: United Nations, 1967), pp. 1–3.

be grouped into four categories: substantive civil liberties, civil rights, procedural rights, and socioeconomic rights. Because the preceding chapters dealt with such socioeconomic issues as education and health care, we will restrict ourselves here to the first three sets of rights.

Substantive civil liberties constitute the most comprehensive of our three categories. Such liberties are primarily political and cultural, especially in the Anglo-American perspective. The term *substantive* refers to the fact that such liberties constitute spheres of thought, expression, or action. These are to be distinguished from procedural rights, which primarily restrict the means used by authorities seeking to limit individual or group enjoyment of substantive liberties. The Declaration affirms the following areas of substantive civil liberties: thought, conscience, and religion; expression; peaceful assembly, association, and political participation; movement and residence within each state's borders; and leaving one's country to seek asylum from persecution.

Regarding civil rights the Declaration proclaims the illegitimacy of invidious legal distinctions and practices based on such criteria as race, color, sex, and ethnic background. Defined in this fashion, civil rights involve areas of both substantive civil liberties and procedural rights. The document stipulates the availability of all rights and freedoms without regard to the above-mentioned social distinctions, stating: "All are equal before the law and are entitled without any discrimination to equal protection of the law." More specifically, it makes provision for the right of equal access to public services, proscribes sex-based discrimination in marriage and employment, and affirms the right to a nationality.

The Declaration's procedural rights or due process of law provisions include prohibitions against cruel and inhuman punishment, arbitrary arrest, detention, and exile. Among the most basic of the procedural rights in the document are fair and public hearings before an independent and impartial tribunal, the presumption of innocence, and the assistance of legal counsel. Further procedural rights include the avoidance of arbitrary interference with one's privacy, family, home, and correspondence and the prohibition of attacks on one's honor and reputation.

As the reader will probably have concluded by now, the rights encompassed in the Declaration are highly commendable. It would indeed be a marvelous world if they were as widely enjoyed as proclaimed. Unfortunately, the Declaration does not constitute directly enforceable law for the UN's member states. Such principles become binding only when a particular state ratifies conventions and treaties that are adopted by the United Nations and other groupings of states.

Further, the enforcement of even this international legislation is largely the responsibility of national officials.[2]

The limited but significant enforcement roles of such worldwide supranational organizations as the United Nations and the International Labor Organization (joint private and governmental) as well as such nongovernmental bodies as Amnesty International, the International Commission of Jurists, and the International Press Institute have been discussed in Chapter 3. It will suffice here to say that such organizations generally depend on publicity and mediation.[3] Unfortunately, the regimes which tend to commit the most serious offenses are usually among the least sensitive to international public opinion. For example, when Amnesty International reported on the situation of political prisoners in East Germany in the mid-60s, that state's leaders responded by denouncing Amnesty International as a monopoly capitalist organ to which little attention need be paid.[4]

We observed in Chapter 3 that the most effective international enforcement of human rights occurs in Western Europe, particularly through the instruments of the Council of Europe. We will now be more specific in noting the nature of the rights protected by that organization. Its European Convention for the Protection of Human Rights and Fundamental Freedoms has been ratified by and is at least partially in force in 15 states that include the United Kingdom, Sweden, West Germany, and Italy, though not France.[5]

The first section of the European Convention is similar to the Universal Declaration in that it contains provisions articulating the substantive and procedural liberties and rights of citizens.[6] It is distinguished from the latter, however, in that limitations on the exercise of these liberties and rights are more explicitly recognized. For example, the Convention's affirmation of freedom of expression is qualified by the following assertion:

---

[2] *United Nations Action in the Field of Human Rights* (New York: United Nations, 1974); International Conference on Human Rights, *Status of Multilateral Agreements in the Field of Human Rights Concluded under the Auspices of the United Nations* (New York: United Nations, 1968), p. 10.

[3] Peter Archer, "Action by Unofficial Organizations on Human Rights," and Armand Gaspard, "International Action to Preserve Press Freedom," in Evan Luard (ed.), *The International Protection of Human Rights* (New York: Frederick A. Praeger, 1967), pp. 160–82, 183–209.

[4] Peter Przybycski, "The Criminal Jurisdiction of the German Democratic Republic Conforms to the Principles of Human Rights," *Law and Legislation in the GDR* 2 (1966): 23–30.

[5] Ralph Beddard, *Human Rights and Europe* (London: Sweet & Maxwell, 1973), p. 1.

[6] Copies of the Convention are published in several sources. The interested reader might consult: Clovis Morrison, Jr., *The Developing European Law of Human Rights* (Leyden, Netherlands: A. W. Sijthoff, 1967), pp. 215–24; or Anna Coote and Lawrence Grant, *Civil Liberty* (Baltimore: Penguin Books, 1972), pp. 299–328.

The exercise of these freedoms, since it carries with it duties and responsibilities, may be subject to such formalities, conditions, restrictions or penalties as are prescribed by law and are necessary in a democratic society, in the interests of national security, territorial integrity or public safety, for the prevention of disorder or crime, for the protection of health or morals, for the protection of the reputation or rights of others, for preventing the disclosure of information received in confidence, or for maintaining the authority and impartiality of the judiciary.

Article 17, which was invoked in a 1957 case to uphold the West German Constitutional Court's ban on the Communist party, denies to any group or person the right to use political expression and organization to seek the destruction of any of the rights and freedoms set forth. In general, the Convention does not contain comparable qualifications in its provisions dealing with the civil rights or the due process rights of persons accused of criminal acts. Yet Article 15 offers the signatory states the right to act contrary to their obligations under the Convention "in time of war or other public emergency threatening the life of the nation."

Despite these limitations, or, depending on your point of view, reasonable qualifications, the Council of Europe's approach has advantages over the UN's. Most important, its Court of Human Rights is empowered to issue rulings that may have the force of law in the relevant nation. This Court may hear a case only after the issues have been investigated by the Council's Commission and the latter body has ruled both that the issue is a proper one for supranational deliberation and that the Commission has failed in its own efforts to mediate the dispute. Any signatory state or group of states may bring to the Commission allegations of Convention violations by another contracting state against its own nationals. In 1967 Denmark, Norway, and Sweden charged the Greek regime with the use of torture and the inhuman treatment of political prisoners.[7] In addition, 11 of the 15 signatory powers have accepted an optional declaration granting their own nationals, as individuals, the right to petition the Commission for redress. In 1975 the Court overturned certain provisions of British prison rules in a case involving the denial of an inmate's access to an attorney.[8]

Since its inception over 5,000 individual petitions have been submitted to the Commission, of which 90 percent have been rejected.[9] Of the remainder the vast majority were resolved by means of friendly

---

[7] Amnesty International, *Report on Torture* (London: Duckworth, 1975), pp. 79–105.

[8] Michael Zander, "European Court Lays Down the Law," *Manchester Guardian Weekly*, March 1, 1975, p. 6.

[9] Beddard, *Human Rights*, p. 5.

conciliation. Thus the Court, which receives cases only after Commission review, has had only a limited case load. Moreover, on the occasions in which the Court has issued rulings, these have not always been against defendant states. Finally, since the ultimate sanction available to the Council of Europe for noncompliance with a Court decision is the expulsion of a member state, the entire process depends on the various parties' willingness to be voluntarily bound by the accords.

It would be wrong to view any or all of this international law and machinery as a substitute for assurance of rights at the national level. This is particularly true for the four countries in our study that are not bound by the European Convention. Yet even in the four Western European signatory states the principles of the Universal Declaration must be enforced and assured primarily through national law and legal practices.

National Legal Systems

An examination of how well the eight states safeguard individual rights through their national legal systems must begin with a brief description of the major variations in those systems. Many domestic factors certainly intrude strongly, as do international and historical influences. A number of these have been discussed in the first half of this book, including war, regime character, and foreign penetration. We have not previously described a more immediate set of influences, the legal traditions with which each of our states approaches contemporary problems of law enforcement and civil liberties.

National legal systems are themselves the products of other basic and underlying forces that affect the state of individual rights. For example, the German and Italian legal systems reflect elements of their countries' authoritarian traditions and the post-1945 reaction against the Nazi and Fascist perversions of those traditions. Other systems may be shaped by such national patterns as federalism, religion, or the degree of homogeneity of the population.

Our designated eight countries represent three distinguishable legal families. The British and American systems are among those based on the Common Law, while the Swedish, French, West German, and Italian systems belong to the large Roman or Civil Law group. In East Germany and the Soviet Union, as in other Eastern European countries, the prevailing legal structures are shaped by the Socialist Law tradition.[10] Although there has been a good deal of interfamily emulation,

---

[10] René David and John Brierly, *Major Legal Systems in the World Today: An Introduction to the Comparative Study of Law* (New York: Free Press, 1968).

with structures and practices originally belonging to one group being taken up by members of another, as well as a substantial amount of intrafamily variation, for example, between the United States and Great Britain, it nevertheless seems appropriate to compare the legal systems in this manner.

What is it about these three families which sets them apart from one another?

Common Law

Historically, the Common Law developed in England after the Norman Conquest as an effort by the royal courts created by the king to articulate a uniform body of law applicable throughout the domain to replace diverse local custom. Over time the principles of law came to be distilled from the judgments of courts in concrete cases with the development of the practice of relying in present cases on prior judicial decisions. Written statutory enactments tended to play a secondary role in this process. Despite the increasing prevalence of written law in the last century, both in Britain and the United States, the Common Law tradition is built around the ability of independent judges to set precedent and assign legal meaning as a consequence of rendering decisions in particular cases. Furthermore, unlike the continental European pattern, the Common Law tradition subjected state organs and private individuals to the same set of judicial institutions.[11] Therefore, notwithstanding the fact that in modern Britain Parliament is constitutionally supreme, theoretically having the ability to make law as it pleases, whereas in the United States Congress and the president are formally constrained by a single documentary Constitution, the legal systems of both countries derive from a common judge-centered and case-centered heritage.

Roman Law

The evolution of the Roman Law family in Europe was significantly different. During the Middle Ages one found, as in England, a plethora of tribal and territorially distinct customary legal practices. Toward the end of this epoch and the beginning of the Renaissance the law taught at major European universities involved the interpretation of Roman Law, in particular the compilations of Justinian, with an eye toward uncovering universal principles of justice. As scholars reflected and commented on this law, other sources of legal understanding were

---

[11] A. V. Dicey, *Introduction to the Study of the Law of the Constitution,* 10th ed. (New York: St. Martin's Press, 1961), pp. 328–405.

introduced into their analyses. These included local practices and the Roman Catholic church's Canon Law, itself derivative of Roman Law.

At the end of the 18th century and the beginning of the 19th century, law began to be applied systematically to the emerging European nation-states. Most notably in France with the Code Napoléon, but also throughout the Continent, over the course of the 19th century legal scholars and practitioners articulated codes defining the major principles of law to be applied in the respective national jurisdictions. Characteristically, the codes represented an amalgamation of Roman Law with nationally distinctive practices. In most countries the outcome was the imposition of four basic codes: civil, civil procedure, penal, and criminal procedure.

By contrast to the case and judge-centered evolution of the Common Law, with general legal principles emerging inductively from the particular case to the general rule, the development of the Roman Law family on the Continent exhibited the opposite tendency. Here the general legal principles were to be found in codes. Judges were to deduce and apply these principles in particular cases. As a result, continental judges never acquired the formal right to set precedent and make law, as did their Anglo-American counterparts.

In addition, the evolving Roman tradition was one in which the regular courts could not hold the state accountable for its actions. Unlike courts in the United States, with their capacity to rule on the constitutionality of legislative and executive action, or the similar ability of English courts to declare the state's actions ultra vires, or beyond its authorized legal powers, regular continental courts were denied such a prerogative. What emerged instead were separate sets of administrative law courts, outside the regular judicial hierarchies, having the ability to determine whether or not state action exceeded lawful requirements in particular cases. As against the regular civil and criminal courts, whose rulings were constrained by codes, the administrative courts developed a body of legal principles which were shaped significantly by their own case-based decisions.

Socialist Law

The legal systems in the states employing the East European brand of socialism are characterized by the relatively recent imposition of something that can be termed Socialist Law onto a fabric that had been based for centuries on Roman and local traditions. As such, Socialist Law remains the most difficult of the three legal families to distinguish and define.

Indeed, for a number of years after the Russian Revolution of 1917 there was some doubt about whether law was appropriate to a revolutionary state in the process of building socialism. Marx and Engels had emphasized the negative character of law in pre-socialist societies, viewing it as a major instrument by which a ruling class maintains its hegemony over an oppressed class.[12]

Beginning in the 1920s the view developed that law had a role to play in the building of socialism. This law might appear in print, much like Roman Law, with appropriate constitutions and codes. Yet its sponsors asserted that Socialist Law had the function of helping to remold a society rather than to preserve one. It was to be interpreted by judges in the context of the ideological goals set out by the leaders of the Communist party, these being dominantly revolutionary.

The resultant revolutionary legal system in the Soviet Union was notable as much for its arbitrary enforcement as for its disrespect for many aspects of the prerevolutionary social and economic patterns. As noted earlier, the Stalinist system was probably more arbitrary and less constitutional than even that of the Nazis.

The full flavor of the Stalinist version of Socialist Law was imposed on the East European–bloc countries after 1945, especially during the period of intense purges in those countries between about 1948 and 1953. However, those states also tended to maintain major elements of their prewar Roman legal systems and retained traditions concerning the rule of law that were stronger than the comparable traditions of either czarist Russia or the Soviet Union.

It is somewhat more difficult now than in previous decades to accept the idea of a separate socialist legal tradition. This is due to the movement of almost all East European states, including the Soviet Union, away from an emphasis on continuing revolutionary change in their social and economic systems in favor of a conservative emphasis on defending and reinforcing previous changes. Law serves the "ruling class" in the socialist states as well as in capitalist states. Indeed, it serves public property rights more zealously than any property rights are served in capitalist systems.

On the other hand, Socialist Law remains distinct from Western patterns by being more directly subject to political interference, by giving less attention to private legal relationships among citizens, and by emphasizing reinforcement of the regime's efforts to plan economic development. It is also distinguished by its constant use as an instrument for educating citizens concerning the regime's rigorous standards of personal and social conduct. Law is expected to help pave the way toward a transition from socialism to communism, the latter being a "higher" level of economic and social relationships.[13]

---

[12] Harold Berman, *Justice in the U.S.S.R.* (New York: Vintage Books, 1963), pp. 13–65.

[13] See the October 1961 Program of the Communist Party of the Soviet Union, quoted in John Hazard, Isaac Shapiro, and Peter Maggs, *The Soviet Legal System* (New York: Oceana Publications, 1969), p. 9.

Since 1956 the Socialist Law countries have reacted to the Stalinist-type perversions of their legal systems by reaffirming new standards of "socialist legality." This refers essentially to the repudiation of many of the worst arbitrary practices, particularly in political cases, and to the development of new codes and due process standards that conform somewhat more closely to those of the West. Unfortunately, such actions have been subject to repeated steps backward in most of these countries, and little real momentum for legal reform has been allowed to develop.

Human Rights Policies

The study of legal families can only introduce the study of the national contexts within which human rights policies are made and implemented. Such policies derive from the interplay of tradition, governmental structures, societal values, and the existing constitutional, statute, and administrative law.

Using the Universal Declaration as the standard of measurement, how well are human rights protected in our eight countries? In addressing this question, we will employ the classification of rights presented at the beginning of this chapter: substantive civil liberties, civil rights, and procedural rights.

SUBSTANTIVE CIVIL LIBERTIES

This comparison of how well basic areas of liberty are protected focuses on belief and expression in their political and religious contexts. In terms of substantive political rights we divide our countries into three leaders: Sweden, the United States, and Great Britain; three Western European nations in which such rights are less well established: France, West Germany, and Italy; and finally, the two highly restrictive Socialist Law countries included in this survey: East Germany and the Soviet Union. Our groupings are consistent, except for Sweden, with the legal families of the eight countries. Yet other factors have made equal or greater contributions to the results.

A significantly different pattern results from comparisons of religious liberty. The separation of church and state is rejected by Sweden, Britain, Italy, and the two German states. The Soviet Union joins the United States and France in proclaiming this significant civil libertarian principle. Freedom of religion, the right to practice any creed without governmental restraint, is quite secure in five of the survey states but not in Italy, East Germany, and especially, the Soviet Union.

Such general comparisons must be interpreted by the reader in the light of particular national policies. Since that is so, we now proceed to describe the state of substantive liberties in each of the eight.

The United States

The best place to begin our observations on the state of substantive civil liberties in the United States is the Bill of Rights of the federal Constitution. These first ten amendments emphasize procedural rights. However, substantive rights of expression and association are stated in the following unqualified language of the First Amendment:

> Congress shall make no law respecting an establishment of religion, or prohibiting the free exercise thereof; or abridging the freedom of speech, or the press; or the right of the people peaceably to assemble, and to petition the Government for a redress of grievances.

Until the 20th century the First Amendment and other Bill of Rights protections were invoked only as barriers against the federal government. The states were restrained only by their own constitutions and courts. Only after World War I did the U.S. Supreme Court begin to extend the standards of the Bill of Rights, with the support of the 14th Amendment, to the states.[14]

The federal courts, especially in recent decades, have interpreted the First Amendment so as to provide strong support for individuals and groups seeking relief from government violations of substantive rights. On the other hand, no branch of government has accepted an absolute version of any such rights. For the courts it has been a question of which grounds for government limitation of particular rights can be accepted in designated circumstances. However, the Supreme Court has generally given the rights themselves a privileged place in relation to competing values and circumstances.[15]

United States constitutional law deals with both freedom of religion and the separation of church and state. The former has enjoyed strong public support during most of the nation's 200 years. In contrast, the recent tendency of the Supreme Court to interpret the establishment of religion clause to prohibit many kinds of government support for religious institutions has split the country down the middle.

With respect to religious belief and expression Americans are guaranteed very wide latitude. These rights have been extended to include such acts as refusing, on religious grounds, to salute a flag in a public school or to take an oath at a citizenship proceeding. Further, one is entitled to refuse to work on a Saturday and still receive unemployment compensation. Limits have been set on some practices that directly threaten public health or outrage public morals (for example, polygamy).

---

[14] Henry Abraham, *Freedom and the Court*, 2d ed. (New York: Oxford University Press, 1972), pp. 29–88.

[15] Thomas Emerson, *The System of Freedom of Expression* (New York: Vintage Books, 1970), pp. 21–41.

Statutes and rulings regarding the separation of church and state reflect a less absolutist approach to the constitutional principle. The courts have only recently struck down the many religious tests for such benefits as military draft exemption and licenses for certain occupations. The enormous benefits that go to religious institutions through tax deductions and exemptions have survived most challenges. On the other hand, the courts have taken a strict stand against the use of public schools for Bible reading and prayers prepared by public officials. Although private parochial schools have been allowed grants for designated services to their students as well as tax exemptions, the Supreme Court has ruled against direct and indirect grants intended to finance instruction.

Efforts to regulate political thoughts by law have typically taken the form of requiring individuals to demonstrate their loyalty to the United States by swearing adherence to certain beliefs and disavowing commitment to others. The taking of oaths and loyalty tests has sometimes been made a precondition for obtaining public or public-related employment and for practicing a variety of occupations. In addition, such requirements have been imposed in connection with the acquisition of passports and investigations by legislative committees. In general these requirements have had little effect on dissidents who might have violated the criminal law but have caused the harassment of many people who reject such tests of political belief in principle.

By and large, the Supreme Court has found that disclaimer oaths, affirmations that individuals do *not* hold particular political beliefs, are unconstitutional. On the other hand, the Court has generally concluded that positive oaths, in which persons are asked to swear their allegiance to the Constitution, are permissible. Moreover, in regard to the freedom of foreign travel, the Court ruled in the 1960s that the State Department had no right to deny persons passports because of their political beliefs.

Witnesses that have appeared before investigatory committees of Congress and state legislatures have been held in contempt and subjected to criminal sanctions when they refused to testify concerning their political beliefs. Federal law makes it a misdemeanor to refuse to testify unless an acceptable claim of possible self-incrimination is made. Nevertheless, since the application of the contempt penalty usually requires a judicial proceeding, the courts have become involved in the process. Although it has been found that individuals subpoenaed to testify have no ability to obtain prior injunctive relief from a committee's decision to question them, the Supreme Court has ruled that committees have no right to expose solely for the sake of disclosure. Investigations must be linked to an authentic, though broadly defined, legislative purpose. In this context the Court has applied a balancing test according to which it seeks to weigh the public good versus the private harm to be derived from the probe. At any rate, relatively few congressional contempt citations have been upheld ultimately by the courts. Also, in recent years Congress itself has exercised greater internal control over committees whose members have been prone to violate witnesses' civil liberties. In 1975 the House of Representatives abolished its Committee on Internal Security (previously named the Committee on Un-American Activities).

Let us move now from the realm of thought and belief to that of expression. Expression involves the communication of thoughts and beliefs to others. To that extent it refers to the freedoms of speech, press, assembly, and petition. Given the breadth of this subject, we shall restrict ourselves to public policies concerning *political* expression. And in reviewing policy in this area, readers should keep in mind that few countries seek to limit the expressions of individuals or groups whose views are identical to those of the prevailing regime. Instead, restrictive efforts are typically directed against those who, in varying degrees, oppose existing practices.

Political dissidents in many nations have often been convicted of treason because of their expressions. Fortunately, the drafters of the U.S. Constitution largely foreclosed this legal device for repression by restricting the definition of treason to overt action in the direct behalf of a foreign power. Nevertheless, the national government and state governments have often sought in the present century to place manifold restraints on American freedom of expression.

Beginning with World War I and the subsequent "Red Scare" a plethora of antisubversive legislation was enacted. State provisions included criminal anarchy and syndicalism laws, acts which made it illegal to advocate the use of force and violence to achieve radical political change. At the federal level there have been the Espionage Act (1917), the Smith Act (1940), the Internal Security Act (1950), the Communist Control Act (1954), and sections of the Military Selective Service Act (1967). What binds these pieces of national and state legislation together is that they not only sought to restrict subversive or seditious action, such as organizing a conspiracy to overthrow the government, but also imposed criminal penalties on the expression of political views.

Supreme Court decisions arising from these measures have shifted over time and have been subject to several competing legal doctrines. The Court has never affirmed the absolutist position that there is no constitutional authority to prohibit political discourse of any kind. In recent decades it has ruled that no criminal liability may attach to membership or association per se, or to the academic or theoretical advocacy of violent overthrow. However, in earlier periods convictions based on expression divorced from action have been upheld.[16]

To understand prevailing policies concerning press freedom in the United States it should be clear that the various media of public communication differ in their relationship to the government. The printed media—book, magazine, and newspaper publishing—are not subject to government licensing. Television and radio stations, however, are licensed and regulated by the Federal Communications Commission.

The broad judicial doctrine governing mass media forms of expression is that of no prior restraint. In general the First Amendment has been interpreted to mean that government may not censor expression before dissemination.[17] There are, however, exceptions and qualifications. Magazines and books are frequently sent through the mails, and there is apparently no unqualified constitutional right to use the postal service. Yet the Supreme Court has nullified a federal statute which permitted the censorship of foreign Communist propaganda.

According to the relevant statutes, radio and television stations are supposed to operate for the "public interest, necessity, and convenience." Although these stations are not formally subject to prior restraint, the FCC's periodic reviews of their licenses, based on the extent to which they comply with this vaguely worded imperative, has occasioned criticism that the commission exercises a kind of prior intimidation. However, if stations believe that their licenses are being revoked as gestures of patently political revenge they may appeal to the courts for relief. Recent federal and state statutes regulate the kind and amount of political advertising that stations may accept.

In recent years public policy treating freedom of expression has been linked closely to the issue of government secrecy, for example, in the *Pentagon Papers* case. Two aspects of this issue should be noted: the right to publish and the question of public employee disclosure of classified documents. Although the Supreme Court eventually ruled (1971) that the *New York Times* and the *Washington Post* could publish the classified *Pentagon Papers,* the attorney general, for the first time in U.S. history, was successful in obtaining an injunction from a lower federal court barring this expression before the final decision was rendered. Moreover, the Supreme Court by no means foreclosed the possibility of prior restraint in subsequent cases where the national security was involved. In fact, the CIA was subsequently able, with federal court approval, to achieve the prior censorship of portions of a book about that agency which was coauthored by a former employee.

---

[16] Nathaniel Nathanson, "The Right of Association," in Norman Dorsen, ed., *The Rights of Americans* (New York: Vintage Books, 1970), pp. 231–51.

[17] Jay Sigler, *American Rights Policies* (Homewood, Ill.: Dorsey Press, 1975), pp. 81–84.

The injunction was obtained because the former employee had signed secrecy agreements with the agency stipulating that he could not disclose any information he secured during his employment.[18] As a reaction against unauthorized disclosures there is now (1976) a bill before Congress, the Criminal Justice Codification, Revision, and Reform Act, which contains a provision that would make a federal employee or former employee criminally liable for communicating classified information to unauthorized persons.

Exercise of the rights of assembly and petition often goes beyond mere verbal expression. Immediate threats to public order and safety often become involved, and the line between political expression and action is often hard to draw. In comparison with its speech and press decisions, the Supreme Court has been far more willing to tolerate prior restraint, through carefully drawn licensing statutes, of parades, open-air assemblies, and other modes of public demonstration. However, it has insisted that neither the statutes nor their implementation permit discrimination among different political causes. It has also upheld the constitutionality of police interventions at public meetings where there is a direct incitement to violence or at which "fighting words" are used.

Finally, in the post–World War II era approximately half of the state legislatures enacted laws prohibiting candidates of the Communist party from appearing on election ballots. Only recently has the Court, in effect, overturned these restrictive statutes.

The United Kingdom

By contrast with the American situation, Great Britain has no single constitutional document in which citizens' civil liberties are asserted. Nevertheless, over the centuries a number of fundamental laws have been enacted which proclaim certain basic rights: Magna Carta (1215), the Petition of Right (1628), the Habeas Corpus Act (1679), the Bill of Rights (1689), and the Act of Settlement (1701).[19] These documents proclaim such things as the subjection of governmental action to law and parliamentary supremacy and independence, and such procedural safeguards as the crucial requirement that a judicial writ of habeas corpus be secured before an individual may be incarcerated. Although some of the substantive civil liberties guaranteed by the U.S. Constitution are contained in one or more of these documents, others are not.

---

[18] Victor Marchetti and John Marks, *The CIA and the Cult of Intelligence* (New York: Dell Publishing, 1975).

[19] John Wuest and Manfred Vernon, eds., *New Source Book in Major European Governments* (New York: World Publishing Co., 1966), pp. 7–25.

Further, because of the doctrine of parliamentary supremacy the individual rights provided in these acts do not enjoy the preferred position relative to other laws that exists under the U.S. Constitution. Thus, in spite of the Habeas Corpus Act, in 1920 the government of Northern Ireland, with parliamentary approval, passed the Special Powers Acts allowing the arrest and detention without trial of persons suspected of endangering public order. In 1971 the British government resumed the use of these acts to intern alleged IRA activists.

If the basic statutes and charters do not articulate each of the freedoms of belief, expression, and peaceful political action, where are these freedoms to be found in the British scheme of things? Dicey's famous view was that "the security which an Englishman enjoys for personal freedom does not really depend upon or originate in any general proposition contained in any written document."[20] He took the position that under the Common Law the English were free to think, speak, and act as they pleased. The only legal constraints on their behavior were those explicitly provided by law. With this view in mind, let us review the present state of substantive civil liberties in Britain.

In regard to freedom of thought, the British are currently free to hold or not hold any religious beliefs they wish. However, in England and Scotland there are established churches (Anglican and Presbyterian) headed by the queen. The sovereign must by law be an Anglican; and a member of the royal family who marries a Roman Catholic, for example, is thereby excluded from the line of succession. Although religious disabilities affecting membership in the House of Commons were ended in the 19th century, bishops of the Church of England are still entitled to sit in the House of Lords.[21]

In sharp contrast to American policy there is direct government assistance to sectarian schools of diverse religious denominations. What is more, under the 1944 Education Act prayer and religious instruction are provided in the regular county primary schools. Pupils and teachers, if they make a formal request, may be excused from these practices.[22] The crime of blasphemy may still be enforced against atheists and religious bigots who articulate their sentiments, though it is rarely applied.

Unlike the United States, Britain did not turn to widespread use of loyalty oaths during the Cold War era. The disavowal of communist or

---

[20] Dicey, *Introduction*, p. 206.

[21] Harry Street, *Freedom, the Individual, and the Law* (Harmondsworth, England: Penguin Books, 1963), pp. 183–96.

[22] J. A. Parry, *The Provision of Education in England and Wales* (London: George Allen & Unwin, 1971), pp. 39–45.

other subversive political beliefs was not made a precondition for public or private employment. Nonetheless, as the result of several well-publicized espionage cases, a system of security checking was instituted during the 1950s. Government and private employees involved in national security-related projects whose political views are shown to be communist or fascist are subject to dismissal. And persons so treated do not have recourse to the courts to challenge the decision.

The political views of English citizens may affect their ability to travel abroad. The granting of a passport is not a matter of right but of royal prerogative which the government may withhold, not subject to judicial review, as it pleases. There have been instances when the withholding was based on the applicant's political beliefs.[23]

In the area of expression there is nothing in the United Kingdom that closely approaches American antiradical legislation. The nearest approximations are the laws defining seditious libel and incitement to disaffection. As stated in the Libel Act of 1792 and interpreted by subsequent judicial dicta, laws against sedition criminalize expressions whose intent is to bring into hatred or contempt the monarchy, the government, or the administration of justice, among other things, and to encourage violent attacks on those institutions.[24] The Incitement of Disaffection Act (1934) makes it illegal for an individual to "maliciously and advisedly" seduce a serviceman from his duty or allegiance. The possession of printed matter intended for these purposes is also made criminal. On the other hand, prosecutions for both crimes have been exceedingly rare and may only be undertaken with the personal approval of the director of public prosecutions.

While prior restraint of expression has rarely been used in the United States, this has not been true in Britain. Until a few decades ago there was severe prior censorship of films and theatrical performances. Although this practice has since been liberalized, particularly in regard to obscenity, the British system remains more restrictive than that of the United States.

Television broadcasting is operated by the publicly owned and directed British Broadcasting Company and by the Independent Broadcasting Authority, which is publicly owned but commercially run and directed. Although very free to criticize public policy, both networks must comply with regulations governing appearances by political candidates and government representatives that are similar to those used in the United States.

The major sources of political censorship applied to newspapers and

---

[23] Street, *Freedom*, pp. 273–74.
[24] Ibid., pp. 197–202.

other printed media, as well as the broadcasting networks, are the Official Secrets Acts.[25] These acts make it a crime for any servant or officer of the Crown to communicate to any unauthorized person information which might be prejudical to state security. Crucially, criminal liability also attaches to an unauthorized person who attempts to pass the information along to others. If such provisions had been in force in the United States, Daniel Ellsberg, the former Defense Department analyst who leaked the *Pentagon Papers* to the press, and numerous editors and reporters for the *New York Times,* the *Washington Post,* and other media could have been sent to prison.

The provisions of the Official Secrets Acts are so sweeping that theoretically the unauthorized disclosure and dissemination of any government information could constitute a felony. In practice the implementation of the statutes has been worked through a "D Notice" system. Under this informal arrangement a committee composed of press and broadcasting representatives and senior civil servants reviews information which the government is either willing or unwilling to make public. Lists of permitted and forbidden topics are then circulated to editors and other media heads. Prosecutions are undertaken only against those who publish information dealing with prohibited subjects. In the last few years an effort has begun to reduce the severity of these measures, and it may very well be that before too long the entire system will be altered.

The judiciary acts as another major source of government restraint on free expression. A statute authorizes British judges to imprison for contempt those who publish any but the most skeletal accounts of legal proceedings before their completion. In the interest of avoiding prejudicial pretrial publicity, even the publication of pictures of the accused may be proscribed. Such restraints are now under severe challenge. Recently the press published without retribution news of litigation regarding the deformities of children whose mothers had taken the drug thalidomide. Nonetheless, such limits on the media are much broader than those enforced by American courts.

The rules governing public assemblies are fixed largely by local community bylaws and such statutes as the Public Order Act (1936). The approach taken in these regulations is similar to American policy in that they make it an offense for anyone at a public meeting to use threatening, abusive, or insulting words or behavior which may result in a breach of the peace. But in conflict with American practice, it is

---

[25] J. A. C. Griffith, "Government Secrecy in the United Kingdom," in Norman Dorsen and Stephen Gillers, eds., *None of Your Business: Government Secrecy in America* (Baltimore: Penguin Books, 1975), pp. 328–49; and Anthony Lewis, "A British Test of the Right to Publish," *New York Times,* August 3, 1975, p. 16.

now criminal conduct under the 1965 Race Relations Act to use words at a meeting or in any public place that are likely to stir up racial or religious prejudice. Proof of guilt does not require any test of direct incitement to violence.

Sweden

The substantive civil liberties of Swedes are only partially set out in the country's Constitution. Other legal sources include statutes and codes, including the redrafted Penal Code of 1965. Sweden's Constitution consists of four separate documents: the Instrument of Government, the Riksdag Act, the Act of Succession, and the Freedom of the Press Act.[26] Aside from the last and a portion of the Instrument of Government, these frequently altered statements are principally devoted to the organization of the powers of the various governmental authorities.

In the realm of religious belief, Article 16 of the Instrument of Government states that the king "shall not constrain or allow to be constrained the conscience of any person, but shall protect everyone in the free exercise of his religion." Although this policy is widely respected, Sweden rejects the constitutional separation of church and state. The Lutheran church is the official state religion and is headed by the king. Although Sweden is a very secularized society with low church attendance, the official religion plays a pervasive role in public life. The king is the Church's head, and the cabinet minister in charge of ecclesiastical affairs must be Lutheran. All Swedish subjects are automatically regarded as church members unless they are born of non-Lutheran parents or, as adults, decide in writing to defect. Taxes, long imposed to support the Lutheran church, now aid other denominations as well. Both prayer and religious instruction take place in the public schools. The various parishes into which the country is divided perform the state function of recording all births, marriages, emigrations, and deaths, even those of nonmembers.[27]

Liberties of expression and peaceful political action are delineated in the Freedom of the Press Act and the Penal Code. The latter contains sections covering sedition, treason, and incitement to disaffection. To what extent are speech, advocacy, and association, as opposed to action, restricted by these provisions? Among the less controversial provisions are those that prohibit the incitement of mutiny or disaffection among

---

[26] Gunnar Heckscher, *The Swedish Constitution* (Stockholm: Swedish Institute, 1959), pp. 3–24.

[27] Joseph Board, Jr., *The Government and Politics of Sweden* (Boston: Houghton Mifflin Co., 1970), pp. 12–13.

soldiers in wartime or the provision of information to foreign powers.[28] However, some major incursions on free expression are suggested by language that defines it as a crime against public order to

> orally, before a crowd . . . or in a publication distributed or issued for distribution, urge or otherwise attempt to entice people to commit a criminal act, evade a civic duty or disobey public authority. . . . If a person publicly spreads a false rumor or other untrue assertion *apt* [emphasis added] to arouse a danger to public subsistence or to public order or security, he shall be sentenced for spreading socially harmful rumor.[29]

Furthermore, Swedish law, like British law, now makes the public expression of racial, religious, or ethnic hatred a criminal deed.

Aside from these restrictions, the country's publicly controlled radio and television industry and privately owned publishing firms are largely free to say what they please. While providing for the conventional protections against libel and defamation found in most legal systems, the Freedom of the Press Act guarantees freedom of expression to publishers and radio and television broadcasters. In contrast to the British Official Secrets Acts, this statute organically links freedom of expression to the right of citizen access to almost all government papers, files, and information.[30] To be sure, there are carefully defined limitations to this right of access in the national security domain. But to Americans concerned by inordinate government secrecy in their country, only partially ameliorated by the 1967 Freedom of Information Act, the Swedish Constitution's century-old tying of free expression to public access still represents a progressive model.

Finally, restraints on political organization and action in Sweden are within the parameters set by the Universal Declaration. No political groups are prohibited per se, and public assemblies, parades, and demonstrations are only restricted by the requirement that there be no immediate incitement to violence. Sweden's Communist party is treated as a respected force in parliament.

France

The substantive freedoms in which we are interested are, as a rule, somewhat less adequately protected in France than in the United States, Great Britain, or Sweden. The Fifth Republic's Constitution has relatively little to say about these matters, and what it does say is not in-

---

[28] *The Penal Code of Sweden*, trans. Thorsten Sellin (South Hackensack, N.J.: Fred B. Rothman & Co., 1972), pp. 53–59, 69–74.

[29] Ibid., p. 47.

[30] Stanley Anderson, "Public Access to Government Files in Sweden," *American Journal of Comparative Law* 21 (Summer 1973): 419–73.

variably for the good. In fact, President Giscard d'Estaing has pledged that his administration will remedy the deficiencies by drafting a charter of individual liberties.[31] On the plus side, the Preamble to the Constitution proclaims the regime's attachment to the freedoms asserted in the Declaration of the Rights of Man and refined in the Preamble to the 1946 Constitution of the Fourth Republic.[32] But prior to a 1971 ruling of the Constitutional Council it was the prevailing view that these rights were only juridically defensible to the extent that they were confirmed and defined by legislation.

Beyond the Preamble, Article 4 of the current Constitution asserts that the right of political parties to organize is unrestricted, but then states that "they must respect the principles of national sovereignty and of democracy." To date, this provision has not been used to dissolve antiregime groups. Other legal mechanisms are available for that purpose.

From a civil libertarian perspective the Constitution's worst feature is Article 16, which invests the president with an almost unrestricted ability to supsend normal protections and rule by decree during national emergencies, as he defines them. During the Algerian crisis, de Gaulle used his emergency powers to issue decrees which, among other things, provided for the administrative internment of suspects and prohibited the distribution of publications that supported organizations "contending with the authority of the State."[33]

In the area of religious belief, a 1905 law provided for the freedom of thought and conscience and the separation of church and state. Thus there are no religious tests for public office. The state does not financially support any religious denomination; and neither prayer nor religious instruction is offered in the public schools. Since 1959, however, the regime has extended monetary assistance to parochial schools from the elementary through the university levels.[34]

May the French suffer legal disabilities solely as the result of their religious or political views? During the Algerian War a number of reservists were called to duty because, apparently, they had been critical of the regime's prosecution of the conflict. Only in the last ten years has the right of conscientious objection to military service been

---

[31] *Economist* (London), August 10, 1974, p. 39.

[32] Frede Castberg, *Freedom of Speech in the West* (New York: Oceana Publications, 1960), pp. 42–45.

[33] United Nations, *Yearbook on Human Rights for 1961* (New York: United Nations, 1963), pp. 130–35.

[34] Albert Menendez, "Church and State in France," *Church and State* 28, no. 1 (1974): 13–17; Charles Markmann, "Freedom à la Française," *Civil Liberties Review* 2, no. 2 (1975): 73–94; and Maurice Duverger, *The French Political System* (Chicago: University of Chicago Press, 1958), p. 152.

recognized. Prior to 1965 a refusal to accept induction was regarded as a crime. Since that year the law has been changed to permit alternative service for persons who object to military service on religious or philosophic grounds.

In some countries, individuals whose political views are thought unreliable are denied employment in educational institutions and other spheres of public service. This criterion is not used in the selection or dismissal of teachers and university professors in France. The situation respecting the admission of candidates into the public administration is a bit more ambiguous. The Council of State has ruled that political belief by itself cannot bar entry but that manifestation or expression may.

As far as freedom of expression is concerned, the Penal Code's provisions covering sedition and treason have not been employed recently to inhibit speech and advocacy. Nevertheless, a variety of other devices are used to limit press and associational freedoms. First, the state radio and television monopoly is subject to far more politically motivated interference than are its counterparts in Britain or Sweden. News reports are often slanted so as to cast progovernment parties in as favorable a light as possible.[35] Recent efforts at reform have thus far proved to be of only limited value.

For a long time film censorship was of the most extreme sort; movies were censored before they were shown and even before they were made. The latter arrangement recently has been abolished, yet the Ministry of Information still exercises a prior restraint, frequently used for political purposes, over what French audiences may view.

Censorship of printed expression is also extensive. Press freedom is defined, basically, by a law enacted in 1881. As amended, this legislation provides that anyone who by speech or writing provokes another to commit a criminal act is to be treated as an accessory and that defamation of public authorities and institutions is a crime. Thus press disclosures of the torture of civilians by the military during the Algerian War, on the order of the My Lai revelations in the United States, were followed, not by suitable investigations, but by public prosecutions against those responsible for uncovering the horrors. The law also authorizes the minister of interior to forbid the circulation, distribution, or sale of journals and other writings in a foreign language or in the French language but of foreign origin.

Beyond these substantial restrictions on liberties the Penal Code and the Code of Criminal Procedure invest the police with very broad

---

[35] Jack Hayward, *The One and Indivisible French Republic* (New York: W. W. Norton & Co., 1973), pp. 143–50.

powers to limit expression in the name of public order.[36] Prefects may, for instance, order the police to ban the further publication of or to seize newspapers considered dangerous to the public peace. And unless a plaintiff can show the act to have been unreasonable, an appeal to the courts will be unavailing. As Hayward reports:

> In the Paris region the prefect of police has power to control the distribution of all publications and he has used this to harass the street-sellers of leftist papers. In the four months between 22 November 1969–22 March 1970, 890 people were detained by the police in the Paris region for selling leftist newspapers and distributing tracts. They are taken away for "verification of their identity" and resistance leads to indictment for "rebellion and violence against a policeman."[37]

The right to freely organize an association is stipulated by a 1901 law. Informal groups do not suffer from prior restraint. However, if groups wish to have a certain legal status (that is, own property or take legal action), the law requires that they file papers at the prefecture. Until recent decisions by the Council of State and the Constitutional Council, a prefect and the minister of interior could deny groups such status because of suspicions concerning their purposes. Although this sort of prior restraint is no longer enforced, sweeping police powers still permit the dissolution of associations for disturbing the peace and offending morality.

There is, in addition, extensive use of prior restraint in the realm of political action. All demonstrations must receive police authorization, which may be denied if the authorities assert the possibility of a risk to public order. But appeal to the Council of State is possible, and in practice the severity of such restrictions varies with the political climate.

Italy

Unlike the French Constitution, the Italian Constitution contains a detailed enumeration of substantive liberties as well as provisions for an effective Constitutional Court with which to defend them. Yet Italy's Penal Code, Code of Criminal Procedure, and Public Security Law were drafted during the Fascist era and consequently contain numerous sections that are incompatible with civil liberties. Moreover, Mussolini's

---

[36] See, for example, Article 30 of *The French Code of Criminal Procedure*, trans. Gerald Kock (South Hackensack, N.J.: Fred B. Rothman & Co., 1964), p. 27.

[37] Hayward, *French Republic*, p. 141.

Concordat with the Catholic church, which continues to restrict the exercise of substantive liberty, grants the Church a preferred legal position in the Italian system.

Although the Constitutional Court has struck down a host of constitutionally questionable provisions in these documents, it has also upheld others.[38] Italy is on the verge of enacting a new criminal procedure code and a new public security law governing police prerogatives. But observers suggest that these instruments may not be much better than those they are intended to replace.

The Constitution (Article 8) proclaims all creeds equal before the law and all religious groups free to organize. However, though the latter provision is generally implemented, the former is not. Under the Concordat the state provides instruction in Catholicism in public schools and crucifixes for schoolrooms.[39] Further, government financial assistance is distributed to parochial schools.

In 1971 the Constitutional Court ruled that where the Concordat conflicted with basic libertarian principles of the Constitution it would be unenforceable. Thus, the Concordat's ban against the holding of public employment or office by defrocked priests has been removed. On the other hand, the Court has usually upheld the constitutionality of criminal and civil restraints on the expression of anti-Catholic views. Thus Article 404 of the Penal Code, which states that whoever publicly offends the state religion is punishable by imprisonment for up to three years, was affirmed by the Court.[40] This and related provisions have been widely used for restrictive purposes, including the banning of the presentation in Rome of Rolf Hochhuth's *The Deputy,* a play that accuses Pope Pius XII of passivity in the face of Nazi atrocities during World War II.

On paper the Constitution offers a commendable list of protections for the rights of expression and peaceful political action. These encompass: free expression without prior restraint; the right to form associations and political parties; the right to assemble peaceably and to petition the government; and the right to travel freely within the country or to leave it. But as in other countries, there is often a large gap between constitutional promise and fulfillment.

Although the RAI radio and television network is a public monopoly, it is not as openly biased as its French counterpart. Both printing presses and journalists require government licenses in order to func-

---

[38] Malcolm Evans, "The Italian Constitutional Court," *International and Comparative Law Quarterly* 17 (July 1968): 602–33.

[39] Paolo Barile, *Corso di diritto costituzionale,* 2d ed. (Padova: CEDAM, 1964), pp. 285–90.

[40] *Codice Penale* (Milano: Hoepli Editore, 1946), p. 75.

tion legally. However, there is no evidence of politically inspired discrimination in the awarding of these permits.

The Constitutional Court has nullified sections of the Penal Code which permitted the exercise of prior restraints on written communications. Films and live theatrical performances, as illustrated above, are still subject to this mode of suppression to a limited extent. Newspapers and the other media of written expression may be restricted, nevertheless, by a variety of legal means. In particular the crime of *vilipendio* has been found constitutional. This criminalizes speech, written or oral, that defames the honor of public institutions, the president, the Church, or the pope. During periods of political turbulence, prosecutions for *vilipendio* have been particularly widespread. Further, editors of two New Left journals were successfully prosecuted for having violated the Penal Code's prohibition against the incitement of class hatred. The Constitutional Court has adopted what in American terms amounts to a "bad tendency" doctrine in affirming the constitutionality of prosecutions. This approach requires only a minimal threat to the public safety and welfare to justify the imposition of sanctions.[41]

Although Italy tolerates an exceptionally wide range of political contestants, there are some limitations on the right of association. Even though a 1952 statute forbade the reorganization of the Fascist party and the dissemination of fascist propaganda, the statute has not yet been used to prevent the Italian Social Movement (MSI), a quasi-fascist party represented in parliament, from operating throughout the country. On the other hand, police emergency powers have been invoked to disband various paramilitary right-wing groups and Maoist formations at the extreme left of the political spectrum.

The rights of assembly and travel have been strengthened in recent years. The Constitutional Court struck down a section of the Public Security Law which required that the police be given three days' prior notice of meetings in private places at which attendance was open to the public. However, the Constitution itself (Article 17) authorizes requirements that the authorities be given previous notice of meetings in public places and permits particular assemblies to be banned for reasons of public safety and security. As regards travel, the Court ruled against provisions of the Public Security Law which made it illegal to leave or attempt to leave Italy for political motives and severely restricted the use of a procedure, widely used under the Fascist regime, by which the police compel an individual to move to and remain in a particular community.

---

[41] Giovanni Bognetti, "The Political Role of The Italian Constitutional Court," *Notre Dame Lawyer* 49 (June 1974): 982–83.

West Germany

Current policies affecting substantive civil liberties in West Germany are based on two somewhat contradictory approaches. First, given the Nazi past, the Basic Law and legislation passed pursuant to it have been designed to protect freedoms treated contemptuously under Hitler's rule. Second, however, the state seeks to curtail freedom of thought, expression, and action for alleged enemies of freedom. As a result, sweeping restraints have been imposed on those regarded as opposed to the existing order.

Freedom of conscience, religion, and political belief are asserted in the Basic Law (Article 4), sections of which incorporate parts of the pre-Nazi Weimar Constitution. This constitutional document sets the pattern, which we have already seen in Sweden, Britain, and Italy, of broad respect for freedom of religion combined with the continued integration of church and state. Respecting the latter, the Basic Law prohibits the establishment of religion on a national basis, forbids religious tests for holding public office or employment, and extends the right of conscientious objection on both philosophic and religious grounds. Yet it permits church establishment by the Länder.

The public schools, which are subject to Länder control, offer prayer and religious instruction in conformity to the given community's dominant religious creed—Protestant or Catholic. Private confessional schools are also state supported and regulated.[42] The Penal Code imposes criminal sanctions for the public expression of antireligious sentiments; it makes blasphemy or reviling a particular religious denomination punishable by a jail sentence of up to three years. The desire to forestall a revival of anti-Semitism appears to have been the major motive behind the latter prohibition.

Certain penalties may be inflicted on individuals on the basis of their political beliefs. For instance, the Basic Law stipulates that "art and science, research and teaching are free," but qualifies this protection by further stating that teachers are not absolved from loyalty to the Constitution. As a consequence of public concern growing out of a wave of radical student activism and disclosures of extensive East German espionage activities, a law was enacted in 1972 which requires the political screening of all persons seeking public employment. This measure has been used at all levels of government to exclude individuals affiliated with allegedly extremist organizations. Further, Article 18 of the Basic Law provides that citizens who abuse the basic rights of others may have all their own rights forfeited if the Constitu-

---

[42] Klaus Obermayer, "Religious Schools and Religious Freedom; Proposals for Reform of the German Public School System," *American Journal of Comparative Law* 16 (1968): 552–62.

tional Court so rules. Although no such prosecutions have been instituted to date, several Germans have been refused passports because of their political views.[43]

Analogously, the general right of free expression is constitutionally protected but is, at the same time, subject to potentially severe legal constraints. In regard to speech, written and oral, the Basic Law invests citizens with uncensored freedom of the press, radio, films, and so on. Yet the Penal Code criminalizes a host of actions which in American law could not be easily suppressed. In particular the law regarding treason offers an extensive array of limitations on speech and advocacy. Defined as treasonable are disseminating propaganda that endangers the state, using symbols of unconstitutional organizations, insulting the federal president, and disparaging the state, its symbols, and its constitutional organs.[44] The Code's restrictions on the transmission of government information go beyond the British Official Secrets Acts. It is treasonable espionage to obtain a state secret in order to transmit it to an unauthorized person or to disclose it publicly in a manner endangering the welfare of the Federal Republic of Germany or one of its subdivisions. The penalties are applicable to public servants who pass along such information and to individuals who simply pry into state secrets with intent to disseminate.

The most publicized case that has arisen under these draconian provisions involved the news magazine *Der Spiegel*.[45] In 1962 that periodical published a story, based on leaked information, concerning the unpreparedness of the West German armed forces. Subsequently, the police seized *Der Spiegel*'s offices at the behest of the defense minister, and the editor and publisher were charged with treason. Although a public uproar eventually forced the government to drop the prosecution, the Constitutional Court earlier refused to declare unconstitutional the relevant sections of the Penal Code.

It is not necessary to search the Penal Code in order to find barriers to the freedom of association. The Basic Law asserts the right of organization for associations and political parties. But such bodies may be dissolved if they seek to impair, undermine, or destroy the constitutional order. Further, the continuation of such activities after legal dissolution can subject members to prosecution. State governments have succeeded in dissolving associations without recourse to judicial authorization. Political parties, however, may be proscribed only on the

---

[43] Castberg, *Freedom of Speech*, pp. 381–84.

[44] *The German Draft Penal Code*, trans. Neville Ross (South Hackensack, N.J.: Fred B. Rothman & Co., 1966), pp. 199–208.

[45] Donald Kommers, "The Spiegel Affair: A Case Study in Judicial Politics," in Theodore Becker, ed., *Political Trials* (Indianapolis: Bobbs-Merrill Co., 1971), pp. 5–33.

basis of Constitutional Court decisions. During the 1950s the federal government obtained bans against a neo-Nazi party and the Communists. But in the warmer international environment of the late 1960s a new Communist party was permitted to reorganize.

As regards action or conduct of a political character, the Basic Law provides that all Germans have the right of peaceful assembly. But open-air meetings may be subject to prior police approval in the interest of public security. The law relating to conduct at such assemblies has recently been liberalized so that public incitement to civil disobedience is no longer punishable except in the most severe cases. Likewise, resisting a lawful order to disperse is not punishable if an individual erroneously believed the order itself to be illegal.[46]

Finally, the history-conscious drafters of the Basic Law sought to insure the freedoms of travel and citizenship which were denied by the Nazis. Germans are free to travel within the Federal Republic's borders, and the state is prohibited from withdrawing a person's citizenship if doing so he would make the person stateless.

The USSR and East Germany

The way in which substantive civil liberties are legally defined in East Germany and the Soviet Union resembles conventional Western practice. Freedoms are broadly enunciated in the 1968 East German and the 1936 Soviet constitutions in language that approximates Western liberal standards. These freedoms are then narrowed substantially by the criminal laws. It also seems clear that the reasons for restrictions on liberty are parallel, these reasons including the desire to inhibit fundamental (that is, regime-threatening) criticism of the political order and to maintain social stability. But there are also obvious differences. Whereas in the West sweeping restraints on various liberties tend to be employed mainly during periods of national emergency and civil disturbance, in the East they are much more likely to be applied in the normal course of things. Moreover, the two Socialist Law regimes possess instruments of very close control over all means of mass communication and routinely employ prior restraint or pre-censorship. Also, the level of threat perception, the theshold at which the state apparatus considers itself or society to be endangered, is generally much lower in the East. Hence controls are typically imposed at an earlier phase and cover a wider range of subjects than in the West.

The Soviet and East German constitutional statements governing

---

[46] Albin Eser, "The Politics of Criminal Law Reform: Germany," *American Journal of Comparative Law* 21 (Spring 1973): 245–62.

religious belief differ somewhat. The East German document asserts that "every citizen . . . has the right to profess a religious creed, and to carry out religious activities." The comparable Soviet provision is more polemical in tone, granting both freedom of worship and freedom for antireligious propaganda. In addition, the Soviet Constitution specifies separation of the church from state and school.

The differences in wording reflect genuine disparities in policy. East German schoolrooms are used for religious instruction. The state supports professional religious education at the universities and directly subsidizes Protestant, Catholic, and Jewish denominations, in proportion to membership, for salaries and operating expenses. Moreover, churches are permitted to collect taxes from their congregants and to base their assessments on tax rolls provided by the government.[47]

The Soviet policy toward religious belief is sharply at variance with these supportive policies. Provisions of the criminal codes of the Soviet republics make it illegal to violate rules governing the separation of the state and school from the church. Further, one may not organize a group which, under the "pretext" of worship, endangers the health of citizens or stimulates them to refuse social activities and duties.[48] In the Russian Republic administrative edicts also proscribe

> compulsory collection of taxes and contributions for the use of religious organizations and clergy; preparation for the mass distribution . . . of appeals . . . and other documents exhorting refusal to observe legislation on religious denominations; commission of fraudulent acts for the purpose of arousing religious superstitions; . . . organization and systematic conduct of classes to teach religion to minors in violation of the regulations established by law; . . . refusal of religious organizations to register . . . in state agencies.[49]

Finally, unlike the German Democratic Republic, the Soviet Union does not allow for conscientious objection to military service on religious or other grounds.

In general, the approach of the German Democratic Republic is similar to that of several other East European states in that it reflects a modus vivendi which leaves the existing churches in a position to carry on with limited restrictions despite an avowed state policy of promoting atheism. The Soviet Union, on the other hand, allows the dominant Russian Orthodox church to carry on its activities at a level that is de-

---

[47] Jean Smith, *Germany beyond the Wall* (Boston: Little, Brown & Co., 1967), pp. 137–59.

[48] *Soviet Criminal Law and Procedure: The RFSR Codes,* introduced and translated by Harold Berman (Cambridge, Mass.: Harvard University Press, 1966), pp. 201–30.

[49] Hazard, Shapiro, and Maggs, *Soviet Legal System,* pp. 81–82.

signed to prevent the development of new believers. Relatively small groups which sometimes seek to circumvent the tight restrictions, such as the Jehovah's Witnesses and the Baptists, receive severe punishments.

The constitutions of both countries offer qualified endorsements to the right of free expression. Thus the East German document (Article 27) grants freedom of speech, including press, radio, and television. But this is modified by the phrase "in accordance with the spirit and aims of this Constitution." The comparable grant in the Soviet Constitution (Article 125) is restricted by the words "in conformity with the interests of the working people, and in order to strengthen the socialist system." Expressions which do not conform to or are not in accord with the spirit and aims of these objectives may therefore be suppressed. The legal instruments available for this purpose are to be found in the criminal statutes.

The German Democratic Republic Penal Code contains such a plethora of restrictive provisions that we hardly know where to begin in describing them. Among the political expressions for which citizens may be held criminally liable are: defaming the state, denigrating foreign personalities, expressing contempt for the state's symbols, engaging in fascist propaganda, inciting opposition to the state and its institutions, disclosing state and industrial secrets to unauthorized persons, and forming or joining treasonable associations.[50] In reality, then, no substantial legal impediments bar the punishment of those who express deviant political views. The machinery of control is always at hand, though international and domestic political considerations result in major variations in its use. As in other Warsaw Pact countries, this machinery is aimed most intensely at such intellectuals as creative artists and scientists.

The Russian Republic's Criminal Code contains three broad provisions limiting expression. They are entitled: (1) Anti-Soviet Agitation and Propaganda; (2) Organizational Activity Directed at the Commission of Especially Dangerous Crimes against the State, and Participation in Anti-Soviet Organizations; and (3) Divulgence of State Secrets. The wording of these provisions is broad enough to criminalize, for example, not only writing or distributing anti-Soviet expressions, but simply possessing them. In the last few years the police have sought, with surprising difficulty, to apprehend the authors, distributors, and readers of the *Chronicle of Current Events* and other underground publications. In 1966 the authors Sinyavsky and Daniel were tried, con-

---

[50] *Penal Code of the GDR*, reprinted in *Law and Legislation in the GDR* 2 (1968).

victed, and sentenced to long prison terms for sending their critical writings to the West for publication, acts which were deemed to constitute "anti-Soviet agitation."[51]

Such developments are part of a campaign of increased repression of dissident writers that began soon after Nikita Khrushchev's ouster in 1964. During the "Khrushchev era" writers critical of Stalin had been encouraged, and increased tolerance had been extended to many kinds of expression. However, since 1965 a pattern of incarceration in labor camps and mental institutions, together with the exile of such leading dissidents as Alexander Solzhenitsyn, has been broadly applied to intellectuals who seek to criticize the regime and its major policies. Such actions supplement the continued institutionalization of censorship, the restriction of publication and support to writers in good standing in regime-controlled writers' unions, and constant calls for even greater conformity to the regime's ideological proclamations.

Not surprisingly, the situation in the two countries with respect to overt conduct is even worse. Although unauthorized protest demonstrations do occur from time to time, such collective manifestations are prohibited by law and those engaging in them are typically treated harshly. Equally severe are restrictions on travel abroad. As is suggested by the Berlin Wall and the plight of Soviet Jews who wish to emigrate, both Socialist Law states violate the Universal Declaration by denying passports and exit permits for various social and political motives. Indeed, any foreign travel is considered a special privilege. Unauthorized attempts to leave are regarded as serious crimes. Domestic travel, especially in the Soviet Union, is also subject to state control through the use, among other things, of an internal passport system.[52]

Summary: Substantive Civil Liberties

It has been shown that in each of the eight countries peaceful action is more likely to be subject to legal restraint than is political expression, and that statements are less protected than is the domain of belief or thought. The Soviet Union and East Germany are substantially less inclined to grant these various kinds of liberties than is the most repressive of the six Western states. Among those Western states, the most serious limitations on political expression and action exist in

---

[51] John Turner, "Artists in Adversity: The Sinyavsky-Daniel Case," in Becker, *Political Trials,* pp. 107–33.

[52] Robert Conquest, *The Soviet Police System* (New York: Frederick A. Praeger, 1968), pp. 62–66; and Joachim Rennebert et al., "Social Foundations of the Fight for the Gradual Suppression of Criminality in the GDR," *Law and Legislation in the GDR* 1 (1966): 55–58.

France, Italy, and West Germany, with the broadest restraints operating in France. Sweden, the United States, and Great Britain, probably rankable in that order, are among the Western industrialized countries in which substantive liberties are most respected.

A major variation from these general patterns occurs in the area of freedom of religion and the separation of church and state. Here France has one of the more liberal policies and Sweden and Britain are among the states with strongly established churches. However, in neither Sweden nor Britain are minority religions as subject to biased government policies as in Italy. East Germany appears to be substantially more tolerant and supportive in the area of religion than is the Soviet Union, although it is not as protective of its major denominations as the four Western European states with established churches.

Finally, variations exist in the sources of the protection and limitation of rights, which include constitutions, penal codes, statutes, and implementing practices. Both Britain and Sweden demonstrate that a generally high level of respect for individual rights in the political sphere need not depend on provisions of a documentary constitution. In both countries a strong tradition of constitutionalism internalized by governmental elites has probably counted more, and this has been reflected in statutes that tend to reinforce constitutional rights more often than they infringe them. On the other hand, the strong American sense of constitutionalism is rooted more in the Constitution itself and in the federal courts' role as its guardian. In sharpest contrast, the Soviet Union and East Germany demonstrate that a liberal constitution cannot ensure substantive rights. However, we have shown that the loopholes foreclosing individual political rights begin with the fine print in the Soviet and East German constitutions.

CIVIL RIGHTS

We intend to treat public policies concerning equality and discrimination under two distinct headings: (1) the rights of racial, ethnic, and other minorities, and (2) the rights of women.

Minority Rights

Broadly conceived, the minority rights policies of the eight countries may be seen as falling into one of three categories. First, there are states which extend vaguely worded constitutional commitments to equality before the law but do not go very much beyond this in terms of statutory law and administrative enforcement machinery. Second, we find countries that supplement constitutional provisions with legislated penalties for discriminatory behavior. Third, there are states which have not only antidiscrimination laws but also articulated specialized governmental institutions to ensure implementation.

The United States and Great Britain belong to the third category. After more than three centuries of white inhumanity to blacks, Indians, and other minorities, after the Civil War, Reconstruction, the Civil Rights movement, and pathbreaking decisions by the Supreme Court, American federal and state laws now prohibit most forms of discrimination in public accommodation, voting, housing, education, and employment. Most of the pathbreaking laws were passed between 1957 and 1968, but recent court decisions have also relied on long-forgotten statutes passed immediately after the Civil War. The Civil Rights Act of 1866 has been used to broaden federal protection against private discrimination. What is more, several federal agencies and many state commissions have been created to ensure compliance with the law. The Civil Rights Division and the Community Relations Service of the Justice Department, the Commissions on Civil Rights and Equal Employment Opportunity, and a variety of units in other executive departments have been created with this aim in mind. In many instances it is unnecessary for individuals who feel themselves to have been discriminated against to bring suit in the courts. Instead, machinery is available at the national and state levels to enforce antidiscrimination policies. A number of techniques may be put to this end, including government-initiated civil suits and prosecutions, and evaluations of the extent to which federal contractors and federal agencies themselves are complying with the numerous laws and regulations.[53]

Furthermore, in recent years the thrust of American minority rights policy has shifted from the relatively passive objective of prohibiting discrimination to that of actively fostering integration, especially in education and employment. This shift has engendered substantial controversy over such issues as busing and racial quotas, with opponents contending that busing will not achieve integrated schools because of the flight of white students to suburban or private schools and that racial quotas deprive majority citizens of their equal protection under the law. In any case, although it has taken centuries to accomplish, current American minority rights policy appears to be relatively vigorous.

Although Britain's racial and ethnic minorities constitute a far smaller proportion of the overall population than those of the United States, since the 1950s the United Kingdom has absorbed a large num-

---

[53] Sigler, *American Rights Policies,* pp. 126–41, 259–69. For background on civil rights in the United States see Richard Kluger, *Simple Justice* (New York: Alfred A. Knopf, 1976).

ber of nonwhite immigrants from Commonwealth countries in the West Indies, East Africa, and South Asia. Their presence in Britain stimulated a host of discriminatory practices. Although the existing Common Law ensured something approaching equality before the law as regards transactions between the individual and the state, until recently there were no effective remedies against bigotry in the private sector.

To rectify this situation Parliament enacted the Race Relations acts of 1965 and 1968.[54] The first act made it illegal to discriminate on the basis of race, color, ethnicity, and so on, in places of public resort, entertainment, or recreation and in public transport. In addition, as mentioned earlier, incitement to racial hatred became unlawful. To enforce this act a Race Relations Board and a number of conciliation committees were established. These bodies heard citizen-initiated complaints and sought by means of benign negotiation to end discrimination in the areas mentioned. If conciliation failed, they could then bring grievances to the attorney general's attention for possible litigation.

As the result of research showing the persistence of discrimination in British life, the Board soon recommended that the law be strengthened. After suitable debate Parliament passed the 1968 act. This replaced all but the racial incitement section of the previous act and declared discrimination in public accommodation, employment, and housing to be unlawful. Further, a Community Relations Commission was set up to advise the government and assist local communities in promoting harmonious race relations, and the Race Relations Board was empowered to bring suit when violations were discovered and conciliation proved unsuccessful.

Although British policy was largely modeled on that of the United States, it is weaker than its American counterpart. For instance, the Board does not, on its own, reach out to insure compliance; it investigates only after receiving complaints. With one minor exception there is nothing in the law which explicitly requires affirmative action to induce integration. Most significant, during the same period that the British government was taking these steps toward ameliorating discrimination it also enacted the 1968 Commonwealth Immigration Act, whose effect was to make racially based distinctions concerning the right of Commonwealth citizens to emigrate to the United Kingdom. This act has been viewed as a major concession to the anti-"coloured" attitudes of the majority population. However, Britain's protection of civil rights may regain some momentum as the result of a new Race

---

[54] Anthony Lester and Geoffrey Bindman, *Race and Law* (Harmondsworth, England: Penguin Books, 1972), pp. 73–149.

Relations Act proposed by the Labour government in early 1976. Although American-type affirmative action programs are still not included, the bill does contemplate government-initiated investigations.

The Swedish and Soviet systems belong under our second category of minority rights legal protection. Given the social homogeneity of Sweden's population, the underlying basis for intergroup prejudice is not very great. Nevertheless, the country's Penal Code makes it illegal to discriminate in business, public services, entertainment, or public assembly. The law applies to civil servants as well as private businessmen. Violators may be fined or sentenced to prison for up to six months.[55]

The Soviet Constitution (Article 123) promises even broader protection than the Swedish code:

> Equality of rights of citizens of the USSR, irrespective of their nationality or race, in all spheres . . . is an indefeasible law. Any direct or indirect restriction of the rights of, or, conversely, the establishment of any direct or indirect privileges for, citizens on account of their race or nationality, as well as any advocacy or racial or national exclusiveness or hatred and contempt, are punishable by law.

Using similar language, the Russian Criminal Code affixes penal sanctions for violations; the constitutions and codes of the other republics treat the matter in about the same fashion.[56] The reader should be aware, however, that these provisions are two-edged swords, since displays of racial or ethnic "exclusiveness" are also subject to prosecution. There have been postwar criminal actions involving ethnically conscious intellectuals who have been convicted of, in effect, trumpeting the historical or linguistic distinctiveness of their nationalities with inordinate ardor.

On the other hand, the Soviet Union's federal structure is itself a recognition of the country's multiethnic character.[57] Many non-Russian nationalities are accorded the symbolic and tangible benefits of having their "own" republic or other political subdivision and of being represented in the Supreme Soviet's second chamber, the Soviet of Nationalities. The degree of cultural and linguistic autonomy enjoyed by such groups as the Ukrainians and the Uzbeks has fluctuated with the vicissitudes of the Soviet political climate. Today, it seems fair to say that the non-Russian nationalities are allowed to learn and express them-

---

[55] *Penal Code of Sweden*, p. 48.

[56] *Soviet Criminal Law and Procedure*, p. 181; and I. P. Tsamerian and S. L. Ronin, *Equality of Rights between Races and Nationalities in the USSR* (Paris: UNESCO, 1962), pp. 28–29.

[57] Robert Conquest, *Soviet Nationalities Policy in Practice* (New York: Frederick A. Praeger, 1967), pp. 61–108.

selves in their own language and to celebrate, within limits, their diverse cultural backgrounds. The limits relate primarily to implications of separatist aspirations, though such aspirations may be visible only to the regime's observers.

The Soviet approach has reduced discrimination in education and employment but has had little impact on bias in social relationships in a multiracial and multinational society with deeply entrenched prejudices and patterns of discrimination. Central and East Asian national groups as well as Jews (legally a nationality) are subjected to discrimination by the majority Slavic community.[58] Additionally, official propaganda that fosters prejudices is not unusual.

The protections in France, Italy, West Germany, and East Germany fall into the weakest category. The constitutions of these countries proclaim racial or ethnic equality or prohibit discrimination. Yet these states lack precise implementing legislation, except for restraints on incitements to group hatred, and they have not developed specialized government enforcement units to eliminate discriminatory practices.

What, then, is the legal status of the constitutional commitments? All subordinate laws and regulations governing state and private transactions are construed by the courts of these countries as conforming to the constitutional requirements. For instance, even though the West German civil and criminal codes do not directly prohibit discriminatory practices, the courts will interpret their application in particular cases so as to make them conform to the Basic Law.[59] The deficiency of this arrangement is apparent. It requires an individual who believes himself to be the victim of racial or ethnic discrimination to initiate a civil suit or lodge an administrative complaint. Given the absence of appropriate statutes, enforcement tends to be haphazard. Thus, despite the French Constitution's avowals, thousands of North African immigrants are being subjected to various forms of housing and employment discrimination, often with the connivance of local authorities.[60] Moreover, such aliens as foreign workers in France and black U.S. servicemen in West Germany are more likely to experience discrimination than are citizens. Language problems and special legal difficulties combine to make the present situation far from satisfactory for noncitizens.

---

[58] Abraham Brumberg, ed., *In Quest of Justice* (New York: Praeger Publishers, 1970) pp. 200–213.

[59] Kenneth Lewan, "The Significance of Constitutional Rights for Private Law: Theory and Practice in West Germany," *International and Comparative Law Quarterly* 17 (1968): 571–601.

[60] Vincent Lalu, "Un Plan pour les immigres," *L'Express*, October 21–27, 1974, p. 31.

The Rights of Women

In no other area of regulation of the individual are laws in such rapid flux as those which pertain to the rights of the sexes. As a result of shifting popular attitudes and the efforts of organized women's groups, particularly in the Western industrialized nations, new legislation and new judicial rulings are overturning old norms. For writers who wish to comment on the new legal status of women, this poses the problem of trying to shoot at a fast-moving target.

Since the Equal Rights Amendment is currently pending ratification in the United States, amid considerable public debate, it seems appropriate to begin by reviewing the comparable constitutional provisions of the other countries chosen for this analysis. The following constitutional provisions approximate the content of the ERA:

> East Germany (Article 20)
> Men and women have equal rights and have the same legal status in all spheres of social, state and personal life.
>
> The Soviet Union (Article 122)
> Women in the USSR are accorded all rights on an equal footing with men in all spheres of economic development, cultural, political and other social activity.
>
> West Germany (Article 3)
> All persons are equal before the law. Men and women have equal rights.
>
> Italy (Article 3)
> All citizens have equal social standing and are equal before the law, without distinction of sex.
>
> France (Preamble to the 1946 Constitution)
> The law guarantees to women, in all spheres, rights equal to those of men.

Interestingly, of our seven European countries only Great Britain and Sweden, the states which were designated as providing the broadest range of substantive civil liberties, lack an explicit constitutional guarantee along the lines of the ERA.

Although the above provisions of the Soviet and East German constitutions do tend to reflect reality, this is less true for the French and Italian provisions. Only in the last few years have France and Italy taken major steps toward equal rights for women. For instance, a 1959 French civil service ordinance barred women from several areas of public employment. French women, allegedly because of their lack of authority, were not eligible for membership in the prefectural or diplomatic corps.[61] In Italy, similarly, such discriminatory code provisions as differences in punishment for adultery and the denial of women's right to become judges have only recently been removed as the result of court decisions and new legislation.

The fundamental question of voting rights was resolved some time ago in all eight countries, so that the current franchise laws apply the same eligibility criteria to both sexes. However, in the two Latin countries women were not permitted to vote on an equal basis until after World War II rather than, as in the other nations, during the decade following World War I (see Table 9–1). Since the right to vote usually precedes the acquisition of other equal treatment rights, the fact that France and Italy were latecomers is fairly indicative of other legal inequities which women in these countries suffered until quite recently.

Next, let us consider the economic status of women. Historically, legal disabilities and disparities with respect to occupational choice and working conditions were often the result of policy-makers' benign intent to shield women from performing jobs to which, it was assumed, they were either physically or temperamentally unsuited. Today these conceptions have changed.

Equal pay for equal work is a concept that has won growing acceptance. It has been established by law in the United States, Great Britain, Sweden, East Germany, and the Soviet Union.[62] An April 1976 ruling by the European Court of Justice gave the principle broad application with the European Communities.[63] This binding ruling will help to make up for a lack of clear protection in the national law of such member states as West Germany, Italy, and France.

Equal pay is not worth very much unless equal employment opportunities are also provided. Statutory guarantees have been enacted in the United States, Sweden, East Germany, the Soviet Union, and most recently, Great Britain. At the national level American equal employment opportunity policy has been fixed by Title VII of the 1964 Civil Rights Act and by several executive orders governing public employment and employment by private firms with government contracts.[64] The 1975 British statute follows many of the lines of the U.S. approach but stops short of the American requirement that affirmative action be

---

[61] Daniele Alexandre, "The Status of Women in France," *American Journal of Comparative Law* 20 (Fall 1972): 647–61.

[62] Leo Kanowitz, *Women and the Law* (Albuquerque: University of New Mexico Press, 1969), pp. 100–131; Olive Stone, "The Status of Women in Great Britain," and Gunnor Wallin, "The Status of Women in the Soviet Union," *American Journal of Comparative Law* 20 (Fall 1972): 592–621, 662–92; and Rudolph Mecklinger, "GDR Passed New Abortion Law," *Law and Legislation in the GDR* 2 (1972): 23–30.

[63] *Economist*, April 17, 1976, p. 54.

[64] Pauli Murray, "The Rights of Women," in Dorsen, *Rights of Americans*, pp. 531–39.

TABLE 9-1
Year Women Acquired Same Voting
Rights as Men

Soviet Union	1917
Sweden	1919
Germany (East and West under Weimar Constitution)	1919
United States	1920
Great Britain	1928
France	1944
Italy	1945

Source: UN, Commission on the Status of
Women, *Constitutions, Electoral Laws and Other
Legal Instruments Relating to the Political Rights
of Women* (New York: United Nations, 1968),
pp. 121–35.

taken to hire women in previously male-dominated posts. Although Swedish, East German, and Soviet law do not go this far, equal employment opportunity has been public policy in these nations longer than it has in the United States. Moreover, the Russian Criminal Code imposes penal sanctions against anyone who seeks to restrain a woman from entering the labor force or any other area of public life.

As in other areas of civil rights, strong government commitments have not secured the end of discrimination against women. Jancar has reported the continued exploitation of Soviet women at home, at work, and in political life. In her view, "An essentially conservative environment has supported the regime in the maintenance of the primacy of the traditional female role."[65]

The current policies of the U.S. government have increased opportunities, but America still lags behind most of Europe in relative pay and many kinds of employment opportunities. Despite weaker legal protection, greater equality exists in most of Western Europe than in the United States. However, the overall legal position of women tends to be weakest in predominantly Catholic Western European countries. Presumably, the European Court of Justice will continue to exert pressure for expanded opportunities for women in the member states of the Communities.

Another set of women's rights issues that has stimulated enormous controversy involves contraception and abortion. At present, the dissemination of birth control information is permitted in all of the eight countries except Italy. This has been public policy for some time in

---

[65] Barbara Wolfe Jancar, "Women and Soviet Politics," in Henry Morton and Rudolf Tokes, eds., *Soviet Politics and Society in the 1970s* (New York: Free Press, 1974), p. 119.

Sweden, East Germany, the Soviet Union, and most states of the U.S., but only in the 1960s and 1970s was such information made legally available in the other countries. Although Italy's Constitutional Court upheld a section of the Penal Code which criminalized public incitement to propaganda for "practices against procreation,"[66] Italian physicians may prescribe birth control pulls for patients on the pretext that their purpose is not contraception.

Nonemergency abortions are legal in all of the eight countries except West Germany and Italy. However, the legalization policies vary considerably in regard to length of pregnancy, the deciding authority and the acceptable grounds. In West Germany a law permitting abortion through the first three months of pregnancy was struck down by the Constitutional Court in 1974. The Court cited the Basic Law's stipulation that "everyone has the right to life and to inviolability of his person."[67] The Italian Constitutional Court recently overturned the Penal Code's criminalization of abortion.[68] Yet the issue has been left unresolved as a result of parliamentary indecision.

Except in Sweden, East Germany, and the Soviet Union, opponents of legalized abortion are well organized and vocal. Thus it is by no means certain that the current pattern of toleration will ultimately prevail, particularly where this rests largely on court decisions rather than legislation. There have been reports that the new abortion law in France, which does not allow for coverage under public health insurance, is being widely ignored by hospitals and physicians who are refusing to perform the surgery. Yet proabortion forces in France and elsewhere are also increasingly active.

Public policies concerning public accommodations, marriage and divorce, and property and other economic rights of women are also in a state of flux. It seems evident that over the next decade most existing inequities will be removed. Even in Italy the parliament in 1975 enacted a new law giving wives full legal equality with their husbands in all key family decisions.

Summary: Civil Rights

Perhaps in part because they did not perceive the granting of equal rights to minorities and women as a threat to political stability or social order, most industrialized states have taken major steps to assure equality in recent years. Indeed, most of the governments in our study

---

[66] Evans, "Italian Constitutional Court," pp. 602–33.

[67] Nan Robertson, "Abortion Argued around the World," *New York Times*, March 23, 1975, p. 52.

[68] "Legalizing Abortion in Italy," *San Francisco Chronicle*, January 7, 1975, p. 10.

have recognized that positive steps to assure substantive rights to all groups are a precondition of domestic stability. In addition, ideological and moral considerations have contributed to this trend.

Voting rights have preceded other legal advances in each of the eight countries. Employment rights have generally preceded such social developments as access by minorities to private clubs and the gaining by women of control over their own reproductive functions.

As in the area of substantive civil liberties, major variations exist in the degree to which the eight countries commit themselves to ensure civil rights. Official policy seems to be strongest in the United States and Great Britain, where special enforcement machinery has been established to protect the rights of minorities and women, and in the Soviet Union, where the criminal law may be invoked to these ends. The weakest protections operate in France, Italy, and West Germany.

Yet strong policies and machinery certainly do not guarantee equality. Since the United States, Great Britain, and the Soviet Union have far more serious intergroup tensions than do the other countries in this survey, their efforts should be viewed in part as remedial action that is not nearly as necessary in the more homogeneous countries. A somewhat different relationship between protection and the intensity of the problems exists in the area of women's rights. The tendency has been to have the strongest protections in countries where women had already made substantial progress toward equal treatment. Thus the greatest lags exist in the Catholic countries, Italy and France, and in West Germany.

PROCEDURAL RIGHTS

As we reported at the beginning of the chapter, the Universal Declaration mentions a number of procedural rights to which all individuals ought by law to be entitled. Essentially these are stipulations which seek to require fair and humane treatment on the part of states in their dealings with their own citizens. These procedural rights include the right to be protected from arbitrary search, arrest, and detention; to have a fair trial; and to be protected against cruel and inhuman punishment.

Privacy and Arbitrary Searches

As recently stated by the U.S. Supreme Court, privacy can be viewed as a substantive as well as a procedural right. The Court has applied this doctrine to the private use of contraception and pornography, limiting government interference in these areas. In addition, the right to be free from government searches of one's home, business establishment, or person is an area of acknowledged, though limited, substantive right. However, the legal history of the right of privacy, and especially the right of freedom from government search, is primarily one of procedural protections against the abuse of government's limited right to invade individual privacy. For example, all governments retain the legal authority to search for and seize material when evidence suggests the involvement of a person in a criminal act. The central issue is whether the government must take certain procedural steps when it seeks to exercise its authority to search or seize property.

In the Anglo-American Common Law countries, protection against arbitrary state intrusions has been built around the requirement that the police obtain a judicial warrant before they may conduct a search. Moreover, the warrant does not confer an unbounded right to search and seize anything the police wish, but is restricted to items specified in the warrant and to clearly visible materials that it is illegal to possess. The types of items for which a search may be made are more limited in Britain than in the United States, although there is some state-to-state variation in the latter country. Observers note that American judges tend to be more lenient in granting search warrants than do their British colleagues.

In both nations, involuntary searches of the immediate premises without a warrant may occur attendant to an arrest. To a more limited extent, searches may take place without an arrest if the police have reasonable grounds to believe, which they must subsequently justify, that an individual is on the verge of committing a crime. Hence the U.S. Supreme Court has upheld the constitutionality, under the Fourth Amendment, of recent "stop and frisk" laws. British practice in this area is more restrictive.[69]

Personal privacy may also be invaded through state monitoring of thoughts and expressions. We refer here to such things as wiretapping (the interception of telephone conversations), bugging (the recording of other conversations), and the interception of mail. With regard to telephone taps, the general rule in the United States is that judicial authorization is required in those circumstances in which the technique is legal. In Britain, wiretapping may be undertaken on the approval of a governmental official, the home secretary. The U.S. Supreme Court has held that electronic listening is not per se forbidden by the Fourth Amendment's prohibition against unreasonable search except if physical trespass has occurred or if a person is located in a place where he or she might normally expect privacy. However, wiretapping and bugging are limited by law. The 1968 Crime Control and Safe

---

[69] Kent Greenwalt, "The Right of Privacy," in Dorsen, *Rights of Americans*, pp. 304–5; and Street, *Freedom*, pp. 20–24.

Streets Act makes most forms of private electronic surveillance unlawful. Nonetheless, upon obtaining judicial approval, both federal and state governments may engage in these practices in coping with certain categories of suspected criminal activity. If they do not secure a warrant, federal and state officials practicing wiretapping and the like are subject to the same penalties as are private citizens. Furthermore, information obtained by illegal taps and bugs is not admissible in court. Although the major exception provided under the act is that the attorney general may authorize electronic surveillance in cases involving national security, the Supreme Court has interpreted this provision quite narrowly.[70] Under federal law the executive must obtain a court order to open someone's mail; however, federal officials may on their own authority record addresses on envelopes to determine with whom a person is corresponding.[71]

British law treating government wiretapping and interception of mail is less restrictive. In Britain the privacy of both telephone and mail communication may be violated on the approval of members of the government without recourse to judicial warrant.

If constitutional stricture were equivalent to actual policy, the right of personal privacy would be well protected in the Soviet Union and East Germany. Provisions of the Soviet Constitution state that the persons, homes, and correspondence of citizens are inviolably protected by law. The Constitution of the German Democratic Republic contains parallel expressions. In addition, the Russian and East German codes of criminal procedure appear to strengthen these commitments by indicating that searches, seizures, and interceptions may occur only under law.[72] Unfortunately, these same codes go on to state that these invasions of privacy may be authorized, not as the result of judicial warrant, but by the procurators alone. This means that police wishing to search need merely to secure a decree from the state prosecutor. The codes' provisions represent an advance over the earlier Stalinist approach of allowing the police routine incursions on their own initiative. However, police officials still may act on their own "in instances not permitting delay."

Search and seizure rules in the four selected Roman Law systems come somewhat closer to Anglo-American requirements. The West German Basic Law and the Italian Constitution make reference to the right of privacy and the secrecy of the mails and telephone conversa-

---

[70] Jethro Lieberman, *How the Government Breaks the Law* (Baltimore: Penguin Books, 1974), pp. 85–92.

[71] Arthur Miller, *The Assault on Privacy* (New York: New American Library, 1971), pp. 59–60.

[72] *Soviet Criminal Law and Procedure*, p. 256. For East Germany see Code of Criminal Procedure, reprinted in *Law and Legislation in the GDR* 2 (1970): 14–15.

tions. However, both documents indicate that certain limitations may be imposed by law. These exceptions are spelled out in the West German and Italian codes of criminal procedure and other statutes. In France and Sweden, codes also define the circumstances for state-authorized intrusions. In West Germany, Italy, and Sweden the general rule is that a judge must be persuaded to grant an order authorizing search and seizure, based on the necessities of criminal investigation. Police may act on their own initiative only if there is danger that delay will entail the destruction of evidence or immediate harm to public safety. And under these circumstances the police must retrospectively justify their actions before a court within a short period of time. The French regulations here are more lax.[73]

In urgent situations each of these four nations sanctions telephone-tapping and interference with correspondence without the prior issuance of a court order. Until 1975 the Swedish law on the subject required that intrusions of this sort must be by court order only, but in the wake of several terrorist acts the Riksdag passed a law waiving this restraint for one year.

The actual protection of individual and group privacy depends largely on the norms of the military, intelligence, police, taxation, and other agencies which are directed to engage in surveillance or may expand their surveillance activities of their own accord. All eight governments maintain organizations with authority to investigate individuals and groups that are suspected of planning subversion, espionage, or sabotage. The distinctions among the eight relate to the extension of such tasks to the surveillance of individuals and groups that are not suspected of criminal activity, the respect shown for national and international standards concerning methods, and the degree to which the investigating agencies are effectively controlled by authorities and can resist illegal political demands.

A real danger exists that any comparisons we make will be based as much on the skill of the investigatory agencies in keeping their own operations secret as on the actual range of their activities. Few such agencies have been subjected to broad and intensive investigations by other government bodies. With this in mind we contend, first, that, although intelligence and police organs are not necessarily more efficient in East Germany and the Soviet Union, they do operate with considerably greater freedom from effective press or judicial controls

---

[73] *The German Code of Criminal Procedure,* trans. Horst Niebler and Manfred Pfeiffer (South Hackensack, N.J.: Fred B. Rothman & Co., 1965), pp. 56–63; Mauro Cappelletti, John Merryman, and Joseph Perillo, *The Italian Legal System* (Stanford, Calif.: Stanford University Press, 1967), pp. 283–84; *French Code of Criminal Procedure,* pp. 48–50; and *The Swedish Code of Judicial Procedure,* trans. Anders Bruzelius and Ruth Ginsburg (South Hackensack, N.J.: Fred B. Rothman & Co., 1968), pp. 115–24.

than do the comparable agencies of any of the six Western states in this survey. They have less need to justify their choice of targets or methods and can use larger numbers of agents and informers.[74] Second, intelligence agencies in most large West European states and the United States have engaged in widespread surveillance of individuals and organizations suspected of political activity that is unwelcome to the regime rather than illegal. U.S. congressional committees have revealed such domestic actions by American intelligence agencies as burglary, broad mail and telegraph surveillance, many illegal wiretaps, and abuse of tax records. Yet the standards of police and intelligence agencies in Italy, France, and West Germany, if not other Western countries, are probably as bad or worse. Further, the known covert domestic operations spinning off from such surveillance activities have been more serious in Italy and France than in the United States.[75] The advantage of the United States has been the independence of its press, judiciary, and legislative branch, and their ability to learn about and report abuses. However, this difference became apparent only after the development of the Watergate scandal.

Freedom from Arbitrary Arrest and Detention

The historical record suggests that in periods of national emergency the usual legal safeguards protecting individuals against involuntary confinement have been breached in almost all of the eight countries. No detailed elaboration of this point is needed with respect to Fascist Italy, Nazi Germany, or the Soviet Union under Stalin. However, even in nations ordinarily regarded as being ruled by law, recent history offers examples of this form of state activity. We need cite only the removal of American citizens of Japanese ancestry from the West Coast during World War II (an act subsequently affirmed by the Supreme Court), the detention without trial of IRA suspects in Northern Ireland, and French practices along the same lines during the Algerian War.

In this section we focus on policies concerning detention in nonemergency circumstances prior to conviction and sentencing at a criminal trial. These policies may be viewed as falling under two headings: detention before and after a person has been formally accused of a crime.

Neither under British nor under American law do the police possess

---

[74] Roy Medvedev, *On Socialist Democracy* (New York: Alfred A. Knopf, 1975), pp. 161–63.

[75] See Philip Williams, *Wars, Plots, and Scandals in Post-War France* (Cambridge, England: Cambridge University Press, 1970); and Domenico Bartoli, *Gli italiani nella terra di nessuno* (Milan: Afnoldo Mondadori, 1976), pp. 163–203.

a general right to detain an individual involuntarily without placing him or her under arrest. Nonetheless, there are a number of exceptions. In both systems there is some latitude in regard to on-the-street detention (for example, stop and frisk) and prearrest questioning. In addition, so long as there is judicial compliance, almost all American states permit the confinement of persons as material witnesses.

Arrests may be made upon the issuance of a judicial warrant or without warrant by police authorities on the basis of probable cause (United States) or of reasonable grounds for suspicion (Britain) if there is no time to secure one. The judicial warrant is intended as a check on arbitrary police confinement. Evidently British jurists show greater reluctance to issue them than do their American counterparts.[76] Also, British judges have the option, even in relatively serious cases, of issuing a summons, a procedure which in the United States is generally restricted to petty offenses.

In both Britain and the United States the citizen may be confined after arrest, but he or she must be brought promptly before a judge for a preliminary proceeding, at which time a decision concerning further pretrial detention is made. If not quickly taken before a magistrate and charged, the arrested person may obtain a writ of habeas corpus and secure release. Both British law and American law make use of the bail system. In Britain release on bail pending trial is almost entirely discretionary. In the United States the constitutions of over 40 states make it a matter of right in all but capital cases to be afforded an opportunity to post bail. Although in most instances American judges cannot deny bail per se, they nevertheless exercise considerable discretion in setting the amount, subject to the weakly enforced constitutional imperative (also prescribed in British law) that it not be excessive. In both countries a judge may free individuals on their own recognizance if the court is confident that they will appear later for trial.

In the United States the question of bail has excited substantial discussion.[77] In many jurisdictions the jails are crowded with impoverished prisoners who have been unable to afford a bail bond. Thus they must remain imprisoned, not having been found guilty of a crime, until such time as their cases are tried. Since court calendars in major cities are crowded, this may take a long time. One result has been the expansion of the practice of plea bargaining, the agreement to plead guilty to lesser charges than are first proposed. In Britain, where judges have greater leeway in determining whether or not bail should be granted, there is at once a greater inclination to rely on release

---

[76] Delmar Karlsen, *Anglo-American Criminal Justice* (New York: Oxford University Press, 1967), pp. 107–10.

[77] Frederic Suffet, "Bail Setting: A Study of Courtroom Interaction," in Richard Quinney, ed., *Crime and Justice in Society* (Boston: Little, Brown & Co., 1969), pp. 292–307.

without bail and, at the same time, a strong tendency to deny liberty to individuals expected to commit further criminal acts.

As was true for search and seizure, current law in East Germany and the Soviet Union in this realm represents an improvement over Stalinist practice. Nevertheless, the Russian Republic and German Democratic Republic criminal procedure codes allow for extensive pre-accusation detention. On their own volition the police may detain an individual for several days. After this, a suspect may be legally confined only on the authority of the procurators while a preliminary investigation is conducted. This form of detention may last several weeks.[78]

Unlike the usual Common Law practice, a person may be detained, charged, and brought to trial in the German Democratic Republic and the Soviet Union without being formally arrested. Under both Socialist Law and Roman Law arrest is a separate procedure, either with or without warrant, based on the likelihood of the suspect's flight. In East Germany and the Soviet Union the law requires that an individual who has either been arrested and charged or simply charged by the procurator, with or without prior detention, must be brought before a court promptly to determine whether there are sufficient grounds to sustain the accusation. Assuming that there are, the judge then has some discretion to grant freedom pending trial. But the choice here is strongly influenced by the prosecutor's preferences, and it is permissible for the accused to be jailed for several months while awaiting trial. In short, though there has been a step away from some arbitrary police state tactics, criminal procedures in East Germany and the Soviet Union still leave much to be desired.

To a considerable extent the jurists who recently redrafted the Socialist Law criminal procedure codes were influenced by their Roman Law counterparts. It is not surprising, then, that pretrial detention practices in France, West Germany, Sweden, and Italy approximate those found in East Germany and the Soviet Union. The major differences concern the length of time involved and the role of prosecutors. In general, shorter periods of preaccusation confinement are permitted in the Roman Law countries and the role of magistrates is enhanced. As a rule the police may only detain an individual for questioning for a few hours without seeking a court order. After this, the suspect must again be brought before a magistrate within at most several days to be formally accused. At this stage the judge may order either further confinement or grant provisional freedom pending trial. Naturally there is some country-

---

[78] Ivo Lapenna, *Soviet Penal Policy* (Chester Springs, Pa.: Dufour Editions, 1968), pp. 105–21; and Hilde Benjamin, "The New Criminal Law of the GDR," *Law and Legislation in the GDR* 2 (1967): 5–10.

to-country variation, but if the judge rules against freedom an accused person may be imprisoned for many months while awaiting trial. French law allows up to eight months. And recently in West Germany an accused forger was kept in jail over three years before his case was tried, an action which the Constitutional Court sustained.

The Italian criminal justice system has a confinement technique which, so far as we can determine, is unique among Roman Law countries (though a variation has been used in such Socialist Law countries as the Soviet Union). Left over from the Fascist era and partly affirmed by the Constitutional Court, *ammonizione* allows an individual suspected of criminal behavior to be subjected to police surveillance and compulsory residence in an area remote from his home. Although the Court now requires *ammonizione* to be imposed only by judicial order, it is still a mode of involuntary confinement without benefit of criminal trial. *Ammonizione* has been used to remove a number of suspected *mafiosi* from their Sicilian habitats and compel them to live in other communities.[79] The effectiveness of this crime control device is questionable, since the residents of the affected localities complain that the suspects simply continue their endeavors in the new, and previously uninfected, communities.

Fair Trial

A variety of ingredients are necessary for a criminal trial to be considered fair. At or near the top of the list is the requirement that such proceedings be conducted openly by regular courts in conformity with clearly stated rules. Special, secret police tribunals are clearly incompatible with this standard. Such organs were common in the USSR under Stalin but were apparently never widely employed in East Germany. Today they are specifically prohibited in East Germany, but the situation in the Soviet Union is somewhat less clear. It is true that Article 7 of the 1958 Fundamental Principles of Criminal Procedure, in accordance with which the codes of the various republics are written, states: "Justice in criminal cases shall be administered only by the court. No person may be deemed guilty . . . of a crime and subjected to criminal punishment otherwise than by a judgment of the court."[80] On the other hand, there exist a variety of "nonpenal" offenses, for example, antiparasite laws, for which penalties other than imprisonment may be inflicted without benefit of a trial in a regular court.

France is the only other country in our group in which special courts

---

[79] Bognetti, "Political Role," pp. 981–99.

[80] *Fundamentals of Legislation of the USSR and the Union Republic,* trans. Murad Saifulin and Yuri Sdobnikov (Moscow: Progress Publishers, 1974), p. 274.

pose a problem. At de Gaulle's behest a special military tribunal was instituted to try the cases of rebellious civilians during the Algerian crisis. Although the tribunal is still in existence, some of the extraordinary rules under which it operates have been modified and its decisions, at least on points of law, are subject to appellate review by the Court of Cassation. However, it is still authorized to detain political suspects longer than the statutory eight-month pretrial limit.

Another high priority is the accused's right to counsel. Each of the eight legal systems has provisions for defense attorneys at the trial stage of serious criminal cases. The systems differ concerning the point in pretrial proceedings at which a suspect is permitted to obtain legal assistance. Here a sharp difference exists between recent Common Law and Roman Law developments on the one hand and East German and Soviet practice on the other. In the Western countries defense lawyers may or must be appointed during the preliminary stages of an investigation. In France, for example, the accused cannot be questioned by the examining magistrate except in the presence of his attorney. A similar requirement exists in Italy as the result of court decision. Article 137 of the West German Criminal Procedure Code states, "The accused may avail himself of the assistance of defense counsel at any stage of the proceeding." Policies in the United States, Britain, and Sweden are similar, though the American protections are delayed if a grand jury is employed.

Under East German and Soviet law, defense counsel is appointed only after the prosecutor has determined that there is sufficient evidence to merit bringing the accused to trial. Up to this point, interrogations and evidence gathering proceed without the benefit of an attorney. What is more, communications between the accused and his counsel are not privileged, as they are in the West, and political constraints may make the defendant's legal representation ineffective.

At the trial stage of serious criminal cases, who determines guilt or innocence? This is another area in which the Common Law countries differ from both the Roman and Socialist Law systems. For most charges in the United States and in some cases in Great Britain a defendant has the right to a jury trial. This is a right which he may waive, in which case the determination of guilt or innocence is made by a judge. In a jury trial, however, the Common Law rule is that the jury decides questions of fact—guilt or innocence—while the judge rules on matters of law and procedure.

For Roman and Socialist Law countries the court's judgment is the outcome of a collective deliberation involving professional judges and lay jurists. Serious criminal cases are usually heard before panels consisting of several magistrates and a number of ordinary citizens chosen along lines analogous to Common Law jury selection. Decisions are rendered on the basis of majority vote. Generally, though with some exceptions, the preferences of the professional judges count no more than the laymen's.

On the issue of what types of evidence may be admitted in court, the American system is distinctive. Although later decisions have altered the policy in part, American state and federal trial courts have been bound by the Supreme Court's 1961 ruling that courts may not admit as evidence material which has been obtained illegally.[81] Recent decisions have opened the way to the use of illegally obtained confessions in some circumstances.

This kind of exclusionary rule does not exist in the other countries. Except for confessions obtained by coercion, even British and Swedish courts will allow the admission of evidence which has been acquired by proscribed means. In these instances, the legal remedy involves the initiation of civil or criminal litigation against the perpetrator of the unlawful act, for example, the police officer. As the reader may suspect, this approach does not tend to provide adequate safeguards. Prosecutors are reluctant to move against individuals who have aided them in securing convictions.

Cruel and Inhuman Punishment

Every civilized state recognizes that the application of certain punishments must be proscribed or limited because of their alleged cruelty or the unfair pattern of their application. One of the leading issues concerning cruel and inhuman punishment is the applicability of this doctrine to capital punishment. Capital punishment is generally tolerated by international law, though particular executions often bring widespread protests in many countries. The issue of whether the death penalty is unusual rests on whether one is dealing with legal authorization or actual use. More than 100 countries currently authorize the death penalty for designated crimes.[82] Yet even in the countries which make the most use of capital punishment, it is rarely the routine punishment for any particular kind of crime.

Efforts to abolish the death penalty have proceeded for a century or more in most of the countries with which we are concerned. At times the abolitionists have succeeded, only to have the penalty restored

---

[81] Karlsen, *Anglo-American Criminal Justice*, pp. 129–33. Some recent decisions of the U.S. Supreme Court have weakened the restraints against illegally seized evidence that were established by the same court in the 1960s. See Leonard Levy, *Against the Law* (New York: Harper & Row, 1974), pp. 61–87.

[82] Kathleen Teltsch, "U.N. Says 100 Nations Use Executions," *New York Times*, March 25, 1973, p. 4.

shortly afterward. In the Soviet Union, for instance, the death penalty has been abandoned and reinstated several times since the Bolshevik Revolution.[83] This is another area of law in which the situation changes rather rapidly. In view of public concern with increasing rates of violent crime, especially air piracy and urban terrorism, some abolitionist states are now under pressure to restore the death penalty.

The states which still execute individuals do so by less cruel and more expeditious means than prevailed in earlier eras. Disemboweling or drawing and quartering are relics of the past. Hanging, gassing, shooting, electrocuting, and guillotining, though also subject to torturous effects, may represent some advance.

At present, capital punishment is constitutionally prohibited in Italy (except in wartime), West Germany, Sweden, and Britain. In Italy and West Germany abolition was based on a reaction to the Fascist and Nazi epochs.[84] Sweden ended executions for peacetime offenses in 1921 and in 1973 eliminated the death penalty entirely. In Great Britain abolition came in stages. The 1957 Homicide Act restricted the death penalty to several types of murders (for example, murders committed during a robbery, by firearms or explosion, or in resisting police officers).[85] Notwithstanding significant opposition, in 1965 Parliament prohibited the death penalty for a five-year test period. Before that phase ended, the law was changed to make abolition permanent.

The death penalty is now part of public policy in France, the United States, the Soviet Union, and East Germany. It is our contention that the capital punishment issue is a major test of public morality in a given society. Yet we recognize that numerous factors are involved in the decision to abolish or maintain this tool.

For France the historical roots of capital punishment are exceptionally deep. The land which developed the guillotine now authorizes the death penalty for premeditated murder, armed robbery, treason, espionage, and other crimes against the integrity of the state.[86] Yet, in part because of strong leftist opposition to this penalty, executions are exceedingly rare; from 1960 through 1969 only three persons were put to death.[87]

The use of the death penalty in the United States reflects the nation's

---

[83] Will Adams, "Capital Punishment in Imperial and Soviet Criminal Law," *American Journal of Comparative Law* 18 (1970): 575–94.

[84] James Joyce, *Capital Punishment: A World View* (New York: Thomas Nelson & Sons, 1961), pp. 84–89.

[85] James Christoph, *Capital Punishment and British Politics* (Chicago: University of Chicago Press, 1962), pp. 195–96.

[86] Marc Ancel and Norval Morris, *Capital Punishment* (New York: United Nations, 1968), p. 41.

[87] World Health Organization, *World Health Statistics Report* 26 (1973): 306–15.

character as an armed country with deep racial divisions and an exceptionally high murder rate.[88] Since World War II, America has retreated from earlier heavy use of the gas chamber and the electric chair. Yet at present nearly 40 states and the federal government authorize the death penalty for crimes ranging from rape to airplane hijacking. The U.S. Supreme Court ordered a de facto moratorium on executions beginning in 1967. However, in July 1976 the latest in a series of decisions by that court reaffirmed the acceptability of capital punishment as long as meaningful guidelines were provided for the review of individual cases. The court deferred to the will of the public and the legislatures—the opposite of the approach taken in more elitist Britain.

The Soviet Union employs capital punishment more than any other nation except South Africa. Its approach reflects the fear of subversion which has been inculcated in both ordinary citizens and leaders. Not even the widespread knowledge of the enormity of Stalin's crimes has generated an outspoken abolitionist movement. Perhaps the most distinctive feature of capital punishment policy in the USSR is the wide range of criminal acts for which the death sentence may be inflicted. An individual may be shot not only for aggravated murder or rape and the political crimes of espionage, sabotage, and treason, but also for a number of property crimes. Thus bribetaking, currency speculation, and the theft of socialist property are punishable by execution.

The policies of the German Democratic Republic are not quite as severe in this area despite a comparable effort by the regime to maintain a siege mentality. Still an individual may be put to death for the crime of "diversion," or deliberately seeking to harm the national economy or the state by damaging or destroying socialist property. We have no systematic data on the frequency of executions for property crimes in the German Democratic Republic, but the language of the relevant code suggests that execution for this reason is an extraordinary measure and that appeals for clemency are usually granted.

Execution is by no means the only form of cruel and inhuman punishment to which governments may subject persons. Unnecessary brutality often occurs in jails, prisons, and other confinement facilities. Within the past several years international agencies have received charges of torture and mistreatment against institutions in the United States, Great Britain, France, East Germany, and the Soviet Union.[89] Strong political motivations for poor treatment appear to operate in Britain (in relation to Northern Ireland), East Germany, and the Soviet

---

[88] See Hugo Bedau, ed., *The Death Penalty in America*, rev. ed. (Garden City, N.Y.: Anchor Books, 1967); and Michael Meltsner, *Cruel and Unusual: The Supreme Court and Capital Punishment* (New York: William Morrow & Co., 1974).

[89] Amnesty International, *Report on Torture*, pp. 105–13, 184–91; and Hayward, *French Republic*, pp. 135–36.

Union. As of this writing, only Chile and South Africa rival the Soviet Union in regard to documented cases of abuse of political prisoners.[90] By contrast, Swedish correctional practices enjoy the reputation of being among the most enlightened in the world.[91]

The Soviet Union's use of involuntary detention in mental hospitals for "treating" political dissidents has drawn much attention in the West. Although in Western nations the committal procedures for individuals judged to be mentally ill do not typically provide the due process safeguards applied in criminal cases, these nations have not used the placement of persons in mental hospitals as a standard device for political repression. On the other hand, there is evidence that Soviet policy has encouraged the involuntary confinement of many intellectuals whose political views do not coincide with those of the leadership.[92]

Since World War II, Western law has come to reflect the view that the involuntary withdrawal of citizenship, especially when it results in statelessness and is accompanied by forced exile, constitutes a cruel and inhuman punishment. In this connection, it is an irony of Soviet policy that at the same time that many individuals who wish to leave the USSR are denied the right to do so, a number of dissenters, Solzhenitsyn being the most prominent example, have been forcibly expelled from their homeland and not permitted to return.

Summary: Procedural Rights

Procedural rights appear to be the most encroached upon of the three spheres discussed in this chapter. In this area the executive generally seeks to maintain and expand what it regards as its own prerogatives. In a climate of high perceived or actual crime or political disorder, legislative and judicial institutions are inclined to support the law enforcer against the suspect.

The two Socialist Law countries in our study were rather consistently limited in their extension of procedural rights to their citizens, although

---

[90] See Peter Reddaway, ed. and trans., *Uncensored Russia: Protest and Dissent in the Soviet Union* (New York: American Heritage Press, 1972).

[91] See John Conrad, *Crime and Its Correction: An International Survey of Attitudes and Practices* (Berkeley: University of California Press, 1970); and Norval Morris, "Lessons from the Adult Correctional System of Sweden," *Federal Probation* 30, no. 4 (December 1966): 3–13.

[92] For a discussion of the Soviet situation see Zhores Medvedev, *A Question of Madness* (New York: Alfred A. Knopf, 1971). Accounts of American and Swedish problems may be found in Thomas Szasz, *Law, Liberty, and Psychiatry* (New York: Macmillan Co., 1963); and Lloyd Moyer, "The Mentally Abnormal Offender in Sweden: An Overview and Comparison with American Law," *American Journal of Comparative Law* 22 (Winter 1974): 71–106.

both have progressed since Stalinist times. In all probability the whole domain of procedural rights in the German Democratic Republic and the Soviet Union is less than the sum of the parts suggested above. Although many similarities exist between the procedures in these Socialist Law countries and the procedures in our Roman Law states, East Germany and the Soviet Union tend to restrict each aspect of individual rights more than it is restricted in the Roman Law states. However, this is much less true for ordinary criminal procedures than for political cases.

The Anglo-American democracies appear to have some advantages over the Roman and Socialist Law countries in the procedural area. This is true in such areas as jury trials and pretrial detention. However, the Roman Law countries tend to match the Common Law states in the use of judges as barriers against most kinds of procedural violations. Sweden stands out from the other three Roman Law states in being more restrictive concerning searches and seizures. Yet even Sweden has been willing to restrict procedural rights when confronted with increased terrorism.

CONCLUSIONS

Let us return to our basic question: To what extent do the individual regulatory policies of our eight countries meet the standards expressed in the Universal Declaration? If we hold up these countries' policies to the ideal measure of what ought to be, their deficiencies become both manifest and myriad. Alternatively, if we answer by comparing them with current practices around the world, our response can be more sanguine. A recent effort to rate most UN member states according to two of our three dimensions — substantive civil liberties and procedural rights — suggests that, except for East Germany and the Soviet Union, the eight countries compare favorably to most other nations.[93] As against global norms, and particularly when viewed in relation to Third World policies, the prevailing practices in our Common and Roman Law systems appear commendable.[94]

Let us approach the issue of the fulfillment of the Declaration's goals by asking whether citizens' liberties and freedoms are better protected today (1976) than when that document was written. On this matter a number of observers have speculated, usually on the basis of the Soviet experience, that increasing state intervention in economic life inev-

---

[93] Raymond Gastil, "The New Criteria of Freedom," *Freedom at Issue* 17 (January–February 1973): 2.

[94] Rupert Emerson, "The Fate of Human Rights in the Third World," *World Politics* 27 (January 1975): 201–26.

itably produces a decline in the range of individual freedom. Our evidence inclines us to believe that this is not the case at all. For the most part, the citizens of our eight nations enjoy more equal treatment, better procedural safeguards, and greater political liberty than they did when the Declaration was promulgated in 1948, despite the expansion of welfare state measures in the intervening period.

Admittedly the trend has not been uninterrupted or uniform — witness the McCarthy era in the United States, the Algerian interlude in France, and post-Khrushchev retrenchments in the USSR. But even contemporary policies in East Germany and the Soviet Union show some bright spots. Clearly, so far as substantive civil liberties are concerned, the prevailing practices in the Socialist Law states continue to be restrictive. Yet in the areas of civil rights and due process in nonpolitical criminal cases, the two socialist legal systems vary more in degree than in kind from their Roman Law counterparts. On balance, then, and in the light of past experience, we must remain optimistic about the future of freedom.

10 Antitrust Policy and Worker Participation: Aspects of Industrial Regulation

Although new candidates for economic and social dominance may be emerging in post-industrial societies, the present leading forces are governments and major business enterprises.[1] The latter operate in agriculture and services as well as industry. The formal and informal relationships between government and enterprises range from full public ownership and control to efforts by large multinational corporations to exercise leverage over governments.

Business enterprises maintain great influence over technological development and product availability. Of greater interest to us here, they are able to manipulate consumers and to exploit and alienate workers. A major function of contemporary government is to minimize such effects by interceding with

Note: In this chapter we shall use the word *firm* interchangeably with the word *enterprise* despite the fact that the former term has a specialized meaning in some countries. The term *corporation* refers to a particular legal status and pattern of organization for a firm or an enterprise.

[1] John Kenneth Galbraith, *The New Industrial State* (Boston: Houghton Mifflin Co., 1967.

business on behalf of consumers, workers, stockholders, and others. This often involves government regulation of business in the interests of greater safety, health, and fairness.

In this chapter it is not possible for us to describe and compare all of the diverse ways in which government regulation of enterprises is applied. These methods vary widely among nations and industries. In Chapter 4 we summarized the broad differences among the eight countries in regard to planning and public ownership. We have also discussed the special problems caused by multinational corporations and the need to reconcile other economic goals with stable currencies.

In this chapter we have chosen to discuss two problems of industrial regulation which help determine the democratic or authoritarian character of a given society. Social scientists have long been aware that democracy cannot be related to the political system alone. As we observed in our discussion of civil rights, the economic, social, and cultural spheres are also involved. Expanding this view a bit further, we now compare the eight countries in regard to their responses to these problems: (1) the highly concentrated control of enterprises, whether in mixed or socialist systems, which limits competition and threatens serious consequences in such spheres as economic opportunity, prices, and wages; and (2) the desires of workers and their representatives to increase their power and autonomy within the industrial firm in order to improve working conditions and increase other rewards.

COMPETITION AND ANTITRUST POLICY

Whatever the virtues of economic concentration, many political analysts view the exercise of economic power by a comparatively small number of private firms to be incompatible with democracy. Those who direct these enterprises are frequently perceived as having an inordinate influence over fundamental societal decisions, an influence, moreover, which is not easily subject to popular control. For some observers the appropriate political reaction is nationalization. This solution settles the question of ownership: the state owns the firm in the name of the public. It does not, however, resolve the question of size itself; whether a firm is owned by the state or by private shareholders, it may still be gigantic and may still dominate an entire sector of industry. In addition, the transfer of control over enterprise decisions from a small group of privately chosen managers to an equally small group of state-selected managers does not necessarily enhance the ability of the public, in whose name the reform was initiated, to influence policy decisions.

If concentrated ownership rather than size and control were the central issue, then there is some evidence that the problem is not as severe as it once was. If we define ownership as the ability to derive income from property, then data drawn from Western Europe and the United States suggest a gradual diffusion rather than a concentration of ownership in the private sector.[2] This deconcentration of ownership rights is a consequence of the growth of such phenomena as mutual funds and pension funds.

It is conceivable that the limited trend toward the deconcentration of corporate ownership will be accelerated through various plans for the purchase of stock equities by workers in the enterprise in which they hold jobs. France, Sweden, Italy, West Germany, and the United States have already enacted or are seriously considering measures which would facilitate such employee acquisitions.[3] That possibility was one of President de Gaulle's principal responses to the 1968 general strike in France. In the United States many firms have developed such arrangements without legislative mandate. For example, the employee pension and profit-sharing funds of Sears, Roebuck have been used to purcahse more than 25 percent of the company's outstanding common stock.

From our point of view this path toward what some have called the democratization of capital, though probably desirable in itself, does not assure either public accountability or sufficient competition among firms. Of course, these premises would be rejected by the leaders of the Soviet Union and East Germany, who consider their public monopolies to be the ultimate answer to public accountability and reject most claims on behalf of competition. However, the six survey countries with mixed economies all have regimes which claim to desire competition as well as efficiency and accountability. A major problem is the apparent contradiction between the need for large and wealthy firms as competitors at the international level and the threat of such dominant units at the national level.

We seek below to describe how the six states with mixed economies have sought to reconcile such conflicting aims through competition policy. A major component of such an effort is termed antitrust law. The term *antitrust* refers to two related but distinguishable sets of public policies. The first set is intended to prevent the creation of private market-controlling enterprises or to dissolve those that already exist.

---

[2] Frederick A. Pryor, *Property and Industrial Organization in Communist and Capitalist Nations* (Bloomington: Indiana University Press, 1973), pp. 90–131.

[3] *Workers' Negotiated Savings Plans for Capital Formation* (Paris: OECD, 1970); and *Prospects for Labour/Management Co-operation in the Enterprise* (Paris: OECD, 1974), pp. 90–91.

The second set is concerned with the restraint of trade or cartel practices, collusive agreements entered into by nominally independent firms in order to restrict competition by, among other things, fixing prices, rigging bids, and allocating markets. Our interest is primarily with the former set.

Antitrust policy may operate together with a wide range of other public policies designed to maintain or control competition. These include particular controls and supports concerning wages, prices, securities, government contracts, exports, and business ethics.[4] Intentionally or not, these various policies often conflict with and negate one another.

The United States: Tradition and Unused Power

Until relatively recently there has existed a substantial difference between American and Western European orientations to antitrust. In the United States the prevalent attitude was perhaps best expressed by Justice Learned Hand's observation that the 1890 Sherman Act prohibited not merely bad trusts but all trusts.[5] The historical American perspective in regard to monopolies and cartels has been one of opposition in principle, at least rhetorically, to all restraints on market competition. In Western Europe, on the other hand, antitrust policies have been based on a desire to control the abusive consequences of monopolies and cartels rather than on an opposition in principle to such organizations. Western European legislation affecting private monopolies and corporate mergers is, by and large, a post–World War II phenomenon, and in several instances it was inspired by the older American pattern. Such legislation, however, was introduced in countries with extended experience in regulating cartels. We suggest that the underlying reasons for the earlier American start in monopoly control policy were the pervasive liberal commitment to individualism and unfettered market competition and liberal hostility toward the agglomeration of power in either the state or the private sector.

The major American antitrust enactments are: the Sherman Act (1890), the Clayton and Federal Trade Commission acts (1914), and the Celler-Kefauver Anti-Merger Act (1950). The Sherman Act was directed against existing monopolies and cartel arrangements but did not invest its administrators with authority to stop the formation of monop-

---

[4] Robert Dahl and Charles Lindblom, *Politics, Economics, and Welfare* (New York: Harper & Row, 1953), pp. 190–91.

[5] Quoted in Walter Adams, ed., *The Structure of American Industry,* 4th ed. (New York: Macmillan Publishing Co., 1971), p. 457.

Comparing Public Policies

olies. The Clayton Act was intended to rectify this deficiency by prohibiting corporate mergers that would tend to weaken competition. But as Richard Barber observes: "The merger provision . . . was so easily circumvented that it was largely meaningless, and it was not until 1950, with the enactment of the Celler-Kefauver amendment, that mergers were effectively proscribed when they threaten to create monopoly or lessen competition."[6]

Yet despite such legislation, the American record of enforcement is one of hesitancy and half-measures. Economic concentrations have not been eliminated or even significantly reduced. Neither the executive nor the courts have sought to repeat the trust-busting achievements of the 1895–1911 era. Although the courts have been willing to strike down monopoly-creating mergers in response to suits filed by the Justice Department, there has not been a strong inclination to break up oligopolistic industries in which the market is controlled not by one but by several enormous firms. Moreover, companies which have grown to gigantic proportions not as the result of merger and acquisition, but as a consequence of their own internal growth, have usually remained unaffected. Also, the bulk of recent size-increasing corporate mergers have been neither *horizontal* (the merging of competing sellers and producers) nor *vertical* (the formation of firms contributing to varying stages, processes, and supplies within a given industry). These sorts of linkages were the original objects of antitrust policy. Instead, Barber estimates that since 1960 more than 80 percent of the significant mergers in the United States have been of the *conglomerate* variety.[7] Conglomerates are firms which place a wide variety of operations under a single corporate umbrella.

The diversification of International Telephone and Telegraph offers a worthwhile illustration. Originally begun, as its name suggests, as a communications firm, ITT has in recent years acquired among other companies: Avis Rent a Car, the Sheraton Coporation (hotels), Levitt and Sons (home builders), and Continental Baking.[8] Only after ITT sought to acquire the Hartford Insurance Group, having previously absorbed several other insurance companies, did the Justice Department's Antitrust Division hesitantly move to block the merger. In short, it is unclear at present whether the existing antitrust legislation is of much use in preventing economic concentrations via the conglomerate route.

---

[6] Richard Barber, *The American Corporation* (New York: E. P. Dutton & Co., 1970), p. 171.

[7] Ibid., p. 176.

[8] Anthony Sampson, *The Sovereign State of ITT* (Greenwich, Conn.: Fawcett Publications, 1973).

The recent energy crisis has stimulated a good deal of congressional discussion concerning the structure of the petroleum industry. The leading firms are organized vertically, controlling the process from well to gas pump. They also control a large part of the alternative energy supplies and related technology. This has led to strong efforts to dismember the companies in one way or another. Yet such actions will require new legislation rather than implementation of existing antitrust laws.

The overall American record is that of a system which has placed some important and effective restrictions on overt restraint of trade while accommodating itself to an economy in which oligopolies and conglomerates continue to develop. In some ways U.S. antitrust policy corresponds to its tax policy. In both cases a progressive policy framework is undercut by hesitant governments and powerful private interests.

Great Britain and West Germany: New and Untried Laws

Two of the Western European states included in this study, Great Britain and West Germany, have recently approved antimerger and antimonopoly laws which could allow strong government intervention. The comparable French and Swedish legislation is weaker, while the Italian is almost nonexistent. Before pursuing our analysis, however, we note that these nations, except for Italy, have separate administrative devices for regulating cartel practices on the order of the Federal Trade Commission and other federal and state regulatory agencies in the United States.

The British effort to prevent private monopoly and to control corporate mergers dates from the 1956 Restrictive Practices Act which, among other things, provided for the establishment of a part-time Monopolies Commission responsible to what was then called the Board of Trade. The Commission's powers were limited to investigating and publicizing; it could not prevent a merger from being consummated or compel subsequent divestiture.

During the 1960s there was a dramatic acceleration in the rate of corporate mergers in Britain with an accompanying increase in market concentration. Unlike the American pattern, most of these mergers were of the horizontal type—the most obvious form of anticompetitive activity.[9] The trend stimulated new legislation: the Monopolies and Mergers Act of 1965 and the Fair Trading Act of 1973. These laws invested the government with the ability to prevent any merger which

---

[9] Patti Saris, *British Antitrust Policies: Competition or Concentration* (Washington, D.C.: Congressional Research Service, 1973), p. 4.

would create a monopoly or produce an enterprise with over £5 million in overall assets if such an amalgamation were deemed to be against the public interest.

One problem in enforcing the acts has been the processes required. Under the 1965 legislation the ultimate approval of both chambers of Parliament was required to forestall a merger. However, firms typically abandoned merger plans well before recourse to Parliament was taken, and the 1973 act streamlined the procedures somewhat. The real impediments to vigorous enforcement have been the attitudes of successive Labour and Conservative governments and their conceptions of the British public interest.

These conceptions have been predicated on the desire, in Harold Wilson's words, "to drag British industry kicking and screaming into the twentieth century." Merger and monopoly policy has been set against the intent to make British industry more efficient and competitive in an international context. In most cases efficiency and international competitiveness have been positively associated with increasing the size of British corporations. Thus in 1966 the Labour Government established the Industry Reorganization Corporation (IRC) which, in several instances, actively encouraged horizontal mergers. Between 1965 and 1970 fewer than ten out of several thousand corporate mergers were declared to be contrary to the public interest. Although the succeeding Conservative government under Edward Heath abolished the IRC, its perspectives in this area were not very different.[10]

For those who favor a more vigorous antitrust policy, the situation in West Germany affords somewhat stronger grounds for optimism. However, the relevant law on merger and monopoly control dates only from 1973 and it is too early to assess its impact on the structure of German industry. Prior to 1973 the Federal Cartel Office had regulatory powers to control the pricing and other policies of market-dominating firms but could do little in the area of merger control. Under provisions of the new law the Cartel Office, assisted by a quasi-independent Monopolies Commission, has been formally invested with extensive authority. All types of mergers—horizontal, vertical, and conglomerate—are subject to its review. All combinations involving firms which have 20 percent or more of the market, employ at least 10,000 workers, or have annual sales of at least 500 million deutsche marks must be registered with the Federal Cartel Office. Significantly, prior government approval is required if a merger involves two or more firms which separately had worldwide sales of one billion DM in the preceding year.[11] The object of this global criterion is the multinational corporation seeking to expand its German holdings.

The Cartel Office can compel the dissolution of a merger up to a year after its registration on the ground that it will either create or strengthen a market-dominating position. Yet such action will not be taken if it can be shown that the merger will improve competition or that the negative effects on competition can be outweighed by general economic advantages or a "paramount public good." If the minister of economics is persuaded that a merger will enhance the German employment picture, or protect key domestic industries threatened by competitors in international markets, he can overrule the Cartel Office and permit the merger to become final.

Even if the 1973 act were to be enthusiastically implemented, it would still leave West German antitrust policy with some major problems. What would be done with an enterprise which grows to market-dominating proportions after a merger is approved? Presumably, it might be subject to regulation with respect to pricing policies and the like, but it could not, as we understand it, be broken up. The same applies to firms which grow, not as the result of merger and acquisition, but as a consequence of internal expansion, as has happened so often in the American economy. Abusive practices in the market can be regulated, but limits on size per se probably cannot.

France and Sweden: Domestic Concentration Welcomed

The antitrust policies of France and Sweden are similar to those discussed thus far in that the respective legislation of these countries invests cartel agencies with the authority to control certain restrictive business practices if they seriously affect prices and other major economic factors. However, in neither country do the cartel agencies have the power to prevent mergers which would create monopolistic enterprises or promote economic concentrations.[12]

The Swedish government has informed the OECD that "there is no antitrust legislation of the American kind in Sweden."[13] Direct prohibitions are minimal, and maximum discretion is reserved to the ad-

---

[11] Mergers and Competition Policy (Paris: OECD, 1974), pp. 28–29; and Paul Heil and Georg Vorgbrugs, "Anti-Trust Law in West Germany: Recent Developments in German and Common Market Regulation," International Lawyer 17 (April 1974): 377.

[12] B. Clement, "An Appraisal of French Antitrust Policy," Antitrust Bulletin 19 (Fall 1974): 587–603; Patti Saris, French Antitrust Policies: Competition, Regulation, and Nationalism (Washington, D.C.: Congressional Research Service, 1973), pp. 1–12; Martin Schnitzer, The Economy of Sweden (New York: Praeger Publishers, 1970), p. 220; and Mergers and Competition Policy, p. 27.

[13] The Industrial Policies of 14 Member Countries (Paris: OECD, 1971), p. 306.

ministrative authorities. A cautious proconcentration orientation operates in regard to the large export sector of the economy.

Because the French economy has been dominated until recently by a large number of small, family-owned firms, cautious in outlook and often inefficient in operation, the government's policy has been directed at promoting consolidation rather than restraining it. Like the British, the French have sought to enhance the ability of domestic firms to compete in the international market. In order to take advantage of economies of scale and to encourage the standardization of equipment and technique, France's fifth national economic plan called for industries to be dominated by one or two firms.

The major French barrier to concentration has not been antimonopoly laws but the government's rules on foreign investment. Generally, the goal has been to retard the acquisition of domestically owned firms by foreign multinationals, especially in industries related to national defense. But the application of this policy has been highly selective and has been limited by the European Communities' rules which seek to foster the free flow of capital among member states.

Italy: The Least Control

Italy is unique among the nations we have considered thus far in that it lacks merger control and antimonopoly legislation and also does very little by way of cartel regulation. Italy's membership in the European Communities subjects Italian enterprises to some restraints, but the regime has done little to augment those controls. This was made evident when the government did nothing to forestall the 1966 merger of the country's two largest chemical firms, Montecatini and Edison, whose amalgamation resulted in the creation of the world's sixth-ranking chemical company.

The European Communities and Antitrust: A Growing Force

Above the nation-state level, Great Britain, France, West Germany, and Italy belong to the European Communities. The EEC Treaty contains several antitrust provisions. Specifically, Article 85 asserts a general prohibition on all restrictive cartel agreements among firms to the extent that such agreements may adversely affect trade among the member states. Article 86 was designed to eliminate the abusive action of one or more enterprises operating in market-dominating positions within the Community.[14]

---

[14] Anthony Parry and Stephen Hardy, *EEC Law* (London: Sweet & Maxwell, 1973), pp. 277–324.

Until 1970 the Economic Community's central administrative organ, the Commission, made little effort to apply these articles, as refined in attendant regulations, to monopoly-creating corporate mergers. But because of growing concern with the takeover of European firms by American-based multinationals, as expressed, for example, by members of the EEC's parliament, the Commission tried to invoke Article 86 against the acquisition of its leading West German competitor by a Belgian subsidiary of the Continental Can Company—thereby creating a Community-wide monopoly. The Commission concluded that such action was inherently abusive and therefore proscribed by the Treaty of Rome. The firm thus restrained appealed the Commission's decision to the EEC's Court of Justice, which in 1973 ruled against the Commission on technical grounds and permitted the merger to be consummated. However, what may prove more significant in the long run is that the Court also judged the scope of Article 86 to be broad enough to permit its subsequent use as a merger and monopoly control weapon.[15] To this end, the Commission later prepared a draft regulation to guide implementation of its newly recognized prerogative.

The proposal, which has yet to receive final approval, approximates the West German legislation in tone and substance. It is important to point out that even if the regulation is put into effect, the Commission would still be able to approve competition-reducing mergers which were found to be in the Common Market's general interest. How is this general interest likely to be defined?

Given current sentiment, it seems likely that the EEC interest will be seen as defensive in nature. That is, efforts by American or Japanese multinationals to absorb European firms will be resisted more vigorously. But the concentration of enterprises of Common Market origin is likely to be encouraged in many instances. The impulse toward extra-European concentration has stimulated a reaction in the direction of intra-European concentration, in the British and French manner.

The expansion of multinational corporations has persuaded a significant number of national representatives that domestic and even regional attempts at regulation will not suffice. As a result, a commission on the multinationals, recently formed under the auspices of the United Nations and the Organization for Economic Cooperation and Development (OECD), has devised a voluntary code of conduct to govern the transnational operations of these corporations. Further, international trade union organizations are assessing the impact of the multinationals on labor markets. Whether these manifestations of in-

---

[15] Stephen Smith, "Control of Concentrations in the European Economic Community: Evolving Restrictions on the Urge to Merge," *Villanova Law Review* 19 (February 1974): 420–69.

terest will evoke suitable international control mechanisms remains to be seen.

Outcomes: Competition Policy

Conflicting aims, timid implementation, and fear of multinational competitors have all contributed to the failure of antitrust or other competition policies to reduce industrial concentration and its negative consequences. As we have seen, the problems appear different from country to country, and the absence or failure of such policies may sometimes spur national economic activity. Yet such outcomes have allowed industrial empires, domestic and multinational, to threaten domination of national governments and the European Communities. These trends also threaten increased exploitation of consumers and employees.

Numerous measures of concentration confirm the overall failure— and none of the countries in our survey is an exception to the pattern. Economic concentration has intensified as regards sales, profits, and employment. Pryor has found that the work force in Western industrialized nations has become increasingly clustered in production establishments employing 1,000 or more individuals. Even larger units are typical of the Communist-ruled East European countries.[16] East Germany was one of the last of these countries to eliminate the private and mixed enterprises which offered an element of competition through relatively small production units. The long-run trend data concerning enterprise size, as opposed to establishment size, yield approximately the same results. Even greater future concentration is indicated by the positive association between growth in enterprise size, as measured by labor force concentration, and the level of technological development in particular industrial sectors. Generally, the more advanced the production techniques of an industry, the greater is the concentration of the workers engaged in it.

In sum, the trend toward bigness seems to be an irreversible outgrowth of modern industrial organization. Antitrust policies, as they have been erratically applied to the private sector in the West, seem capable only of mitigating some of the uneconomic consequences of market concentration. They are not reversing this trend.

If giantism is an inescapable fact of life, then we must ask whether any available policies would reduce its undesirable political, economic,

---

[16] Pryor, *Property and Industrial Organization,* p. 133, defines a production establishment as "a business or industrial unit at a single physical location." He defines an enterprise as "a business organization . . . consisting of one or more establishments under common ownership and control." For data on concentration in production, see Pryor, pp. 132–66, 167–213.

and social consequences. Suggested remedies for the loss of individual and popular control include the development of new forms of worker participation and codetermination within firms.

THE POSSIBILITY OF INDUSTRIAL DEMOCRACY

The modern business enterprise, private or public, is subject to three fundamental forms of control. There are two types of external controls — controls imposed by the market, which operate if the structure of an industry permits meaningful independence on the part of competitors and consumers, and governmental controls, including such indirect instruments as monetary and fiscal policies and such direct ones as antitrust laws, wage and price controls, and directive planning. And there are internal controls, imposed on the enterprise by its own managers.[17] External controls, whether of the market or governmental variety, can mitigate only some of the deleterious economic efforts of giantism. The consumer must depend entirely on such externally imposed restraints. But the employee may look beyond these to the possibility of sharing the internal control of enterprises.

The idea of worker participation or shared control in management is rooted in 19th century syndicalist conceptions.[18] Subsequently various forms of worker participation and control were experimented with in the Soviet Union soon after the Russian Revolution and transformed into control devices by various Fascist regimes between 1930 and 1945. After World War II worker participation was championed by the British occupation regime in Germany and by the Tito regime in Yugoslavia.

Within Europe this course of action has been the source of long and often ideologically hardened debates. Some Western European Communist leaders have argued that worker participation in management is a device to artificially reduce the enduring class struggle, by paternalist means, and thus reconcile workers to monopoly capitalism. Some representatives of private business, especially in France, have regarded the prospect with equal suspicion, seeing power-sharing or participation as a means of destroying capitalism. Further, various non-Communist Western European trade union leaders have evinced skepticism, fearing a reduction in the power of independent unions to achieve their ends either by collective bargaining or by pressuring national governments for prolabor legislation.

Despite these expressions of doubt and hostility, the momentum of

---

[17] Robert Dahl, *After the Revolution?* (New Haven: Yale University Press, 1970), pp. 119–41.

[18] See Harry W. Laidler, *History of Socialism* (New York: Thomas Y. Crowell Co., 1968), pp. 277–315.

such changes has accelerated in the past decade. In the following survey of industrial democracy in the eight nation-states, attention will be paid to policies which offer employees opportunities, through job enrichment and restructuring, to control their work situations. We emphasize especially efforts to place worker representatives on enterprise executive boards.

Participation in "Workers' States": The Soviet Union, Yugoslavia, and East Germany

For a time the promise of Eastern European socialism was the achievement of a high level of economic democracy that would provide the base for a parallel layer of political democracy. However, after Eastern Europe's flirtation with experiments in worker participation and control, its dominant economic model, developed and imposed by the Soviet Union, precluded advanced approaches to industrial democracy.

In the Soviet Union the question of worker control, or the role of workers in the management of state enterprises, was highly controversial during the early phases of the country's postrevolutionary experience. Various experiments begun during the first decade after the Revolution included direct control of enterprises by worker committees; power-sharing between relatively apolitical managers and party-selected workers; and shared management by state managers, local party officials, and trade union representatives.[19] However, with the advent of the First Five Year Plan, in 1929, these experiments were brought to an end. In tune with more autocratic political trends and Stalin's desire to clarify responsibility for production failures, control was then placed in the hands of state-appointed managers. To be sure, the managers' power was circumscribed by party and higher state officials. Yet the trade union apparatus was purged and its new leaders were warned against seeking to intervene in the running of industry. Instead, Stalin instructed the trade unions to confine themselves to encouraging workers to meet production goals and maintaining labor discipline.

Although the role of trade unions in Soviet industry has been expanded somewhat since the 1930s, the principle of excluding workers and their representatives from major roles in enterprise management has not been seriously challenged.[20] The trade unions now have some

---

[19] Jeremy Azrael, *Managerial Power and Soviet Politics* (Cambridge, Mass.: Harvard University Press, 1966), pp. 12–102; and Merle Fainsod, *How Russia Is Ruled* (Cambridge, Mass.: Harvard University Press, 1963), pp. 503–25.

[20] Adolf Sturmthal, *Workers Councils* (Cambridge, Mass.: Harvard University Press, 1964), pp. 87–139.

administrative and consultative responsibilities. The primary units of trade union organization are the factory and local committees. The members of these committees are elected by enterprise employees, though with local party officials taking an active part in putting together acceptable slates of candidates. The committees are responsible for administering such social measures as workmen's compensation, health insurance, old-age pensions, vacation pay, maternity leave, and worker housing assignments. Further, they are invested with the power to negotiate collective agreements with management. However, since there is no effective right to strike, and wage rates are determined largely by national-level decision-makers, the room for bargaining and maneuver is minimal.[21] Beyond these matters, such committees enjoy the right to advise and be consulted on issues affecting an enterprise's work force at periodic labor-management conferences. The manager maintains the authority to hire and fire, though disputes may be taken to such external bodies as state arbitration commissions and local party organs.

With some authority from Lenin's writings, Stalin began in the 1920s to declare direct worker control a heresy against Marxism-Leninism. This view was further developed in the 1950s under both Stalin and Khrushchev when Tito's Yugoslavia developed a version of such direct control in the aftermath of that country's departure from the Soviet camp.[22] Yugoslavia's trade unions have been given strong representational powers. All workers participate in referenda, and their representatives decide such basic issues as prices, production plans, and budgets. Yugoslavia can thus claim a considerable degree of genuine worker participation. Unfortunately, this record of industrial democracy has not been matched by a comparable development of democracy in that country's political system.

In the official Soviet view Yugoslavia's model is an extremist one which must not be emulated in the USSR or elsewhere in East-Central Europe. Although a more pragmatic approach has been taken by some Soviet commentators in recent years, it has been made clear to the bloc regimes that their experiments in economic reform should not emphasize worker control. In the absence of such warnings the East Germans might well have moved quite far in that direction.

---

[21] Roy Medvedev, *On Socialist Democracy* (New York: Alfred A. Knopf, 1975), pp. 260–66; Emily Brown, "The Local Union in Soviet Industry: Its Relations with Members, Party, and Management," and A. Piatakov, "The Purposes and Functions of Trade Unions in the USSR," in Harry Shaffer, ed., *The Soviet Economy* (New York: Appleton-Century-Crofts, 1963), pp. 223–40, 240–50; and Arvid Brodersen, *The Soviet Worker* (New York: Random House, 1965).

[22] See Gerry Hunnius, "Workers' Self-Management in Yugoslavia," in Hunnius et al., eds., *Workers' Control: A Reader on Labor and Social Change* (New York: Vintage Books, 1973), pp. 268–321; and Paul Lendvai, *Eagles in Cobwebs: Nationalism and Communism in the Balkans* (Garden City, N.Y.: Doubleday & Co., 1969), pp. 108–211.

The leaders of the German Democratic Republic did provide for expanded participation by worker's representatives as part of their economic reforms of the early 1960s. The employees of large-scale enterprises now elect production committees which, among other things, participate in devising and implementing the firms' annual and long-term development plans. Also, the same law which provided for the establishment of production committees stipulates that the 80-odd cartellike industry associations of enterprises in the same economic sectors install social councils to see to it that the associations' objectives do not conflict with those of society. Officials of the Free German Trade Union Federation are represented on these bodies. The roles of the production committees and social councils are primarily consultative, with power and responsibility retained by the state directors at the two levels of industrial organization.[23]

West Germany and Sweden: Advanced Approaches in Western Europe

Although no Western European country has implemented a complete system of worker codetermination in enterprises, West Germany and Sweden have taken the most advanced positions in that area. Through statutes, both countries provide or are committed to near-equality for worker representatives on certain policy-making bodies within certain firms.

In order to explain the role of workers in West Germany we must note certain special features of that country's economic organization. Corporations in the German Federal Republic exhibit a two-tiered management arrangement. Usually the shareholder and others select the members of a supervisory board, a body which meets periodically and has charge over broad policy matters. The supervisors, in turn, select individuals to serve on another collectivity, the management board, which is responsible for the day-to-day running of the business.[24]

Since 1951 the law has required that in the iron mining and steel industries the supervisory boards of corporations must be composed of equal numbers of shareholder and worker representatives plus a neutral figure agreeable to the two sides. The employee members are chosen by trade union bodies either by themselves or in consultation with plant-level works councils. In addition, the management board includes a labor director who cannot be appointed or dismissed with-

---

[23] David Childs, *East Germany* (New York: Frederick A. Praeger, 1969), pp. 130–33; and Thomas Bayliss, "Economic Reform as Ideology: East Germany's New Economic System," *Comparative Politics* 3 (January 1971): 211–29.

[24] Charles De Hoghton, ed., *The Company: Law, Structure, and Reform in Eleven Countries* (London: George Allen & Unwin, 1970), pp. 41–45, 366–68.

out the approval of the worker representatives on the supervisory board.[25] In other sectors of West German industry, a firm which employs over 500 workers is required by law to grant one third of the membership on its supervisory board to employee representatives. What is more, these positions are filled by direct vote of all the firm's employees.

This pattern will be taken several steps farther as a result of legislation approved in March 1976. The new law requires 50 percent worker representation on the supervisory boards of all firms with more than 2,000 employees. However, the measure does not go as far as the trade unions had wanted. One major concession, insisted on by the Free Democratic party, leaves the shareholders in control of selecting board chairmen and able to prevail when labor and the owners cannot find a basis for agreement.[26]

In addition to this strong position on managerial boards, West German workers are represented by their unions in the negotiation of collective bargaining agreements and by internal works councils which are formally independent of trade union organizations. All business establishments having at least 20 employees must provide for directly elected works councils. Until the original law was strengthened in 1971, the councils' activities included the following: supervising the observance of all laws, regulations, collective agreements, and individual contracts affecting employees; and taking part in decisions about working hours, employee behavior, and welfare and related matters when these are not covered by collective bargaining agreements. The councils, however, were criticized for becoming "talk shops," strong on rhetoric but weak when it came to asserting employee interests with management. Since 1971 the prerogatives of these units have been enhanced. Today, for example, employer decisions dealing with hiring, firing, and promotion must undergo advance scrutiny by the councils. Thus if a firm wishes to discharge an individual employee it must seek the council's consent. If this is not forthcoming, the case will be taken to a labor court for adjudication — with the affected person retaining his or her job until a ruling is made. And in planning major layoffs, the employer is now obliged to submit, well ahead of time, a social plan detailing how this is to be accomplished. If the works council's members object, a neutral arbitrator will be brought in to devise an appropriate formula.[27]

Until the present decade the Swedish labor movement, comprising

---

[25] Executive Board of the West German Trade Union Federation, "Co-Determination in the Federal Republic of Germany," in Hunnius et al., Workers' Control, pp. 194–210.

[26] International Herald Tribune, March 19, 1976, pp. 1, 2.

[27] Innis Macbeath, The European Approach to Worker-Management Relationships (New York: British–North American Committee, 1973), pp. 5–7.

both blue- and white-collar trade union federations, preferred to use the collective bargaining agreement as the basic instrument for the achievement of enterprise-centered worker objectives. Although the issue of direct worker participation in management had been discussed on and off since the 1920s, the unions' preference was for a clear division between management, from whom benefits were to be won, and labor, in whose name the unions bargained. But despite Sweden's impressive record of industrial peace and growing affluence, the prevailing sentiment has changed.[28]

As a reaction to a wave of wildcat strikes which began among miners in 1969, leaders of the blue-collar trade union federation (LO) adopted a program in 1971 calling for the democratization of companies through worker representation on their boards of directors. At first the LO sought to accomplish this objective by means of negotiation with the national employers' association. When its proposal was rejected, the LO in conjunction with its white-collar counterpart approached the government with a request that the goal be achieved through legislation. A 1973 act provides for worker representation on the directorial boards of all enterprises employing over 100 persons except banks and insurance companies. In 1976 the law was extended to all firms with 25 or more employees. Swedish unions are now authorized to appoint two board members to represent blue- and white-collar interests, respectively. Thus the board participation of worker representatives falls far short of codetermination and the West German arrangements. This limited approach was adopted in part because the unions feared that a greater role in management at the board level would diminish their ability to act as independent units in the collective bargaining process.

However, Sweden's unions and the Social Democratic government decided in 1976 to expand employee participation by seeking to achieve codetermination through a different route than those taken by West Germany and Yugoslavia. The new joint determination law, scheduled to become effective in 1977, requires management to accept the views of union representatives on all decisions concerning the organization of production and the setting of working conditions.[29] Management will not be able to hire, fire, or reallocate work without prior union consent. Thus Sweden has moved to create a new variation on both worker codetermination and collective bargaining that can be expected to provide at least as much industrial democracy as now exists in West Germany.

---

[28] Wilfred List, "In Sweden the Byword Is Cooperation," and Lars Karlsson, "Industrial Democracy in Sweden," in Hunnius et al., *Workers' Control*, 164–76, 176–92.

[29] *International Herald Tribune*, June 21, 1976, p. 9; and Erich Jacobs, *European Trade Unionism* (New York: Holmes & Meier, Publishers, 1974), pp. 73–74.

The potentialities of such changes in Swedish management-labor relations are indicated by recent internationally noted experiments in modifying assembly line routine in order to lessen worker alienation from work and employers.[30] Among other approaches, production tasks are rotated among workers and made more diverse. Studies indicate that individual employees gain a higher degree of job satisfaction through a feeling of greater personal autonomy and initiative. These reforms have been stimulated by the labor-management works councils.

France, Italy, and Britain: Ambivalent Labor Positions

France, Italy, and Britain have adopted cautious positions on the extension of industrial democracy through participation and codetermination. France and Britain have developed limited board-level participation by labor in the enterprises of their large public sectors. Italy has an advanced system of plant-level participation through works councils. However, in all three countries the unions have not been enthusiastic advocates of codetermination, and the governments have responded accordingly.

In the immediate wake of the liberation (1944–45) there was considerable enthusiasm in France for worker control of industry. Particularly in those sectors of French industry where the wartime managers had records of collaboration with the Nazis, worker committees assumed control of a significant number of enterprises. But shortly after the conclusion of hostilities, other views, notably Gaullist ones, prevailed. The worker committees were replaced by works councils whose prerogatives were almost exclusively consultative.

As a residue of this era of employee participation, union representatives and consumer advocates are to be found on the boards of directors of nationalized firms. The worker representatives are either directly elected by employees or appointed by the unions. But according to Sturmthal, the structure of control is such that basic decision-making power rests in the hands of government-selected managing directors who, in most instances, need not receive board approval for their actions.[31] As to private corporations, the workers are entitled by law only to send union observers to board meetings.

After the explosive student-worker uprising in the spring of 1968, French workers acquired new bargaining rights at the plant and enterprise level. Elected shop stewards have been authorized to negotiate with management as representatives of local union organizations. These changes were designed by de Gaulle to pacify discontented workers.

---

[30] Macbeath, *European Approach*, pp. 79–86.
[31] Sturmthal, *Workers Councils*, pp. 51–52.

However, they appear increasingly modest in relation to steps toward codetermination in West Germany and Sweden.

In Britain the labor movement has long approached participation with great skepticism. Yet worker participation has a foothold in the public sector and the British unions have recently moved to expand this considerably.

The British trade union movement has placed great emphasis on the collective bargaining agreement as the basic device for the attainment of worker objectives. For example, while in most Western European countries such matters as the length of paid vacations and the amount and duration of sick leave benefits are addressed by national legislation, in the United Kingdom they have been included under the scope of collective bargaining agreements.[32] And until recently union leaders have sought to strengthen worker influence within the enterprise through such agreements. Because collective bargaining has been a powerful tool for protecting British workers' interests, this has tended to downgrade joint management-worker bodies in enterprises.[33]

Yet this negative orientation has been changing. In 1967 the Trade Union Conference submitted a report to the Royal Commission on Trade Unions and Employers' Associations calling for revisions in the laws in order to encourage employee representation on the boards of private corporations. Following the renationalization of the steel industry in 1968, union-selected employees were appointed to that industry's four managing boards. Perhaps most significant, the Trade Union Conference has endorsed the principle of worker participation as embodied in a proposed European Communities company law and the Confederation of British Industry, the major employers' organization, has recorded itself in favor of a one-third presence for worker representatives on the boards of large firms.[34]

All of this movement does not assure new national law on behalf of participation. The unions have been promised a version of "closed shop" mandatory unionism and already command exceptional power within plants through union organizations built around the shop stewards. Given their frequently exercised ability to call brief work stoppages, their influence on management's labor practices has been formidable.[35] Joint labor-management production committees, obligatory in the public sector and voluntary in the private, have consultative

---

[32] Everett Kassalow, *Trade Unions and Industrial Relations: An International Comparison* (New York: Random House, 1969), pp. 130–34.

[33] *Economist*, March 24, 1973, pp. 66–67.

[34] *Economist*, March 13, 1976, p. 95.

[35] For an illustration taken from one firm see "Upstairs/Downstairs at the Factory," *Time*, September 15, 1975, pp. 58–69.

functions that add to labor's presence. If British labor decides to pause or retreat on the road to participation, this will probably be due to the strong available alternatives.

The situation in Italy resembles the French and British patterns. As in France, during and immediately after World War II the Italian anti-Fascist resistance movement and provisional government were dominated by forces—Communist, Socialist, and Christian Democratic— which were largely hostile to the interests of the traditional private business sector. In Italy these forces agreed to include in the new Constitution a loosely worded endorsement of worker participation (Article 46) that reads as follows:

> In order to promote the economic and social dignity of labor, and in harmony with the needs of production, the Republic recognizes the right of the workers to participate, in the ways and within the limits established by law, in the management of business enterprises.[36]

This article was not self-fulfilling, but required implementing legislation to make it effective. Although the provision was used to help legitimate works councils, to date no legislation has mandated worker representation on the boards of directors of either private or public enterprises.

This outcome is in part a reaction to the Mussolini regime's commitment to corporatist notions of worker-management collaboration. The Fascists viewed limited participation as an alternative to the institutionalization of class conflict. In the last days of Mussolini's regime a new law was promulgated which called for joint owner-employee-state management of large firms.[37]

Given this heritage, it is not surprising that the Marxist-oriented Italian labor movement has not pursued the idea of codetermination with much enthusiasm. Instead, the Italian union leadership, as is also true for its French counterpart, has sought to emulate the accomplishments of the British unions by broadening and strengthening the collective bargaining process, especially at the plant level. Since the late 1960s the Italian unions, through a succession of strike waves, have succeeded in wresting from management powers over work rules, hiring and firing practices, and profit allocation, and have negotiated wage and salary indexing agreements in many industries in the hope that such agreements will raise income levels at a rate fast enough to

[36] Mauro Cappelletti et al., *The Italian Legal System* (Stanford, Calif.: Stanford University Press, 1967), p. 291.

[37] F. W. Deakin, *The Brutal Friendship* (London: Weidenfeld and Nicholson, 1962), pp. 665–77.

keep up with price inflation. Thus the Italian unions are as powerful an influence in the country's economy as their British counterparts and a substantially stronger influence than the French labor movement.

The European Communities and the Acceleration of Industrial Democracy

The Commission of the European Communities has been developing a European company statute that would provide for rather extensive worker representation. Firms doing business within the nine member states will be offered the option of being voluntarily incorporated on a Community-wide basis rather than in any one member country. They would thereby be subject to a single and simplified set of operating rules.[38]

The draft statute contemplates a two-tiered management structure on the West German model. It proposes that one third of the seats on the supervisory board go to elected worker representatives, another third to shareholders, and the remaining third to independents chosen by the common agreement of the employer and worker representatives. Predictably, reactions to the proposed arrangement have been mixed. Some spokesmen for industry have cried "socialism," while the trade unionist responses have ranged from endorsement to "not enough" and "a capitalist trick." Thus the chances for ultimate approval by the member states are uncertain. But even if the European company law is not adopted in the form proposed by the Commission, the proposal will have served to accelerate the movement toward direct worker participation in management in several member states.

The United States: The Narrowest Approach

Among our six Western countries, the prospect for statutory or voluntary worker participation on corporate boards seems smallest in the United States. The demand for full industrial democracy was articulated at the beginning of this century by the Industrial Workers of the World (the "Wobblies") and other marginal left-wing groups. However, the American Federation of Labor and the Congress of Industrial Organizations, now combined, have consistently rejected worker participation in favor of collective bargaining.

American corporations, no less than those of Western Europe, are being confronted increasingly by expressions of employee dissatisfac-

---

[38] Edmund Fawcett, "European Companies," *European Community* 188 (July–August 1975): 3–7; Dennis Thompson, *The Proposal for a European Company* (London: Chatham House, 1969); and Campbell Balfour, *Industrial Relations in the Common Market* (London: Routledge & Kegan Paul, 1972).

tion with authoritarian work routines which were designed in an earlier era for poorly educated and unskilled labor forces. Numerous studies have shown a strong positive relationship among authoritarian workplace rules, lack of employee discretion, and poor worker morale and low productivity.[39]

As a result of such pressures and the example of European unions in the same industry, the progressive and independent United Automobile Workers has decided to seek representation on the board of directors of at least one major American auto manufacturer.[40] Further, some large firms have encouraged efforts at plant-level involvement of worker representatives in the allocation of work assignments. The managerial stimulus has come not so much from union locals imbued with a participatory ideology as from management's desire to reduce absenteeism and employee turnover and to increase productivity. Given the long-run advantages, it would appear that many more of these reformed labor practices will be adopted, with or without the involvement of the conventional trade union apparatus: shop stewards, grievance committees, and locals.

Notwithstanding these developments, few labor or business leaders have exhibited much interest in the concept of worker participation on executive boards. Legislation is not in the offing, and the United States will not be directly affected by such developments in the European Communities. However, some pressure for participation has been mounted on behalf of American consumers.

The lack of American leadership in industrial democracy appears surprising if we view industrial democracy as an aspect of post-industrial reform. The post-industrial status of the United States has been confirmed in various aspects of education, civil liberties, and pollution policies that are discussed in this book. Yet American workers have not gained substantial control over their workday or over employer decisions that lead to job losses and other vitally important outcomes.

This peculiar situation appears to be rooted in the limited horizons, sometimes compounded by corruption, of major figures in the U.S. labor movement. It also arises from the myth of uniquely generous American salary and other benefits, belief in which makes alternative processes and goals seem unnecessary. Yet American workers have not increased their job satisfaction in recent years and the outlook is for stronger pressures on labor and political leaders to take some initiatives beyond the present aims of higher salaries, fringe benefits, and

---

[39] David Jenkins, *Job Power: Blue and White Democracy* (Baltimore: Penguin Books, 1974), pp. 155–75.

[40] *International Herald Tribune*, May 15–16, 1976, p. 5.

union or closed shops. The collective bargaining process has been re-fined in regard to the indexing of wages and the binding arbitration of disputes. Yet little interest has been expressed in going beyond collective bargaining.

CONCLUSIONS

The modern business enterprise has been changing rapidly in its relationship to government, consumers, and employees. We have examined two of the most notable trends in public policy affecting firms and have found that in most of the surveyed countries great attention has been given to participation by workers in management and that the problem of maintaining competition among firms has become salient in much of Western Europe as well as in the United States.

It was found that in each of the countries with antitrust laws a major gap exists between paper commitments and the effectiveness of implementation. Even in the United States, West Germany, and Great Britain — the countries with the strongest legislation — public policy has not prevented either continued concentration within industries or concentration across industries through conglomerates.

Numerous reasons may be offered for this record, but the most apparent one is the awareness that large corporations can serve national needs by promoting export earnings, financing research and development, and resisting domination by foreign-based multinational enterprises. Other factors include the enormous difficulty of proving the anticompetitive motives of mergers, acquisitions, and acts of collaboration.

Given the continued interest of the European Commission and the U.S. Justice Department, competition policy will continue to be a central area of industrial policy development. Despite this increased attention, the trend toward progressively larger private and public enterprises appears likely to continue.

From our review of employee participation practices in the eight nations it seems clear that the center of current attempts at innovation, certainly as they pertain to executive-level decision-making, is in Western Europe. Despite traditions of class-based social and occupational distinctions, the impulse for change has come from West Germany, Sweden, and the EEC Commission rather than from the United States or the Soviet Union, the two industrial giants. Why should this be the case?

Interest group power relations can be held partly responsible in both instances. Trade unions are weaker in the Soviet Union than in any of the other seven countries. In the United States labor controls many congressional votes and can exert strong pressure on the Democratic party and Democratic presidents. Yet the proportion of unionized workers is low and the lack of party discipline limits the effectiveness of labor's political pressures.

Ideology also seems to be a likely influence.[41] Historically, the trade union movements in Western Europe have been heavily influenced by two sorts of doctrines which encourage worker participation. On the one hand, there have been the syndicalist, anarcho-syndicalist, and guild socialist doctrines, which have emphasized direct worker control of the firm as the central objective of working-class movements. On the other hand, and in contrast to these views promoting industrial conflict, there has been the social teaching of the Catholic church, with its stress on class reconciliation, social harmony, and the responsibilities of property. As expressed in the papal encyclicals *Rerum Novarum* and *Quadragesimo Anno,* and as manifested in the programs of Europe's Catholic unions and political parties, that teaching encourages amelioration of the socially destructive consequences of laissez-faire capitalism through peaceful consultation and the sharing of power between owners and workers.

These conceptions are largely missing from the Soviet and American experiences. Deriving from Lenin's doctrinal assumption of the proletariat's need for external leadership and Stalin's massive plans for industrialization, the crucial debate with respect to Soviet industrial management has been over how much power is to be exercised by party officials or national planners in relation to local managers of production establishments. After some early and unsuccessful experiments with worker control the idea was not only abandoned but transformed into a heresy. In the official Soviet view the workers do not need direct participation in management discussions because the state officials who direct the enterprises have no interests in conflict with their employees. This myth has been contested elsewhere in Eastern Europe. Yet the Soviet regime has thus far managed to resist emulation of developments in those countries.

The experience of the American labor movement offers something of a paradox because of American labor's early 20th century support for the doctrine of voluntarism. After early attempts to achieve labor's objectives through the political process failed, the AFL, under Samuel Gompers' leadership, adopted the position that the most effective route for the attainment of labor's goals was through union organizational efforts. The government was perceived not as a political ally but, based on past experience, as a likely enemy. Thus it was believed that linking the unions to a socialist or social democratic political party would prove fruitless.

---

[41] Daniel Bell, *The End of Ideology* (New York: Collier Books, 1961), pp. 355–92.

The U.S. experience has centered on the belated but successful effort of the post-1945 labor movement to win high wages for workers in organized industries through collective bargaining. The unions have been slow to enlarge their membership or to conceive new approaches to industrial relations. The Democratic party has been called on principally to help extend basic benefits and to undo Republican-sponsored restrictions on labor practices.[42] Corruption in the Teamsters Union and divisions among the AFL-CIO, Teamsters, and UAW components of the labor movement have contributed to a lack of interest in industrial democracy despite growing indications of alienation among young assembly line workers. Geographic and political isolation from European patterns of industrial democracy has also kept this issue area out of American politics.

Underlying each of these factors is the exceptional American attachment to long-established beliefs concerning the sanctity of private property and the legitimacy of private enterprise. This is associated with a widespread abhorrence of socialism and an emphasis on individual rather than class-centered social mobility. All of these elements have contributed to an approach that has been termed business unionism. Just as the company sells goods at the price that the market will bear, so the unions sell labor at a price decided by collective bargaining. To a greater extent than in Western Europe, American unions fear that participation or codetermination would place labor representatives in the contradictory roles of buyers and sellers of the same product.

Sweden and West Germany are notable for the strength of their labor organizations, for close union ties to the ruling political parties, and for the absence of ideological barriers to innovative approaches to greater worker power. France, Britain, and Italy differ from Sweden and West Germany in one or more of these respects. Yet, partly as a result of West German leadership in the European Communities, they will also see important movement toward industrial democracy within the next several years.

Let us raise a final question: To what extent do participation and codetermination offer a meaningful solution to the problems posed for society by large-scale enterprise? These modes of industrial democracy offer the possibility that workers, as citizens of a firm, will have a voice in the formulation of its policies. But the enterprise's constituents, those who are affected significantly by its actions, include such other segments of the population as the consumers of its products and the victims of its pollutants. At present, these constituents may affect the firm's policies through the marketplace and governmental regulation.

---

[42] J. David Greenstone, *Labor in American Politics* (New York: Vintage Books, 1969), pp. 25–29.

Yet without direct representation of such groups in management, all the objectives of industrial democracy cannot be achieved.

Moreover, as anyone who owns a few shares in a vast corporation can attest, the ability to vote for members of its board of directors does not result in very much control over the firm's policies. Now shareholders may lose some of their limited influence as a result of increased employee power. Workers' lives are more intimately linked to the fate of their employer than is the life of the average shareholder. Yet more should be done in the Western democracies to protect and expand the influence of small shareholders.

Finally, what if the worker representatives on a management board come to view the firm's problem from the perspective of efficiency, production, and cost-consciousness rather than from the perspective of worker interests? For instance, and this is a recurring theme in the Western European debate, suppose the firm's products were not selling well enough to justify current employment or salary levels. How would or should the worker representatives vote on layoffs, salary reductions, and the like? No totally satisfactory answer to this problem seems to be available. Yugoslavia has pioneered in the use of such devices as voted recall of representatives. Other devices of direct democracy could also be employed. Yet the basic problems of allocating benefits and deprivations among workers would remain.

11 Protecting the Environment: Pollution Control Policy

Protection of the physical environment involves a common human need that is rarely matched in other issue areas. All of us, regardless of geographic, political, and social subdivisions, are threatened by some of the same dangers to our survival. Industrial pollution, nuclear catastrophe, natural disasters, the spread of disease, imbalances between population and needed sustenance—these are still among the most elemental human problems and policy issues of our time.

We focus here on a dimension of this area of policy that is associated with industrialization to a high degree and is closely tied to the questions of scale and the control of enterprises that were addressed in Chapter 10. We refer to the tendencies of the industrialization process and post-industrial patterns of resource use and abuse to threaten the physical environment. In order to narrow the subject to a manageable scope, we emphasize air and water pollution problems and provide only brief references to such other aspects of environmental protection as noise, working conditions, and land use.

INTERNATIONAL POLLUTION REGULATION

As noted in Chapter 3, pollution control has been a policy area that has benefited considerably from a wide range of multinational influences. It would be easy to argue that such processes have been too little and too late. Yet in no other sphere have the governments of both industrial and developing nations depended as much on international forces for stimulation and expertise.

These multinational influences range from bilateral intergovernmental treaties to major multilateral conventions and the varied activities of numerous international organizations. The substantial growth of regional approaches is indicated by the existence of more than 200 international agreements concerning control over water use and pollution in rivers and lakes which border more than one country.[1] For example, the United States is party to an agreement with Canada which commits both nations to clean up the Great Lakes. What is more, environmental control treaties cut across ideological camps. Thus the European nations bordering the Baltic Sea, including West Germany, Sweden, East Germany, and the Soviet Union, signed an agreement in 1973 to minimize pollution damage in order to preserve the "live resources" of that body of water. Extraregional bilateral cooperation is reflected in agreements by the United States and the Soviet Union, as one relatively cost-free manifestation of détente, to cooperate in this sphere by exchanging scientists and technological information and by undertaking joint research projects.[2]

Numerous international conventions, open for ratification by all nations, seek to protect the earth's environment from various pollution hazards. One notable illustration of this sort of international law is the 1963 convention banning nuclear testing in the atmosphere, underwater, and in outer space, a document to which all countries in our analysis, except France, have adhered. Other conventions seek to prevent pollution of the seas by oil and various wastes, to end the manufacture and stockpiling of bacteriological and toxin weapons, and to block a variety of other threats to human survival.

A number of international organizations, global and regional, have taken an active role in promoting pollution-control policies by stimulating discussion and research, monitoring pollution levels, passing resolutions, and drafting treaties and conventions for adoption by their members. Beginning in 1968 the United Nations broadened its consid-

---

[1] Samuel Bleicher, "An Overview of International Environmental Regulation," *Ecology Law Quarterly* 2, no. 1 (Winter 1972): 31.

[2] James Barros and Douglas Johnston, *The International Law of Pollution* (New York: Free Press, 1974), pp. 332–35.

eration of physical environmental issues. After several years of debate, planning, and preliminary meetings, a UN Conference on the Human Environment was held at Stockholm in 1972 which, despite extensive disagreement between the representatives of rich and poor nations, produced a report containing a long series of recommendations for promoting national and UN action.[3] One of the Conference's principal outgrowths was the establishment of a specialized agency, the United Nations Environmental Program (UNEP), to assist in the coordination of international environmental policy-making.

Beyond this expanding UN role, many regional organizations have recently become involved with the problem. The Soviet-bloc Council for Mutual Economic Assistance (CMEA) has approved a Comprehensive Integration Program which provides for the collaboration of member states in the protection of the environment. Several "coordination centers" have been created to investigate CMEA-wide pollution problems.[4]

In the industrialized West, the Council of Europe, the European Communities, the Organization for Economic Cooperation and Development, and even the North Atlantic Treaty Organization have all, in varying degrees, taken up the cause of environmental protection. This involvement has produced several tangible results. For one, the Council of Europe's Consultative Assembly passed a European Water Charter in 1969.[5]

The strongest regional authority lies in the European Communities. With powers based on the Economic Community's Treaty of Rome, the Commission has been able to apply regulations binding on all member governments and firms. Thus in 1972 the EEC was able to impose common standards on automobile exhaust emissions and on the production of detergents. During the following year a broad environmental action program was adopted and a permanent working group, the Conference of Senior Government Advisers on Environmental Problems, was established to oversee its implementation.[6]

Although the involvement of various international bodies in the promotion of multinational pollution-control policy is unquestionably desirable, this activity suffers from certain deficiencies and handicaps.

[3.] "World Environmental Newsletter," *World* 1, no. 2 (June 1972); and *Report of the United Nations Conference on the Human Environment* (New York: United Nations, 1973).

[4] B. Gorizontov, "Collaboration of COMECON Countries in the Protection of the Environment and the Utilization of Natural Resources," *Problems of Economics* 9 (1974): 37–59.

[5] Council of Europe, *The Management of the Environment in Tomorrow's Europe* (Strasbourg: European Information Center for Nature Conservation, 1971).

[6] "World Environmental Newsletter," *World,* September 12, 1972; and "Programme of Environmental Action of the European Communities," *Bulletin of the European Communities* (March 1973).

Perhaps the most visible shortcoming has to do with the division of the world's nations into those which are already industrialized versus those which aspire to industrialization. Representatives of many of the less developed countries view the imposition of pollution-control restrictions as costly impediments to the achievement of their national economic objectives. After all, they contend, the advanced countries went through the process of industrial growth without paying very much attention to its destructive effects on the environment. Now that these advanced nations are concerned with the problem they are asking, in effect, that poor countries with many other developmental problems also bear the costs of environmental control. On the basis of such reasoning Brazil, with one of the fastest-growing economies in the Third World, refused to participate in the UN's Stockholm Conference.

Although the leaders of the industrializing nations do not all subscribe to the foregoing definition of the situation—Singapore is a notable exception—enough of them perceive the situation in this way to produce "pollution havens."[7] Countries with minimal environmental restrictions become attractive locations for multinational firms unwilling to operate plants in nations which have been inclined to make pollution-control requirements a cost of doing business. To be sure, there are pressures going the other way. For example, Third World countries in which tourism is a major industry are sometimes reluctant to become pollution havens for fear of the impact on the flow of visitors.

Hypothetically, the problem that pollution havens represent could be met through an acceleration of international regulation. If uniform environmental standards could be devised and enforced, or if, in their absence, compensatory import duties could be imposed on goods produced in nations with weak controls, the production cost advantages now operating to stimulate pollution havens could be reduced. But given the existence of conflicting national interests, based on differing levels of economic development, the chances of achieving this goal are not very great.

The above discussion points to another and related problem with international regulatory policy: national sovereignty. Although there is a general rule of international law according to which a state which damages the citizens or property of another state is liable, the existing enforcement procedures are usually either cumbersome (for example, taking the case to the International Court of Justice) or ad hoc and dependent on the goodwill of the offending party.

---

[7] Cynthia Enloe, *The Politics of Pollution in a Comparative Perspective* (New York: David McKay Co., 1975) pp. 111–41.

Several examples of independent national action illustrate the current limitations on international regulation. Until President Giscard d'Estaing's recent and temporary decision to suspend atmospheric nuclear bomb testing, France had conducted a series of such tests in the South Pacific during the 1960s and the early 1970s. The explosions were carried out over the repeated protests of such nations as Australia and Japan and despite the existence of an international convention seeking to ban such environmentally harmful experiments. China continues to ignore the convention, and it appears likely that other nations will follow Peking's course. In another area, France, Britain, and the Soviet Union have ignored strong warnings from scientists in various countries and have built and promoted supersonic commercial aircraft. Moreover, in 1974 France refused to stop dumping salts from its potassium mines into the heavily polluted Rhine River, thus frustrating the cleanup efforts of the five other countries through which it flows. In the face of such national behavior, there is little that international regulatory bodies can do at present.

Finally, the pattern of international environmental regulation has been piecemeal and uneven. The attempt to regulate waterborne effluent has been more extensive and has proceeded at a faster pace than the effort to control the no less damaging air-carried emissions. But even as regards the former, there is the inevitable problem of enforcement in a situation of competing national sovereignties. In 1972, for instance, 12 European states which border the North Sea and the North Atlantic signed an agreement to curb the dumping of waste products into those bodies. However, the nations involved created no supranational machinery to monitor compliance. National policies as such must be viewed as the core of pollution control.

NATIONAL POLLUTION CONTROL POLICIES: AN OVERVIEW

The Stages of Development

Although it is clear that the eight countries in our analysis vary in the extent and vigor with which they have sought to deploy and enforce environmental control measures, it also seems true that their attempts at regulation tend, over time, to go through roughly similar stages of development. We are not suggesting that national policies go through these stages at the same time or at the same pace, even though it is evident that the late 1960s and the early 1970s have been the peak years to date of environmental concern for most national policy-makers. Rather, it is our view that a common dynamic has pushed the various national environmental policies through roughly similar phases of historical experience which have been related to, but not exclusively caused by, when and how fast the nations involved went through the process of industrialization.

During the first stage the policy focus is on conservation and public health.[8] Either by royal decree, as in czarist Russia, or through national legislation, as during Theodore Roosevelt's Administration in the United States, areas of natural beauty or historical significance are set aside and foreclosed to economic development. Further, as a result of soil erosion, deforestation, and the damage to agricultural cultivation caused by periodic floods and droughts, projects are undertaken to conserve a nation's primarily renewable natural resources so as to more rationally exploit their potential. As compared to public health policies, such conservationism usually involves national-level decisions and budgetary allocations.

Although this early conservationist focus was essentially rural in character and not always related to industrialization, the public health concern was clearly rooted in urban industrial development. Thus, as Ridgeway observes about England:

> The laboring people who packed into towns during the nineteenth century lived in abominable conditions. The drinking water was foul, and drainage for sewage and garbage was often nonexistent. Of fifty large towns, only six had a good supply of water. In London, where nine companies controlled the water supplies, three quarters of a million poor people begged or stole their drinking water for want of money to buy it. People hauled water for miles, oftentimes collecting it from ditches.[9]

Under these circumstances it should come as no surprise that diseases such as cholera reached epidemic levels. Charles Dickens' novels are illustrative here. Thus public sanitation and communicable disease prevention became crucial public policy concerns.

In some countries nationwide measures were undertaken to cope with this problem, such as Britain's succession of public health acts, beginning in 1846. However, since the immediate impact was felt initially at the local level, the first policy responses tended likewise to be municipal. Hence we witness the enactment of community ordinances attempting to regulate and control land use, garbage collection, and sewage treatment. The intent of either the national or local decision-makers was to maintain a sufficiently sanitary environment to prevent the spread of disease.

---

[8] James Ridgeway, The Politics of Ecology (New York: E. P. Dutton & Co., 1970) pp. 18–69; Earl Murphy, Governing Nature (Chicago: Quadrangle Books, 1970), pp. 4–121; and William Berbert, "The Historical Framework of Environmental Politics" (paper prepared for Duquesne University History Forum, Pittsburgh, October 1971), pp. 1–18.

[9] From The Politics of Ecology by James Ridgeway. Copyright © 1970 by James Ridgeway. Reprinted by permission of the publisher, E. P. Dutton & Co., Inc.

Public health implementation and enforcement practices during this stage also exhibit certain commonalities. For one thing, there is an emphasis on private and local governmental remedies. Under both Common and Roman Law systems, individuals whose property or person was damaged because of the polluting actions of other persons or of enterprises sought as plaintiffs before the courts to have nuisances abated and/or to receive monetary compensation. Municipal governments often resorted to this type of tactic as well. In addition, whether the level at which public health rules were written was national, intermediary, or local, there was a strong tendency to rely on voluntary compliance, with relevant parties informed of the regulations and the potential penalties for violating them, but then not compelled to take the necessary ameliorative steps.

The next stage in the evolution of environmental protection policy is reached as the result of diverse stimuli. Jurisdictional conflicts between, say, upstream polluters and downstream users of a watercourse lead to the realization that local regulations will not suffice. There is a felt need for national intervention as environmental protection becomes a national political issue. Several things typically happen to put the issue on a nation's policy agenda. There may be one or several dramatic incidents—a killer smog in London or Los Angeles, an oil spill in the Santa Barbara Channel, the pollution-caused corrosion of centuries-old sculpture in Venice—which attract public attention and create alarm. When scientists, other private environmental advocates, and issue-seeking politicians or government advisers link the disturbing events to their sources, reaching a broad public or a national policy-making elite, action is at least possible.

Typically the action taken involves the formulation and deployment of a series of separate national laws on water, air, and other types of pollution. Enforcement authority is then invested in various national ministries, departments, and agencies which, in conjunction with subnational bodies, are supposed to see to it that the policies are executed.

The effort to apply the new regulations frequently creates enormous administrative problems. There is a lack of coordination, with different bureaucratic entities uncertain about where their jurisdictions end and the jurisdictions of others begin. Moreover, the authorities with new pollution-control responsibilities often retain conflicting missions in economic development. The appropriate Russian proverb has it that the goats are now asked to guard the cabbage patch. For example, a ministry of agriculture whose main task has been the stimulation of food production finds itself in the position of having to limit the use of particular pesticides and herbicides that enhance crop yields. The outcome of this sort of conflict over objectives is often weak pollution-control enforcement, coupled with a kind of institutional schizophrenia.

Dissatisfaction with this piecemeal approach to environmental regulation is frequently accompanied by a growing awareness of the interconnectedness of pollution problems. Scientists brought in to help establish program standards, outside critics of existing practices, and the practical difficulties evoked by the enforcement effort all contribute to a broader ecological perspective. A third stage is reached when there is a governmental response to the difficulties of the second stage.

Administratively, the third stage is characterized by the establishment of a separate organization within the national government to oversee and coordinate pollution-control policy. Many offices, agencies, and bureaus that were previously located in diverse ministries are now brought together under a single overall rubric. In some countries, as in France under Pompidou or in Great Britain during the Conservative Heath government, a new cabinet-level department of the environment is installed. In other nations a functionally specialized lead agency, below the cabinet level, is created to perform the task of coordination. The establishment of the Environmental Protection Agency under the Nixon Administration is an example of the latter approach.

The policy-making perspective during the third stage of development is more broadly ecological. The predominant view, in accordance with which policy is formulated, has it that resource conservation, public health concerns, air and water pollution, solid waste disposal, and land use control are all parts of a whole, segments of an overall environmental problem. Therefore, the impulse is toward comprehensive and integrated environmental planning.

There are other tangible indications during this period that governments take environmental problems seriously. Budgetary allocations for relevant control programs are increased significantly, often at the expense of other policy objectives. Furthermore, enforcement practices are strengthened. Industrial and governmental polluters and resource users become aware that the new regulations require the alteration of long-established patterns through, for example, the installation of new equipment or manufacturing techniques and the diversion of monetary resources to pollution-control purposes. What is more, violators become aware that they will be punished, routinely, for failure to comply with the law.

The fourth and, to date, final stage in the evolution of environmental protection policy is one of retrenchment. Most of the Western countries in our study moved into or toward the third stage in the late 1960s or early 1970s. Those were the years of prosperity and high employment that preceded the onset of the energy crisis. It seems apparent that by the mid-1970s priorities had changed. Many national policy-makers are now preoccupied with reviving economic growth, reducing unemployment, and exploiting domestic energy sources, and the consequent tendency has been to relax or weaken control standards. Although the retrenchment has not typified all national policy outlooks—Sweden does not appear to have followed this path—it nevertheless seems fair to say that for many nations a noticeable decline of enthusiasm has occurred among both decision-making elites and mass publics. On the other hand, even in the countries where decline has set in, the advances achieved earlier have not all been wiped out. Nor does it seem likely that the fundamental problems will go away.

Potential Sources of Policy Variation

By arguing that different national environmental control policies tend to pass through similar stages of development, we have accentuated the shared experiences of the eight nations. All have large industrial sectors, and all have become aware of threats to the air, water, and other elements in their environments. Yet the various national efforts to reduce pollution and regulate the environment exhibit some rather meaningful differences, especially as regards the implementation of programs and the enforcement of rules. What are the likely sources of these variations?

First, an obvious source of policy differences is the severity of the pollution problem in a given country. At least with respect to industrial production, observers suggest that the more sophisticated the industrial process, the greater is the environmental hazard. Although some older industries are highly pollutive, the manufacture of synthetic fibers generates more contaminants than does the manufacture of cotton. Modern petrochemical and metallurgical industries are major offenders. In the third stage technology can be focused on the reduction of pollution produced through basic and advanced industrial processes. But in no country has the pollution-control capability of technology yet matched its overall pollution-producing influence.

From a global perspective, all eight countries in this survey should be regarded as highly industrialized. Yet, as noted in Chapter 4, major variations exist in their levels of technological advancement. For example, the United States deployed an array of sophisticated and highly polluting industries earlier than did the Soviet Union, and it has taken a great lead over the Soviet Union in regard to private automobiles. As a result of such factors, a substantially smaller quantity of air pollutants is emitted annually in the USSR than in the United States.[10]

---

[10] Donald Kelley, Kenneth Stunkel, and Richard Wascott, *The Economic Superpowers and the Environment: The United States, the Soviet Union, and Japan* (San Francisco: W. H. Freeman, 1976), pp. 65–66.

Some observers, notably from Communist-ruled countries, stress the importance of ideology. From the Marxist-Leninist viewpoint, pollution and the desecration of the environment are inevitable consequences of the private ownership of the means of production. Capitalists are motivated by the desire to maximize profits and minimize costs to the exclusion of all other considerations. Where the use of air and water in the production process are cost-free, the private entrepreneur will have no incentive to economize on their use. He will therefore use them, for example, as repositories for waste by-products. In this way the costs of cleaning up the ensuing pollution are externalized, becoming social costs which must be borne by the community. Alternatively, the argument continues, when ownership of the means of production is socialized, this logic no longer applies. When the people, through the state, are the owners, there is a reconciliation of the interests of the producers and of society. The public interest in the curtailment of environmentally harmful pollution is incorporated, as a high priority value, within the decision-making structure of enterprises.

How valid are these observations? First, irrespective of the ideological forecasts to the effect that "it can't happen here," the Communist leaders recognize that pollution problems exist in their own countries as well as in capitalist countries. Second, the seriousness with which various governments enforce pollution-control policies seems to vary independently of ideological bloc membership. Among capitalist nations, Sweden's performance has been good whereas Italy's has not. And on the other side, East Germany's enforcement record appears more praiseworthy than that of the Soviet Union's.[11] Furthermore, the ideological distinction built around the notion of externalized pollution costs is far from being clear-cut in practical terms. Thus air and water are generally regarded as free goods in the Soviet Union, and there has been little effort to apportion the costs of cleaning up pollution among the production establishments responsible for generating it. The incentive structure for Soviet factory managers does not encourage environmental restraint; bonuses and promotions go to those who meet or exceed production goals, regardless of the environmental consequences. On the other hand, in several capitalist countries the recent thrust of environmental policy planners has been toward finding fiscal devices by which pollution costs can be internalized and thus made part of the overall cost calculations of private producers.

A few ideology-related differences produce advantages for Eastern European systems. Communist-ruled states benefit from the inclina-

---

[11] Marshall Goldman, *The Spoils of Progress: Environmental Pollution in the Soviet Union* (Cambridge, Mass.: MIT Press, 1972).

tion of their decision-makers to downplay the production of private consumer goods. To the extent, for instance, that Communist systems emphasize the use of mass transportation as against the private automobile, with the latter's obvious role in raising air pollution levels, they would seem to have an advantage. Such systems also place enormous power in the state planning apparatus with respect to such environmentally sensitive issues as natural resource use and the zoning of industrial and residential housing. When such power is used to protect the environment, there is little that can stand in its way. However, at least in the Soviet Union there has been little inclination to use the planning machinery with this end in mind until quite recently.

There may be something positive to be said for private ownership and capitalism in the cause of environmental protection. Given the propensity of people to protect property they own more vigorously than property they do not own, the public is likely to demand that the government act to prevent damage to private property before it acts on behalf of public holdings. In addition, capitalist systems have the advantage of long experience with the use of prices as measures of scarcity relationships among commodities, and to the degree that price calculations are pertinent in assigning and internalizing pollution costs this experience is likely to prove very useful. Communist-ruled systems are latecomers here. For ideological reasons centering on the labor theory of value, prices have been assigned to goods without direct consideration of the costs of production.

Beyond these ideological considerations, several cultural factors seem to help account for the varying national commitments to environmental protection. One such factor may be the extent to which the underlying cultural values and popular attitudes of a given national population facilitate or retard environmental protection.[12] For instance, in the heavily industrialized English Midlands it is frequently said that "muck is money." That is, when smokestacks are emitting great quantities of soot, or slag heaps are building up to substantial heights, industry is prospering and there is full employment. When such beliefs are widespread, the pollution-control cause is bound to suffer.

Important cultural values in at least some of the eight nations apparently support environmental regulation. Observers of Swedish society, for example, note the existence of deep-seated beliefs in the intrinsic beauty of nature, the values of science, and the desirability of collective social action.[13] Public opinion studies of Swedish attitudes on environmental control seem to reflect these underlying values.

---

[12] Enloe, *Politics of Pollution*, pp. 13–21.

[13] Richard Tomasson, *Sweden: Prototype of Modern Society* (New York: Random House, 1970) pp. 271–92.

Thus a 1969 poll revealed that close to 70 percent of Swedes favored an increase in local taxes for the purpose of fighting water pollution.[14]

Conversely, observers of the French and Italian societies report the presence of certain cultural themes which we would expect to reduce national commitments to effective environmental regulation. We have in mind the absence of a strong spirit of civic-mindedness which would encourage people to cooperate in antilitter campaigns and ventures of that character.

Several parallels between traditional Soviet and American attitudes toward nature may have an impact on pollution-control enforcement. In particular, for both nations popular perceptions of nature were affected by the countries' enormous size and seemingly limitless natural resources. The derivative belief in the inexhaustibility of the environment, coupled with strong emphases on industrial development, is hardly supportive of control efforts. To be sure, some values may cut both ways. Although a belief in the uses of technology to promote material well-being and rapid economic growth may have negative environmental consequences, such a view may also help stimulate innovation and production in the field of pollution-control equipment.

The social structure of a particular country contributes both to the severity of the pollution problems and to the development of policy responses. Nations with a large middle class produce more energy-intensive goods and generate more waste than do countries with a predominantly lower-class population. Fortunately, the higher educational level of the middle class contributes to earlier and more intensive support for environmental protection.

It may also be argued that some characteristics of political systems evoke variations in antipollution enforcement. In terms of governmental structure, we would expect public bureaucracies with long-standing reputations for honesty and general effectiveness to be better at environmental regulation.[15] In this connection, we should point out that the Italian public administration, which has a horrendous reputation, recently reported "losing" several million dollars which international organizations had contributed to help save Venice from further deterioration. And during the 1973 cholera epidemic in Naples, an outbreak caused by the consumption of infected shellfish from the polluted bay, public health officials contributed to civil disturbances by not having enough vaccine on hand to immunize worried citizens.[16]

---

[14] Lennart Lundqvist, "Environmental Policy and Administration in a Unitary State: Sweden," in *Organization and Administration of Environmental Programmes* (New York: United Nations, 1974), p. 127.

[15] Robert Putnam, "The Political Attitudes of Senior Civil Servants in Western Europe: A Preliminary Report," *British Journal of Political Science* 3, no. 3 (July 1973): 257–90.

[16] William Murray, "Report from Naples," *New Yorker,* August 26, 1974, pp. 55–65.

The effective application of pollution-control policies requires co-ordination between national and subnational governmental units. Therefore, political systems in which regional and municipal governments are either weak and inept or hostile and resistant to national initiatives would seem unlikely to do a good job. To the extent that federal systems, such as are found in the United States, West Germany, and Switzerland, promote vigorous subnational governmental activity, they are likely to create institutions with the necessary tools to perform essential regulatory tasks. On the other hand, as evidence from these countries suggests, federal structures may also impede coordination by stimulating jurisdictional jealousies and constitutional conflicts.[17] Alternatively, in unitary systems having extended traditions of bureaucratic centralization, as in France and Italy, local governing bodies may be so atrophied in their powers or so lacking in financial resources that they are unable to respond effectively to national initiatives.

We might hypothesize that political systems with independent mass media, autonomous interest group organizations, and strong oppositional political parties would be more likely to respond to popular pressures for effective antipollution rules than would authoritarian systems with relatively poor feedback mechanisms. Much as we might expect this to be the case, it does not necessarily follow. The hypothesis assumes that popular pressures will inevitably push decision-makers in a proenvironmentalist direction. Yet this is not always the case. Although procedures for accurately registering public sentiment may promote the pollution problem into a visible political issue, they may also report conflicting preferences. For example, U.S. television pictures showing long lines of irate motorists at gas stations may have encouraged politicians to weaken controls on offshore drilling or strip mining in order to expand energy sources. The underlying attitudes themselves rather than the structures which report them may be of greater significance.

Finally, the patterns of interest group power can be expected to have a major impact once the physical environment emerges as a major policy area. Although all gain from a clean and healthy environment, the politics of pollution directly affects the allocation of costs and the distribution of benefits in regard to jobs, production, and other values. Industrial interests resist changes that they cannot pass on to consumers. Yet some companies recognize that pollution control is itself an industry and others can derive a competitive advantage from industry-wide investments. Labor is often split over environmental issues, seeking to balance the benefits of greater health and safety with the threat of short-term loss of employment. Farmers seek to protect the

---

[17] Enloe, *Politics of Pollution*, p. 101.

availability and utility of agricultural land, but often defend questionable uses of chemicals.

Policy Options

A limited number of policy alternatives have been considered thus far by decision-makers seeking curtailment of pollution. Most systems use fiscal or monetary levers to promote improvement in air and water quality. Two broad patterns fall under this rubric: the "pay the polluter" and the "polluter pays" principles.[18] The first and more widely used approach involves direct or indirect payments by the state to private or public entities in an attempt to induce them to abate their pollution-causing activities. Here we have in mind such measures as direct grants to local governments and industrial establishments to subsidize the purchase and installation of suitable equipment: for example, giving localities money to defray the costs of primary- and secondary-level sewage treatment facilities. The pay the polluter principle may also be applied through manipulation of the tax laws. In many nations enterprises are given tax advantages, in the form of write-offs and depreciation allowances, when they use prescribed anti-pollution devices to meet specified emission and effluent standards.

Analysts, most often economists, argue that paying the polluter has a number of serious drawbacks. One major objection is the enormous public costs which are typically involved.[19] Related to this argument is the view that paying the polluter is highly inequitable, with the community in effect bribing the polluter, with public funds which could be used for other programs, to stop doing things which should not have been permitted in the first place. Further, this approach has been criticized for being inefficient. Given attendant information-gathering problems, the polluter may have an incentive to overestimate the costs involved in order to receive greater benefits. In addition, since payments and tax breaks are usually given for the installation and use of relatively specific equipment, there is often little incentive for an enterprise to alter its production techniques or switch to alternative and less environmentally hazardous raw materials, procedures which might be less costly in the long run.

The second approach, to which many economists are attracted, is the polluter pays principle. The most frequently employed but usually less than effective implementation of this approach is the fine. Often

---

[18] *The Polluter Pays Principle* (Paris: OECD, 1975), pp. 28–34.

[19] Allen Kneese and Charles Schultze, *Pollution, Prices, and Public Policy* (Washington, D.C.: Brookings Institution, 1975), pp. 69–84.

an industrial air or water user, after suitable warnings, will be fined for not reducing pollution discharges to the prescribed levels. Fines as used in the United States and the Soviet Union, for example, are remedial rather than preventive measures and are typically unrelated to the amount of environmental damage being inflicted on the community by the polluter. In several countries it is cheaper for an enterprise to absorb the cost of the fine than to comply with the antipollution regulation. Clearly, this is not what the economists have in mind.

Advocates of the polluter pays principle see it as a means for shifting the total costs of pollution from the external community to the source, the polluter. This involves assessing and levying charges on the polluting enterprise equivalent to the amount of damage it is doing to the surrounding environment. This prevents the firm from treating the use of air and water in the production process as cost-free and compels it to enter the charges for their use into cost of production calculations. There is then an automatic incentive to economize on the use of air and water resources so as to reduce discharges to tolerable levels.

Yet the approach is hardly problem-free. A crucial difficulty in applying the polluter pays principle has to do with the determination of appropriate charges. If secondary or remote effects of pollution are to be measured, the problem becomes exceedingly complex. The principle has been used most often to combat water pollution because it is technically easier to arrive at rational cost calculations for water pollution than for air pollution. It is possible that charges for air and water use will be passed along to consumers, in the form of higher prices, unless this is specifically prohibited. Industry-wide costs will inevitably show up in prices, but those of specific high-pollution enterprises should not.

The next cluster of antipollution policies involves the imposition of direct governmental controls. These are usually but not invariably employed together with some form of monetary incentive. We have in mind here permits, licenses, environmental impact statements, decrees, ordinances, and other legal restraints. A requirement that no new plant be permitted to go into operation until it has installed appropriate pollution-control equipment, a rule which bars certain toxic chemicals from being manufactured in particular sections of a country, and a decree prohibiting the sale of automobiles without catalytic converters after a specified date, would all be illustrations of direct controls. In one form or another, and in combination with different sorts of monetary inducements, such controls are perhaps inevitable. Nonetheless, the effectiveness of direct controls is dependent on the ability of various public agencies to apply appropriate standards to a range of problems of enormous complexity and uncertainty. Frequently this must be done in situations where there is a significant time lag between the point at which the rule is applied and the date at which its impact, in terms of pollution reduction, can be assessed accurately. Then, too, effective enforcement requires that the agencies applying the direct controls resist a host of pressures from the public, industrial managers, and other governmental bodies for a general relaxation of standards or greater flexibility in their application to particular cases.

Despite these difficulties, the policies currently deployed by our eight nations to control air and water pollution are almost all composed of different mixes of direct controls and monetary levers. With this perspective in mind, we will now examine the central characteristics of air and water pollution control in the eight nations.

VARIATIONS IN THE EIGHT STATES

Pollution control is more difficult to evaluate than are most other policy areas. Measurements are often unreliable and are rarely comparable on a cross-national basis. We can compare the eight survey nations in regard to basic elements of what we termed stage three policy development. But the whole of such policies is usually greater than or different from the sum of such parts as whether the given country has developed a consolidated or lead agency, passed new laws which recognize the interrelationships among environmental factors, applied strong and innovative enforcement mechanisms, and resolved conflicts among interest groups and the various levels of government. It is perhaps most important to discover whether a given political system means business when it drafts and implements its policy instruments. We shall seek to offer some comparisons for each of these aspects of national policies.

All eight countries have recently introduced or revised statutes or regulations that seek to take a broader and tougher approach to air and water pollution. However, Italy has not yet approved a broad statute to protect its highly vulnerable water resources. The most comprehensive approaches to legislation have been taken in Sweden, the United States, and East Germany, each of which has passed since 1968 omnibus environmental protection acts that both contributed to the consolidation of government authority and set broad standards for enforcement. Each of these countries has also developed separate legislation for particular aspects of air and water pollution control. France, Britain, and West Germany have depended on revisions of more narrowly focused legislation, and the Soviet Union depends on centrally promulgated "fundamental principles" which must be elaborated in administrative decrees and republic-level enactments.

The effectiveness of such laws and regulations can be greatly increased if they are implemented within the context of national economic planning. This appears to be most advanced in France and East Germany, though Sweden and the Soviet Union also link environmental and economic planning and the United States comes closer to a planning approach in such areas as water, air, and energy than in broader economic matters.

We have suggested that advanced environmental control requires the coordinating and innovating role of a dominant or lead agency. No country places all environmental responsibilities in a single structure. Yet France, Great Britain, and East Germany have established ministries with omnibus jurisdiction; Sweden has given broad responsibilities to a board within the Ministry of Agriculture; and the United States has established its Environmental Protection Agency as a lead agency outside the system of cabinet-level departments. West Germany, the Soviet Union, and Italy lack this consolidation of power and responsibility, and this has apparently contributed to the weaknesses of their enforcement patterns.

All things considered, pollution control is more effective—though sometimes less flexible—when the central government drafts and directly implements regulations. All eight countries divide pollution-control responsibilities between central and local authorities to some extent. However, the British and the West Germans emphasize local autonomy to an exceptional degree and Sweden stands out for centralized implementation. Formal federal or unitary patterns are not always decisive in the allocation of such powers. For example, the United States has developed impressive central authority in this area.

Our earlier discussion of policy options emphasized the benefits of the polluter pays principle. The planned application of this principle has been evident in both East and West Germany. The user charge is a German contribution to this area of policy, having been employed in the industrialized Ruhr area since the beginning of the century. Charges were assessed on various users of the river by local water management associations. East and West Germany have recently applied the principle to water pollution at the national level, and the German Democratic Republic has also levied such charges on industrial air polluters. In addition, France has acted under its 1971 Rectifying Finance Act to assess annual charges against firms which "because of the nature or the volume of their activities require extensive and regular controls."[20] Sweden and the United States have taken smaller steps toward such user charges, particularly in the area of sewage treatment.

---

[20] Stephen McCaffrey and Françoise Borhenne-Guilmin, "The Use of Law in Environmental Regulation: A Survey of Legal Responses to Selected Problems," in *Organization and Administration of Environmental Programs*, p. 113.

The principal fiscal techniques used to curtail pollution are subsidies and fines. Given the enormous costs of effective pollution control, either approach can involve large sums and huge programs. The United States has led the way by appropriating billions of dollars in grants to local governments for sewage treatment and other purposes and has provided limited grants to private firms through tax benefits. Direct grants and tax subsidies are utilized in most of the eight countries, with Sweden, West Germany, East Germany, and France all providing considerable aid to firms and local governments. Such subsidies are a lesser factor in Italy, Great Britain, and the Soviet Union, and this has apparently contributed to the comparative lag in the overall impacts of their programs. Fines are typically part of the antipollution arsenal, but they are easily shrugged off by enterprises in the Soviet Union and Italy and are applied on a sporadic basis in most of the other six surveyed countries. Some of the largest fines have been assessed in the United States.

Although each of the eight employs a version of the permit or license as a regulatory tool, major variations exist in regard to the licensing authority and the standards that must be met. Since pollution control depends on evolving technology, it is extremely difficult to be specific about standards. The United States and Sweden both use such terms as *economically achievable, technically practicable,* and *best available technology.* These concepts are subject to conflicting interpretations and lend themselves, especially in the United States, to prolonged legal battles. The American-derived environmental impact statement is a major advance in the evaluation of the various effects of substantial projects. It has been applied to all national budgetary expenditures in France. With such reports the more careful regimes can avoid social and physical damage that goes beyond specific indicators of pollution. Differences in enforcement patterns are as evident in licensing as in fines. The Soviet Union and East Germany have similar requirements for new and expanded industrial plants, but these are enforced more rigorously in East Germany than in the Soviet Union.

All elements considered, we offer the following ranking of the eight countries in regard to pollution-control policy:

1. Sweden.
2. United States.
3. France.
4. East Germany.
5. Great Britain.
6. West Germany.
7. Soviet Union.
8. Italy.

We do this with some hesitation because pollution control is more complex and difficult to assess than are most of the policy areas discussed in this book. Sweden impresses us with its unwillingness to retreat in the face of economic pressures. The United States stands out for its heavy direct investment. East Germany and France have both created consolidated enforcement agencies and have adopted many of the best ideas from progressive countries. Britain and West Germany have not shown very much consistency, though each has major achievements to its credit. The Soviet Union has not really backed away from a single-minded emphasis on production, and Italy has been unable to mobilize a coherent national policy.

This summary picture needs to be enlarged upon with some details concerning particular national efforts. As such, we take up some further aspects of air and water pollution policy in each of the eight nations. These countries are presented in the order of our ranking.

Sweden

The administration of Swedish policy has been invested in two principal bodies: the National Environment Protection Board, with general supervisory duties, and the Franchise Board, whose task is to issue permits and licenses. The National Environment Protection Board is part of the Ministry of Agriculture, while the Franchise Board is an independent entity.[21] The major piece of legislation which these agencies are charged with implementing is the Environmental Protection Act of 1969. This comprehensive law covers air, water, solid waste, and noise pollution. Instead of trying to state precise emission and effluent levels for various pollutants, the Riksdag left such calculations to the law's implementers.[22] Although the act listed the pollutants whose use the legislators wanted controlled, it left the development of appropriate standards to the government agencies in collaboration with industry representatives and others.

Once established, these standards were applied through a permits system. Since 1974, municipal and industrial air and water users have had to receive permission to build new facilities or expand old ones. If the two boards find that all "economically feasible and technically practicable" measures to meet the established standards have been taken, a permit will be forthcoming.[23] This is the general practice, but

---

[21] *Sweden's National Report to the U.N. Conference on the Human Environment* (Stockholm, 1971), pp. 60–63.

[22] U.S. Department of Commerce, *The Effects of Pollution Abatement on International Trade* (Washington, D.C.: U.S. Governnment Printing Office, 1973), pp. 72–74.

[23] Lundqvist, "Environmental Policy," pp. 136–37.

the use of some hazardous substances (for example, certain pesticides) has been banned outright or, at a minimum, has become subject to special licensing procedures.

Sweden's methods for financing the implementation of these policies have stressed the pay the polluter principle. That is, substantial grants have been made to local communities for sewage treatment facilities and private industries have also been directly subsidized to induce their compliance. However, a Royal Commission on Environmental Costs, set up in 1971, issued a report which advocated the gradual elimination of such payments and their replacement by a system of user charges. Right now, it is uncertain whether the Commission's recommendations will be broadly adopted or whether user charges will be employed only for particular sectors of the economy.

What is certain, though, is that the Swedish reaction to the recent global business recession as it effects the pollution question has been unlike the American reaction. While the tendency in the United States has been to restrict the antipollution commitment in the name of saving jobs and cutting costs, the Swedes have responded to the economic downturn by strengthening their antipollution efforts. Under the Keynesian assumption that more not less public spending is called for during recessionary phases of the business cycle, the government has increased its antipollution expenditures in the hope that this provide an economic stimulus.

Another Swedish departure from American practice lies in the realm of land use planning. Specifically, Sweden has devised a national land use plan which contains provisions for the zoning of industrial plants and other facilities. A weaker measure of this type was defeated recently in the U.S. Congress. Only widely varying state and local laws guide land use in the United States.

The United States

In the United States the Environmental Protection Agency (EPA) has been responsible since 1970 for the overall supervision of air and water pollution control. The principal statutory weapons at its disposal are the National Environmental Policy Act (NEPA) of 1969 and the 1970 and 1972 amendments to the Air Quality Act and the Federal Water Pollution Control Act.

Under the National Environmental Policy Act federal agencies and local government or private seekers of federal funds are required to file environmental impact statements. The law stipulates that no money will be forthcoming until the EPA has been assured that proposed projects will not have a deleterious effect on the environment.

The present legislation to control water pollution represents a significant strengthening of previous policy in a number of respects. All navigable waters within the country are now covered by its provisions. States are required to write water pollution control plans which meet EPA standards before these plans may be put into effect. All municipal and industrial water users must obtain permits based on prescribed discharge standards. It is mandated that all facilities use the best available and economically achievable control technology. Fines imposed on violators may range up to $50,000 a day for repeated offenses. Private firms receive some tax concessions for complying with EPA standards, and the federal government may absorb up to 75 percent of the total costs incurred by municipalities in meeting sewage treatment standards. It is envisaged, however, that localities will rely on self-financing after their current capital equipment needs are met.[24]

The new policy is not without its critics.[25] A major thrust of the criticism concerns the gap between the broad goal stated in the law, "that the discharge of pollutants into the navigable waters be eliminated by 1985," and the enormous costs involved in reaching this and shorter-term objectives. For example, although the EPA can compel companies to stop discharging particular pollutants, on pain of being shut down ultimately, the legislation makes no provision for reimbursing individuals, communities, and firms for the dislocations which would result from such a shutdown. Interposed between the 1985 target and the enormous costs required to achieve it are escape hatch phrases, such as *best available technology* and *economically achievable*, which provide room for bargaining and maneuver. When EPA, the states, and individual users cannot reach agreement on the meanings of such provisions in particular situations, lawsuits routinely follow.

The 1970 Clean Air Amendments are directed at both stationary dischargers and motor vehicles. In regard to the latter, the law contains specific emission standards for such harmful substances as carbon monoxide. To assure adherence, the EPA was authorized to carry out compliance tests, establish fuel standards, and receive performance warranties from manufacturers. Further, tight deadlines for meeting the standards were imposed, and manufacturers unable or unwilling to meet the 1975–76 standards could be fined $10,000 per vehicle. Since the law's enactment, however, carmakers have had some success in lobbying before Congress and the EPA for more time and lower standards and, given the auto industry's crucial role in the American economy, the imposition of the draconian fines called for under the law

---

[24] Kneese and Schultze, *Pollution,* pp. 53–57.

[25] Bruce Ackerman et al., *The Uncertain Search for Environmental Quality* (New York: Free Press, 1975), pp. 319–25.

is virtually unthinkable. The government's pressure has been reduced to negotiation and arbitration.

Insofar as stationary (mainly industrial) sources of air pollution are concerned, the law empowers the EPA to set limits, "threshold values," on the discharge of certain pollutants into the atmosphere. States are charged with the primary responsibility for achieving ambient air quality standards. They were to prepare implementation plans for EPA approval by 1972 so that the initial set of standards could be met by 1975. Congress also recognized the existence of a group of especially hazardous pollutants immediately dangerous to human health. The EPA was given the task of drawing up a list of such substances, setting appropriate emission levels, and then applying them without the necessity of state involvement. Finally, all newly constructed plants were required to meet EPA source-performance standards by using "the best adequately demonstrated control technology."[26] But in response to industry pressure, in 1973 the EPA lowered its original standards on some types of emissions.

Several aspects of American air and water pollution control policies stand out. First, they are enormously complex to administer. Second, the costs involved in attaining the congressionally sanctioned objectives are astronomical. Third, they often evoke intense federal-state conflicts. Fourth, state government commitments vary greatly; some states, including Oregon and Colorado, evince environmental concerns even stronger than those of the national government, whereas others hardly recognize that an environmental problem exists. Fifth, Congress and the EPA have displayed uncertainty in the selection of management instruments to enforce the laws. Finally, given the complexity, the costs, and the uncertainty, there has been a tendency either to make the application of standards the result of shifting political bargains or to leave it to the courts to decide what the laws mean—after years of litigation.

France

In France, public awareness of the severity of the nation's pollution problems was stimulated by the "100 measures" campaign launched by President Pompidou in 1969. This highly publicized national discussion involved the government's solicitation of proposals from concerned private individuals and groups. Some of these proposals were incorporated into a comprehensive environmental protection program developed by an interministerial committee assisted by a joint public-private advisory commission. In 1971, overall responsibility for co-

---

[26] Kneese and Schultze, *Pollution*, p. 52.

ordinating the program's implementation was invested in a new Ministry for the Protection of the Environment, which was at first headed by a prominent Gaullist politician.

Prior to Pompidou's undertaking, French pollution policy had been based on three fundamental pieces of legislation. The first, which dates from 1917, provides for the classification of commercial and industrial establishments according to the likelihood of their posing public health hazards. Those categories deemed harmful may be operated only with the approval of a departmental prefect and must be constructed within specially designated industrial areas. The 1961 Air Pollution Law stipulated that "all buildings and industrial, commercial . . . or agricultural establishments, vehicles . . . , possessed, operated or held by any private person or body corporate, shall be constructed, operated or used in such a manner as to prevent both the pollution of the atmosphere and smells which constitute a public nuisance, endanger health or public security."[27] Follow-up ordinances for regulating auto emissions, fuel use, and plant construction, as well as a special set of zoning protections for Paris, were issued before 1969. Finally, a basic law on water pollution, enacted in 1964, empowered the establishment of discharge standards and the creation of six regional river basin agencies, with accompanying financial support to assist municipal and industrial entities.

Rather than start afresh, the post-1969 French environmental protection program has, by and large, used these earlier laws as enabling legislation on the basis of which the government has issued a series of regulatory decrees and ordinances. Thus, since 1970 the executive has limited or prohibited the dumping of certain waste products into the water, granted prefects the authority to compel certain industries to cease operations during air pollution alerts, and given several ministries the responsibility for determining the conditions for the use of incineration, combustion, and thermal equipment throughout the country.

The French system of direct controls relies on the same kinds of permit and licensing arrangements that are employed at present in most other nations. Prefects, aided by local inspectors from national ministries, have tended to perform this function in the field of air pollution control. The administration of water pollution regulations, on the other hand, is performed by the river basin agencies along with newly created coastal control units which handle the problem in each of the country's 24 sea-bordering departments.

---

[27] Government Research Laboratory, *Profile Study of Air Pollution Control Activities in Foreign Countries: First Year Report* (U.S. Department of Health, Education, and Welfare, 1970), p. 31.

However, the protection program has involved more than the elaboration and implementation of executive decrees. For one thing, pollution abatement has been included as a high-priority item in France's recent national economic plans, an important factor in determining the allocation of public resources. Related to this development is the fact that in the preparation of the government's annual budget, the environment ministry (renamed the Ministry on the Quality of Life under Giscard d'Estaing) must be consulted on the environmental impact of proposed expenditures.

When it comes to paying for pollution control, France is among those countries that extend substantial subsidies. Companies investing in suitable equipment can receive subsidies and soft loans (4 percent interest over 18 years) from the government to cover up to 50 percent of their costs; and they have also been able to qualify for accelerated depreciation allowances on such installations. Like the two Germanies, France has combined subsidies and tax benefits with aspects of the polluter pays principle. However, France is unique in assessing variable user charges against firms for their general impact on the environment and not only their specific emissions.

East Germany

The German Democratic Republic is the only state in our survey which includes environmental protection as an explicit constitutional objective. Article 15 of East Germany's 1968 Constitution contains the following statement:

> In the interests of the welfare of citizens, the state and society shall protect nature. The competent bodies shall ensure the purity of the water and the air, and protection for flora and fauna and the natural beauties of the homeland; in addition this is the affair of every citizen.

One reason for the provision is that the Constitution was drafted at a time when the country's party and state leaders were becoming increasingly concerned about the deterioration of air and water resources, itself a consequence of rapid industrial growth during the 1960s.

In response to the nation's substantial pollution problems, the East Germans have fashioned environmental protection measures and enforcement machinery which compare favorably with those deployed by other European Communist-bloc states, including the Soviet Union.[28] Although ostensibly inspired by the Soviet example, the East German effort has been far more extensive than that of its "guide." East Ger-

---

[28] Peter Sand, "The Socialist Response: Environmental Protection Law in the GDR," *Ecology Law Quarterly* 3 (Summer 1973): 451–505.

many's approaches have been influenced by the work of Western ecologists and economists to an extent that the country's leaders would find politically difficult to admit.

In conformity with the constitutional imperative, the Council of Ministers established in 1969 a standing committee on the environment for policy planning and coordination. In 1970 the committee's basic recommendations were embodied in a comprehensive law approved by the Volkskammer: the National Environment Act.[29] Various institutional means have been employed in the enforcement of this act. At the national level, a new Ministry for Environmental Protection and Water Management was created in 1971. The ministry's responsibilities include the supervision of regional water basin authorities, whose own powers to regulate users were extended by the 1970 act. The act also specified that county and municipal governments had to enact antipollution ordinances (primarily in the fields of solid waste disposal, noise abatement, and public sanitation) in conformity with overall national designs. Municipal governments were also invested with the authority to compel local factory managers to include environmental protection goals in their production plans. The national five-year economic plan and the various county-level land use master plans also encompass pollution-control objectives.

The direct controls of East Germany's enforcement bodies comprise an array of licenses, permits, and approvals. New plants are not permitted to go into operation until supervisory bodies have been assured that appropriate air and water purification steps have been taken.[30] Unlike the Soviet Union, the German Democratic Republic apparently applies such regulations routinely.

East German authorities have relied on two types of monetary levers: fines imposed on violators and subsidies offered for antipollution capital outlays. Such subsidies have involved granting enterprises exemptions from production fund payments (East Germany's equivalent of corporate taxes). Also, firms have been authorized to include control-related capital and operating costs in their price calculations, and goods manufactured by means of waste recycling techniques have been accorded preferential prices.

These pay the polluter measures have generally been used to encourage facilities to introduce requisite equipment or alter production practices so as to reduce pollution discharges. But like their counterparts in West Germany, East Germany's decision-makers have also seen advantages in the user charges approach. Under a 1971 decree,

---

[29] Rolf Kachelmaier, "About the Legal Safeguards Governing the Protection of the Environment in the GDR," *Law and Legislation in the GDR* (1971): 24–41.

[30] *Governmental Measures in the GDR to Keep Waters Clean and to Rationally Use Ground and Surface Waters* (Stockholm, 1972), pp. 1–10.

a water use charge has been imposed on enterprises that discharge specified environmentally harmful substances into the nation's waterways. And in 1973 another decree applied the same principle to air pollution. Under the 1973 decree, a charge (calculated on a per kilogram per hour basis) is imposed on plants which emit any of 113 contaminants. Unlike positive environmental improvement outlays, such charges cut directly into enterprise profits since firms are specifically prohibited from passing the costs along to consumers. As might be imagined, this procedure offers a strong inducement to reduce effluent and emission levels. It is as yet unclear whether this user pays approach will ultimately replace the combination of direct controls and pay the polluter practices or whether it will continue to be used in conjunction with the other devices. What is clear, however, is that East German policy has moved away from the idea that air and water are free goods — a perception which still obtains in the Soviet Union.

Great Britain

Prime Minister Heath's decision in 1970 to create a new super-ministry, the Department of the Environment, led to the establishment of the first cabinet-level body of its kind in the industrialized world.[31] This Conservative step followed the decision by Heath's Labourite predecessor, Harold Wilson, to set up a Royal Commission on Environmental Pollution shortly before his government was defeated at the polls.[32] Earlier, broad public concern had been aroused by the dramatic Torrey Canyon oil spill disaster in the English Channel, much as American opinion was influenced by the spills at Santa Barbara.[33]

The major British enactments in the field of water and air pollution have been the Alkali Act (1906), the Water Resources Act (1963), and the 1968 Clean Air Act. The latter two statutes represent modifications of earlier and weaker laws: the Rivers Pollution acts (1951 and 1961) and a 1956 Clean Air Act. With respect to inland water pollution the 1963 law required the creation of river authorities to regulate developments along the country's important waterways. These authorities are composed of appointees from local government councils and several national ministries. (The Department of the Environment is now responsible for the overall supervision of the river authorities.[34]) The authorities are empowered to regulate the discharge of effluents

[31] Enloe, *Politics of Pollution*, pp. 147–48, 269–70.

[32] Royal Commission on Environmental Pollution, *First Report* (London: Her Majesty's Stationery Office, 1971), pp. 1–3.

[33] J. Clarence Davies, *The Politics of Pollution* (New York: Pegasus, 1970), pp. 48–49.

[34] J. McLoughlin, *The Law Relating to Pollution* (Manchester: Manchester University Press, 1972), pp. 16–36.

through the granting of use licenses and the issuing of "consents." The sweeping language of the 1963 law makes it an offense "to cause or knowingly permit to enter any stream any poisonous, noxious or polluting matter." Such an action, however, is deemed permissible if a river authority consents to it.

Except for their regulation of the Thames River, the authorities do not seem to have been especially forceful in limiting pollution. In practice, "consents" are granted liberally to industries. And if a local government permits a new factory to be built, the authorities can do little to prevent the factory from using the community's sewage system. Furthermore, even when the authorities find that violations of the law or of their own consent rulings have occurred, they have been reluctant to take action. Although they may impose small fines on violators and, in some instances, take them to court in order to recover additional damages, the authorities have been hesitant to pursue either course of action.

Two distinct policies are used to control air pollution. The first derives from the 1956 and 1968 Clean Air acts and is directed at stationary pollution sources, primarily domestic heating units.[35] The 1956 act empowered local governments to designate "smokeless areas" within which only smokeless fuels could be used for home heating. It further provided that part of the domestic users' costs for installing the necessary equipment be defrayed by national and local government subsidies. Enforcement was on a voluntary basis; that is, it was left to the local authorities to decide whether or not areas would be designated as "smokeless" and how vigorously the rules would be applied.

Overall, the results were uneven, since some communities complied with the law and others opted not to. Generally, the localities having the greatest financial resources, including Greater London, made the most substantial efforts. In poorer but equally dirty communities, enforcement was minimal. A locality's inability to pay for homeowners' subsidies and the public health personnel needed to inspect premises was one significant element affecting such failures to comply. In mining areas another important factor was the issue of "concessionary coal." In Wales and other regions, miners receive coal as part of their wages. In such instances, election-conscious local councilmen have been reluctant to demand that the miners heat their homes with smokeless fuels.

The 1968 act tightened the policy somewhat by giving the Housing Ministry the power to force local governments to submit plans for the designation of smokeless zones within which violators could be prosecuted and fined after a suitable period. However, the ministry has not

---

[35] Howard Scarrow, "The Impact of British Domestic Air Pollution Legislation," *British Journal of Political Science* 2, no. 3 (July 1972): 261–82.

exercised this power when smoke-free fuels have been in tight supply. And like the river authorities, many local governments with designated zones have been slow to invoke the available legal sanctions.

The second type of air pollution control policy is built around the 1906 Alkali and Works Regulation Act and the supplementary order of 1966.[36] Unlike the Clean Air acts, these rules are administered not by local authorities, but by the Department of the Environment's Alkali Inspectorate. The regulations apply to almost all air-polluting industries, those which use what are known as "scheduled processes" in their production. Enterprises whose production activities may involve the emission of harmful substances are required to register annually with the Inspectorate. They may not continue to use "scheduled processes" unless the Inspectorate is persuaded that they are employing the "best practicable means" to prevent unacceptable emissions from being discharged into the atmosphere. When the Inspectorate decides that such means have not been used, an offense has been committed and the owner may be fined. In contrast to the Clean Air acts, the Alkali and Works Regulation Act makes no provision for direct governmental subsidies for the purchase of the necessary control equipment. Since 1969, the manufacturers of motor vehicles have been subject to a similar type of regulation in regard to the emission standards that their vehicles must meet.

West Germany

West Germany shares Britain's problem of exceptionally intensive industrial activity in a middle-sized country. It has long had the advantage over Britain of booming profits, but it has been slow to overcome many problems rooted in its political institutions.

From an organizational point of view, West German environmental protection arrangements are not advanced. At present no functionally specialized ministry or lead agency within the national government has overall administrative responsibilities. Pollution-control policy-making is shared by several ministries, notably interior, health, and economics. The country's ten Länder governments plus West Berlin are responsible for enforcing both their own policies and most of the policies made in Bonn. Further, the West German states, unlike many of their American counterparts, have also failed to create separate environmental protection ministries. In North Rhine–Westphalia, for example, the job of environmental protection has been assigned to the Ministry of Labor and Social Affairs, a body which obviously has other duties.[37]

---

[36] Government Research Laboratory, *Profile Study*, pp. 64–68.
[37] Ibid., p. 60.

The most recent effort to strengthen West German antipollution policy was begun in 1969. That effort was stimulated by the election year commitment of the victorious Social Democrats, under Willy Brandt's leadership, to do something about the country's environmental deterioration. One campaign slogan pledged: "Clear skies over the Ruhr again." To fulfill his party's commitment Brandt, as chancellor, appointed a cabinet committee on environmental problems with the task of preparing a comprehensive policy statement. The document was approved by the full cabinet in 1971 and has become the basis for the government's subsequent legislative proposals and subsidiary regulations.[38] The proposals typically have amended preexisting laws.

In the field of air pollution, West German practice, as spelled out in 1971 and 1974 parliamentary enactments, involves a reliance on permits and licenses and follows the Swedish pattern of leaving the elaboration of precise emission standards to the administrators.[39] Since the regulation of motor vehicle discharges involves interstate activity, it has been undertaken by the central government for some time. But until 1974 the responsibility for executing the permit system on stationary air pollution sources, though based on nationally determined standards, belonged exclusively to the Länder. Since that year the policy has been slightly modified so that today the Bonn Ministry of Interior has the authority to issue or deny permits for certain types of transportation-related equipment. Nevertheless, the enforcement of nationally determined emission standards on plants, commercial facilities, and homes is still done by the states. Licenses are awarded by the Länder if a plant has: (1) installed the latest technical equipment for limiting discharges, and (2) the resulting ambient air pollution levels do not exceed limits for the surrounding area. In 1973 the government submitted to parliament a proposal to amend the existing Federal Water Law (1957) to apply the polluter pays principle to the entire country.

> The scheme levies fees on discharges in accordance with the damaging effect of their waste waters, and sets the fees so that they will provide a strong stimulus to reducing waste discharges to watercourses. The choice of technologies for reducing or eliminating waste water discharges is to be left to the discharger. . . . Payments are to be made by all public and private dischargers of waste water to surface waters and coastal waters without regard to the legality of the discharge, or to the size or quality of the watercourses to which discharges are made.[40]

---

[38] *National Report of the Federal Republic of Germany on the Human Environment* (Stockholm, 1972), pp. 1–74.

[39] For a description of the 1974 act see Environmental Protection Agency, *Summaries of Foreign Government Environmental Reports*, vol. 4, no. 25 (September 1974), p. 7.

[40] Allen-Kneese and Charles Schultze, *Pollution, Prices, and Public Policy* (Washington, D.C.: Brookings Institution, 1975), pp. 69–84. © 1975 by the Brookings Institution, Washington, D.C.

The payments go to the Länder and are used to reduce the damages caused by the polluters.

Other types of monetary levers are still being used. Currently both central and state governments offer direct outlays, loan guarantees, and tax relief to local agencies and private industries to facilitate the necessary capital investment. However, it is expected that these allocations will eventually be phased out.

The Soviet Union

Observations by Western writers concerning the pollution problem in the USSR emphasize two things. First, official rhetoric notwithstanding, the problem is severe. There is an abundance of horror stories involving increasing pollution levels in the Black and Caspian seas, Lake Baikal, and most major navigable rivers as well as accounts of serious health hazards posed by air pollution in many industrial cities. Second, Western analysts, and Soviet environmental specialists if spoken to privately, concur that the political system's response to the problem has been inadequate. State ownership of enterprise per se is no guarantee of high environmental standards. Some critics even go as far as to resurrect the convergence theory — the view that, given the common characteristic of advanced industrialization, the American and Soviet polities are moving closer together — in maintaining that both systems have proved equally incapable of dealing effectively with environmental deterioration.[41]

But from an organizational perspective, the Soviet system is unlike the American, or the East German for that matter, in that it has not yet developed a specialized ministry or lead agency to apply and coordinate protection measures. The closest approximation in the areas of air and water pollution control is the Public Health Ministry. In conjunction with comparable agencies in the country's 15 republics, it operates the State Sanitary Inspectorate, whose functionaries have the primary responsibility for enforcing existing regulations. But at both the national and republican levels, other ministries (for example, Agriculture, Fishing) have their own inspectors with analogous duties. In addition, such organs as the All-Union Gas Purification and Dust Removal Association, attached to the Petroleum Ministry, and the Council of Minister's Chief Administration for the Hydrometeorological Service are involved in research, equipment design, and other aspects of the pollution-control effort. The results of this fragmentation of bureau-

---

[41] David Powell, "The Social Costs of Modernization: Ecological Problems in the USSR," *World Politics* 23 (July 1971): 618–34; Enloe, *Politics of Pollution*, pp. 190–220; and Kelley, Stunkel, and Wascott, *Economic Superpowers*, pp. 285–93.

cratic authority are "overlapping jurisdictions and rivalries, with no single agency competent to coordinate the efforts of all."[42]

These organizational difficulties in Moscow are often compounded by problems deriving from the regime's federal character. Although both national and republican units are supposed to operate within the context of broad national guidelines, there is apparently enough "give" in the system to allow for significant variation in the elaboration and enforcement of operative standards.[43]

The style of Soviet environmental protection legislation parallels that of other policy domains. The practice is for a set of "fundamental principles" to be adopted by national decision-makers, often followed by a set of administrative decrees, in accordance with which the republican governments are supposed to enact complementary legislation for their jurisdictions. The major "fundamental principles" affecting pollution control are those governing land use (1968), public health (1969), and water (1970).

On paper, the character of the Soviet system of direct controls is largely indistinguishable from comparable patterns in the other countries in our analysis. New industrial plants must be licensed by sanitary inspectors before going into operation; ultimately, the inspectors have the right to compel plants to cease production when they are found to be violating prescribed effluent and emission standards. In practice, enforcement is spotty. Even when the national party leadership takes a stand on the protection of a national treasure, such as Lake Baikal, new polluting factories are built and only partially controlled. Inspectors who determine that economically important establishments are violating the law are often dissuaded from taking action through the intervention of local party and government officials or of leaders in the heavy industry ministries with production goals at stake.

The application of monetary levers also leaves much to be desired. The Soviet enforcement approach places great emphasis on the use of fines and punitive sanctions. As Goldman puts it:

> When a determined stand is taken and a stiff fine is levied, the fine may still not serve as a deterrent even under the criminal code. In most cases the fine is not taken out of the plant director's pocket but out of the enterprise fund. Under these circumstances the plant manager hardly feels any personal loss. . . . One of the Soviet Union's most respected ecologists reports that funds to pay fines were frequently included in the financial plan of the enterprise at the beginning of the year.[44]

---

[42] Powell, ibid., p. 627.

[43] Philip Pryde, *Conservation in the Soviet Union* (Cambridge, England: Cambridge University Press, 1972), p. 137.

[44] Goldman, *Spoils of Progress*, p. 35.

In addition to levying fines, state agencies allocate direct grants to industries for antipollution purposes. But enterprise managers exercise considerable discretion in the use of these grants. Since the managers' careers and salaries are linked to their ability to achieve predetermined production goals rather than to their success in maintaining a healthful ambient environment, they often delay the installation of purification facilities and sometimes divert the funds for production-enhancing purposes. In short, as is often true in the United States, industrial managers are inclined to regard the whole array of environmental protection measures as a bureaucratic nuisance to be evaded wherever possible. What appears to distinguish the two political systems in this regard is the presence on the American scene of independent interest groups and government authorities which exert a restraining influence on actions stemming from such sentiments.

Italy

Italy has the reputation of being the most heavily polluted country in Western Europe and the one whose government has done least to combat the problem.[45] A few illustrations are suggestive. As of 1972, Milan, the nation's major industrial center, lacked a sewage treatment plant—thereby allowing raw sewage from that community's several million residents and several thousand commercial and industrial establishments to flow into local rivers. As a result of such uncontrolled discharge of untreated sewage, the Italian Riviera, an important resort area, is in danger of losing its tourist business. The petrochemical plants in the communities surrounding Venice have emitted pollutants in sufficient quantities to cause irreparable damage to many of the city's priceless historical buildings, monuments, and art treasures. Turin, the international headquarters of FIAT, has frequent smog alerts. Finally, Italy has the smallest percentage of national parkland and the largest number of oil refineries of any nation in Western Europe.

Despite the efforts of Italia Nostra, the country's leading environmental interest group, and expressions of concern from the mass media and parliament, the governmental response has been less than overwhelming. This is most apparent in the field of water pollution: Italy currently lacks any comprehensive legislation covering this subject. In the absence of such legislation, local officials have sought periodically to take court action against polluters through the application of various fishing, hygiene, and sanitation regulations. But observers suggest

[45] John Navone, "Italy—An Environmental Disaster Area," *America* 126, no. 21 (May 1972): 592–94; William Murray, "Letter from Rome," *New Yorker*, April 8, 1974, pp. 113–29; and Claire Sterling, "Italy," *Atlantic Monthly* 232, no. 4 (October 1973): 12–30.

that these measures are clearly inadequate without suitable national coordination.[46]

The picture is not quite so grim, at least in terms of legislation, when it comes to air pollution. In 1966 parliament enacted a basic "framework law," covering heating plants, fuels, industries, and motor vehicles. Under the law's general provisions the government was empowered to issue decrees and regulations containing specific standards and enforcement procedures.

The law and the resulting regulations are enforced by such diverse national authorites as the health, interior, industry, labor, and transportation ministries as well as subnational agencies. Each of these authorities and agencies is supposed to be formally advised by central and regional air pollution commissions. Regulations now in force set emission standards for domestic heating, industry, and motor vehicles. In applying these standards, the authorities have divided the country into three "zones": heavily industrialized, moderately industrialized, and rural. The zone in which a particular community is placed affects, for example, the type of fuel that heating plants are permitted to burn.

The crucial problem so far as enforcement is concerned is funding. The Italian government has not opted for either a system of user charges or one of special tax incentives for the installation of control equipment. In fact, pleading poverty, it offers no form of direct monetary assistance to induce complaince. Since a substantial percentage of pollution emissions comes from the plants of small firms, which often lack the necessary capital for equipment purchases, the current situation appears to encourage evasion of the law rather than compliance with it. Large firms with greater resources are better able to respond. For example, the state-owned oil and gas company, ENI, has created an $85 million program to control liquid and gaseous discharges at its facilities over the next several years.

CONCLUSIONS

Each of the eight surveyed countries has reacted to growing domestic and international concerns about environmental pollution by strengthening its statutes, regulations, and implementing agencies. However, significant variations exist in the scope of such laws and in the degree to which enforcement authority is concentrated. The mix of policy options is not very varied, but only a few states apply the pollution pays principle other than in regard to fines. The mix of direct controls and financial inducements is similar, but the intensity of their utilization varies greatly.

---

[46] U.S. Department of Commerce, *Pollution Abatement*, pp. 42–47.

Strong policies involve such elements as large subsidies, user charges that are not routinely passed on to consumers, lead or consolidated environmental agencies, the support of local governments and major interest groups, and a broad approach to environmental impacts. On the basis of these tests we were most impressed with Sweden's overall record and most critical of Italy's.

The variations that we found seem to result much more from such political factors as interest groups, elite perceptions, and bureaucratic adaptiveness than from ideology or obvious geographic or sociopolitical factors. However, we recognize the relative affluence of the leading countries as compared to the laggards, and credit this variable as both a direct and an indirect force. Effective pollution control is a response of post-industrial societies to a lingering and intensifying problem of industrialization.

12 Conclusions

Recent events in the Western world—the Vietnam War, the energy crisis, economic recession, acts of political terrorism, mounting rates of violent crime—have combined to create a mood of deep pessimism among many intellectuals, national political leaders, and ordinary citizens about the future of Western civilization. Certainly, some aspects of our analysis lend support to these gloomy perceptions. Nevertheless, in thinking about the various distributive, extractive, and regulatory policies we have described in this book, we come away believing, rather unfashionably, that the picture which emerges also affords substantial grounds for optimism.

Although there are meaningful variations among the survey countries in pace, style, and commitment, several tendencies in the evolution of public policy give us reason to believe that the future need not be as bleak as it is often portrayed. We have several phenomena in mind here. The welfare state has been broadened and standards of support increased to or above subsistence levels in the majority of the countries studied. Each nation in our survey has also improved the quality and availability of health services.

Trends in militarization have also been quite positive in relation to the value system of the authors that influenced this book. Significant declines in defense spending as a proportion of GNP were most evident in the United States, Great Britain, and France. Each of our eight countries participated in a movement away from dependence on military conscription, some through all-volunteer forces, others through reduced terms of service. It is evident that demilitarization benefited public social programs as well as investment and private consumption.

Further, the early agenda items of post-industrial politics seem to be taking a progressive course. Environmental pollution undoubtedly poses a severe problem in all of our eight nations. Yet it is also true that many of these countries' political decision-makers have recognized the problem's severity and have responded by imposing restrictions, creating governmental agencies, and increasing budget allocations. These steps have rarely, if ever, been as effective as environmentalists would wish or as the situation demands; yet it would be hard to deny that, at the very minimum, a level of awareness and concern now exists which was lacking previously.

We also discern some bright spots in the domain of industrial relations. In particular, we have reference to the current reform efforts to enhance the influence of workers on their working environments and to give them representation in managerial structures.

In general, the rights of women and of minority ethnic, racial, and religious groups appear to be better protected now than earlier in this century in almost all of the eight nations. The case for improved civil liberties is perhaps more problematic; but even here we would argue that, at least in most countries in Western Europe and North America, freedoms of individual thought, expression, and peaceful political participation have continued to increase in recent decades.

The broadened "critical consciousness" that has spurred progress in relation to each of these post-industrial issues has been bolstered by expanded and reformed secondary and higher education. In turn, the school systems have been given a higher priority and assigned a multitude of new functions.

Despite these grounds for optimism we do not mean to sponsor a rose-colored view of the world. Few positive trends were uncovered in the critical area of taxation. The state of civil liberties in liberal and social democratic Western Europe was less positive than we had anticipated. Resistance to the democratization of education continues to hold back major reforms in several member states of the European Communities. In the mid-1970s serious economic pressures and political instability were threatening to markedly disturb evolutionary progress in much of the Western world. Neither of the two Communist-ruled states demonstrated sustained progress toward political liberalization, demilitarization, or greater satisfaction of the consumer demands of their citizens.

Which country or group of countries has led the way in the more positive developments? The value preferences noted in Chapter 1 of this volume corresponded most closely to those ascendant in Sweden. In relation to virtually every policy area discussed in this book the Swedish approach emphasized generosity, equality, and efficiency. In Sweden one finds a comprehensive welfare state that is also one of the world's leaders in attacking the post-industrial agenda. Swedish economic success appears to refute claims that personal and corporate incentive has been destroyed. However, the recent defeat of the long-ruling Social Democrats adds credence to contentions that the Swedes have paid a high price in taxation, bureaucratic control, and loss of individuality.

The record of the United States is marked by inconsistency. There is much to criticize in regard to health care, social insurance, and urban policy. Yet in at least a few spheres, including public education, the protection of civil liberties and civil rights, and control over restraints on trade, the American performance appears to be superior to that of most or all of the other countries surveyed. The American welfare state has grown rapidly, while military allocations have been reduced in relative terms. The majority of post-industrial issues, ranging from university reforms to women's rights to environmentalism, first stimulated mass movements and achieved high visibility in the United States. America's performance in such widely criticized areas of U.S. public policy as environmental control and taxation proved to be progressive in comparison with that of most of the other countries surveyed.

The leadership roles of other countries have been far more limited than those of Sweden and the United States. West Germany stood out in social security and industrial relations, Britain in health care and some aspects of civil liberties, and the Soviet Union in health care and opportunity for higher education. East Germany ranked high in environmental policy, health care, and education, and France and Italy rated well in social insurance.

Adding the dimension of change in recent decades, we note that leadership roles can be short-lived. For example, Britain gave up its earlier pathbreaking role in social welfare, and West Germant in education. In contrast, several areas of Swedish, Soviet, and East German leadership have emerged only since the 1960s. Although Italy has advanced considerably in such areas as education and social insurance in recent decades, that country has remained far behind many other Western European nations in most major public services as well as in such post-industrial issues as environmentalism and women's rights. At present, France appears to be determined to achieve a leading position in several policy areas, including social security and secondary education. Yet it may need much time to make up for its earlier "immobilism."

The case for the Soviet and Eastern European brands of socialism is frequently stated in terms of a trade-off between civil libertarian guarantees and extractive and distributional justice. According to this argument, Soviet-style regimes sacrifice Western liberal standards of individual freedom but are more inclined than their democratic counterparts to offer high levels of public services and to narrow the range of income differences among their citizens. The first part of this proposition seems to be incontestable; civil libertarian protections are weaker in East Germany and the Soviet Union. But the welfare state is not consistently more developed in the Communist-ruled nations. Commendable progress in health and educational systems is offset by lags in taxation and income maintenance programs. In its approach to most policy problems the East German regime, despite its reputation for slavish adherence to Moscow's directives, was shown to be more flexible and innovative than the Soviet regime.

It is evident that the scope of governmental involvement has continued to grow in each of the eight countries. Is there an optimal level of governmental intervention, and has that level been exceeded? These have crystallized as two of the central political questions of our time. Our answer must be complex. Most governments are doing too much for and to some people in particular spheres of policy, yet not meeting the needs of other people in other areas. Versions of the post-industrial agenda place more stress on change in the processes used to provide services than on the expansion or contraction of programs. Much room exists for fairer taxes, more efficient social programs, and less intrusive police practices. Failure to move in these directions will jeopardize the basic support for big government in each of the eight countries.

Throughout this study we have addressed the question of influence and cause in public policy formulation. This book appears at a time when a lingering debate continues between those who emphasize socioeconomic factors and those who stress political influences. Although little new evidence correlating factors and outputs has been presented here, we are able to review a substantial literature that ranged widely across the public policy agenda. As a result, we can offer some pointers for avoiding excessively simplistic conclusions on causation which might be based on research in a single policy area.

Each issue offers a different mix of influential factors. Levels of per capita income and demographic trends relate importantly to standards for basic educational and social welfare services. However, these factors have smaller impacts on military spending levels, the character of the tax system, and many other aspects of extraction and distribution. Socioeconomic factors generally have more influence on the setting of the policy agenda than on the determination of particular solutions. As one moves away from budgets to the organization of services and patterns of regulation, the impact of a wide range of political variables becomes more evident. Few would suggest that political variables are unimportant for the development of particular health service structures or for the protection of the rights of political dissidents.

Particular political factors have varying effects from issue to issue and from nation to nation. The extent of organization of service-providers may be decisive in the health area and less crucial in income maintenance. A military-industrial complex may have its equivalent in the area of education but not in the area of public assistance. Similarly, the ascendancy of presumably more innovative and progressive leftist political parties has had an inconsistent impact on policy. As measured by national voting patterns (see Chapter 4), the level of popular support for left parties shows no unequivocal relationship to the application of "progressive" solutions to the policy problems with which we have been concerned. Apparently, the majority of conservative ruling parties in our sample of countries have demonstrated a considerable ability to anticipate the need for new directions.

Yet other political factors appear to be consistently influential. Among these are bureaucracies, cross-national emulation, and the priorities given to particular values. Executive bureaucracies play crucial roles in studying emerging problems, proposing solutions, blocking approaches that they oppose, protecting favored clients, and maintaining incremental patterns of policy change.

Emulation, often spurred by international organizations, is important for virtually every issue area discussed in this study. The impact of emulation is perhaps most dramatic in regard to industrial democracy and environmental protection. Yet major emulative patterns were also evident in taxation, education, social security, and militarization.

Variations in national values also contribute a good deal to policy outputs. Such values often have deep roots in national experiences. Among the most evident linkages of this kind are those which relate to social security, pollution control, and industrial democracy.

The future is as difficult as ever to forecast. The most reliable projections are based on the continuation of certain present trends. We do not seek to go very far out on a limb at this juncture. Yet some trends seem sufficiently clear. The first is that the developed states will increase their tendency to learn from one another and to emulate the policies that work best in other countries. The institutionalization of exchanges of experience has progressed quite far and is affecting more and more policy areas. Second, major efforts will be made to close glaring gaps among the advanced nations in access to such programs as postprimary education in Western Europe and health care in the United States. In these two cases there is substantial awareness of the need for further development and the largely political barriers can be expected to crumble soon.

Further, the political agenda can be expected to shift to new topics after present issues are resolved. Industrial democracy, sexual discrimination, and the possible need to choose between industrial growth and environmental quality have been among the most hotly debated issues of the 1970s. Energy shortages, inflation, unemployment, and budget deficits have also been among the leading problems of the present decade. Some, but not all, of these issues will be resolved or given a reduced emphasis during the coming decades. New issues will emerge out of unmet needs, newly created demands, and future global developments ranging from food and energy shortages to war, economic and political integration, and the impact of possible greater affluence.

In projecting the future, one can as easily present an optimistic picture of stability and affluence, in which major new issues might relate to leisure, as a pessimistic scenario of starvation, industrial and political instability, and global war. The progress described in this book depended on 30 years dominated by peace and economic growth. Little progress will be possible if the generally positive environment for innovation and change is reversed.

Index

419

Organization for Economic Cooperation
and Development (OECD) — *Cont.*
education, 253–54, 256, 260–61
and energy, 96
and physical environment, 98, 380
taxation, 278–79
Organization for European Economic Cooperation (OEEC), 72, 86, 88; *see also*
Organization for Economic Cooperation and Development
Organization of Petroleum-Exporting
Countries (OPEC), 78, 95–96
Outcomes, defined, 7, 11
Output, defined, 7, 11
Owen, Robert, 167

P

Pareto, Vilfredo, 48
Parliament, 138–43, 308–9, 312, 359, 396,
399, 402, 410
Peacock, Alan J., 57, 170
Pechman, Joseph, 295
Peel, Robert, 180
Penetrative processes, 67–78
Pensions; *see* Income maintenance
Peter the Great (Russia), 155, 160
Peters, B. Guy, 51
Petroleum, 89; *see also* Energy
as economic weapon, 61, 95–96
reserves, 102–3
Physical environment, as policy determi-
nant, 6, 25–27
Physical environmental policies; *see also*
particular countries, Physical resources,
Public health, *and* Urban policies
historical patterns, 81–82, 160–61, 178–
80, 199, 382–86
international influences on, 81–82, 98–
99, 379–82
policy processes, 50
recent policies, 64–65, 385–86, 391–411
sources of policy variation, 386–91
Physical resources, 21, 25–27, 101–4
protection of, 93, 383
Physiocracy, 162
Pickles, William, 91–92
Pinder, John, 95
Piven, Frances Fox, 231
Planning; *see* Economic planning
Poland, 7, 42, 70, 272
Polanyi, Karl, 169
Police
origins of, 159, 181
practices, 151, 197, 341–44
Policy; *see* Public policy
Political authorities, 35–36
influence on policy, 46–49, 135–149
Political community, influence on policy,
35–42, 120–24

Political culture, influence on policy, 120–
24, 389
Political executive, and public policy, 135–
37, 317
Political parties, 3, 39–41, 46, 66, 77, 123–24,
129–35, 145, 147, 166–68, 182–83, 197,
293, 321
Political regime, 35–36
influence on public policy, 42–46, 199
Political scientists, 1–2
Political system, as determinant of public
policy, 5, 35–51, 120–49
Pollution control; *see* Physical environmental policies
Pomper, Gerald, 41
Pompidou, Georges, 93, 385, 399, 400
Pope Pius XII, 320
Population; *see also* Social cleavage *and*
Urbanization
density related to policy, 28–31, 104–6
growth, impacts of, 31–32, 104
size related to policy, 31–32, 104–5
Post-industrial state
definition, 5, 246–47
and convergence of societies, 249–52
and education, 252–64
elements, 5, 201–2, 245–49
elite, 49, 246
emulation, 250
trends, 413
Powell, G. Bingham, 125
Prisons; *see also* Crime and punishment
reform, 82, 180–81, 348–49
Privacy, from search, wiretapping, 337–41
Private ownership; *see* Capitalism
Procedural rights, 337–50; *see also* Civil
liberties *and* Crime and punishment
definition, 299
Progressive movement (U.S.), 168
Pryor, Frederic, 23–24, 228–29, 231, 238,
239, 362
Public administration; *see also* Executive
bureaucracies
influence on policy, 45–46, 389
Public assistance; *see* Income maintenance
and Welfare state
Public enterprise; *see* Public ownership
Public expenditures, 23–24, 26, 36, 57; *see
also* Distributions, *specific countries,
and specific areas of spending*
collective goods, 202–3
grants, 202–3
impact of war on, 56–60
interwar period, 192–95
in liberal era, 169–75
in mercantilist era, 156–58
Public health, 28, 161, 163, 178–70; *see also*
Physical environmental policy *and* Urbanization